POSTMODERN MOMENTS IN MODERN ECONOMICS

POSTMODERN MOMENTS
IN MODERN ECONOMICS

David F. Ruccio and Jack Amariglio

PRINCETON UNIVERSITY PRESS   PRINCETON AND OXFORD

Copyright © 2003 by Princeton University Press
Published by Princeton University Press, 41 William Street,
Princeton, New Jersey 08540
In the United Kingdom: Princeton University Press,
3 Market Place, Woodstock, Oxfordshire OX20 1SY
All Rights Reserved

Library of Congress Cataloging-in-Publication Data

Ruccio, David F.
Postmodern moments in modern economics / David F. Ruccio,
Jack Amariglio
p. cm.
Includes bibliographical references and index.
ISBN 0-691-05870-9
1. Economics—History—20th century. I. Amariglio, Jack. II. Title.
HB87.R83 2003
330.1—dc21   2002193066

British Cataloging-in-Publication Data is available

This book has been composed in Sabon

Printed on acid-free paper.∞

www.pupress.princeton.edu

Printed in the United States of America

10 9 8 7 6 5 4 3 2 1

The end of one journey is simply the start of another.

—José Saramago, *Journey to Portugal*

Where there are people my business is certain to thrive
Yo', I've got a lifetime job, baby,
You know, my trade must be plied by the last man alive.

You see,
    I am a gravedigger.
        I dig,
            Gravely . . .

—Kent Foreman, "Tradesman"

Contents

Preface   xi

Acknowledgments   xvii

Chapter One
An Introduction to Postmodernism, for Economics   1

Chapter Two
Knowledge, Uncertainty, and Keynesian Economics   55

Chapter Three
The Body and Neoclassical Economics   92

Chapter Four
Feminist Economics: (Re)Gendering Knowledge and Subjectivity   137

Chapter Five
Values and Institutional Economics   171

Chapter Six
Capitalism, Socialism, and Marxian Economics   216

Chapter Seven
Academic and Everyday Economic Knowledges   252
 Appendix A   283
 Appendix B   285
 Appendix C   287

Chapter Eight
Economic Fragments   289

References   301

Index   333

Preface

THE JOURNEY that culminated in this book began without a fixed destination. As if on one of those hallowed road trips along interstates and meandering back roads, through out-of-the-way towns and stunning landscapes, Jack and I let the imaginary born with the new day determine the direction we would travel. We struck up conversations in roadside diners, or boarded a train and talked with the other passengers, stepping off now and then to soak up the sights and sounds around the station. The journey—the unexpected conversations, the growing and changing collaboration, the unpredictable discoveries—is what mattered. Only in its midst did an idea emerge: a study, written in collaboration, of the relation between postmodernism and economics.

When exactly the journey began is hard to say. We've known one another since graduate school, in the Ph.D. program at the University of Massachusetts at Amherst. (Jack was a fourth-year student when I entered in 1977, one year out of college.) We worked with the same advisers (Stephen Resnick and Richard Wolff) and in the same intellectual tradition (a nondeterminist approach to Marxian theory that was being produced at UMass from the work of Louis Althusser and Barry Hindess and Paul Hirst), but we took it in somewhat different directions: Jack, an inquiry into "primitive communism" in relation to the Iroquois; I, a critique of the methodological and epistemological underpinnings of the "optimizing" approach to socialist planning. Our first real collaboration emerged from our membership in the "journal group," a monthly seminar that aquired an official name (AESA, the Association for Economic and Social Analysis), grew to sponsor academic conferences and summer retreats, and, eventually, gave rise to the editorial board of the journal *Rethinking Marxism* (of which we were both founding members and have served as editors).

But we did not actually start writing together until much later, when we decided to invent a paper called "Postmodernism and the Critique of Political Economy" and present it at the Allied Social Science Association meetings (where both the American Economics Association and the Union for Radical Political Economics hold their annual gatherings) in 1992. Around that same time, we had been discussing the possibility of writing a book on the "problem" of postmodernism in relation to economic discourse in the work of Fredric Jameson and others with two close friends and intellectual companions, Bruce Norton and Julie Graham. For a variety of reasons, that particular volume never came to pass (nor did

Jack and I ever publish that first, joint paper), but all of us did go on to explore various dimensions of the problem, in separate articles, chapters, and books.[1]

The roots of our curiosity about postmodernism, together with our shared sense of its potential significance for economic and social discourse, can, of course, be traced back to earlier periods. Growing up and going to college at roughly the same time but in very different places, both of us were interested in the arts, involved in theater, active in the antiwar and other left-wing movements, disenchanted with traditional versions of economics and radical social theory, and looking to challenge and transform the terms of the existing conversation—in many areas. And in the special setting of the Ph.D. program at UMass during the 1970s and early 1980s, we were allowed to explore those interests and concerns in directions that were not limited by the usual (then as now) disciplinary protocols of economics. Althusser's *Reading Capital* and other, related texts that we worked our way through both opened up the question of the philosophical distinctiveness of Marxian theory (beyond the strictures imposed by modernist versions of economics and social science) and acquainted us with other intellectual currents generally considered to be unrelated to economics, whether mainstream or radical. These included texts in postpositivist history of science and philosophy, structuralism and poststructuralism, deconstruction, linquistics, anthropology, psychoanalysis, and postmodernism, written by Thomas Kuhn, Richard Rorty, Maurice Godelier, Michel Foucault, Jacques Derrida, Jean-François Lyotard, Jacques Lacan, Alan Badiou, George Bataille, Dominique Lecourt, and many others. (This is perhaps one of the reasons why our own reactions to modernism have much more of a "French inflection"—focused as they are on questions of discourse, indeterminacy, and power—than do those of our colleagues and friends Arjo Klamer and Deirdre McCloskey.) And then we were pleased to find that the situation in economics (at least in the areas of methodology and history of thought) had begun to change, with the publication of Klamer's *Conversations with Economists* (1983) and McCloskey's "The Rhetoric of Economics" (1983). If we found ourselves at (or, according to some, outside) the margins of the discipline, at least we had some company!

I certainly don't want to imply any necessary trajectory or teleology, whether of our individual efforts or of our eventual collaboration, based on these "initial conditions." But the fact is (as I look back and stitch together a more or less coherent narrative) both of us did begin exploring the relation between postmodernism and economics and, eventually,

---

[1] See, e.g., Norton 1995, 2001; J. K. Gibson-Graham 1996; Amariglio 1998; Ruccio 1998; Ruccio and Callari 1996; and Ruccio, Graham, and Amariglio 1996.

working together on this project. As it turns out, we composed our first papers devoted to the topic at roughly the same time but quite separately: Jack's for Warren Samuels's edited volume *Economics as Discourse* (published in 1990) and mine for a special issue of the *Journal of Post Keynesian Economics* (published in 1991). As we steered our way through these largely uncharted waters, our new collaboration began to take shape. During telephone conversations and visits to one another's homes, over restaurant meals and between sessions at academic conferences, we traded ideas on teaching, discussed various aspects of economic and social theory, considered relevant conferences, and formulated potential paper topics.

The initial draft of chapter 6 was a paper on postmodernism and the Marxian critique of political economy for the conference "Marxism in the New World Order: Crises and Possibilties," sponsored by *Rethinking Marxism* in 1992. Later, a brief conversation while we were walking through a parking lot (after dinner in a Northampton, Massachusetts, Mexican restaurant) was the impetus for an essay on a disorderly conception of capitalist competition for a conference on volume 3 of *Capital* in Bergamo, Italy, in 1994; parts of that essay are also included in chapter 6. Chapter 2 is largely based on a paper for a 1993 conference, "Keynes, Knowledge, and Uncertainty," held at Leeds University and organized by Sheila Dow and John Hillard. "Why not?" we asked ourselves as we considered a submission, though we were nervous about stepping onto the terrain of those better schooled in Keynes. Still, we wondered, why not see what use we can make of postmodern theory in exploring the various reactions to Keynes's own writings on uncertainty? We were pleased by a generally warm reception to our intellectual trespassing, although one participant did comment later that ours was a "dangerous strategy" (Backhouse 1995, 365).[2]

An invitation to participate in "Knowledges: Production, Distribution, Revision," a conference at the University of Minnesota in 1994, led us to the problem of nonacademic economic knowledges and to the work that is the backbone of chapter 7. Fortunately, we had the opportunity to further develop our ideas on that topic when, in 1998, Evan Watkins kindly asked us to present some recent work in a seminar session with his students and in public lectures at Pennsylvania State University. Our first attempt to theorize the role of the body in relation to economic discourse,

---

[2] An even stronger reaction has recently been expressed by Yanis Varoufakis, who, in the *Post-autistic Economics Review* (2002), argues that postmodernism "not only lets neoclassical economics off the hook but, more worryingly, reinforces it copiously before dissolving into it." Therefore, he concludes, "the postmodern turn will be chosen by pseudo-dissidents whose prime interests lie in acquiring a chic image; one that the self-effacing postmodern criticism is good at imparting." Given the trajectory of our academic careers, if we have sought to acquire a "chic image," one would have to conclude that we have failed miserably.

especially neoclassical economics, took the form of a paper for a conference on the so-called new economic criticism at Case Western Reserve
University, also in 1994. This was a pioneering attempt, by Mark Osteen
and Martha Woodmansee, to gather people from the largely separate academic worlds of economics and literature to discuss, on one hand, economists' use of the methods and protocols of literary criticism to analyze
"economic texts" (including the idea that economic institutions and practices could be read as texts) and, on the other hand, literary critics' use
and production of economic concepts and theories (including many that
are not recognized as such by most practicing economists). Much was
made at the time of the difficulty in communicating across disciplinary
boundaries. In the case of our work on the body, which is set forth in
chapter 3, the problem was exactly the opposite: while literary theorists
generally greeted our approach with enthusiasm, many mainstream economists considered it irrelevant, and our heterodox companions challenged
it as wrongheaded.

As our collaboration changed and developed, it also expanded to include others. Some of the most valuable shared work has been with Stephen Cullenberg. In 1995, the three of us organized a conference "Postmodernism, Economics, and Knowledge" at the University of California,
Riverside. Our joint work on the edited volume that emerged from that
conference included an introduction that, in revised form, appears here
as chapter 1. Jack's paper with Julie Graham, prepared for the 1993 "Out
of the Margins" conference organized by the International Association
for Feminist Economics, was the starting point for our reflections on postmodernism and feminist economics in chapter 4. That leaves chapter 5
(which builds on Jack's 1987 unpublished paper on Nietzsche and Marx)
and chapter 8, the conclusion (which, in the words of one of the outside
readers for the press, represents our attempt to provide "coherence without closure").

In this way the individual passages and sections of this book emerged,
at diverse places and moments, from within the collaboration that we've
nurtured and sustained for the better part of the past two decades. But
the idea of the book itself—writing a single volume on the postmodern
moments in modern economics—did not arise until the summer of 1994.
Our first idea was to edit a volume of others' writings, since no such
collection existed at that time. Then we decided that separately and together the two of us had written (or were planning to write) enough to
consider editing a volume of our own essays. Finally, we discarded that
idea in favor of a more cohesive monograph that borrowed from our
previous work but explored new topics and was written as a single text.
An interested publisher, a patient and insightful editor, many other proj-

ects and diversions along the way, and the book we hoped someday to write now exists.

The research project itself has allowed us to develop a new relationship both to the discipline of economics and to the work that is currently taking place in other disciplines. The two of us, with doctoral degrees in economics, have always been outsiders—sometimes even by choice. Oddly enough, however, postmodernism provided a way for us to become more engaged with the discipline, especially in areas and schools of thought where we hadn't spent much time (including, much to our surprise, topics like the Arrow-Debreu general equilibrium theory). It thus helped us create spaces in which other ways of thinking and other conversations—still having to do with economic questions and themes—could take place. Reading, talking, and writing about the connections between postmodernism and economics also encouraged us to seek out discussions within academic settings outside and beyond economics. We have therefore spent a good bit of time and energy crossing disciplinary borders, especially into literature and literary criticism, anthropology, cultural studies, philosophy, and social theory. We hope to have assembled a text that, in the end, is interesting and relevant to our colleagues and friends on (and beyond) both sides of the disciplinary divide.

David F. Ruccio

Acknowledgments ———————————————————————————

A LARGE PART of the pleasure of both the collaboration and the intellectual project that find expression in this book can be attributed to the many people we have met and talked with along the way. We have benefited from their comments and encouragement, their suggestions and support, in ways of which we may still be only dimly aware. Rather than the vaunted "death of the author," our work emerges from and dissolves into this larger collaboration, as part of ongoing and expanding conversations.

We have chosen to minimize the distinctions among the various roles our friends and colleagues have played in the history of this book, in an attempt to avoid the hierarchy and differentiation that are often implicit in these kinds of acknowledgments. Instead, we want to use this space to publicly express our gratitude in the form of some relatively unadorned lists.

Together, we want to thank the following individuals: Enid Arvidson, Radhika Balakrishnan, Drucilla Barker, Ricardo Bellofiore, Carole Biewener, Mark Blaug, Ted Burczak, Antonio Callari, S. Charusheela, Victoria Chick, Joseph Childers, Brian Cooper, Stephen Cullenberg, John Davis, Neil de Marchi, George DeMartino, Jonathan Diskin, Sheila Dow, William Dugger, John Dupré, Susan Feiner, Rebecca Forest, Regenia Gagnier, Rob Garnett, Kath Gibson, Ilene Grabel, Julie Graham, Ulla Grapard, Jean-Joseph Goux, Stephen Gudeman, Wade Hands, Sandra Harding, Shaun Hargreaves Heap, Gillian Hewitson, John Hillard, Susan Jahoda, Donald Katzner, Serap Kayatekin, Arjo Klamer, Henry Krips, Amitava Kumar, Tony Lawson, Lee Levin, the late Don Lavoie, Allan MacNeill, Yahya Mete Madra, Uskali Mäki, Stephen Marglin, Deirdre McCloskey, Richard McIntyre, Ed McKenna, Judith Mehta, Ellen Messer-Davidow, Will Milberg, Phil Mirowski, Warren Montag, Margueritte Murphy, Julie Nelson, Bruce Norton, William Olson, Mark Osteen, Cecilia Rio, Bruce Roberts, John Roche, Jane Rossetti, Warren Samuels, Antonio Santucci, Mark Setterfield, Anwar Shaikh, David Shumway, Jackie Southern, Gayatri Chakravorty Spivak, Diana Strassman, Paul Turpin, Marjolein van der Veen, Evan Watkins, Roy Weintraub, Lucas Wilson, Martha Woodmansee, and Diane Zannoni.

Individually, we want to thank many other people. Bill and Demetra Allen, Ernie Bartell, Saibal Basu, Suzanne Bergeron, Gerry Berk, Dwight Billings, Joseph Buttigieg, Peter Buttigieg, Chuck Craypo, Fred Dallmayr, Eray Duzenli, Kent Foreman, Teresa Ghilarducci, Denis Goulet, Janet Hotch, Carla Ingrando, Marc Jarsulic, Gilberto Lima, Ryan Mason,

Anne Montgomery, Tom Scheiding, Esther-Mirjam Sent, Larry Simon, Roger Skurski, Jacinda Swanson, Juli Tate, Karen Tice, Chuck Wilber, Marty Wolfson—and, *muy particularmente*, Lisa Markowitz—have made David's work on this book not only possible but enjoyable. For their contribution to his work, life, worklife, and lifework, including this book, Jack is indebted to Hans Abbing, the late Paola Beck, Evangelos Charos, Al DeCiccio, Elaine Donovan, Christina Hatgis, Sue Ellen Holbrook, Sandor Horváth, Caroline Janssens, Kerry Johnson, Monica Kjelman, Anthony Laramie, Art Ledoux, Theodore Long, Ellen Longsworth, Larry Looney, Joanneke Lootsma, Michael Mascolo, Marijke Prins, David Raymond, Rose-Mary Sargent, Charles Tontar, Bregje van Eekelen, Irene van Staveren, Olav Velthuis, Doris Weichselbaumer, and Peter-Wim Zuidhof

The production of this book was made possible in part by support from the Institute for Scholarship in Liberal Arts, College of Arts and Letters, University of Notre Dame.

Peter Dougherty is a more patient, understanding, and helpful editor than any author can rightly expect. He also cares and knows more about economics than most practicing economists. He deserves a great deal of credit for imagining—and doing his own part to create—a larger conversation.

It is impossible to express in words all that we feel for the friendship, encouragement, and inspiration unstintingly offered by Stephen Resnick and Richard Wolff over the years. We hope that dedicating this book to them will begin to indicate our gratitude.

Jack Amariglio. "Economics as a Postmodern Discourse." In *Economics as Discourse*, ed. Warren Samuels, 14–46. Boston: Kluwer Academic, 1990.
Jack Amariglio. "Give the Ghost a Chance! A Comrade's Shadowy Addendum." In *The Question of the Gift: Essays across Disciplines*, ed. M. Osteen. New York: Routledge, 2002.
Jack Amariglio, Stephen Cullenberg, and David F. Ruccio. Introduction to *Postmodernism, Economics, and Knowledge*, ed. S. Cullenberg, J. Amariglio, and D. F. Ruccio, 3–57. New York: Routledge, 2001.

David F. Ruccio and Jack Amariglio. "Keynes, Postmodernism, Uncertainty." In *Keynes, Knowledge, and Uncertainty*, ed. S. Dow and J. Hillard, 334–56. Aldershot: Edward Elgar, 1994.

David F. Ruccio and Jack Amariglio. "Postmodernism, Marxism, and the Critique of Modern Economic Thought." *Rethinking Marxism* 7 (fall 1994): 7–35.

David F. Ruccio and Jack Amariglio. "The (Dis)orderly Process of Capitalist Competition." In *Marxian Economics: A Centenary Appraisal*, vol. 1, ed. R. Bellofiore, 94–108. London: Macmillan, 1998.

David F. Ruccio and Jack Amariglio. "The Transgressive Knowledge of 'Ersatz Economics.' " In *What Do Economists Know? New Economics of Knowledge*, ed. R. Garnett, 19–36. New York: Routledge, 1999.

David F. Ruccio and Jack Amariglio. "From Unity to Dispersion: The Body in Modern Economic Discourse." In *Postmodernism, Economics, and Knowledge*, ed. S. Cullenberg, J. Amariglio, and D. F. Ruccio, 143–65. New York: Routledge, 2001.

David F. Ruccio and Jack Amariglio. "Modern Economics: The Case of the Disappearing Body?" *Cambridge Journal of Economics* 26 (January 2002): 81–103.

POSTMODERN MOMENTS IN MODERN ECONOMICS

1

An Introduction to Postmodernism, for Economics

Funeral by funeral, economics does make progress.
—Paul A. Samuelson, "Credo of a Lucky
  Textbook Author"

IN THIS CAUTIONARY epigraph—or epitaph, as the case may be—the doyen of modernist economics suggests how it becomes the queen of the social sciences, one shovelful of dirt on a coffin after another. For Samuelson, the "Darwinian impact of reality melts away even the prettiest of fanciful theories and the hottest of ideological frenzies" (1997, 159).[1] Modernism as dirge; economic knowledge as its fossil remains.

Samuelson is only the latest to conclude with morbid optimism that, in the end, the evolutionary nature of scientific practice amongst economists does lead to the growth of economic knowledge—even if it grows as an unintended consequence of practice. There is a utopia in this dystopic rendition; a faith in the idea that, as long as economists remain committed to the norms of scientific practice, the knowledge they produce will illuminate historical reality and enlighten future generations.[2] This grizzled confidence is a hallmark of modernism itself, those discourses and practices

---

[1] Samuelson's reformulation of Planck's credo, substituting "economics" for "science," occurs in this 1997 essay paying tribute to his *Economics* textbook; it occurs as well in his (1998) fiftieth-anniversary paean to his "lucky" book *(Foundations of Economic Analysis)*. This time, though, he not only credits Planck for the loan, but also proceeds in paraphrasing a different adage, as when he tells us that, in economics, "often the dance must proceed Two Steps Forward and One Step Back" (1998, 1379). Whether digging or dancing, though, Samuelson labors just the same in his confident assertion that "soft and hard sciences are cumulative disciplines" in which "we each bring our contributions of 'value added' to the pot of progress" (1378).

[2] It seems that there must be thousands (perhaps tens of thousands) of easily accessible statements by economists in which this optimism is a necessary component. One does wonder why it is necessary to keep incanting such confidence. One of these thousands is the following: talking about his own theory of "bounded rationality" and its relative neglect to date by practicing economists, Herbert Simon (1991) reflects that "science, viewed as competition among theories, has an unmatched advantage over all other forms of intellectual competition. In the long run (no more than centuries), the winner succeeds, not by superior rhetoric, not by the ability to convince or dazzle a lay audience, not by political influence, but by the support of data, facts as they are gradually and cumulatively revealed. As long as its factual veridicality is unchallenged, one can remain calm about the future of a theory" (364–65).

that have been associated with ideas such as "progress" and "knowledge" since the Western Enlightenment.[3]

Yet despite the prevalent optimism among economists and philosophers over the past one hundred and more years, many of them have nervously surveyed the standing of economic knowledge in modernist culture and science: "[C]laimed to be the most 'effective' or 'mature' of the social or human sciences, or described as the 'hardest' of the 'soft' sciences, economics seems destined for a somewhat ambiguous and problematic place in the spectrum of knowledge" (Hutchinson 1979, 1).

There is no need to lament this ambiguity, for it speaks to the effervescent vitality (and not Samuelson's recursive life through incessant death) of the different discourses that comprise economics. This vitality may be most attributable to the "undecidables" and "aporias" that characterize modern economics, the fact that pure scientificity always seems out of reach as the ostensible achievement of the discipline.[4] In some versions of this ambiguity, the point is to clean up economics by removing the vestiges of past "errors" ("prettiest of fanciful theories") and opinion ("hottest of ideological frenzies") that still remain in the debates between various schools.[5] Other versions have it that as long as economics remains a "human" science, it will be impossible to accurately model economic behavior since humans confound models in their resort to just plain inexplicable actions.[6] And there are others who consider economists' attempts

[3] In the course of his discussion of the citing of precursors for one's own authoritative stance, E. Roy Weintraub summarizes "Whig" histories of economic thought like this: "Science as the exemplar of the march of reason, and economics, as science, leads the Whiggish historian of economics and the typical economic scientist to think in terms of successes and failures, precursors and blind alleys, heroes sung and unsung, and all manner of retrospective gold medals and booby prizes" (1997, 186).

[4] Compare the view that ambiguity means absence of scientific precision (and thereby progress) with Paul Feyerabend's emphasis on "the essential ambiguity of all concepts, images, and notions that presuppose change. Without ambiguity, no change, ever. The quantum theory, as interpreted by Niels Bohr, is a perfect example of that" (1999, viii).

[5] Consider, for example, this blast at "neowalrasian theory" leveled by Robert Clower (1994). After declaring this theory "scientifically vacuous" and concluding that there "is no way to make progress in economic science except by first discarding neowalrasian analysis" (810), Clower really gets down to business: "in my opinion, what we presently possess by way of so-called pure economic theory is objectively indistinguishable from what the physicist Richard Feynman, in an unflattering sketch of nonsense 'science,' called 'cargo cult science' " (809). Clower, by the way, goes on to make a pitch for a reversion to "induction," as though this would indeed provide a straight shot to science.

[6] This confounding of science due to human behavior includes, of course, the all-too-humanness of the economic scientists themselves. Or, at least this is the gentle conclusion of Tjalling Koopmans (1957), who sees in the supposed discrepancy between the logic of correct scientific procedures and the persistent departures from this norm by economists a kind of understandable human failing in wanting to cut to the chase, a failing that could be called uncharitably the "will to distort." In Koopmans' own (understated) words: "often

to model human behavior pure blasphemy, seeing such desire for mechanistic control as a violation of the basic freedom of human beings and of the dignity and meaning of human life.

We are not partial to any of these ways of thinking through the problematic of ambiguity that T. W. Hutchison announces. Instead, we take up the challenge of unearthing and engaging the "undecidables" and "aporias" of economic discourse, as part of a new phase of self-conscious thought, a new phase perhaps of society and history: that which has been labeled the postmodern.[7]

Categorizing the Postmodern

Postmodernism is a relatively new development within economics, but one that has promise in calling economists' attention not only to the epistemological conditions of existence for their theorizing, but also to the general cultural milieu within which modern economics has both expanded and contracted. Modern economics certainly has a right to claim, as Samuelson says, the growth of knowledge. But it has run up against anomalies and fragmentations that have proliferated diverse knowledges, in addition to putting on the agenda concepts and approaches that lead away from rather than toward a unified, universalist science. While some may regard current economic discourse as "converging," we argue that—more than a century after the marginalist revolution—economic discourse is more heterogeneous than one might expect a unified science to be.[8] This heterogeneity is nothing to bemoan. It speaks instead to the limits of modernism in economics, and just as much to the emergence of "postmodern moments" within the discipline.

---

we are more preoccupied with arriving at what we deem to be true statements or best predictions, in the light of such knowledge as we have of the phenomena in question, than in exhibiting the postulational basis, and thereby the ultimate observational evidence, on which our statements rest" (143).

[7] We have found the following surveys of postmodernism useful in our teaching and research: Sim 1999; Bertens 1995; Rosenau 1992; Best and Kellner 1991; Docherty 1993; Connor 1989; Rose 1991; and Nicholson 1990. Our depiction here of postmodernism thus draws on all of these, but also differs in important respects.

[8] Of course, there are studies (e.g., Alston, Kearl, and Vaughan 1992) showing a great degree of "consensus" among a sample of economists on numerous theoretical issues. As Fuchs, Krueger, and Poterba (1998) argue, though, their own studies dealing with questions of policy based on parameter estimation techniques demonstrate considerable amounts of disagreement among economists within particular fields. This result is interesting since it suggests that the empirical and practical implications one draws from common theoretical outlooks (that is, even if one concedes this point) can vary widely among aspiring scientists because of differences in estimates, but even more so because of the economists' "values."

Many commentators have challenged the Samuelsonian vision by attacking the neoclassical orthodoxy with which progress in economic theory is most often associated. Yet these criticisms also treat economics as an autonomous field, unconnected to such trends as formalism, historicism, and scientism that have comprised the transdiscursive horizon of Western modernism during the past 125 years. Our own challenge to Samuelsonian progress starts from the premise that modernism is not only an exhausted project, but a destructive one. One form of damage is its silencing of theoretical disagreement under the rubric of the unity of science and "correct" scientific protocols. This has led to disdain for, neglect of, and hostility towards nonmainstream thought.

Additionally, the Samuelsonian vision has kept in place the fetishism of the unified rational subject, the bottom line of "prediction," the reliance on mathematical "rigor," and much else that has given economics its specifically "modern" character. An engagement with postmodernism implies giving up this ground. It means taking seriously the evanescent concepts and experiences of disunity and dispersion in everything from macroeconomic theorizing to economic actors, now devoid of central, organizing motivations. These concepts and experiences have shown up even in the modernism that dominates economics. However, the conceptual possibilities opened up by these postmodern irruptions have not been mined to much purpose. Our hope is that the postmodern can push economists and others to talk about the discipline and conduct their theoretical practices differently. Many lines of research are opened if postmodernism is taken seriously, as we show in subsequent chapters.

We will discuss postmodernism as historical phase, as existential "condition," as style, and as critique. Most of the debates surrounding the term *postmodern* can be rendered intelligible according to these four headings.[9] Postmodernism has been seen, by some critics, as a particular stage in the life history of modern capitalist economies. It has been seen as a "condition," or state of existence, describing the cultural/social dominant within which we experience the contemporaneous. Some writers view postmodernism as a literary/rhetorical or practical style (especially in the arts and architecture), one that affects even the philosophical stances that characterize current discussion regarding the nature of knowledge and scientific method. Finally, postmodernism has been a critique, that is, an attempt

---

[9] Stephen Brown (1995) speaks of the seven "key features" of postmodernism. He lists them as "fragmentation, de-differentiation, hyperreality, chronology, pastiche, anti-foundationalism, and pluralism" (106). As readers can ascertain, these features are dispersed throughout our treatment of the "four categories" that follow. For another list of distinguishing characteristics of postmodernism (or at least of poststructuralism), see Amariglio 1998.

to create thought and action "outside" of the constraints of modernism (and here, modernism ranges from modernization and economic development strategies in a postcolonial world to the "high modernism" of formalist literature and mathematics). In what follows, we elucidate each of these categories. This will set the stage for a brief synopsis of the postmodern moments that have arisen within economic discourse and provide a context for the chapters that comprise the remainder of our book.

Postmodernity: The Latest Phase of Capitalism?

It needs to be said straightaway that we do not pursue an approach that sees postmodernism as a particular world-historical phase. Nothing in our treatment invokes the "postmodern" as the latest stage in "late capitalist" (or "post-Fordist") economies, and especially the process of "globalization."

The main reason for our neglect of this approach is that we reject its basic premises, first, that capitalism has morphed within the past half century into a distinct socioeconomic phase captured by the concept of "late capitalism" and, second, that "postmodernism" as a *noneconomic* phenomenon illustrates the existence of such a phase, or that postmodernism refers to a historical rupture in the global economy. Since our main objective is to address the ways in which postmodernism currently appears, or could guide new developments, within the discipline of academic economics, we have chosen not to elaborate our objections to this line of thought.

Still, this work is ubiquitous in the fields "outside" of academic economics, and a few words on it will put the rest of our analysis into clearer relief. It is not our aim to disparage this literature or to dissuade economists from interacting with it. To the contrary, economists should read it, partly because its picture of present world economic circumstances is so far from the mainstream neoclassical orthodoxy (and so much closer to heterodox, especially Marxist, views) that it can be engaged productively as a bona fide challenge, not only to that orthodoxy, but to cross-disciplinary dialogue. Our own interests in postmodernism and its contributions to the field of economics, though, lie elsewhere.

The best-known advocate of the "late capitalist" approach is the literary and cultural theorist Fredric Jameson. Jameson (1991) captures the flavor of treating postmodernism as the cultural form of the latest phase of capitalist development in his frequent reference to three identifying aspects of "late capitalism": mass commodification, a shift in the location and conditions of global production, and the rise of new industries (mostly in information technologies) that allow for the unbroken worldwide expansion of capitalist markets and, hence, profitability.[10] Jameson, it should be noted, is a devotee of the late Belgian Marxist economist Ernest Mandel (1975), whose book on "late capitalism" is the bible for those (cultural critics mostly on the left) who are looking to define capitalism's most recent trajectory.[11] Following in the footsteps of both the Marxian-inspired Frankfurt School of sociocultural analysis (Theodor Adorno, Max Horkheimer, and Herbert Marcuse, among others) and the great Hungarian cultural theorist Georg Lukács, Jameson analyzes the forms of cultural expression that have aided this phase of capitalist development, partly by becoming commodities themselves.[12] Hence, everything from the arts to philosophical thinking is seen to relate to this unyielding commodification and postindustrialization of the industrialized nations, paralleling the shift in economic production and ecological impact brought about by the globalization of capital.[13]

It is the idea of commodification that connects postmodernism most intimately to late capitalism.[14] Not only has capitalism inexorably ex-

[10] Manuel Castells's monumental three-volume analysis (1996–98) of globalization, information, and identity foretells of a new global information age that might be understood as the phase of postmodernity par excellence.

[11] For a first-rate depiction of the way Jameson utilizes Mandel, see Norton 1995. Norton also argues that Jameson "contains postmodernism within a modernist narrative" (66) by invoking the unifying vision of a stage-theory of capitalism. The concept of post-Fordism (Amin 1994) rivals late capitalism within literary theory and cultural studies as a way of making sense (again, from a left-wing perspective) of the supposed economics of postmodernism. Gibson-Graham (1996) develops a critique on grounds similar to those of Norton. She notes, in particular, that "theories of post-Fordism, centered as they are on the conditions and consequences of the flexible industrial paradigm and stable capital accumulation, present a world in which capitalist development is the only road" (164).

[12] Culture here should be understood to include the forms of subjectivity that global capitalism is said to produce. Needless to say, in the Jamesonian vision, postcolonials seem increasingly to hold identical subject (or should we say, subjected) positions, including of course that of class. Kayatekin and Ruccio (1998) challenge the idea that processes of globalization create a single subjectivity and argue, instead, that it is both possible and desirable to locate/produce multiple social (including class) identities in the postcolonial world.

[13] A similar frame of analysis marks David Harvey's *The Condition of Postmodernity* (1989). If not on a par with the influence of Jameson, then Harvey must be seen as not far behind in affecting investigations of postmodernism in terms of the latest phase of capitalism. For an alternative take on capitalism and globalization, one that challenges from a feminist, poststructuralist viewpoint the totalizing vision implicit in Jameson, Harvey, and others, see Gibson-Graham 1996.

[14] Bruce Pietrykowski (1994) provides a different reading from Jameson and others who have argued for a one-to-one correspondence between consumer culture and postmodernism. Pietrykowski presents evidence that many of the elements of "fast capitalism" and "ephemerality, fragmentation, juxtaposition, surface, and depthlessness" that are currently attributed to post-Fordism and postmodernism can be seen clearly in the rise of consumer services and the particular aesthetics or designs of many commercial sites, from gas stations to department stores, during the heyday of Fordism in the early twentieth century in the

panded markets, both geographically and in quantity of objects marketed, but culture has lost its relative autonomy and become almost entirely oriented toward the sale of commodities. This is apparent, according to some critics, in the growth of markets for cultural artifacts and the shrinking number of them produced outside of an exchange economy. More importantly, it is apparent in the increasing shallowness and slickness of the arts, culture, and thought, as they uncritically mimic—as with pop art, such as Warhol's *Campbell's Soup, 1*—or propagate commercial images. Indeed, an emphasis on "image" or "surface" as opposed to "content" or "depth"—characteristic of previous artistic forms, such as van Gogh's *Still Life*—is said to mark art forms that express this postmodern shift.[15]

It is noteworthy that Jameson identifies Gary Becker (1991) as the quintessential postmodern economist. Becker represents, in Jameson's view, the recognition among economists that most if not all areas of contemporary life are now prone to the logic of capital, including the vagaries of market forces. According to Jameson, Becker captures the spirit of the age, as everything from marriage to drug addiction to death becomes fodder for market-inspired calculations. Jameson does not present Becker as the latest disciplinary "imperialist," seeking to displace other noneconomic approaches to culture by advocating economically rational principles, especially individual choice, as the foundation of all social life.[16] Instead, Becker's theoretical oeuvre gives voice to that which has transpired "in reality": the unfettered spread in the last century of capitalist markets and the commodification of just about everything. In Jameson's eyes, Becker's postmodernism consists mainly in marking the extent to which market logics have seized any and all noncapitalist, nonmarket social domains.

This take on Becker contrasts with the interpretation of feminist economists and others who consider his work in the vein of "high modernism,"[17] as representative of the neoclassical paradigm committed to for-

---

United States. Pietrykowski's main point is that there is no clear-cut division, when it comes to commodity culture, between modernity and postmodernity.

[15] For an excellent overview of the many art forms that have characterized the postmodern during the last thirty years, from diverse postminimal styles to deconstruction and commodity art, see Sandler 1996.

[16] For an excellent evaluation of Becker's notion of culture as it enters economic analysis, see Koritz and Koritz 1999. Amartya Sen names Becker as one example of economists whose understanding of establishing "close relations" with different disciplines takes an "imperialist" form. As Sen states more generally, "Sometimes the proposed relation has been given a rather 'imperialist' form, with economic theorists adhering strictly to their astonishingly narrow methodology and then applying, with remarkable confidence, that slim methodology to other disciplines as well" (1991, 76).

[17] One exception is McCloskey, who, while critical of the strategies of formal modeling, or "blackboard economics" as she has called it elsewhere (1996), supports the neoclassical metaphor of the rational individual, at least in major part.

Figure 1.1. Andy Warhol, *Campbell's Soup, 1* (1968). One from a portfolio of ten screenprints on paper, 35" x 23". (Credit: The Andy Warhol Foundation, Inc./ Art Resource, New York.)

mal modeling and the reduction of human motives to a single purpose: individual gain. Motivations such as "altruism," for example, produce "psychic gain." Be that as it may, we note again that for many literary and cultural theorists like Jameson, the postmodern denotes rampant commodification, unchecked by oppositional forces—avant-gardes, say—that find themselves subverted by the power and allure of the market. This world, structured according to the object-life of the commodity, has received an enormous boost by new information technologies, especially the Internet. Accordingly, computers have made commodity time and space ultimately traversable in ways unthinkable for past generations of producers and consumers. In addition to the use of computer technology in such "post-Fordist" production methods as "flexible specialization," one need not leave one's chair (in front of one's screen, of course) to be bombarded by commodity images and the cornucopia of goods in cyberspace. This obliteration of constraints of time and geographical location in buying and selling (lowering transactions costs and reducing to rubble other past barriers to the international flow of financial capital and goods) reconstructs all notions and experiences pertaining to community and nation—hence the rise of the "global economy" that is said to be the hallmark of the postmodern.

Figure 1.2. Vincent van Gogh, *Still Life with Apples, Meat, and Bread Roll* (1886). Oil on canvas, 46 x 55 cm. (Credit: Collection Kröller-Müller Museum, Otterlo, Netherlands.)

Opponents of this global spread of capitalist commodity production often counter by seeking spaces for economic life, if not for economic thought, in pre- or noncapitalist social processes, such as gift giving.[18] As capitalism seeps into every pore of the worldwide social skin, these critics hail the gift and any other realm of economic activity not reducible to market exchange. If in the postmodern age culture is merely an accompaniment to capitalist economic expansion, then it is legitimate to ask if it is possible to think about such issues as value and exchange in any register "outside" the regime of the commodity as "the general equivalent."

[18] Or, consider, for example, this understanding of postmodernity as resistance to "economics," a resistance that is informed by the experience of postcolonial subjectivity: "Postmodernity already exists where people refuse to be seduced and controlled by economic laws. It exists for peoples rediscovering and reinventing their traditional commons by re-embedding the economy (to use Polanyi's expression) into society and culture; subordinating it again to politics and ethics; marginalizing it—putting it at their margins: which is precisely what it means to be 'marginal' in modern times" (Esteva and Prakash 1998).

Postmodernism as the "Condition" of the Contemporary

The idea of the postmodern as a "condition" of life today is sometimes connected to the notion of postmodernism as a historical stage. Yet in the work of the best-known theorist of this "condition," Jean-François Lyotard (1984), most of the conceptual baggage of "late capitalist" discourse is discarded for a different emphasis, one that connects living in a postmodern world with changes in discourse itself, especially those that concern knowledge, technology, and science, and thus economics. Lyotard's focus on science and knowledge is matched by still others who describe the current state of social existence (mostly in developed Western capitalist nations) as characterized by the decentering of individual selves and society, a shift from "global" to "local" politics and ethics, the "saturation" of psyches and imaginations by an amazing array of discontinuous images and events, and much else. However, Lyotard in *The Postmodern Condition* describes a shift in the ways in which knowledge and science are both conceptualized and practiced—a shift, we note, that opens up a chasm between modernity and postmodernity.[19]

Lyotard's "report on knowledge," as he calls it, is concerned largely with two interrelated issues. One is rejection of what he terms the "grand metanarratives" that have structured much thought and practice since the Enlightenment. Hence, to the degree that modernity is contemporaneous with the rise and spread of Enlightenment thinking, Lyotard is offering a diagnosis of life *after* modernism. These metanarratives have ranged from the promise of political independence and human liberation through representative democracy or the victory of the masses to the claims for scientific knowledge as the harbinger of social progress through victory over nature and through social engineering. Lyotard calls particular attention to those metanarratives, like liberalism and Marxism, that have held out the hope for total change in society through advocacy of particular principles and perspectives. Both liberalism and Marxism, for example, have measured progress partly in terms of the ability to harness technology and science to human designs, most especially the end of political oppression and economic exploitation. Lyotard is hostile to such stories insofar as they themselves contribute to a "totalizing" vision of the world, one in which progress is in the nature of history, and in which social practices

---

[19] Dow (2001) and Klamer (2001) both interrogate the tenuous links between modernity and postmodernity as it affects discourse. For Dow, the postmodern is the dialectical emergence of the antimodern, while for Klamer the turn of neoclassical economics to "high modernism" augurs its immanent/imminent implosion. Amariglio's (2001) commentary treats the ultimate success (or not) of Dow, Klamer, and also McCloskey in steering a path between or away from modernism and postmodernism.

are linked in a kind of reinforcing signifying chain in the name (or cause) of freedom, happiness, and autonomy. That is, Lyotard sees that much damage has been done in the advent of such grand causes, and he identifies them with the narratives, broadly held and interpreted, that give them their power. But Lyotard also sees the attempt to reduce the relative autonomy of science and culture in the service of these master narratives as illusory or dangerous or both.

Thus Lyotard eschews the story, so prevalent in the history and philosophy of economics, that greater knowledge has propelled social progress, as truth inevitably drives out error and knowledge replaces ideology.[20] A distinguishing aspect of modernist thought is belief in narratives about the benefits of scientific knowledge.[21] Lyotard argues that current scientific preoccupations and practices are no longer wedded to narratives about the ultimate knowability of the world and the beneficial dimension of such knowledge. The world of science that he describes is more taken with images, concepts, and activities of discontinuity. It is a world of nearly infinite and diverse information flows (abetted by the computer revolution) and is rife with scientific "games" in which meaning and consequence are always in play or at stake.[22] This is a world, according to Lyotard, that is developing with a view to chaos and uncertainty, to indeterminacies and fracta, rather than presuming the unified structure of nature and the sanguine results of scientific knowledge.[23] In this world the fundamental discursivity

[20] Cullenberg and Dasgupta (2001) show that the "high modernist" debate over capital theory between the two Cambridges was as much about a contestation of mythologies as it was about the logical correctness of various theoretical propositions put forth. McCloskey (2001) also challenges the view of the progressive and inevitable triumph of "better" theory.

[21] A chemist who is a colleague declared recently in a public audience that the only thing in the entire past century he could identify as clearly contributing to a "better" world was science; all other spheres of human endeavor, from the arts through social and political movements for enfranchisement and sexual revolutions to the spread of the marketplace, have experienced mixed results, at best, and most probably social devolution!

[22] If there is an icon of postmodernism, it is likely the computer. According to Wise (1995), computer science ironically holds much the same position in regard to high theoretical science as did mathematics before the last part of the nineteenth century. Wise states: "Not until the end of the nineteenth century did mathematical expression by itself attain high status among natural philosophers, ultimately as the very foundation of 'modern' physics. (Its formerly suspect boundary position has now been taken over by computer science, halfway between proper science and practical engineering, which in turn is rapidly becoming the foundation of 'postmodern' science)" (357).

[23] Paul Cilliers in *Complexity and the Postmodern* (1998) brings together developments in neurosciences, logic, linguistics, computer science, the philosophy of science, and deconstruction and poststructuralism to provide an interdisciplinary approach to questions of representation and organization in postmodernity. Building explicitly upon Lyotard, Cilliers argues that postmodern societies meet all of what he specifies as the main criteria for "complex systems."

of science is celebrated in a new narrative, as everything from biotechnology and human genome research to contemporary astrophysics may be seen as a "reading" or a Wittgensteinian game. Lyotard identifies these considerations and games as the postmodern condition, at least where production and dissemination of knowledge are concerned.

The postmodern condition Lyotard describes has its corollaries in a variety of human activities. Regardless of the originating causes of this condition (capitalism's most recent developments or the information revolution or the decline of community and the evaporation of universal moral norms or the effects of affluence for some and continued agony for others, etc.), many others have noted the changed conditions of life in more developed societies during the past forty or more years.[24] Lyotard's "report" highlights in many ways the central terms of this altered life experience (that is, compared to the modernism that is said to either precede or coexist with it).[25] These terms include a sense that individual lives and social entities have been "decentered"; that we live in a variety of psychological and social states/positions, each of which "overdetermines" our identities and subjectivities; that modern science and technology contribute possibly as much to "barbarism" and destruction (the atom bomb, pollution, germ warfare, etc.) as they do to the betterment of human life and the natural environment; that the metanarratives of progress and liberation have either failed or contributed to sociopolitical outcomes that are repulsive; that knowledge and ethics are context-specific and time-specific; that there are radical discontinuities in the way we experience most everything we encounter; that little in culture can or ought to be considered "original" or "authentic"; that power is dispersed rather than concentrated; that the search for unique meaning and transcendent truth is no longer meaningful or constructive; and that social inequalities continue, despite modernism's promises of freedom, justice, and equality for all.

This list speaks to modernism's putative exhaustion and anomie, but also to altered circumstances, some of which are happily embraced by

[24] In his 1986 book, *The Control Revolution*, which treats the rise of "the information society" during the past forty or so years, James Beniger produces a daunting list (on pages 4 and 5) of names given by a wide range of social theorists to the "major social transformations identified since 1950." This list, which stops at 1984, includes such labels as *postindustrial society, postliberal age*, the *age of discontinuity*, the *new service economy*, and much more, posited by such writers as Peter Drucker, Alvin Toffler, Daniel Bell, Michael Piore, and Charles Sabel. Of course, the past two decades have seen even more terms and many other authors who could easily be added to his list.

[25] In an earlier text, *Libidinal Economy*, Lyotard (1993, original French edition in 1974) ventures into discussions about the nature of economic crises during the past century (though, of course, this venture follows a different agenda of subjecting modernist economic discourses to poststructuralist interrogation). Brian Cooper and Margueritte Murphy (1999) conduct an insightful close reading of Lyotard's "libidinal economics."

theorists of postmodernism. These changed circumstances, expressed perhaps most fully in recent art and literature, signal the extent to which
the touchstones of modernist culture and society are being decomposed,
discarded, or "deconstructed." While the "postmodern condition," therefore, spans a wide spectrum of social, cultural, and economic currents, let
us discuss three areas in particular that are of primary concern for the
postmodern moments in modern economics: the nature of the contemporary "subject," the state of scientific knowledge, and the sense that we
live in a world pervaded by uncertainty.

The Postmodern Subject

Much talk about postmodernism has commented on the increasingly fragmented human subject, on the dissolution of psychosocial unity.[26] In some
postmodern strands, the subject is said to be overloaded, or "saturated,"
by images, identities, cultural events, and social relationships, force-fed
by the increased volume and pace of market transactions, electronic mail,
MTV, and so on. Changes in our experience of time and space have both
expanded the social world and compressed it (because it is now "global").
Cultural psychologist Kenneth Gergen (1991) gives examples that depict
this saturation of the prototypical postmodern subject through the
"lengthening" of social experience and the shortening of time and space.

> [A] call to a Philadelphia lawyer is answered by a message recorded in three
> languages. (2)
> I gave a short speech at a birthday party in Heidelberg last year. When I returned
> to the United States three days later, a friend on the opposite coast called to
> tell me about the guests' reactions to the talk. He had gotten the gossip two
> days earlier via electronic mail. (2)
> Fred is a neurologist who spends many of his spare hours working to aid fami-
> lies from El Salvador. Although he is married to Tina, on Tuesday and Thurs-
> day nights he lives with an Asian friend with whom he has a child. On week-
> ends he drives his BMW to Atlantic City for gambling. (171)

Gergen claims to be describing a growing phenomenon. In his view, the
compression of time and space accomplished by technological achievements like jet travel and the Internet, along with the possibility of crossing,
or even living, in a variety of "cultures," has now pervaded the everyday

---

[26] The idea of the decentered or fragmented subject has certainly received much attention
in feminist literature. We discuss the role of the feminist subject—fragmented or not—*in
opposition to* neoclassical theory in chapter 4 below and the emergence of a decentered
body *within* neoclassical economics in chapter 3.

lives of a vast worldwide populace. The assault on singular personality and focused rationality and the dispersion of the putative "unity" of the ego and the intentional subject are the consequence of the fragmenting of social life that is considered the hallmark of postmodernity.[27]

For those who believe that the condition of existence for most people has changed in the direction of increased fragmentation but also increased "possibility," the passing of the unified subject and its replacement by the "decentered subject" constitutes a world-historical change. The emergence of the decentered subject has been hailed or reviled depending on whether one sees the resulting dispersion of self and society as an evil, brought about by the insidious commodification that Jameson describes, or a good, announcing the abandonment of the modernist, humanist metanarratives that Lyotard has elucidated. Be that as it may, the perception that the subject is not as unified and rational, as modernist science and literature had once supposed, marks one of the keys to tracing the postmodernist impact on economics and other fields of social theory.

For generations of mainstream economists, the rational subject capable of representing a consistent (at a moment in time) set of preferences is the starting point of economic theorizing.[28] But the postmodern condition opens up a very different research agenda for economic scientists should they choose to disown (what many regard as a necessary fiction) the unified self and move, instead, to a fiction supposedly more in tune with contemporary reality, the decentered self. We return to these issues below. This psychic fragmentation—and here we are not describing a supposed "irrational pathology," as is said to be the case with schizophrenics—is one of the strongest challenges that the postmodern condition, if one accepts its reality, poses to the discipline.[29]

[27] Simon (1991), no theorist of postmodernism, yet describes the situation of a less-than-unified, dispersed self (our words, not his) this way: each of us is "a committee of urges, wants, and needs, housed in body and mind" (362); "each of us 'time-shares,' alternating our many selves" (363).

[28] We have chosen to keep our comments about the rationality assumption, here and in the remainder of the book, to a minimum and instead focus attention on the presumption of a unified form of subjectivity for the economic agent. One reason for our choice is that there is a vast literature by now defending and contending against the notion of rationality as the starting point for economic analysis. This theme has been overworked to a degree that we feel confident that postmodernist approaches add little to what has already been said on one side or another of this debate. However, here is a smattering of references presenting different points of view for those who are looking for a place to start mulling over this issue: Arrow 1987; Sen 1977, 1987; Bausor 1985; Simon 1978; Sugden 1991; Sent 1997; Gerrard 1993; England 1993; and Hollis and Nell 1975. For some who explicitly consider postmodernism and rationality as it is used in economics, see Hargreaves Heap 1993, 2001; Varoufakis 1993; and Sofianou 1995.

[29] Louis Sass (1992) is a clinical psychologist who has years of experience working with schizophrenics in institutional settings. His book constitutes the most serious treatment of

The recognition that subjects may in fact be "decentered" in the contemporary world has spillover effects on the status of knowledge in the postmodern condition. On one hand, subjects may be thought to occupy so many different positions and hold such a bewildering variety of perspectives that stable and commensurable knowledge is seen as impossible. This view sees knowledge as local (not universal) and subject to persistent uncertainty. The fragmentation of subjects (within as well as among themselves) leads each and every one to hold mostly incommensurable concepts and notions, as universal truths retreat into the background or remain a thing of a supposed past, one in which homogenizing forces were presumed to be more decisive in constituting a horizon of transcendental intelligibility.

On the other hand, subjects may be seen to reflect the particular locations in which they find themselves, thus leading to the idea that the unique experiences either of individuals or of the groups to which they belong are productive of "situated" knowledges that, while not entirely translatable or transmittable, are at least stable enough to contribute to well-developed, "standpoint"-based understandings. This view relies on the idea that fragmentation or decenteredness is not pure solipsism. Instead, knowledge may be "relative" to the diversity of cultures and experiences that determine human consciousnesses. The plurality of such identity-based knowledge, often reflecting the particular experiences people may have because of race or gender or class or national distinction, makes it impossible for knowledge to pass itself off as "unsituated" and "uninterested." This view rejects the "god's eye perspective" that was thought to be the underlying premise of modernist notions of knowledge and science. In its place is substituted the notion that knowledge is always/already influenced by the "standpoints" that various and discrete subjects may hold.

The standpoint approach brings certain postmodern theorists close to feminists, multiculturalists, and those who stress the importance of postcoloniality for the "social construction" of knowledge and science. Thus, while one may argue that the postmodern condition is characterized by rampant globalization, caused primarily by multinational capital flows and the increased mobility of worldwide labor, subaltern voices have re-

---

the loose claim that schizophrenia is an apt trope for describing the general state of "postmodern" subjectivity and its manifestation in the arts. An example of the more casual (but not necessarily incorrect) use of this idea is the following discussion of channel surfing—a prototype for postmodern subjective activity—from the composition theorist, Lester Faigley (1992): "The experience of flipping across television programming approximates the consciousness of the schizophrenic living in the intense, eternal present. The viewer watches a series of spectacles from around the world—'smart' bombs exploding buildings, sports heroes in the elation of victory, royal marriages, plane crashes, assassinations, rock concerts, ranting dictators, shuttle launches, hurricanes, scandals, earthquakes, revolutions, eclipses, and international terrorism—all issued in an economy of images competing for attention" (13).

jected their own assimilation and the formation of a globally agreed-upon knowledge. The globalization that Jameson and others have described may be occurring apace, but this has only meant increased differentiation in the field of discourse and culture, as identities and standpoints turn out to be resistant to integration.[30]

Hence, the postmodern condition not only calls attention to the race, gender, class, and national privilege that made possible the "scientific revolution" brought about by the Enlightenment. It may also keep in play irreducible differences as the bases for all contemporary knowledge, even in the "hard sciences." As subjects and societies are decentered by the proliferation of experiences and cultural identities, so too is knowledge and science. And the effects of such a decentering accompanied by a profusion of voices, in which one's standpoint matters, include the possible indeterminacy and/or multiplicity of knowledge(s) not only for the subjects described within any field of thought, but of course—and perhaps even more importantly—for the scientist/observers themselves.

Economic agents, living in a postmodern world, are thus considered to be both situated and saturated—giving voice to the confusion, but also the clarity, that results from an overload of possibilities, from being situated in the multiple positions and identities that globalization has enhanced. Agents are not irrational. They possess different, simultaneously experienced rationalities, expressing the cultural locations and histories whence they arise. Choice in this scenario often appears like a crapshoot (some Marxian theorists would call it an "overdetermined conjuncture"). Scientists, too, are confronted with a welter of choices. Theories contend and overlap, but they also are just plain different and not reducible by a transdiscursive Method. Theory choice may be a matter of aesthetic taste, as the playing field for knowledge games is a collage of relatively autonomous tactics and their outcomes. Thus, the postmodern condition for knowledge production is often represented as a kind of relativism, without ultimate appeal to a predetermined or attainable Truth. Instead, taste and power and interest explain why one theory flourishes while another dwells in the shadows (see Foucault 1980 on the relationship between power and knowledge).

The postmodern condition, as it is often described, evinces indeterminacy and uncertainty rather than limpidity and predictability. Agents and observers of their behavior constantly think and act in the face of "just not knowing." So as might be expected, the issues of how to behave or

---

[30] Arif Dirlik (2000), for example, argues that "any account of the emergence of globalization as paradigm needs to recognize an awareness of the simultaneous unification and fragmentation of the world" (18), including the "proliferation of alternatives to Eurocentrism" (16). Both Gibson-Graham (1996, chap. 6) and Bergeron (2001) introduce difference into existing—unified and totalizing—treatments of globalization.

how to theorize under conditions of uncertainty have risen to the top of the agenda for natural and social scientists, that is, if postmodern theorists like Lyotard are to be believed. Indeed, it is arguable that for the past seventy-five or more years the theme of uncertainty has been central to new developments in the arts and sciences, and this includes economics, of course.[31] From the sheer randomness of dada poetry to the indeterminacy of quantum physics to the role of uncertain expectations in organizing behavior in a market economy, this theme emerged during the twentieth century as opening up a new range of creative possibilities for thought and action.[32] Thus, some argue, postmodernism is simply the recognition of this reality, as theory brings up the rear in self-reflection on already changed world historical circumstances.

The Style of the Postmodern: Deconstructive and Self-Reflective

The preceding comments bring us to our third category for postmodernism, that is, postmodernism as a "style"—of writing, thinking, acting, creating, and so on. In this vein, postmodernism has been associated with a vast number of stances, genres, and movements, from self-reflexivity and bricolage to deconstruction and pastiche.[33]

Postmodern styles in music, art, architecture, literature, philosophy, and culture have brought to the fore the undecidability of meaning, the textuality or discursivity of knowledge, the inconceivability of pure "presence,"

---

[31] Sizing up the state of economic analysis in the mid-1950s, Koopmans concluded that "our economic knowledge has not yet been carried to the point where it sheds much light on the core problem of the economic organization of society: the problem of how to face and deal with uncertainty" (1957, 147). Writing thirty years later, Amartya Sen indicates that the issue of uncertainty had become the primary context for much economic analysis, such that the all-important notion of agent rationality had to be framed in terms of the general case of decision making in the face of uncertainty: "behaviour under certainty can be formally seen as an extreme case of behaviour under uncertainty . . . in this sense, rational behaviour under certainty must be subsumed by any theory that deals with rational behaviour in the presence of uncertainty" (1990, 199)

[32] Some reading on the question of how uncertainty, "indeterminism," and disorder became central themes across the cultural and disciplinary landscape during the past two centuries includes Hacking 1990b; Stigler 1986; Plotnitsky 1994; Dupré 1993; Sass 1992; Kern 1983; Hayles 1991; Krüger, Daston, and Heidelberger 1987; Krüger, Gigerenzer, and Morgan 1987; and Krips 1987.

[33] Nigel Wheale (1995) attempts a summary of postmodern style in the arts like so: "A definable group of strategies and forms recur in the description of postmodern arts and this lexicon orders them into a hierarchy. An all purpose postmodern item might be constructed like this: it uses eclecticism to generate parody and irony; its style may owe something to schlock, kitsch or camp taste. It may be partly allegorical, certainly self-reflexive and contain some kind of list. It will not be realistic. Now construct your own program to meet these demands (42–43).

the irrelevance of intention, the insuperability of authenticity, the impossibility of representation, along with the celebration of play, difference, plurality, chance, inconsequence, and marginality. Such an agglomeration of styles contributes to the sense that there is indeed a postmodern condition to which all these styles refer. And, of course, some of these styles are presented as oppositional to—as critiques of—the prevailing sensibilities and formations that are thought to make up the various modernisms in these fields and disciplines. Whether or not these all speak to a set of changed historical and empirical circumstances, and indeed whether or not the emergence of these styles refers to some central historical cause, like the spread of global capitalist commodity culture, it remains the case that one can document the rise of the "postmodern" in aesthetics and ethics within the past forty or more years. That is, postmodernism as style affects the fundamental determinations of "value" and "meaning" as they are encountered throughout the social and cultural landscape.[34]

It is impossible to render intelligible such diverse stylistic movements in the questions of value and meaning in a brief introduction. Since our investigation in the remaining chapters draws upon certain strands of postmodern styles of thought and presentation, we dwell upon just a few here. One, of course, goes under the name of deconstruction. This approach, sometimes converted into a method, was pioneered by the French philosopher Jacques Derrida (1976, 1978). Like everything else discussed under the rubric of postmodernism (and its close relation, poststructuralism), deconstruction as literary, philosophical, and artistic style has meant many different things to many different people. We encounter it most often, though, as a textual reading and composition in which the play of words and signs within a text is shown to undo such stable and intelligible meanings. For many who practice deconstruction, the goal is to demonstrate the impossibility of pure presence, that is, the inability of any sentence or text to stand for singular meanings and, hence, to eliminate contradiction, ambiguity, multiplicity, and so forth—which was precisely the goal of much modernist design, as in T. M. Cleland's layout for *Fortune* magazine.[35] In a Derridean approach, texts can be "deconstructed" by means of a close and careful analysis to reveal the "aporias" and the "undecidables" that are ever present. Hence, a text is always gesturing—

---

[34] For a recent collection of essays that interrogates the relationship among value, culture, meaning, and art, see Klamer 1996.

[35] According to Cleland (1930, 180, 181), writing in the first issue, "The design of *Fortune* is based upon its function of presenting a clear and readable text profusely illustrated with pictures, mostly photographic, in a form ample and agreeable to the eye. . . . The size and proportions of the magazine are designed to give scope to its illustrations and text without crowding and margins to its pages which shall be in accord with the best principles of fine bookmaking."

Figure 1.3. T. M. Cleland, *Fortune* magazine (1932). Photo: Preston Thomas for Visual Ear. (Permission: *Fortune*.)

mostly in spite of itself—to other texts and to other referents, as it is shown to be the site of *différance* (a mixed word that attempts to connote both "difference" and "deference"—the act of deferring).[36]

Deconstruction as a style of textual analysis calls attention to the radical indeterminacy of meaning, the inability to reduce the incessant play between signifiers (such as words and symbols) that never settles down into univocality. Deconstruction as a style of writing and design is a deliberate attempt to bring forth all those things that can be said to undermine—deconstruct—the supposedly central and fixed meanings of textual compositions. So, for example, Derrida and others have often composed texts that are seemingly dialogic in nature, with simultaneous columns that in some way refer (or defer) to one another (if for no other reason that they occupy a privileged space on the same page). Likewise, these columns and other devices (marginal notes, cross-outs, and so forth) are utilized to show that there is something both arbitrary and even concealing about textual composition—as in David Carson's 1995 design for his own book, *The End of Print*. It is arbitrary since words and images produce random possibilities simply by occupying the same space. It is concealing because the eradication of erasures and the placing in margins of notes and other references hides the conditions of production of texts and the importance of marginalia in determining the range of possible meanings. That is, deconstruction as literary/philosophical style is often employed to show that what at first seems secondary to the main meanings turns out to displace those meanings in a reversal of signification.

A recent text by the economist Judith Mehta shows some of these elements at work in the composition of a piece of economics writing. In "A Disorderly Household" (2001), Mehta stages for readers the "noise" that she finds expressed in most experiments involving economic bargaining games. Rather than the formulaic representations that game theorists are used to in modeling such strategic situations, Mehta runs dual columns, one of which contains the "actual words" of participants in a bargaining game experiment, the other a neoclassical game theorist's abstract rendering of it. The point is to "voice the noise," and to show that these two columns are not reducible to one another and that they signify different things that are unrecoverable in acts of "translation" and synthesis. In opposition to the idea that there are few authorized and acceptable ways to "represent" such experiments, Mehta invokes a cacophony of voices

---

[36] Useful overviews of Derrida's work include Caputo 1997; Norris 1988, 1991; Norris and Benjamin 1989; Gasché 1986; and Culler 1983. See Ruccio 1998 for a discussion of the implications of deconstruction and *différance* for economics. Jane Rossetti must be named as among the first to declare a deliberately deconstructive reading of economics texts, as she does in her important 1990 essay on Robert Lucas; see also Rossetti 1992.

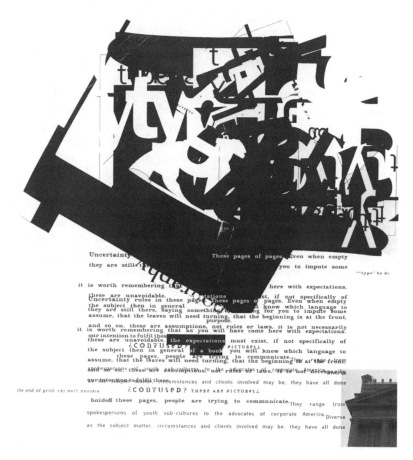

Figure 1.4. David Carson, *The End of Print* (1995). Photo: Preston Thomas for Visual Ear. (Permission: David Carson.)

in order to model in a different way, thus deconstructing a game theorist's modernist text.

It is possible to see this text as being concerned with several additional points. One is the idea that all texts achieve meaning by reference and deference to other texts (hence the deliberate quotation of other game-theoretic articles and books). Another is that knowledge production is a messy affair, one that has as a condition of existence a multiplicity of sources and strategies. There is no single or sure road to meaning. Finally, Mehta's text demonstrates that both participants and readers are active (rather than passive) in constructing meanings in and out of texts. This is achieved by reproducing the actual words of the participants in the original experiment and by making the text unfamiliar in ways that challenge readers to be more engaged and conscious of their roles in "discovering" what a text is trying to say.[37]

Indeed, more generally, deconstructive styles of writing give vent to discursive and semiotic play—a kind of play in which discursive layers are tossed down on top of other layers with no clear "reason" for doing so. Thus, while some deconstructionist texts deliberately embody indeterminacy, other texts are seemingly more slapdash and take the form of a bricolage, a mishmash of presumably unrelated elements and images. The "jokey," "ersatz," and even "nihilistic" quality of such writing and construction (as with postmodern architecture, such as Charles Moore's Piazza d'Italia, which is often linked to an excess of "quotation," ornament, and playfulness, in contrast to a primary concern with function, as in Mies van der Rohe's Lake Shore Drive buildings) unleashes a host of possible revaluations, or, if one is critical of these strategies, the very demise of value itself.[38] As opposed to the minimalism and parsimony characteristic of "high modernist" moments in culture and theory, postmodernist, deconstructionist style is overflowing with meanings, causes, and effects. The saturation we describe above is an effect of some postmodern creations, and this excess of everything is seen, alternatively, to signal a new age of possibility, a proliferation of meanings, a voicing of previously repressed desires, the cultural emergence of marginalized "others," or the destruction of intelligibility, knowledge, and community.

While deconstruction may be a preferred stylistic strategy within postmodernism, a similarly adopted stance has been called "self-reflexivity." One rendition of this idea is the practice of agents or authors "locating" themselves in the process of producing artifacts and actions. Agents and authors, then, seek to show not only that they are themselves "implicated" in their works and deeds, but also that these productions cannot be separated from such constituting aspects as one's histories, identities, interests, values, and so forth. Warren Samuels states that in matters of

[37] In another essay, "Look at Me Look at You" (1999), Mehta makes use of other familiar deconstructionist textual strategies of composition. She combines images with texts, and has fragments of text overlapping on the page. At times, there are multiple columns. She writes with a variety of typefaces and font sizes. She intersperses quotations that, at first, may seem to be tangential to some other parts of the text. The "voice" of the text toggles back and forth between more "personal" and more "objective" modes of presentation. There is little if any deference to disciplinary boundaries, as economic ideas freely mingle with discourse concerned mainly with photography, art history, and much else. And so forth. Indeed, looking over her text, it is hard to "center" it either on the page or even in terms of what constitutes a primary argument. (Thus, deconstruction as a style of literary or artistic creation deliberately conjures up the notion of "decentering" we discuss above.)

[38] The history, languages, and styles of postmodern architecture are explained and illustrated by Klotz (1988), Portoghesi (1983), and Jencks (1987).

Figure 1.5. Charles Moore, Piazza d'Italia (1975–80). (Credit: © Norman McGrath/Esto.)

knowledge, postmodernism "points out the fundamental assumptions of all claims to knowledge, including, in a self-reflexive manner, its own" (1996, 66).

Self-reflexivity may be something other than subjective self-awareness. It is more concerned with the argument that all things, from politics to philosophy, are intimately bound up with the situatedness of those en-

Figure 1.6. Mies van der Rohe, 860–880 Lake Shore Drive
(1949–51). (Credit: Ezra Stoller © Esto.)

gaged in these activities. And identifying the locations from which people
speak, write, and act matters for the kinds of meanings and values that
can be produced. In our own field, E. Roy Weintraub argues, for example,
that "all knowledge a fortiori economic knowledge, is local and contingent and connected to a community in which that knowledge was produced or interpreted or otherwise made significant." He goes on to state
that it is "not useful to speak about economic knowledge without also
speaking about economists and the communities in which economic
knowledge was produced and communicated" (1992, 53–54).

In a different way, a self-reflexive style can be said to be at the heart of
the "discursive turn" that commentators on postmodernism and poststructuralism have noted for the past twenty years. In this view, postmod-

ern forms of theorizing and fictionalizing have in common an inward focus, a focus on the conditions of writing and discoursing, as opposed to the words just "revealing" the world in all its fullness and glory. Thus, postmodernism has been very closely associated with the self-conscious, incessant play with words and images that comprise an assault for some and a celebration for others of modes of discursive creation and representation. The "self-consciousness" of postmodern writers and thinkers that takes the form of showing the discursive conditions of a text's existence— and of showing that one is showing—has been seen either as a retreat of philosophy, art, and social theory away from the pressing issues of the day (presumed to exist "outside" of these realms) or, more benignly, as a new appreciation for the way rhetoric, metaphor, speech acts, and other figures of writing and speech shape the ideas and events of both the discursive and the nondiscursive dimensions of the world.

The inward focus also entails a refusal to "hide" the desires and wills of economic scientists that can be seen to determine their own "preferences" in theory, methodology, and so much else besides.[39] Thus, it is incumbent upon authors who write in a postmodern style to make clear the positions from which they believe they are writing, and what privilege or authority they seek, express, or are trying to subvert—and, along the way, to "out" all other economists, especially those who maintain that one's politics or morals or cultural identities should have no bearing on the kinds of economic analysis one disseminates.

One important way that postmodernist style has entered economics has been through exhortations or attempts to put language and sign systems in general (like mathematics) under scrutiny in the formation of economic analysis. Monographs and collections in economics with titles such as *Adam Smith's Discourse* (Brown 1994a), *Economics as Discourse* (Samuels 1990), *Economics as Literature* (Henderson 1995), *Economics and*

---

[39] One common criticism, which is not at all limited to those who pledge allegiance to postmodernism, is that the desires and wills of economists, like others, is largely a function of prestige, power, and even relative wealth. Donald Katzner (1991a), in his thoughtful defense of formalization within economics, admits the point that at least some of the obsession with formal modes of presentation in economics occurs because "that is where the rewards of publication, recognition, support money, promotion, and tenure are . . . [E]ven the selection of the problem to work on is subject to the same reward pressures. And the structure of these rewards tends to be set by the established standards of what constitutes relevant and significant questions, and what makes up the appropriate assumption-content of analyses which purport to provide answers. Clearly the existence of established standards provides a powerful rationalization for the continued use of formalization" (22). Bruno Frey (2001) echoes this view in arguing that "scholars in academia are strongly motivated by extrinsic incentives. Most of them seek to pursue a career leading them to the top—a full professorship at a good university—and a corresponding income. In addition they wish to enjoy a good reputation and fame with their colleagues" (42).

Language (Henderson, Dudley-Evans, and Backhouse 1993), *Economics and Hermeneutics* (Lavoie 1991), *John Maynard Keynes: Language and Method* (Marzola and Silva 1994), *The New Economic Criticism* (whose subtitle is *Studies at the Intersection of Literature and Economics*) (Woodmansee and Osteen 1999b), and of course *The Rhetoric of Economics* (McCloskey 1985a), *The Consequences of Economic Rhetoric* (Klamer, McCloskey, and Solow 1988), *Knowledge and Persuasion in Economics* (McCloskey 1994), and *Conversations with Economists* (Klamer 1983) have appeared in the past twenty years and mark this self-reflexive moment in economic thought.[40] By showing that economists think and write according to well-known literary and semiotic devices, these texts give the lie to the claim that words, equations, models, and so on are simple transparencies—or, alternatively, privileged languages—allowing economic scientists to apprehend truths that are simply "out there."

Self-reflexivity is witnessed as well when the problem of knowledge is posed largely in non- or antiepistemological terms. Or rather, the problem of knowledge, for many postmodernists, is not an issue since they refuse the polar opposites that have structured most epistemological dissertations at least since the Enlightenment. The problem for many "modernist" philosophers of knowledge had been to specify how a knowing subject could apprehend a dumb and intractable world of objects. But postmodernists have often taken the view that this problem is a red herring. That is, they claim that the problem of knowledge in classical epistemology is built upon a misspecification of the nature of the subject and ignores the impossibility of ever pulling apart the knower from the known.

In this light, postmodernists have argued that knowledge production is not a matter of a subject or scientist finding the right "tools" to "penetrate" the world of objects, finding the nuggets of truth contained within the outer sheaths of extraneous dross. To the contrary, subjects are active in the construction of truths, and their very observations and perceptions structure those truths irresistibly.[41] Subjects therefore can see themselves or their practices and their effects in the truths they produce (a classic

---

[40] Though the title may not be as suggestive as the others we cite, we should add Salanti and Screpanti's edited volume, *Pluralism in Economics*, in which some of the essays call for or employ self-reflexivity within economics. In addition to McCloskey 1983a, an important early article reflecting on language in economics that is cognizant of postmodernism and poststructuralist thought is Milberg 1988.

[41] Cullenberg (1994) discusses this issue in more general terms as the "codetermination" of theoretical discourse and material reality. He concludes that this co- or overdetermination implies the impossibility of an independent standard of truth since "a standard of truth requires an independent or absolute point of reference. But in this case the independence has been corrupted by the mutual interaction between theoretical discourse and material reality" (13).

reference is to Heisenberg's uncertainty principle), and this gives rise to another moment of self-reflexivity.[42] Unable to claim any disentanglement from other texts or the world under analysis, postmodernist practitioners give full voice to their own "presence" in their constructions.

Postmodernism as Critique: From Antimodernism to "Postmodern Moments"

Self-reflexive and deconstructive styles of writing are most often used in the service of critique. Modernism is the object of the critical stances and styles that comprise postmodernism. Now, of course, there are divergent understandings about what modernism means.[43] Here, we will specify those aspects insofar as they show up as the foil for our own work. First, however, we need to clarify exactly what it means to regard postmodernism as a critique of modernism and modernity.

For some postmodernists, the forms of social and cultural life that have been ushered in as part of the "modern age" are sufficiently debilitating and faulty as to warrant simple opposition. That is, postmodernism is sometimes encountered as an antimodernism. In this case, postmodernism often joins forces with neotraditionalists (neo-Aristotelians, for example—see the discussion of this tendency in Klamer 2001) who see modernism as having brought about the demise in older values—some even promised as a feature of modernism—that stressed (local) community, moral goodness, tolerance, social justice, and individual freedom. Since modernism is seen to have failed in cultivating and upholding such values, postmodernism provides a perspective from which to critically evaluate and ultimately transcend modernity. The tendencies to be sensitive to difference and alterity; to question expertise and authority, especially in the name of the state or science; to value conversation and discourse; to desire ecological conservation rather than economic transformation; to refuse the prerogatives usually accorded to technological progress; to criticize the fiction of the self as an independent, unified entity; and to see the murderous flaws in global schemes for human liberation are dimensions of postmodernism in its criti-

---

[42] Indeed, the very meaning of a "fact" has been shown in a number of instances to be socially constructed, thus imbricating the knowing subject/scientist in what modernist discourse considers the objective character of natural or social reality. See Latour and Woolgar 1986; Poovey 1998; and Porter 1995 for detailed studies of the construction of social and natural facts.

[43] We refer readers to texts that summarize aspects of modernism that are of most concern for postmodern theorists and practitioners: Toulmin 1990; Kern 1983; Gablik 1984; Sass 1992; Xenos 1989; and Berman 1982. Ross 1994 is one of the few volumes devoted to exploring modernism "as a critical category interpretation" in relation to the human sciences.

cal moments. As we say, often these moments amount to a hope of recovering elements of a premodern world of values and characters and community and sociality. At the very least, modernism is seen here as presenting the opportunity for a future, in suggesting exactly the points at which modernism can be opposed.[44] Postmodernism as antimodernism takes modernity as the negative blueprint for much of what it hopes to erect.

Yet, for other postmodernists, being simply "against" modernism is both impossible and beside the point. In this view, postmodernism's critical bearing leads towards a "nonmodernism," that is, an attempt to escape the oppositions that structure so much of modernist thought (subject/object, essence/appearance, and so forth). The pressure to be "either/or" is taken to be precisely what modernism presents as the only option. Hence, postmodernism, to be truly "other," cannot be reduced to the play of modernism's oppositions, just the other side of the modernist coin. And, for many who write and create in this postmodern critical mode, the point *is* to be "truly other," to be so radically different as to suggest a sea change rather than a search-and-recovery mission (finding the remnants of a discarded premodernism at the bottom of the vast modernist ocean). The critical edge in this type of postmodern work consists of elisions, of escaping the snares presented by modernist ways of thinking and behaving, of being just out of reach of either/or couplets. This type of nonmodernism is often infuriating to modernist and other critics since postmodernists seem to avoid the kinds of battle that their critics desire. Hence, postmodernism as a nonmodernism often appears as avoidance behavior, a retreat into nonconfrontational stances distinguished by an emphasis on play, the relativity of perspectives, self-absorption, and the inconsequence of theory, interest, value, and meaning.

Elements of both these attitudes—postmodernism as an anti- and a nonmodernism—appear in the work of many scholars, inside and outside economics. There is, however, another possibility worth exploring. This is to view modernism and postmodernism as always "incomplete," unable to achieve the pure presence that we discuss above. That is, we take seriously the deconstructionist idea that it is impossible for various modernisms to totalize any field of discourse, art, or work because their meanings and effects are unequivocal and determinate. To the contrary, we prefer to think of modernism and postmodernism as constituting horizons or, better said, "moments" that are, themselves, transient and porous, lacking the ability to suture time and space—to create discernible boundary lines for historical ages or social terrains—in discursive and nondiscursive

---

[44] The sociologist Anthony Giddens is one who has argued that the modernist project (e.g., justifying a commitment to reason in the name of reason) fails to complete itself. Thus, "modernity turns out to be enigmatic at its core" (1990, 49).

realms. One critical component of such a view lies in the idea that one can show the tenuous, even if tenacious, hold on imaginations and institutions that attends the appearance of modernism (or postmodernism, for that matter) in any field of inquiry or action. Another critical element consists of demonstrating that, despite its best efforts, modernism is unable to close the circle, to completely hegemonize political, economic, and cultural spaces, and that crucial postmodern moments beckon us toward alternative ways of thinking "beyond" modernism. The postmodern moments that have emerged within fields dominated by modernism adumbrate the paths of its supersession. Thus, to the extent that modernism is seen to produce less than salutary effects, highlighting the postmodern moments within a field can be an immanent critique.

Two additional remarks: One is that our interest in exhibiting the postmodern moments within economics is not much directed to the obvious point that modernism and postmodernism coexist in the present. Nor, really, is it directed to the point that postmodernism might profitably be viewed as the latest stage of modernism, a continuation in some sense of many of the themes developed over the course of the past century in art, literature, philosophy, and so forth. Indeed, some cultural critics have belittled the overarching notion of modernism and postmodernism found in other, nonliterary fields (in economics, for instance) since, in their view, including such elements as indeterminacy, the critique of representation, and the decentered (if not the alienated) subject within the confines of postmodernism misses badly the emergence of these and other themes within what they regard as the "high modernism" of their own fields of work and study. In this view, postmodernism is a strengthening rather than a weakening of crucial components of modernism, that is, a moment in the continuous development of modernism. Or the term *postmodern* might be reserved to describe still other irruptions.

This brings us to the second remark. Our use of the term *postmodern moments* is also directed at the idea that there are "uneven developments" within and between fields of thought and practice. So, perhaps it makes more sense to label as postmodern the attack on such notions as the unified subject, the presumption of certain knowledge, a privileging of order over disorder within a field like economics, where modernism may appear as a dogged adherence by a majority of practitioners to these notions. Yet in other fields—literary studies, say—postmodernism may be more concerned with the process of interpretation, the openness of the text, and deconstructive techniques, as a way of critically engaging modernism's preoccupation with timeless meaning, aesthetic autonomy, and closed reading strategies. Hence, to bring forth the postmodern moments in any field or endeavor is to acknowledge that modernism may have many faces, with no single visage ever "full-blown" (whatever this fullness may consist of). And, by extension, postmodernism is (or postmodernisms are) likewise dispersed and multiple, and follows no logic that mandates it appear everywhere in the same form at the same time.

Much of our interest in this book is discipline-specific. Therefore, we steer the remainder of our remarks toward the postmodern moments within economics, paying attention to postmodernism's critique directed at modernism within economic discourses.

The Objects of Postmodern Critique: Modernity's "Isms"

Whether anti- or nonmodernist, or dedicated to showing postmodern moments, what does it mean to treat postmodernism chiefly as a critique of modernism? What elements of modernism within economics are found by critics to warrant opposition or transcendence? What moments of postmodernism disturb the modernist waters of economics as a discipline?

First, we enumerate the primary objects of postmodern critique. These include essentialism, foundationalism, scientism, determinism, formalism, humanism, and the notion of the unified, intentional, rational agent.[45] Postmodernism shares with other schools of thought (and here we include feminism, Marxism, institutionalism, and other "heterodox" approaches within economics) an attack on one or another of these objects. Yet there is also a connection between the critiques that are considered specifically postmodern, and so we attempt to show, for example, that the postmodern critique of the unified agent may weigh heavily in postmodern considerations of the process of producing knowledge.

Representation and Essentialism

Modernism is thought to be imbued with representational logics and forms of display. Here we mean that there are at least two levels of

[45] In what follows, we discuss formalism (or, rather, mathematical formalism) in passing. We note though that for many commentators and critics, the rise of modernity occurred hand in hand with a mathematized culture. And modernism in certain disciplines certainly has meant the move from prose to probability distributions. There are some excellent and diverse discussions, such as Mirowski 1989, Morgan 1990, Porter 1995, and Stigler 1986, of this and related theoretical moves and what they have meant within the discipline of economics and elsewhere; see also Ruccio 1998. In addition, we provide the following sentences from Katzner, the respected mathematical economist, who nicely links modernity and math: "we moderns, it seems, attempt to measure everything . . . [M[easurement is relatively easy and convenient. It has become natural for us. It makes us feel good because it imparts the (frequently illusory) impression that we know something. And it is often not difficult, and even tempting, to ignore what cannot be measured. We seem to be caught up in a culture of measurement which we are unable to let go" (1991b, 18).

thought or practice for every object. A shorthand way of looking at the relationship between these levels is to call them "appearance" and "essence." Now, it is possible to show that modernist notions of science and culture focus on this crucial distinction. In much modernist philosophy of science, for example, the world of appearances is incapable of yielding up the meaning or true nature of objects and their relationships. The role of the scientist is to perceive the patterns that reside within objects or the interactions between them or, alternatively, in the "deep" structures that give rise to the "surface" objects and relations. "Discovery" is all about finding the essential order that lies within or beneath a chaotic and even ornamental surface. Indeed, the scientific critique of common sense and other supposedly nonscientific thought consists of showing that, in these discourses, appearances are mistaken for essences (or, rather, that there is no discernible difference observed between them).

Representation structures as well the self-consciousness of scientific practice. The scientist's words are thought to correspond, in some important way, to the world they describe. That is, language is seen to be representational, at least in the hands of scientists who are trained not to let "mere words" obfuscate the truths that have been discovered.[46]

Whether that language is professional prose or mathematics or formal logic, the modernist conceit is that language is capable of representing truths about the world in an undistorted fashion. There are two sides to this modernist coin. In some hands, particular forms of language are wielded as "special codes," qualified to depict the rational order that governs the objects under investigation or, alternatively, to separate rigorous knowledge from imprecise ideas.[47] In other hands, signs and linguistic

---

[46] Compare this view with that of the Physiocrat disciple and French state bureaucrat Turgot, who saw language as the essential ingredient, bar none, for the emergence of genius. Manuel and Manuel (1979) summarize Turgot's theory, which postulated that the progress of language would make it "destined to become an even better instrument; it would be stripped of its rhetoric, cleansed of its ambiguities, so that the only means of communication for true knowledge would be the mathematical symbol, verifiable, unchanging, eternal" (471). They proceed with this wonderful account of Turgot's view of what happened to scientific genius with the fall of the Roman Empire: "In the past one of the unfortunate consequences of the conquest of a decadent higher civilization by vigorous barbarisms had been the linguistic confusion which followed the disaster. A long period of time elapsed before the victors and the vanquished merged their different forms of speech and, during the interval, language, the only receptacle for the storing of scientific progress then available, was lacking. Geniuses continued to perceive new phenomena, but since they were deprived of a stable body of rational linguistic symbols their observations were stillborn. . . . The babel of languages resulted in a protracted period of intellectual sterility during which it was impossible for a creative genius to express himself because there was no settled linguistic medium for scientific thought" (471–72).

[47] In economics, it is commonly believed that practitioners who eschew mathematical forms of expression are engaged in, to use Samuelson's words, "the laborious working over

conventions are useful or necessary to communicate truths that have been discovered through other means and that require representation through language. The idea here is that language is a neutral medium that can be utilized when and where it does not "distort" the essential truths that science has unearthed.[48] Hence, language is either essence or appearance, but in both cases a necessary convention if the gems of truth excavated from the world are going to be put on display.[49]

One form of this cult of representation, then, is what has been called essentialism. The idea is that there are essences to discover, that there are tried-and-true methods of uncovering these essences, and that appearances are to be probed for the truths hidden beneath their surface. Much postmodern critique has taken the form of a refusal of representational schemas and logics, and a rejection or subversion of essentialism.[50] In place of these schemas and logics is an aesthetic or ethic of "depthlessness." Postmodernism repudiates the search for and representation of essences, proclaiming in contrast notions of juxtaposition, simultaneity, and so forth. That is, for many postmodernists, there are no meanings hidden in texts or in the world, and therefore no hierarchies of elements, some living as appearances and others as essences, some as causes and others as effects. Nothing waits for just the right technique or act of genius or accident to be discovered in this nonrepresentational logic; there is instead an appreciation of the play of elements that comprise pure surface. Attention to the constructedness, arbitrariness, and contingency of meaning and value marks many postmodern approaches. The world is not necessarily meaningless or valueless. But meaning and value are not "essential" or at least implicit in objects and their relations. Looking at how knowledge is produced rather than how a subject/scientist extracts truth from glittery appearances is, once again, the postmodern turn.[51]

---

of essentially simple mathematical concepts" that is "not only unrewarding from the standpoint of advancing the science, but involves as well mental gymnastics of a particularly depraved type" (1983, 6).

[48] Robert Solo, in fact, criticizes the use of mathematics in economics and advocates the use of a "natural language" precisely because the latter "alone conveys an image in the mind that can be checked against the observed and experienced" (1991, 103).

[49] With evident approval, James Buchanan (2001) argues that the replacement of the language of calculus by that of game theory represents a fundamental shift in the definition of economics from a maximizing framework to that of a "science of exchanges."

[50] According to Jane Rossetti, in an essay explaining the relevance of deconstructive view of language for feminist economics, "without an essence, the words themselves have no fixed meaning. . . . Objects have no essence; language cannot convey them, but rather creates them through a series of specific and contingent categories" (2001, 308).

[51] One good example is Andrew Pickering's "posthumanist" account of Rowan Hamilton's construction of the mathematical system of quarternions in which "the center of gravity . . . is positioned between Hamilton as a classical human agent, a locus of free moves, and

Much else is implied in this postmodern critique of representation and essentialism. For example, formalism as a preferred mode of presentation is based on the presumption that some languages are better suited than others for representing truths.[52] The idea that there is, in fact, an important distinction between form and content belies the notion that form can be adequate to content if and when the appropriate linguistic or semiotic devices are employed. The defense of formal modeling and reliance on mathematics in economics depends on the view that such forms of presentation are better able to allow truths to shine through (or at least hypotheses to be tested for their potential veracity or acceptability) than nonformal devices.[53] If there are no truths waiting to be discovered and displayed by the right formal language, then the power and privilege ac-

---

the disciplines that carried him along" (1997, 63). There are, of course, many more examples, as during the past twenty years there has been much written about the "social construction" of knowledge, though not all of this discussion embraces postmodernism. For just two accounts with different foci, see Longino 1990 and the essays in Lynch and Woolgar 1990.

[52] Formalism also connotes, for many, "rigor." And this attribute is often seen to comprise the acid test for deciding if a statement is possibly scientific or otherwise. It is interesting to note that in the same issue of *Methodus*, we get two different accounts of the place of the value of rigor for modern economic science. The first, by Sen (1991), amounts to the claim that furors about formalization sometimes are blown out of proportion since, by now, most economists have some formal training. And, "furthermore, the aura of glory that was associated once with being 'rigorous,' 'exact,' and 'modern'—available only to the chosen mathematical few—has rather dimmed in recent years" (73). The second, by Solow (1991), is directed to the confusion sometimes between abstraction and rigor. Losing patience (Solow's comments come as a response to a "debate" of sorts between McCloskey and Katzner over formalization in economics), Solow blares, "there is no excuse for lack of rigor. You can never have too much rigor. To make non-rigorous statements is to make false statements" (31). And finally, "there is not a category of non-rigorous truths, not in theory" (31). It seems Professor Sen hadn't yet spoken to Professor Solow. One more view on rigor will suffice. This is from Mark Blaug's recent salvo aimed at formalism in economics: "If there is such a thing as 'original sin' in economic methodology, it is the worship of the idol of mathematical rigor, more or less invented by Arrow and Debreu in 1954 and then canonized by Debreu in his *Theory of Value* five years later, probably the most arid and pointless book in the entire literature of economics" (1998, 17). Professors Sen and Solow, meet Professor Blaug.

[53] We have gotten used to the very familiar soliloquy in which famous economists, many of whom pioneered the use of these models and near-pyrotechnical mathematics, late in their careers wonder how in the world such "tools" ever got so out of hand in the training and consequent work of economists as to displace all other forms of argumentation, a concern for "reality," and discursive borrowings. One such example is the recent confession by the new economic historian Richard Easterlin (1997), in which he bemoans that "model building is the name of the game. Empirical reality enters, if at all, chiefly in the form of 'stylized fact.' Econometrics, though a formal course requirement everywhere, plays a surprisingly small part in economic research—showing up in perhaps one dissertation in five. There is no such thing as descriptive dissertations or theses devoted to the measurement of economic magnitudes. Although topics in disciplines other than economics are not uncommon, there is little or no use of the work done in the other disciplines" (15).

corded to mathematics are likely denied. Formal presentation and modeling become just another means of knowledge production, with no better access to underlying essential truths than any other such means. Formalism produces economic knowledge, but it is production once again (and not representation) that is in evidence.[54]

The postmodern critique of essentialism resounds as well in thwarting attempts to escape some forms of representation, as can be seen in some versions of economic philosophy in which words and numbers are said not so much to represent or describe a real world outside of discourse as to present testable propositions for their ability to predict outcomes. The shift from the "realism" of assumptions to the "as if" hypotheses of Milton Friedman and his followers is often defended as an implicit critique of essentialism. This is because Friedman and others may claim not to have any particular notion of the correlation between words, numbers, and underlying truths but, instead, seek accuracy (or at least less falsehood) in prediction that follows from a causal hypothesis. Yet this response fails to eliminate the recourse to some notion that it is possible to discern transdiscursive truth via a method of ascertaining regularities through scientific observation. Such observation "reads" essences (now discussed in the form of abstractions) in the myriad perceptions that are picked over for what is necessary or useful in testing the proposition and what is not. Appearances still are suspect, and need to be arranged and interpreted properly in order for the scientist to verify or falsify the proposition in question.

Friedman's "as if" approach is only one of many such alternatives in the philosophy and methodology of economics, indeed, in all scientific disciplines. We are aware of the view that, at least since the advent of positivism, Humean skepticism about the notion of essence—where essence is equated with "necessity" thought to regulate the relations among and between events, captured in the language of cause and effect—has been the main advance in the philosophy of science. In this view, essentialism is understood mostly as a problem for rationalist epistemologies, or at least those for which causation exists as a necessary relation between events. It may also be a concern for those approaches to epistemology for which universality is less a matter of the conjunctural coincidence of a perceived sequential pattern in observations about those events and more a matter of what must logically be the "underlying cause" of that which

---

[54] On this point, postmodern approaches in economics have much in common with critical realists such as Tony Lawson, who emphasizes that "knowledge is a social product, actively produced by means of antecedent social products" (1997, 25). Indeed, while there are obvious disagreements between postmodernists and critical realists, we are moved here more by important similarities regarding the social production and distribution of economic knowledge, a commitment to (at least some forms of) nonreductionism, a dislike of scientism, and much else. For more on critical realism, see also Fleetwood 1999.

appears to follow. Although they do provide relief from some aspects of the assertion of necessity and the adequate representation of that necessity in a "correct" (read scientific or logical or mathematical) language, these approaches are themselves enmeshed within discursive structures in which essentialisms remain the norm.

In order to make our position clear, perhaps an example will help. Let us take the considerable efforts of the philosopher of science Rudolf Carnap. In *An Introduction to the Philosophy of Science* (1966), Carnap elaborates a position on facts, laws, causes, and determinisms that owes its impetus to Humean skepticism. Among Carnap's substantial contributions are his "perspectivist" view of observations (the fact that many different people will, rightly, advance different causal explanations based on their initial location and circumstances relative to an event), his consequent vision of causation as complex and multiplied (he rejects the notion, in most if not all cases, of single causes that lead to unique effects), and his view that "laws" are mostly the temporary acknowledgment of no disconfirming observations. Carnap is justified, in our view, in calling critical attention to the linguistic or semantic regime in both ordinary and scientific discourses that lend meaning to the ideas of cause and effect through such terms as *leads to* or *follows*. Of course, Carnap sees the problem of deterministic and essentialist versions of causation—those that attribute causation to an essence of the objects/events involved, or those that attribute a necessity of sequence because of a perceived logic of the universe—as a failure of linguistic effect. So in his distinction between facts (statements of singular occurrences) and laws (statements of universality that emerge from the comparison and perception of a regularity in observations dispersed over time and space) he laments the "ambiguity" of language that creates the "misunderstanding" in which factual statements are confused with universal laws. Carnap appeals to the notion that such ambiguities do not so much attend "symbolic logic"—the language of scientists—as they do "ordinary word language," so that there does thankfully exist some kind of linguistic convention that mirrors/represents more adequately the distinction between fact and law.

Much of Carnap's philosophy depends on the familiar resort to forms of prediction and disconfirmation—a testing of laws vis-à-vis careful and constant observations. There is much here that can be questioned regarding essentialism. First, there is the "cult of the fact"[55] that prevails in the

---

[55] While this phrase may live in many different places and texts, we lifted it from an inviting book by Liam Hudson (1972), an experimental psychologist who, in the liberatory, humanist days of the early 1970s, subjected his own Cambridge-Oxford career and his consequent immersion within his becoming-scientized field to a soul-searching "self-criticism." The tenor of his "autobiography" is established in the first page of his "preamble": "This is a book about professional psychologists and the visions they pursue. It expresses a growing dissatis-

accumulation of scientific knowledge. It remains untheorized for Carnap, not to mention many other philosophers of science, how and why facts— singular observations—are granted the privilege of being the arbiter of the "truth" value of perceived regularity. There is the faith—which takes the form of "obviousness"—that observation is *the* standard against which causal, possibly lawlike, statements may be judged to be appropriate (and therefore productive of knowledge). In Carnap's philosophy of science, factuality serves as the essence of truth value, that is, for all putatively empirical statements. Facts and observations are accorded the singular privilege of determining—"causing," keeping in mind all the Carnapian warnings about this term—the willingness to treat shared perceptions of a sequence of events as "true." They are, in any case, a "necessity." (Is there a way or even a will to test the hypothesis that testing predictions by reference to observations is the leading—if not exclusive— means to establish veracity?) Facticity is given pride of place in the determination of truth value, and this reduction of scientific knowledge itself to a "necessary cause" or determination reveals one prevalent form of essentialism: the idea that "the essence" of truth value for lawlike statements with presumably empirical content is comparison with/by facts.

---

faction with the self-consciously scientific psychology in which I myself was trained—an activity that, increasingly over the last ten years, has taken on the air of a masquerade. It has been written in the hope that, somewhere behind the paraphernalia of false science and apparent objectivity, there lies the possibility of a more genuinely dispassionate study of human nature and human action" (11). Much of the charm of Hudson's book lies in his own psychologizing—gently but perhaps significantly—of the psychic processes that lead one to a "cult of the fact" (today, one could even call these processes "disorders" according to the current DSM, for which it seems there is a disorder that corresponds to nearly every imaginable human behavior and mood). Again, while empathically, Hudson narrates critically his own cultivation (he later terms it "indoctrination") in the philosophy of science at Oxford. "As a student, I was certainly left with the belief that all knowledge consisted of facts: hard little nuggets of reality that one could assemble like building blocks into patterns. . . . This 'building block view' in which all elements are inert and equal, is called, I have since learned, 'atomistic.' . . . Our preoccupation with evidence, similarly, made us unnecessarily clumsy . . . [I]t was on to 'the facts,' the evidence, that we homed. The impulse was healthy, in that it short-circuited discussion of woolly generalities. But it was also philistine, in that an appeal to the evidence can easily deteriorate from an attempt at dispassion—a noble venture—into a verbal destructiveness that is both cheap and facile. Only more recently have I realized that the appeal to 'the facts' can also herald an altogether less wholesome enterprise: that of rendering 'scientific' or legitimate a view that is at heart ideological" (38–39). Without commenting on the brave naïveté expressed here, or the "modernist" shibboleths that remain intact, we just want to note that Hudson goes on in his text to provide a welcome and open exploration into what kinds of psychological demeanors are inscribed within the modernist "will to facts" (our phrase). We implore the reader, though, not to see this exploration as a "bottom line" that mercilessly reveals the "real" modernist heart of darkness. It is one of many ways to show that what may seem evident and transcendent from a "no place because everyplace" point of view has, of course, its own overdetermination in and through very specific historical conjunctures and discourses (psychological processes included).

There are other such forms of reduction and essence in Carnap.[56] An-other occurs in his discussion of what is meant by necessity and the prob-lem that arises when a single observation or experience is used to dispute a metaphysical presentation of a law of nature. He writes: "Suppose that on visiting a city for the first time you use a street map to help you find your way about. Suddenly you find a clear discrepancy between the map and the city's streets. You do not say, 'The streets are disobeying the law of the map.' Instead you say, 'The map is wrong.' This is precisely the situation of the scientist with respect to what are called the laws of nature. The laws are a map of nature drawn by physicists. If a discrepancy is discovered, the question is never whether nature disobeyed: the only ques-tion is whether the physicists made an error" (207). Carnap goes on to say that "it should be clearly kept in mind that, when a scientist speaks of a law, he is simply referring to a description of an observed regularity. It may be accurate, it may be faulty. If it is not accurate, the scientist, not nature, is to blame" (207).

Let's consider this formulation. Leaving aside the assertion of the "bruteness" and opacity of nature, its relative "fixedness" insofar as only *it* can change its own laws (and of course, not human discourse), we are left with both an untested proposition—the fact that nature is not disobe-dient in respect to a description of it—as well as a notion that the scientist can either more or less "accurately" describe these laws, by which Carnap means universal statements that are based on the regularity of observa-tion. The essential qualities and characteristics of nature are posited here without regard to testing the veracity of nature's agency in determining the "error" or discrepancy. Nature, we are told, is not capable of "dis-obeying" whenever an "error" or discrepancy exists between the repre-sentation of a law (a map, for example) and the behavior of nature that is signified and condensed in that representation. Hence nature's "natural-ness"—which of course is its "essence"—is asserted in the fact that scien-tists, and never nature, may be "to blame" whenever descriptions are inaccurate. While it may seem absurd to readers to suggest anything dif-ferent, what we are concerned about here is simply the habit of mind that essentializes nature and finds that language, in this case description, can either be accurate or faulty but, in any event, a secondary and reflective response to the primacy of nature itself.

---

[56] It is not feasible for us to elaborate here all of these essentialisms, at least as we see them. But among them would surely be the essentialism that is bound up with the scientific "problem of knowledge" itself and, of course, the fact that the knowledge is seen largely to be a matter of a cognitive relation between a thinking subject and an object that is subjected to scrutiny. For our money, Althusser (Althusser and Balibar 1970) provides the most telling critique of the essentialisms involved in "the problem of knowledge," scientific or otherwise.

But this example brings us to a more wide-ranging problem. And that is the problem in which scientific knowledge is seen primarily to be not only an accumulation of universal laws, but also only a moment in this accumulation process. This issue arises in the context of Carnap's helpful discussion (187–95) of the many-sided determinations of the "cause" of an event. There are at least two components here that bear on our discussion of essentialism.

In the first case, Carnap shows that it is impossible for mere mortals to capture all the "causes" of some events. The problem here is one of the limits to knowledge that result from no one's having the "view from everywhere." Nor is it possible to state the *definitive* composite—the ultimate totality—of all the different "right" observations that come from all the different perspectives. At any moment in time, the prevailing composite is all that can be said to be "the cause" of an event. But consider Carnap's move here. Carnap regards this prevailing totality as the best that can be done under the circumstances, implying, of course, the possibility or at least the norm of a complete set of observations that would finally comprise the real cause. (To ward off possible objections that we misconstrue Carnap here, let us make clear that we fully understand that "real cause" has only the meaning of that which is useful for prediction.)[57] The second component to which we want to call attention is the view that such observations are incomplete, and that science is always engaged in a process of adding to the laws of causation. This implies that the current state of knowledge is forever less than perfect.

While this may be helpful in establishing some relief from the arrogant stance that posits that some specific explanations of events are eternally necessary and exist for all times and places, it is also a modernist maneuver. Its modernism consists of the humble assertion of the mere factness of limitations, such that limits are seen as unyielding and as "given" in and through nature, or at least in and through the scientific endeavor itself. In this view, it is the essence of science not to be able to ever end discussion and investigation of any law because of the ever-present impos-

---

[57] This is how Carnap (1966) describes it: "*Causal relation means predictability.* This does not mean actual predictability, because no one could have known all the relevant facts and laws" (192). Why not, we ask? What is being asserted here as the necessary limit to knowledge? Is it, itself, a fact of nature? A law? Carnap goes on to say, "It means predictability in the sense that, *if* the total previous situation had been known, the event could have been predicted. For this reason, when I use the term 'predictability' I mean it in a somewhat metaphorical sense" (192). How could it have been otherwise? Carnap finishes by stating that "it does not imply the possibility of someone actually predicting the event, but rather a potential predictability. Given all the relevant facts and all the relevant laws of nature, it would have been possible to predict the event before it happened. This prediction is a logical consequence of the facts and the laws" (192–93).

sibility of having complete knowledge, since we can never know now what observations will come tomorrow that may disconfirm any universal statement today. In our reading of postmodernism, the possibility of "complete knowledge" in and for any discourse does in fact exist. And this is precisely because in postmodern approaches to science and epistemology, the universalism involved in the projection of this empiricist essentialism—ironically of the necessary "contingency" and presentness of universal laws—is of course *within* one or more scientific discourses, but perhaps not others. Complete or incomplete knowledge, for that matter, is intratheoretical, not something that simply exists by virtue of a transcendent fact of nature.

We can put this point differently. There are very well developed traditions in the philosophy of science—not, for the most part, Anglo-Germanic—that present more "internalist" or, to use Althusser's phrase, "relatively autonomous" notions of scientific discourse. Thomas Kuhn's work (1970), of course, is another example of such a tradition, as is that of Paul Feyerabend (1978). As Resnick and Wolff (1987) depict, in many of these alternative traditions to mainstream Anglo-Germanic philosophy of science (and building on the work of Gaston Bachelard and Georges Canguilhem), the epistemological norms, protocols, methods, and so on that establish the truth value of any proposition are contained, largely if not exclusively, within a particular discursive formation, scientific or otherwise.[58] The perceptions of the limits to knowledge—or rather, the fact of the contingency of universal causal laws stated by Carnap—are neither transdiscursive nor given "in nature." In contrast to Carnap's view, we are willing to propose that the combination of perspectives that go into the description of an event are, in fact, "total" and perfect, at least within some norm of thought in which knowledge has no "outside" or extension into the future, or in which the future is thought to be completely mapped in advance. In every conjuncture, for example, we can imagine some advocates of particular discourses arguing that their capturing of a causal law, through description or some other device, is complete. This contrasts with discourses that encourage their purveyors to long— as lonely seekers who survey the long, arduous road ahead—for a day in which completion is promised, but alas for whom an arrival at a final resting place will never occur.

It is a form of essentialism to assert the irreducibility of *the* limits to knowledge, as though this assertion would necessarily hold in any en-

---

[58] For us, Dominique Lecourt's *Marxism and Epistemology* (1975) remains a groundbreaking text in elucidating the importance of Bachelard and Canguilhem for both contemporary philosophy of science and a distinctive Marxist epistemology. Of course, Lecourt is himself deeply indebted to the critique of both empiricist and rationalist epistemo-

deavor labeled scientific. It is at best a disputable claim to assert that the essence of scientific knowledge is for it to be forever incomplete and likewise essentially contingent because of the eternally repetitive inability to predict future observations. But such a claim requires a world picture in which uncertainty pertaining to a unknown (in advance) future is a natural fact and is not itself discursively produced and constituted, a point to which we return in chapter 2.

Foundations for Knowledge

Postmodern critique in areas dominated by ideas concerning scientific knowledge has concentrated largely on an assault on foundationalism, the notion that there is a transdiscursive basis upon which such knowledge can be erected.[59] The foundations in question usually range from certain modernist epistemological positions (which include empiricism and rationalism and their offshoots, like positivism) to "proper" experimental methods. What postmodern criticism amounts to, in light of the refusal of essentialism, includes an alternative view that there are multiple bases for the production of knowledge; that there can be no ultimate conceptual arbiter of different truth claims (though there may indeed be the perception that these claims have different effects, some of which can be preferred to others); that discourses concerned with knowledge production are often irreducible, largely nontranslatable, and therefore mostly incommensurate; and that settling the priority or hierarchy of different truth claims must always be connected to persuasiveness and power. Though relativist nihilism is certainly one possible outcome of this antifoundationalism, it is not the only one.[60] Postmodern critique calls attention not only to the play of power and persuasion in the current or past

---

logical essentialism that can be found in Althusser's great contribution to *Reading Capital* (Althusser and Balibar 1970).

[59] There is no question that a defense of foundations for knowledge consists largely of the view that establishing bases expands the realm of what can be considered worthy of scientific study. Yet postmodernists often follow the line of reasoning found in Rorty 1979, in which foundationalism is seen to be about constraint and exclusion. In Rorty's words, "the desire for a theory of knowledge is a desire for constraint—a desire to find 'foundations' to which one might cling, frameworks beyond which one must not stray, objects which impose themselves, representations which cannot be gainsaid" (315). We cannot overemphasize, by the way, the impact of Rorty's work on postmodern philosophies.

[60] Indeed, Bruna Ingrao charges E. Roy Weintraub with plunging into an "extreme relativism" because of his insistence that the "sequence of 'facts' in the history of the discipline is fluid and mutable, according to the contingent problems with which each community of scholars is concerned" (1997, 227). In our view, Weintraub's work does not lead to "extreme," "radical," or "nihilistic" relativism precisely because it involves the production of concrete stories about specific episodes in the history of economic thought.

status quo within scientific practice.[61] It also calls attention to the fact that such forces are considered, in a sense, legitimate in the adjudication among and between discourses.[62]

Rather than shying away from, or simply decrying, the way rhetoric, privilege, authority, and networks of power are entwined in knowledge production and especially in claims for any one discourse's superiority in constituting truth, an alternative position, one embraced by the French philosopher Michel Foucault (1972, 1980), is to acknowledge precisely that this is the way the world of knowing and convincing (and enforcing) works. The imbrications of power and knowledge, in fact, were the focus of much of Foucault's work, and postmodern critics have taken from him the view that there is nothing much to be ashamed of in the recognition that "wills" and "desires" to knowledge have as much to do with power as they do with anything else.[63] Power can be contended over; it can be the object of struggle over who gets to speak and produce authoritative knowledge and who doesn't. This, of course, is exactly what is at stake in the attempts to storm the citadels of knowledge production occupied and controlled by those (usually Western and white men) who disseminate their "normal sciences" in the form of canonical knowledge. That is, power to produce, speak, and disseminate, as well as to subvert and displace, traditional notions of knowledge and particular conceptual content are often the objectives of oppositional forces—in economics comprised of heterodox thinkers and doers, including Marxists, feminists, postcolonialists, and many others.[64] It is true that some of this opposition holds

---

[61] The mathematical microeconomist David Kreps admits that "the rise of mathematics" in economics can be explained, at least in part, by the fact that "the use of a powerful and somewhat obscure tool confers power on the user. As economists became convinced of the value of mathematical rigor, the reward system (based on peer review) reinforced this tendency" (1997, 64).

[62] Weintraub (1992) asserts that "power does matter" (55). Yet, of course, some like Roger Backhouse (1992) aren't persuaded. Though Backhouse admits that the dependence of knowledge on power may be a "fact of life," he concludes there is still "no place" (by which he means no legitimate place) for power in economic methodology (73).

[63] As Chris Weedon explains, "the theory that all discursive practices and all forms of subjectivity constitute and are constituted by relations of power is . . . only disabling if power is seen as always necessarily repressive" (1997, 175).

[64] Postcolonial theory has become an important literature over the last twenty years and shares in many ways concerns similar to those of some postmodernists, feminists, and Marxists, though, of course, there are important differences as well (for one comparative treatment, see Appiah 1992). Postcolonial theorists are concerned with the literary and cultural constructions of those in the former colonized nations as well as those diasporic locations outside these countries. Postcolonial theory often builds upon the idea of "subalternity," "otherness," and "resistance." The idea of the subaltern and the other refuses the binary of the postcolonial subject and experience in simple opposition or contrast to the West. Rather, otherness is often conceived in a nonessentialist and nontotalizing recognition of the myriad

precisely the same modernist view that scientific knowledge ought to be disinterested, unsusceptible to power, unmoved by rhetorical flourishes, unattached to other networks of power in society, and so forth. But, in effect, the postmodern position à la Foucault is that power and persuasion are *not* science's dirty little secret, and postmodern critique has attempted to bring them into the light (sort of like a previously perceived deviant behavior, which has now been shown to be undeserving of ostracism), not in the form of sensational revelation or staged revulsion, but as an assertion of the norms necessarily operating in the everyday life of scientific disciplines.

Science or Scientism?

What this postmodern critique makes possible, though, is a sweeping rejection of scientism, the view that scientific concepts, methods, protocols, and the like are exclusively entitled to the power and privilege they have achieved with modernization. If the growth of scientific knowledge is the key accomplishment of the past three centuries in the West, it has been accompanied by an elaborate philosophical defense of a variety of exclusionary practices by which those deemed to be untrained in or unreceptive to such science are shunted aside or even denied opportunities to speak (since they are considered to be the voice of unreason). We need not belabor this point here since so much of the controversy surrounding postmodernism—indeed, many of the visceral reactions it has provoked—has been in the challenges it has thrown up in contending over the exalted status of science within modernism. However, again it should be noted that the attack on scientific privilege does not necessarily imply a refusal of scientific practice.[65]

---

differences between and among postcolonial people and groups and their colonial pasts and postcolonial presents. Resistance is often thought of as subversion or mimicry, often with the recognition that the act of resistance cannot be separated from what is being resisted. The idea of hybridity is an important conceptual marker signaling a recognition of the integration of cultures and practices and the impossibility of a fully self-referential or "authentic" postcolonial life. Postcolonial writers are also concerned with many of the other concepts that have occupied postmodern theory, such as identity and difference, subjectivity, fragmentation, and representation. For an excellent collection of essays dealing with many aspects of postcolonial theory, see McClintock, Mufti, and Shohat 1997. Gayatri Chakravorty Spivak (1999) provides a brilliant critique of postcolonial studies, and she pushes the field to consider seriously the conditions of transnational culture and globality. S. Charusheela (2001) explores the implications of postcolonial theory for feminist economics.

[65] David Hollinger (1994) is right in his claim that "scientism is sometimes taken to cover a range of ideas broader than either naturalism or positivism, but the common denominator of its many definitions is a highly censorious tone . . . [S]cientism is normally an opprobrious epithet directed at what the speaker regards as an arrogant or naive effort to extend the

Indeed, the postmodern critique has often focused on the self-congratulatory aspects of the philosophy of science and the attempts to insulate scientific practice from scrutiny of its own rules of discursive formation, its implicit epistemological norms, its own situatedness in contemporary culture and social life, and much else. Postmodernism as critique of scientism then connects up with other, perhaps nonpostmodern, critics of science and the philosophy of science, such as Thomas Kuhn (1970), Paul Feyerabend (1978), Bruno Latour (1993), Sandra Harding (1986), and Barry Barnes (1985), who can each be read to have promoted the idea that "agreement" in science needs to be investigated, and that those theories that shape a field of thought are bound to more general social institutions and patterns of status, wealth, and power, or are able to hegemonize the field by "normalizing" the conditions under which theory arises. The postmodern critique of scientism is close as well to the view of Feyerabend that there are no singularly exceptional methods that are productive of science, and even that scientific progress is the result of scientist's refusal to follow any prescribed road toward truth.[66] As we have said, when one empties the world of the distinction between appearance and essence, and any method that claims to uniquely bridge the gap, one gives vent to a plurality of approaches that are potentially productive of knowledge.

The critique of essentialism and foundations opens up the question, then, of the privileged status of scientific discourse. If science has no prior purchase on uncovering embedded and veiled truths, then it is not possible to sustain the hierarchy of discourses in which only science is productive of knowledge and all else—opinion, faith, ideology, art, and so on—is productive of, well, all else. If postmodernist critique is effective in the attack on essentialism, then one possible repercussion may be the leveling of the field of knowledge. Thus, as we argue in chapter 7, postmodern critique encourages one to start from the premise that what are today regarded as ersatz or commonsense or everyday—read, confused, aberrant, and irrational—understandings of economics can be shown to be likewise productive of knowledge worthy of analysis and consideration.[67]

---

methods or authority of science into a field of experience where it does not belong" (34). Hollinger, in his defense of some variant of modernism in the human sciences, is also correct in stating that not all "aspirations toward a scientific culture" have been scientistic. But, again, we argue that the negative connotation in the term *scientism* is precisely oriented toward defenses of science that, when faced with people who do not buy into this form or thinking or its presumed results, lead either to a sneer or the advice (often followed by an enforcement) to "shut up."

[66] Of course, one does not have to buy into postmodernist critique to hold a pluralist methodological position. For a spirited defense of methodological pluralism in economics, see Caldwell 1982.

[67] In his interesting and valuable collection of Austrian, neo-Austrian, and libertarian essays about the possible and actual contributions of economists to public discourse, Daniel

In other words, the trappings of science do not amount to a protective shield, and much of importance would be achieved, we think, if all would-be knowers treated seriously the possibility that truth and useful knowledge can come from these "other" discursive formations and locations.

We note that this leveling of the field of knowledge makes it also impossible to sustain a meaningful distinction between metadiscourse and discourse. To take just one example, there exists a hierarchy that is well established and respected within academic economics such that talk about economic discourse (which includes such specializations as the history of economic thought and the philosophy and methodology of economics) is seen as "second order," while "doing" economics (which involves mostly formulating and testing economic models) is seen as primary, the stuff the discipline is essentially made of.

Now, one presumption here is that economic model building and even "high theory" (which often has no particular testable model as its consequence) have a priority in defining professional economic discourse since they are not commentary on texts but, in contrast, have direct access in some way, shape, or form to the "content" of economics (either the "real world" or mathematically derived abstract truths). Here we see that if we conjoin the critique of essentialism with other poststructuralist tenets regarding the textuality of any world "read" by a scientist/observer, then we can appreciate the impossibility of maintaining the "meta" distinction that accords, once again, so much power and privilege to those thought capable of doing economics as opposed to merely talking about it. If doing economics is just one other means of "reading" the world, and consists of no more nor less than "commentary" on it, then one can at least challenge the first-order, epistemological privilege that is accorded to high economic theory and/or econometric analysis. Admittedly, the objects of

---

Klein (1999) describes the practitioner of economics as "Everyman." Now, this label is a tip-off for what is to follow: "the practitioner of political economy is typically highly ignorant of basic economic ideas" (2). This diagnosis leads surely to a prescription. Klein quotes Adam Wildavsky: "It is up to the wise to undo the damage done by the merely good" (7). We hope that readers will forgive us for wincing when we read Klein's follow-up: "The economist's good works rarely bear fruit in any direct way. The economist's advice seems to fall on deaf ears. When good advice is rejected, the rejection is brusque and ignorant. Even in the rare case when the advice takes root, the sage's influence is long lost and he receives no credit. For the most part, participation in public discourse is like tutoring an ornery and spoiled child. The economist must plead to get attention; once he has attention, his appeals consist of elementary ideas, rehearsed earnestly and painstakingly, and illustrated by imaginative stories and examples. Just when he thinks the public and policymakers are taking his precepts to heart, they suddenly abandon his instruction and for no good reason. His only recourse is to keep on hoping and pleading" (8). For a different story about the possible ways economists might interact with "everymen" (and women), see the essays in Garnett 1999b and chapter 7 below.

such discourse may be different from the objects of the history of economic thought, but perhaps that is all that can be said. Neither tells the truth better or worse, and neither is closer to (or further from) the supposedly primordial "real" with its hidden meanings.

Determinism

Modernism is accused by postmodern critics for its persistent recourse to deterministic arguments where questions of cause and effect are concerned. In some versions of this critique, modernist explanation consists mostly of establishing the necessary or, less strongly, probabilistic patterns that link particular events as causes with other events as effects. Indeed, theory is the realm in which such explanations reign, and the absence of causal explanations is often viewed as the absence of theoretical activity. Now, while it is by no means necessary for causal explanation to be consistent, unilinear, and determinate, postmodern critics see the reduction of causation to these elements in most of what they observe in modernist discourses and disciplines. Determinism is a way of summing up these elements, as deterministic arguments are characterized by the search for principal causes that are said to have the largest weight (sometimes the only weight) in consistently bringing about a particular cause. In the idealized world of the "marketplace of ideas," causal explanations are preferred if they either identify an essential, underlying, and necessary cause (hence, determinism can be another form of essentialism) or capture a statistically predictable correlation between two distinct events, where one event is seen to nearly almost always follow in time and perhaps in space from the other. Postmodernist thinkers, though, have proposed alternative ways of conceiving of causation that avoid, in their view, the destructive consequences of determinism (and these range from the intolerant fanaticism of those who feel that they have found the one and only explanation for events to the passivity produced in human agency and social action when deterministic understandings posit the impossibility of alternative courses of behavior).

Determinism comes in many shapes and sizes. Within modernist social and natural sciences, everything from biology to culture to the economy to subjectivity has been pronounced, often simultaneously, to be the first, last, and perhaps efficient cause of many different events and human actions. In economics, of course, determinism has a variety of familiar forms, the most common being economic determinism, in which the economy or some subparticle of it is seen to structure an array of predictable effects. Hence, "It's the economy, stupid" is not just taken by many economists as an adage of what should count in the political opinions of social agents. It is put forward to describe a grand chain of social causation, in which "the economy" (here including alternative entry points as labor, utility, rational choice, and so forth) is seen as the motivating agency behind all consequent social outcomes.[68] Indeed, as we discussed above, the extension by Becker, Richard Posner (1992), and others of economic reasoning into cultural and social spheres is based on a type of privilege economists think redounds to economic explanation, since, by this logic, most human activity can be reduced in explanation to a matter of economizing, maximizing choices.[69]

The attack on determinisms of all sorts has been among the main contributions of postmodern critique. Alternative, specifically postmodern interrogations have emphasized the randomness of causation and the effectivity of chance, the indeterminacy of events, the multiplicity of possible causes, the fluidity of the relationship between seeming causes and their effects, and the reversibility of positions between putative causes and effects. Such interrogations have proceeded through the use of such notions as overdetermination, juxtaposition, synchronic simultaneity, fundamental uncertainty, and so forth. But, rather than surrender to the claim that theory is all but impossible if causation is not rendered in some form of determinism, postmodern nondeterminists have answered by stressing the role of theory in positing rich conjunctural analyses, limited, of course, to more "local" and specific occurrences. Some, for example the Marxist economists Resnick and Wolff (1987), have argued further that the rejection of determinism does not require even a different "entry point" into analysis. What it does require, though, is the idea that this entry point—which is a discursive "choice," often connected to a multitude of other values and desires—not be presented as favored cause in the world one is describing. Borrowing the term *overdetermination* from the French Marxist philosopher Louis Althusser, Resnick and Wolff show that entering a discourse with any privileged concept such as class does not mandate causal explanations in which class then is said to determine

---

[68] In a recent survey, Gary Miller (1997) argues that the "effect of economics has been felt more strongly in political science that any other social science," a move that has involved "the creation of a sub-discipline—denoted 'positive political theory,' to distinguish it from the more traditional political theory—that is grounded in rational choice modeling and uses analytical techniques from economics" (1173–74).

[69] The latest variant of this extension, of course, is the claim that all human behavior worth studying can be crammed into game theory. As the Nobel Prize winner John Harsanyi (1995) states, "in principle, *every* social situation involves strategic interaction among the participants" (293). In fact, Harsanyi argues that, paradoxically, the assumption of perfect competition in markets was one of the chief obstacles to the ascendance of game theory since it implied the inability of any particular agent to effect much in the way of change in market price.

(either directly or even in a mediated but distinguishable form) other social processes and events.[70]

In economics, of course, economic determinism is less a function of the reduction of the social world to effects of class and much more a similar reduction to the effects of individual economic agency. Postmodern critique adds one more voice to an already noisy chorus of objections to the idea of *homo economicus*.[71] The notion of subjectivity that founds much economic (particularly neoclassical) theorizing has been railed against and dissected for its faultiness by dissenting voices for most of the past century. Postmodern critique, though, identifies the rational, maximizing agent as only one element within the context of a broader theoretical humanism, another distinguishing aspect (according to postmodernists) of the rise and dominance of modernist modes of thinking and being.

Theoretical Humanism

Much of the postmodern critique of theoretical humanism has been closely connected to the writings of Foucault, Althusser, Lyotard, Derrida, and other "poststructuralist" analysts. Perhaps Foucault, though, is best known for his thoroughgoing offensive against humanism, or rather, his claim that recent writing and philosophizing (in the postmodern vein) has shown glimmers, blessedly, of the "death of Man."[72] Foucault (1973) outlines what he terms "epistemes" that he believes have structured Western thought since the Middle Ages, and when he gets to the Enlightenment and thereafter, he sees many roads in thought and practice leading to representational modes in which what is represented and/or signified is most often humanity as the originating subject of all knowledge and consequent history. Placing humanity, rather than God, say, at the center of a discursive universe is, in Foucault's writings, one noticeable characteris-

---

[70] According to Gibson-Graham, Resnick, and Wolff (2001a), "the question of the choice between different theories or entry points involves not which is more accurate or true, but the consequences of choosing one rather than another" (5). Thus, "Marx's language of class highlights certain processes and obscures others, potentiates certain identities and suppresses others, and has the capacity to energize certain kinds of activities and actors while leaving others unmoved" (9).

[71] Among more recent critics, feminist economists have been prominent. Some readings include Feiner 1999; Grapard 1995; Strassmann 1993; Nelson 1996; and Hewitson 1999. Hewitson's book, especially, is written from a self-consciously poststructuralist point of view. See our extended discussion of feminist criticisms of homo economicus in chapter 4 below.

[72] There is an enormous literature that treats Foucault's work. We recommend the following as an introduction to this commentary: Rabinow 1984; Dreyfus and Rabinow 1983; Smart 1993; and Shumway 1992.

tic of post-Enlightenment thinking (that is, perhaps until the middle of the twentieth century). Foucault argues that much social thinking and cultural activity is directed to knowledge of and control over human subjectivity (and here, subjectivity becomes again the motivating agency in tracing all historical movement). Foucault (1979) identifies the human body as the site of much surveillance and discipline, and he sees this desire to "know Man" and his or her body as behind projects of knowledge and social ordering—the exercise of power—varying in subject matter from utilitarianism to existentialism.[73]

The idea that the human subject is the sine qua non for all thought and practice in the modern era is taken up as well by Althusser (1970; Althusser and Balibar 1970), who concentrates some of his own critique on the idea that history is most frequently understood within modern thought as a process with a subject (usually, but not exclusively, a human subjectivity, like individuals seeking progressive freedom from natural or social constraint, or classes seeking the overthrow of exploitation and oppression). Placing humans at the center of schemas of progress and history and meaning is what distinguishes theoretical humanism, as the human subject is thus the beginning and ending point of all movement from the growth of knowledge (which is now understood as undertaken by, for, and through human subjectivity) to the transformation of the natural world (through science and technology oriented to human desires and ends, such as happiness).

Poststructuralist feminism contributes another major voice to this critique of humanism. While of course not all feminisms have been interested in challenging the presumptions of the essential commonality of humans or the notion that progress must be human-centered, quite a few strands of contemporary feminist thought move beyond expanded enfranchisement and "equal rights" (battles still mandatory to fight) to interrogations of the humanist (read masculinist) assumptions and practices in the wake of the Enlightenment. One group most committed to rethinking issues of subjectivity and identity through a focus on the ambiguous meanings of sex and gender has been poststructuralist feminists. Here we have in mind such writers as Judith Butler (1990, 1993), Jane Flax (1990, 1993), and Elizabeth Grosz (1994).[74] While differing in important ways, each of these thinkers rejects the assumption that progress for women is a matter of establishing a stable subjective identity of their own—looking a lot like the

---

[73] For one discussion within economics that evaluates the Foucauldian themes of power/knowledge and their effects on the human body, see Amariglio 1988.

[74] Readers can also evaluate arguments for and against poststructuralist feminism and postmodernism more broadly in Nicholson 1990. Carole Biewener (1999) offers a valuable assessment of the hoped-for effects of poststructuralist feminism on a decentered Marxism (and vice versa).

model of the human subject that was formulated with modernity, or based on the modernist assumption of irreducible biological difference. Butler and the others trouble the notion that subject positions and identities can be stable, and thereby challenge the essentialism (either in the form of cultural determinism or biological destiny) that sometimes accompanies the claim that gender produces clearly distinguishable subjects. Not only do poststructuralist feminists call attention to the masculinism (or "phallocentrism") that one can "read" in the notion of the human subject and the cult of Reason as they have evolved over the past three hundred years in the West. They go on to question the possibility of finding an alternative construct of the human, and certainly one that fixes sexual and gender identity in a bipolar fashion, that can be utilized strategically or not for struggles against sexism, discrimination, and the oppression of women. As Gillian Hewitson (1999) has described it, stressing "performed" as opposed to inherited or natural gender difference (and actually placing greater emphasis on the body than on "consciousness" in the determination of performed identity), poststructuralist feminists have refused the "add women and stir" conception of expanding the modernist notion of humanity as a way to remedy sex and gender affliction. Thus, such feminists "view the ideal of equality, which involves reducing difference to sameness, and the ideal of difference, when reduced to biological difference, as problematic, since both replicate phallocentrism" (128).

If nothing else, postmodern critique has identified the ubiquity of theoretical humanism in characterizing the modern age, but it goes on to propose a much-needed decentering in which the human subject is not only displaced from its structuring role as entry and exit point, but also in which human subjectivity is shown to be capable of deconstruction and fragmentation. Not only, then, are "forces," "processes," and "wills" (along the lines specified by Nietzsche) disembodied in some postmodern thought—going even beyond "structuralism"—and shown to construct subjects rather than being "emissions" or manifestations of subjectivity. Subjectivity itself is seen to be indeterminate and unstable, in an incessant process of decomposition and recomposition. The decentered subject, found in Foucault, Althusser, Butler, and others, and the decentered social totality (with the subject no longer that which seeks its own representation in and through art, philosophy, technology, etc.) are unsuitable because troubling essences for much existing modernist social thought, and this is why for some critics of postmodernism, the assault on theoretical humanism makes theorizing itself impossible.

Yet, of course, postmodern critique shows precisely how one can incorporate the ideas that human subjectivity is complex, uncertain, and irreducible and that this same subjectivity is as much effect as it is cause in scenarios of historical movement. We note, by the way, that the attack on humanism implicates many critics of the notion of homo economicus along with its mostly neoclassical purveyors. So, for example, complaints that neoclassicals and others haven't captured the "real" human subject in championing homo economicus starts from similar premises that there is some such previously unrepresented, unified, and distinguishable human subjectivity that can be properly specified. Postmodern critique, then, should be distinguished from those forms of humanism (found in all sorts of heterodox schools of economic thought, including Marxism, feminism, and institutionalism) that seek to reinstall rather than end the primacy of human subjectivity in economic discourse. One can see in our discussion in chapter 4 below, for example, the tensions felt by those unhappy with neoclassical (and often masculinist and Western) notions of economic agency, but hesitant to go the way of a thoroughgoing antihumanism. We expect these tensions to persist into the foreseeable future.

Postmodernism and Economics: A Stylized Genealogy

Most surveys of postmodernism in the contemporary scholarly landscape say little about the discipline of economics, though as we have stated, there are lots of attempts in cultural fields to talk about a postmodern economy.[75] In her 1991 article, Sheila Dow in fact asked whether there were signs of postmodernism within economics. More than a decade later, we can answer vigorously in the affirmative. For not only have there been important essays, like McCloskey's article on the "rhetoric of economics" (1983a), that have set off a wave of discussions about modernism within economics, but as our previously edited volume (Cullenberg, Amariglio, and Ruccio 2001) attests, there are by now a significant number of different scholars within the field of economics who are either writing about postmodernism or who employ postmodern approaches. For some of these economists, postmodernism enters in its critical guise, as they roundly censure the modernism of mainstream economics.

While not all those who are attracted to postmodern critique are outside of the mainstream of the profession, it has been the case that postmodernism has been useful for those who seek more visibility for their approaches or who wish to displace entirely the long tradition of neoclas-

---

[75] While Rosenau observes that "even in psychology and economics post-modernism is making enormous gains that will be reflected in publications appearing throughout the next few years" (1992, 4), more recent multidisciplinary surveys, such as the *Routledge Critical Dictionary of Postmodern Thought* (Sim 1999), which covers areas of thought that run from philosophy to popular culture, still fail to mention (let alone treat at any length) economic discourse.

sical economic theory as dominant within the field.[76] Much is at stake, some of the critics feel, in the struggle to obviate the centrality of homo economicus, to decenter notions of economic totalities, to revive interest in morality and values and power as determinants in economic discourse, to scale down the pretensions of economics as a "science," to open up spaces for plural perspectives, and to resist the "imperialism" of economics as a master discourse capable of shaping cultural fields.[77] These are often, and rightly we feel, linked to other struggles, such as those dedicated to breaking down barriers to entry of women and minorities into the economics profession, or those that attempt to redress the excessive exercise of expertise and authority, with their pervasive exclusionary effects, that can be found within pecking orders of universities, journals, and so forth.[78]

Parts of what we describe here as postmodern critique can be traced to different movements within economics over the past twenty-five years. Certainly, if one is looking for progenitors, then one must mention at the very least Keith Tribe's often overlooked 1978 treatise on Smithian and

[76] This is true of most of the essays that composed the special symposium entitled "Postmodernism, Economics, and Canon Creation" that appeared in the *Journal of Post Keynesian Economics* in 1991 (see Beed et al. 1991). Post-Keynesianism has turned out to be a welcome ground (relatively speaking) on which to raise issues of postmodernism. The influence of Keynes (especially his 1937 article) and Shackle (1961, 1966, 1990) in particular on questions of uncertainty and the indeterminacy of agent choice, not to mention ideas stemming from Keynes on persistent tendencies toward disequilibria, have been felt within some branches of this school.

[77] In an unpublished paper, Uskali Mäki defines the disciplinary imperialism of economics as "a form of economics expansionism where the new types of phenomena are located in territories that are occupied by disciplines other than economics, and where economics presents itself hegemonically as being in possession of the right theories and methods, thereby excluding rival theories and approaches from consideration" (n.d., 18), for which Jack Hirshleifer (1985) provides the warrant: "There is only one social science. . . . What gives economics its imperialist invasive power is that our analytical categories—scarcity, cost, preferences, opportunities, etc.—are truly universal in applicability. . . . Thus economics really does constitute the universal grammar of social science" (53).

[78] Easterlin (1997) captures again nicely some of the arrogance and exclusions, supposedly in the name of science, practiced by economists in this summary of what he terms his own "indoctrination" to the economics profession in graduate school: "And then there was my education in the values of the economics profession. I learned that economics is the queen of the social sciences. I learned that theory is the capstone of the status hierarchy in economics. I learned the brand names whose research I was to revere and respect. I learned that tastes are unobservable and never change. I learned that subjective testimony and survey research responses are not admissible evidence in economic research. I learned that what was then called 'institutional economics' (Commons, Veblen, etc.) was beyond the pale, as were other social sciences more generally. I learned that there is a mere handful of economics journals really worth publishing in, and that articles in inter- or extra-disciplinary journals count for naught. I learned that economic measurement as then practiced by the National Bureau of Economic Research was to be denigrated as 'measurement without theory' " (13).

pre-Smithian economic discourse. In this book, Tribe employed specifically poststructuralist critiques of humanism and other forms of essentialism in modernist histories of economic thought (shaped by the idea,
which we saw in Samuelson, of the inexorable growth of knowledge,
funeral by funeral) to rethink the claim that Smith was the initiator of a
new, modernist economics. And, one can look at the entire body of work
of Resnick and Wolff over the past twenty-five years as well, as they
have advocated, with others, everything from the critique of classical
epistemology to economic determinism in their attempt to refound a
postmodern Marxian theory as something distinct from neoclassical and
other mainstream economic thought, as well as distinct from Marxism's
own inscription within its past modernist projects. And, of course, for
many McCloskey's (1983a) article on the rhetoric of economics point-
edly criticized at least the official methodologists and epistemologists
among economic philosophers for their modernism, even if it did not
make the concepts and constructs of neoclassical economics its primary
object of scorn.

There may be other progenitors as well, and in fact the onset of postmodernism has led some historians of economics to find similar critiques
of the tenets of modernism in a wide variety of writers and thinkers, often,
however, out of the mainstream.[79] And, of course, there is fertile ground
in economics to find such critiques since, in fact, the braggadocio that has
accompanied "advances" made possible by formalism and other supposedly "scientific" methods of analysis and proof has often been met with
annoyance and resistance by those left out of the resulting conversations.
Perhaps the next few decades of work in the history and philosophy of
economics will be dedicated at least in part to "unearthing" the anti- or
nonmodernist sympathies of past and present economists and others who
are made to live in the margins of the official discipline.[80]

While postmodernism has been mainly available to economists as anti-
or nonmodernist critique of the modernist mainstream, the "postmodern
moments" approach has a somewhat different emphasis. Here, the point
is to show those elements of postmodernism that have arisen in the midst

---

[79] This, for example, is what Ulla Grapard (2001) does by locating Charlotte Perkins
Gilman's "social constructivism" as an early expression of this more or less postmodern
element.

[80] In addition to our prior citations, such work includes Hands's (1997) rediscovery of
Frank Knight's contextualist pluralism and Burczak's (1994) focus on the postmodern moments in Friedrich von Hayek's work. In a similar way, Cullenberg (1999) points to the
postmodern moments and similarities in certain traditions within Marxism and institutionalism by emphasizing their decentered affinities, and Garnett (1999a) takes this Marx-
ist-institutionalist dialogue about postmodernity a step further in his consideration of heterogeneous approaches to nonneoclassical value theory.

of economics as a modernist enterprise. That is, in addition to evaluating and criticizing neoclassical and other schools for their pervasive adherence to modernism, "finding" the postmodern moments with these schools of thought is tantamount to deconstructing economic discourse to demonstrate, in the end, troublesome anomalies that pertain to uncertainty, the instability of subjectivity, the possibility of various rationalities, simultaneous multicausality, persistent and irreducible disequilibrium, and still more. The intention of calling attention to these postmodern moments is to show that, despite proclamations to the contrary, economic discourse in much of the past half century has not been able to build a stable consensus around a "core" of ideas and approaches.

Or, differently, discussing postmodern moments is likewise aimed at depicting even mainstream economic discourse as, perhaps unwittingly, increasingly preoccupied with postmodern themes and ideas despite the claims that fundamental uncertainty, decentered subjects, and so forth are either negligible or manageable within existing theoretical approaches. There are now numerous articles, for example—three that immediately come to mind are by, respectively, Varoufakis (1993), Mehta (1993), and Hargreaves Heap (1993)—that attempt to show the lacunae pertaining to problems of assuming stable, directed, contained, and unfragmented rationalities that become evident in economic game-theoretical approaches. Varoufakis, in particular, argues that anxiety about modernist rationality assumptions are pervading the field, and that in their wake postmodernist approaches to subjectivity have been considered, even if they are still underrepresented.

In the remainder of the present book, we identify and investigate the postmodern moments evident not only in heterodox schools of economic thought but perhaps just as much within neoclassical and Keynesian orthodoxy. Our approach focuses on key concepts and issues within economic thought, locating the "disruptions" that have emerged within and that point beyond the economic modernism that has characterized diverse theoretical traditions in economics. Thus, without claim to exhaustive or final treatment, we discuss, in successive chapters

The role of uncertainty with respect to the work of Keynes and numerous post-Keynesians

The human body as a site of decentering and dispersal within neoclassical theory

The fragmentation of knowing and acting subjects in recent feminist economics

The problem of values as understood by institutionalist economists

The interplay between order and disorder within Marxian conceptions of capitalism and socialism

The differences between academic and everyday economic discourses

Our purpose is to call attention to these elements both as a recognition of modernist economics' inability to exclude or address its own aporias and undecidables, and as the prolegomenon to a research program, in which these postmodern moments are embraced as worthy of direct consideration.

We realize, of course, the "threat" that such a reception represents. The historian of economic thought Mark Blaug puts it succinctly: "in one way or another, postmodern arguments always amount to 'anything goes' " (1998, 29). But, from our perspective, the dissolving effects of uncertainty, decentering, fragmentation, epistemological relativism, and the like on well-formulated economic models are already in process, for better or worse, and are just as much the unintended consequences of modernist formalism, essentialism, scientism, and so forth as they are "imports" from postmodern critics. Though we are not interested in prognostication (our postmodern training, perhaps), we do propose at least one improbable hypothesis: modernist economic discourse, so intent on maintaining its scientific identity, may be seen through the perspective of postmodern moments to be in the process of becoming "other."

Perhaps, then, postmodernism in economics allows for a paraphrased restatement of Samuelson's maxim: funeral by funeral, economics does become other. While modernism still has a death grip on the imaginations of many in the profession, postmodernism beckons those with breath left in them to another site—another graveyard, possibly. Be that as it may, we are willing at least for now to pick up our shovels and relocate, if only as gravediggers, to this other site. Postmodernism cannot, and will not, promise "progress" in economic knowledge as a result of all that repositioned digging. All it can do is show that, even if the quest for progress is dead and buried, still the excavation goes on, and transformations of this different terrain present—funeral by funeral—new opportunities and new discourses for economic knowledge.

2

Knowledge, Uncertainty, and Keynesian Economics

> I had once said to my father, "But there would
> still be no certainty." He had said, "Oh no, but
> what a thing to want, certainty!"
> —Nicholas Mosely, *Hopeful Monsters*

IN THIS FIRST "CASE STUDY," we explain how postmodernism can help make sense of uncertainty, especially in relation to contemporary economics. Our discussion is centered around a particular reading of Keynes's treatment of uncertainty and probability and develops the argument that, following on our discussion of postmodern "moments" in chapter 1, uncertainty turns out to be one of the shifting boundaries in economics between modernism and postmodernism.

Our postmodern approach to the "problem" of uncertainty is provoked by a particular irony that has characterized much of modern—late-nineteenth- and twentieth-century—economics. On one hand, certainty has been an important characteristic of modern economists' conceptions both of the economy and of the role of economics over the course of the last one hundred years. Oscillations have taken place, especially back and forth between neoclassical and Keynesian economists—on matters of both theory (from microeconomic approaches to macroeconomics and now back again) and policy (from free markets to more state-centered approaches to the current celebration of markets). Yet the confidence and self-assuredness (some might say "arrogance") expressed by participants on both sides of the debate seem to have been guided, at least in part, by the presumption of certain knowledge (or, at a minimum, the possibility of such knowledge) predicated on a distanced, objective cognitive relation to the world.[1] It might also be argued that the precise limits of those oscillations—of the theoretical positions and policy options that have been allowed into the debate—have been based on the modern "episteme" of certain knowledge.

---

[1] According to Mark Blaug (1980, 221), "the Keynesian-Monetarist debate of the last two decades must rank as one of the most frustrating and irritating controversies in the entire history of economic thought, frequently resembling medieval disputations at their worst. Again and again, violent polemical claims are made, which are subsequently withdrawn."

On the other hand, economists have both witnessed and (even more important for our purposes) been active participants in the movement to study the phenomena of randomness, risk, probability, and uncertainty, especially from the 1920s and 1930s onward. Much like their counterparts in other areas of modern culture, from physics and biology to art and literature, economists set out to "explore," and in some cases to "conquer," the hitherto unknown "continents" represented by uncertainty and related notions. It was precisely the modern spirit of "economic science"—the certainty that, by wielding all of the instruments available in the economic tool-kit, they would be able to record empirically and formulate theoretically the immutable laws of economic behavior—that led to economists' "discovery," and hence knowledge of, uncertainty, probability, and the like.[2] In this sense, the "normal" functioning of the modernist protocols of economic science can be credited with having given rise to the preoccupation with the "rules of chance" on the part of contemporary economists.

If we are right in characterizing at least some important parts of modern economic discourse in terms of this irony of certainty and uncertainty, we may then be in the position to understand both the emergence of uncertainty in the work of Keynes and the unsettling implications of that concept—especially of what has come to be called "true uncertainty"—for contemporary economists. It is our contention that Keynes's investigations of uncertainty and probability were part of—as they emerged from and, in turn, participated in producing and extending—the modern concern with risk, uncertainty, and related ideas. However, his investigations produced notions of uncertainty and probability some of whose effects were inconsistent with and ultimately could not be "controlled" by the modernist protocols within which they were produced. And it is these elements of "undecidability" or "indeterminacy" that threaten to overrun the boundaries of modern economics and that, therefore, represent the postmodern "moments" of uncertainty.

Or, to put our message differently, there is nothing inherently unsettling, much less "nihilistic," about uncertainty. Rather, it is only the modernism that continues to inspire much of contemporary economics that gives rise to the anxiety occasioned by the significant presence of true uncertainty. This anxiety, born of the modernist tension between certainty and uncertainty, often serves to blunt—by invigorating economists to attempt to control or "domesticate"—the more disruptive implications of uncertainty initially set forth by Keynes.

---

[2] Mary Morgan (1990, 9–11) argues, for example, that econometrics was developed in the early twentieth century as economists searched for an appropriate substitute for the experiments that had, in their view, made physics into a scientific discipline.

Knowledge and Uncertainty

According to many economists, on or about February 1936 the character of economics changed. And, as with the case of Virginia Woolf's allusion to the transformation in human character coincident with the inauguration of the first postimpressionist art exhibition in London, there was open disagreement among economists about the nature of the change occasioned by the publication of Keynes's *General Theory*.[3] While some economists considered it "vigorous and stimulating," many others found it quite troubling. This is especially true of the central role accorded to uncertainty. For the next fifty years, most economists (G. L. S. Shackle being a notable exception) attempted to come to grips with the challenge posed by the new theory of employment, interest, and money by downplaying or ignoring altogether the disturbing implications of Keynes's notion of uncertainty. Instead, the novelty of Keynes's contribution was often cast in terms of the presence and effects of known psychological "laws," "irrational" behavior on the part of some economic agents, and/or the rational actions of agents in disequilibrium situations. And when mainstream Keynesian economists (together with their neoclassical colleagues and others) did attempt to grapple with the problem of uncertainty, they tended to focus on the insurable risk associated with economic actors' uncertain knowledge about actual "states of the world," coupled with their certain knowledge of the probability distribution of such outcomes[4]—or, in the case of Shackle (1961, 1966, 1972), on the freedom associated with the "creative imagination" exercised by uncertain market participants.

However, that situation has now begun to change. To judge by the recent spate of publications on "true" Keynesian uncertainty,[5] not to mention the fact that the conference for which we drafted an earlier version

---

[3] The full quotation, "And now I will hazard a second assertion, which is more disputable perhaps, to the effect that on or about December 1910 human character changed," is from *Mr. Bennett and Mrs. Brown* (Woolf 1924, 4). This "observation" serves as the basis of Woolf's contention that Georgian literary conventions were no longer capable of creating "real" characters and, consequently, needed to be overturned in favor of a new approach to literature, especially the novel. The postimpressionist art exhibition, which included the works of Cézanne, Gauguin, and van Gogh and which apparently was greeted with hostility by a good many British art critics of the time, was organized by Roger Fry in November 1910. See Mini 1991 and Skidelsky 1983 for insightful discussions of Keynes's involvement in the Bloomsbury group.

[4] This is how uncertainty is introduced into the neoclassical general equilibrium model by Debreu, resulting in "the formal identity of this theory of uncertainty with the theory of certainty" (1959, 102). Similarly, Peter Hammond's view is that "uncertainty *per se* really introduces little that is fundamentally new into economics" (1990, 92).

[5] See, e.g., the extensive list of references that accompanies Hillard 1992.

of this chapter was devoted entirely to the issue of uncertainty,[6] we seem to find ourselves in the midst of a decisive shift in thinking. Now, true uncertainty—as distinguished from certainty, probabilistic knowledge, and the like—is accorded a central place in the Keynesian oeuvre, an important marker of the gulf that separates what was original and decisive in Keynes's outlook not only from neoclassical and new classical economics but also from much of what has passed for Keynesian macroeconomics in the postwar period.[7]

What is particularly interesting about the renewed focus on the role of Keynesian uncertainty is that it dovetails with, but ultimately has implications that exceed, recent criticisms of economic modernism that have stayed mostly at the level of epistemologies and discursive structures. Not that such criticisms are unimportant or have not engendered far-reaching debates concerning the standards of knowledge and procedures for scientific verification that have long exercised a decisive influence in the philosophy and methodology of economics. However, in our view, the treatment of uncertainty serves to provoke something more: a postmodern moment at the very core of modernist economic discourse that is, in turn, productive of alternative economic discourses. Precisely because uncertainty threatens to overturn modernist concepts of rationality and subjectivity— on the part both of economic agents and of economic scientists—it has the power to deconstruct any economic discourse that presumes or starts from such entry points.

As we saw in chapter 1, modernist epistemological positions have been criticized and increasingly displaced, outside as well as inside economics, during the course of the past two decades. Rorty, Derrida, Althusser, Lyotard, and Foucault have been joined by such economists as McCloskey, Klamer, and Resnick and Wolff in challenging post-Enlightenment empiricist and rationalist theories of knowledge (and their recent variations, including positivism) both for treating discourse as a "mirror of nature" and for positing a subject-object relation as the point of departure for knowledge. It is because of their work that new, nonpositivist ways of thinking about knowledge production—including the rules of discursive formation, the play of signs, the role of rhetoric and metaphors, and the overdetermination of theory—have come to challenge modernist epistemologies and to point in the direction of postmodern alternatives.

The "discovery" of true uncertainty certainly reinforces the emergence of postmodern theories of knowledge within economics to the extent that

---

[6] The papers from that conference can be found in the excellent volume edited by Sheila Dow and John Hillard (1995).

[7] Paul Davidson (1978) put forward this view twenty years ago; it has recently been restated by James Crotty (1994). This focus on true uncertainty, notwithstanding the contin-

it focuses on the thorny issues surrounding the limits to knowledge. But, in our view, uncertainty is productive of even more disturbing implications for modernist economics: it calls into question not only the usual knowledge claims concerning the way we think about economic discourses but also the conceptions of subjectivity and rationality on which the *content* of much of modernist economics has been predicated. For example, if economic agents are considered to be fundamentally uncertain (if only with respect to future events), then it becomes increasingly difficult to use the processes of rational intellection that are invoked within a wide range of economic models—from neoclassical utility-maximization and Keynesian wage-determination to game theory and new classical macroeconomics—to explain the future (and perhaps even present and past) behavior of such agents. Moreover, allowing uncertain economic actors implies a movement away from traditional notions of a unified, singular subjectivity toward more decentered, postmodern conceptions: for example, subjects that operate with multiple, incommensurable knowledges and rationalities (such that any "I" is comprised of a variety of overlapping and intersecting "I's") and the idea that subjectivity itself is constituted within discourse.

Now, if these postmodern effects on economic agency are "immanent" within the notion of uncertainty, we also believe that they pose unsettling questions with respect to economic scientists. It is new classical economics in recent years that has attempted to bridge the gap between the knowledge claims of economic agents and economists, by supposing the essential identity, under competitive market conditions, between expert knowledge (economic science) and subjective knowledge, at least in regard to rational expectations. However, if this "symmetry" is allowed to operate in the *opposite* direction, then we would find that economic scientists are characterized by the same kinds of uncertainty that have been "discovered" in the case of consumers, producers, and other economic agents. It is here, perhaps, with the recasting of the rationality and subjectivity of the practitioners of economics themselves, that the nihilism of uncertainty will be most acutely felt. If economists are allowed to operate with multiple minds and to have contradictory apprehensions and hopes with respect to all events—past, present, and future—the forms of information and learning that are conditions of the unified, rational mind associated with modernist conceptions of scientific analysis and objective truth will have to be relinquished.

But, as we will see, economists who have been engaged in the discursive production of the "unknown" have tended to shy away from these impli-

---

uing debate about the exact meaning of the term, has become one of the defining characteristics of post-Keynesian economics.

cations. Uncertainty, therefore, continues to represent one of the key sites in economic discourse in which the contrasting conditions and effects of modernism and postmodernism can be identified.

Uncertainty and Economic Modernism: Knight and Shackle

Keynes, of course, was not the first economist to introduce uncertainty into economic discourse. The issue of economic decision-making in the face of uncertainty has a lineage that can be traced back at least as far as mercantilist thought regarding the early stock endeavors of colonial trading companies and the problems of hazard and, therefore, insurance in the event of catastrophe or failure. That is, the notion of uncertainty in economics can be linked historically with the questions of risk, indemnity, and the appropriate profit or loss that presumably derives from investment choices in the face of danger and unknown future outcomes.[8]

Closer to our period, the issue of uncertainty gained importance, though not as a central concept in defining ordinary market situations, in the bringing together of probability theory and economic analysis during the course of the nineteenth century.[9] According to Claude Ménard (1980), however, some of the most notable "mathematical" economists of the nineteenth century balked at the application of probabilistic and statistical analysis to economic problems. Both Augustin Cournot and Léon Walras, while expertly conversant with statistical theory, were unenthusiastic about its use in economic analyses of individual rational choice and market equilibrium. Walras, for example, preferred analytic geometry

[8] Lorraine Daston (1987) discusses the ways in which mathematical probability grew out of and, in turn, changed the theory of risk-taking in the late seventeenth and early eighteen centuries. In particular, Daston argues that "modernity is in some way linked with new attitudes toward the control of the future and the possibility of life relatively secure from the disruptions of chance" (244), although prevailing attitudes toward risk and uncertainty were incompatible with the idea of mathematical approach to either insurance or gambling.

[9] To be clear, we do not mean to imply that uncertainty, randomness, risk, probability, and so on all mean or refer to the same thing, or that there is a unique or agreed-upon understanding of any one of these terms (whether inside or outside economics). However, as Ian Hacking (1990b) has effectively demonstrated, there are important historical connections between the emergence of a "logic of chance" and the rise of statistical conceptions of individuals and society which, in the first half of the twentieth century, culminated in the pervasive influence of "probability" in many spheres of thought, economics included. At the same time, Morgan (1990) argues that probability theory was not joined with statistical and, later, econometric work in economics until the 1940s: "even though these early econometricians used statistical methods, they believed that probability theory was not applicable to economic data. Here lies the contradiction: the theoretical basis for statistical inference lies in probability theory and economists used statistical methods, yet they rejected probability" (228).

and calculus for investigating and presenting the effects of market choices at the margin. In Ménard's view, Walras's reticence to embrace statistical theory signified the economics discipline's commitment to notions of certainty and invariant laws. Only when economics experienced a change in its "vision inspired by the statistical equilibrium suggested by thermodynamics" did economists embrace the sensibilities of "variety, of probability, of approximations" (1980, 541). Frank Knight was one of the first to assert that the application of probabilistic and statistical theory to rational choice was fundamental, if problematic.

Knight

In 1921, Knight published his classic work *Risk, Uncertainty, and Profit*. This modernist text left no doubt that a full account of rational behavior on the part of consumers and entrepreneurs depended on a delineation of the motives for and different types of choice taken in the absence of "certain" knowledge. Indeed, Knight solves one of the most pressing issues of economics, at least to his satisfaction, by showing that profit arises from a condition of "true uncertainty." The wide use Knight made of the concepts of risk and uncertainty has disturbed many later modernists, such as Kenneth Arrow, who faults Knight not only for basing his theory of profit on the existence of uncertainty but for overextending the use of concepts of risk and uncertainty to the point where the entire "free-enterprise system . . . arises as a reaction to the existence of uncertainty" (1971, 7).

That Knight was a modernist should not be doubted. The first chapter of his text contains one of the more careful discussions before Lionel Robbins of "scientific" epistemological and methodological procedures. Although Knight's arguments about the unreality of assumptions and the separation of concrete prediction and abstract theorizing might give pause to contemporary positivists, Knight clearly enunciated his belief that the method of economics "is the scientific method" (1921, 8). Knight's constant comparison and recourse to physics throughout his text suggests his fascination—albeit with reservations—with modernist conceptions of knowledge.

Knight is also the author of these sentiments: "The basis of a science of conduct must be fixed by principles of action, enduring and stable motives. It is doubtful, however, whether this is fundamentally the character of human life. What men want . . . is to have interesting experiences. And . . . an important condition of our interest in things is an element of the unanticipated, of novelty, of surprise" (1921, 53–54). These sentiments do not contradict Knight's admiration for science. On the contrary, Knight poses this view for the twofold purpose of (1) establishing the

challenge for science in coming to grips with the arbitrary and the unknown and (2) indicating that rational knowledge, too, finds its natural
limits in humans' "preference" for chance and uncertainty.

Knight's procedure for handling the issue of uncertainty is exemplary.
He sets out to show that uncertainty is a "normal" condition for human
existence. This is true in part because the future cannot be known in advance with absolute certainty; but it is also true because humans prefer
to structure their knowledge and "adaptations" not on past events but on
expectations about the future. The "human condition" Knight presents is
consonant with modernist culture: human beings are future oriented; they
prefer to transcend time and space and leave both the past and the present
behind. Knight stresses the inherent paradox in all of this: "We live only
by knowing *something* about the future; while the problems of life, or of
conduct at least, arise from the fact that we know so little" (1921, 200).

Knight does see the potential danger in opening up modern economic
discourse to concepts of uncertainty. What is at stake, most of all, is rationality, not only of the economic agent but of the economic scientist as
well. Thus, while Knight admits his sympathies with a type of "irrationalism" that questions the validity of logical principles, he concludes that
"there is to my mind no question of understanding the world by any other
method" (1921, 209). The threat to economic theory posed by "irrational" understandings of uncertainty requires a careful distinction between
risk and uncertainty.

Knight understands the distinction in the following way: whereas a
rational agent could approach risky situations either with an a priori calculation of probable outcomes or, for unique events, with a statistical
estimate based on the accumulation of relevant data, true uncertainty
means that neither probability nor statistical estimation can fully operate.
For Knight, uncertainty marked the limits of probabilistic calculation,
since truly uncertain outcomes were immeasurable. However, Knight han-
dles this problem of uncertainty by claiming that *(a)* agents facing true
uncertainty do, indeed, make statements of probable outcomes; *(b)* agents
generally prefer uncertainty over certainty, because of their interest in the
unpredictable; and *(c)* despite this preference, agents seek to minimize
uncertainty by finding ways, over time, to control the future through
learning and other methods. Utilizing these means, agents can successfully
transform uncertainty into a situation of probability or of statistical guess.

Knight's distinction between risk and uncertainty undermines potentially "nihilistic" understandings of uncertainty. Indeed, it is only
with Keynes (and, later, Shackle) that these more nihilistic understandings are given voice. Knight, however, has anticipated some of the subsequent debate among economic modernists in his text. Three other points
are notable.

First, Knight anticipates Shackle's concern to ground the experience of uncertainty in subjectivity rather than in the natural world (cf. Simon 1976 and Arrow 1971 for similar statements). Though Knight often treats uncertainty as a "fact" of nature, he turns repeatedly to the subject's self-experience and self-consciousness to explain the peculiar ways agents respond to this "fact." Knight, therefore, presages Shackle's more detailed discussion of the critical function of uncertainty for the "freedom" of the subject. For if the world is truly uncertain and "indeterminate," then the subject will have meaningful choices open.

Second, in his response to the "real indifference" of risky and uncertain situations, the essence of rational subjectivity is affirmed. As Knight explains, real indifference means that "mind" is the only helpful guide to action. In encountering uncertainty, the "mind"—in contrast to emotion or instinctive reaction—manages the behavior of agents. As Arrow puts it, for Knight, "human consciousness itself would disappear in the absence of uncertainty" (1971, 1). Rather than signifying the limits to intellectuality, as Keynes's reference to "animal spirits" that our discussion below suggests, Knight's conception of uncertainty confirms the hierarchy of mind over body.

Third, Knight asserts that the rational behavior of economic agents is necessarily of a different order from the reasoning of economic scientists.

> The opinions upon which we act in everyday affairs and those which govern the decisions of reasonable business managers. . . have little similarity with conclusions reached by exhaustive analysis and accurate measurement. The mental processes are entirely different in the two cases. . . . There is doubtless some analogy between the subconscious processes of "intuition" and the structure of logical deliberation, for the function of both is to anticipate the future and the possibility of prediction seems to rest upon the uniformity of nature. Hence there must be, in the one case as in the other, some sort and amount of analysis and synthesis; but the striking feature of the judging faculty is its liability to error. (1921, 230)

This statement anticipates the later furor over rational expectations.

For many economic modernists, however, Knight's discussion is lacking in one critical respect. Knight's is not a formal presentation. As a result, the clarity normally won by a formal, rigorous (need we add, mathematical) language is sacrificed to often muddy and inconsistent prose. In Arrow's view, "Knight's analysis is so lacking in formal clarity that it is difficult to be sure" of his classification system regarding the differences between probabilities and statistical inferences (1971, 17). Arrow excoriates Knight for failing to give "a formal description of uncertainty situations" and for lacking "a rigorous proof" for some of his more important theorems (30). Thus, ironically, the absence of formal procedures calls Knight's modernist text into some question.

Knight's modernist approach to uncertainty marks the beginning of a long tradition in which the more radical (and, in our view, postmodern) aspects of the concept of uncertainty have been avoided. The modernist way has been to "recuperate" uncertainty by treating it as negligible or as a condition of existence for rationality or, in some cases, as instrumental certainty (if outcomes in the world are truly unforeseeable, what difference does it make to rational choice?).

In contrast to Knight, Shackle's work on uncertainty shows that the twin achievements of modernism—the discovery of the essential principles of time and space and the demonstration of the primacy of reason—are instrumentally incompatible. In this sense, Shackle's discussion tends toward postmodernism. In the end, however, Shackle, like Knight, upholds economic modernism.

Shackle

Shackle's modernism consists mainly of his preservation of neoclassical theory's "entry point." Neoclassical analysis begins with a theory of subjective preference that expresses the knowledge subjects possess and their creative desires. Shackle does not question choice-oriented subjectivity as a starting point for theory. In Shackle's work (like Knight's), creative impulses and freedom to choose result from the subject's perception of uncertainty. Far from replacing unified subjectivity with a notion of fragmented, decentered, socially constituted agency, Shackle sees uncertainty as a necessary condition for a subject's escape from determinacy and his or her leap into purposeful action. Although reason (in the sense of full or probable knowledge) may not be effective, a form of rationality does emerge as the sole basis upon which economic actions take place.

But Shackle's postmodernist tendencies are evidenced in his attacks on the formalism of economic theory, the reduction of uncertainty to probability (and, therefore, to "certainty-equivalents"), and the treatment of time and reason as complementary. In regard to the formalism of modernist economic thought, Shackle writes that "economics has virtually turned imprecision itself into a science: economics, the science of the quantification of the unquantifiable and the aggregation of the incompatible" (1972, 360). For Shackle, formalism is wholly inappropriate for an analysis of situations involving uncertainty (which seem to be the majority of circumstances) because it starts from the premise that agents and theorists make decisions with certain (or probable) knowledge.

On this score, Shackle resorts to empiricism, for he accuses formalism of being unable to perceive correctly the essential vagueness of agents' thoughts and the impenetrability of the future. This has led some, like

Marco Magnani (1983, 249), to accuse Shackle of criticizing neoclassical theory for its lack of realism and of remaining hostile to scientific abstraction. If, as Shackle states, the world is perceived as "imprecise," then one captures the truth about that world through similarly "imprecise" discourse. As Coddington points out, Shackle is not licensing "muddled or slipshod or woolly thought" (1975, 158). Rather, Shackle's view "leads to the seemingly paradoxical . . . idea that carefully imprecise concepts can give a more *accurate* expression of the economic world than precise ones" (158). Thus, in standing modernism on its head, Shackle wants economic science to acknowledge "the manifoldness, the richness and the detailed particular variants and individual facets of humanity, rather than dismissing them as the contingent outcomes of some original and essential principles which it is the real purpose of science to identify" (1972, 29). This acknowledgment will bring about greater rigor and clarity and will reflect reality better than most formal models.

As Brian Kantor notes, "Shackle's attempts to abandon strict logic has not found many friends in the economics profession" (1979, 1428). Yet, Shackle's critique of formalism is restricted mostly to the models and empirical methods of the neoclassical-Keynesian synthesis. In the spirit of modernist aesthetics, Shackle chooses to formulate his own contributions in an axiomatic system. Shackle explains: "it became fashionable in the 1950's to set out deductive arguments about human conduct in the strict form of numbered axioms and theorems. This method . . . has a beauty and incisiveness, and offers safeguards against loose reasoning; which amply justify it" (1961, 79).

If Shackle finds fault with the "mechanistic" metaphors of formal economic models, such as general equilibrium schemas, it is because they promote a deterministic view. Such metaphors obliterate the possibility of subjects' decisions. General equilibrium, in particular, excludes uncertainty because "it assumes that economic man knows all he needs to know, can feed his tastes alone into a mental computer and obtain unambiguous directions about what to do to secure their maximum satisfaction" (1966, 9). Man is not like a computer, nor is the "economic cosmos" like a machine. Here, Shackle counters one facet of modernist culture—the metaphor of the machine—with another—the primacy of individual subjectivity.

This is the sense, then, of Shackle's treatment of uncertainty. Since we cannot know what we do not know, we must concern ourselves with the creative process—decision taking—whereby imagination, and not reason, rules. Decisions are taken as a creative act in the face of uncertainty. These acts reflect subjects' desires to pursue paths that will bring about an outcome they feel to be possible. They neither know with certainty the outcomes of their actions, nor do they rule out alternative possible paths, which they can rank order in terms of preference. Most importantly, they do not view the set of possible paths to be complete. Or rather, they remain in doubt about the possibility or impossibility about actions and their outcomes. In this sense, probability is not true uncertainty, since the probability calculus stipulates that the set of mutually exclusive paths is complete (i.e., it sums to unity).

Thus, there is no clear separation between the possible and the impossible, but there are degrees of possibility, giving rise, when an act brings about a result that was anticipated or not, to degrees of "potential surprise." Shackle's possibility calculus shows both the necessity and open-endedness of subjective decision-taking. The existence of uncertainty forces us to imagine the possible paths for altering our circumstances or anticipating their alteration. However, these paths are not simply "probable," for it that were true, we would be little removed from the world of determinacy (we would know in advance all the options available to us). As Paul Davidson comments, "replacing the concept of certainty by the concept of a known probability distribution merely replaces the assumption of perfect foreknowledge by the assumption that economic agents possess actuarial knowledge" (1981, 160). For Shackle, "knowledge and uncertainty are mutually exclusive" (1961, 60).

The concept of uncertainty must not imply the powerlessness of subjectivity. "If history is determinate," Shackle tells us, the subject "cannot alter its predeterminate course." But, equally, "if history is anarchy and randomness, [the subject] cannot modify this randomness nor mitigate the orderlessness of events" (1966, 86). Uncertainty must be understood, as Shackle terms it, as "bounded uncertainty." In "a world where, in short, events are only partly shaped by what has gone before," in such a world "a man cannot know what will happen, as the sequel to this or that act of his own, but he feels able to form judgements about the sorts of things that can happen, he can set bounds to the range and diversity of the consequences that he can conceive for each act amongst those open to him. In face of this bounded uncertainty his choice of act is not empty and automatic, but calls for thought and something more, and matches that meaning implied, by the thoughts by which we seem to ourselves to conduct our lives, for the word 'decision' " (74–75).

Frederic Schick (1988) discusses at length Shackle's notion of bounded uncertainty. The boundedness of uncertainty is to be distinguished from a situation where an agent, in Shackle's words, "can discern no pattern of association between act and sequel, so that it appears to him that any sequel (out of a finite list or an infinite list or altogether without limitation) can follow any act" (1966, 74). In such a case, where the agent therefore would find "no purpose" in choosing among possible actions, the uncertainty that pertains is "unbounded." Schick explains, as we have seen, that Shackle's way out of this situation (that is, assuming that an agent will in fact act and therefore "choose") is that the agent has some possibility of indeed acting. But this action or decision is based neither on knowledge of the actual consequences of his or her action, nor on conditional consequences corresponding to probabilities, but instead is grounded in a supposition—an imagining—by the agent that the contingent consequences of his or her actions are finite, but no numerical likelihood can be assigned to them. This, in Schick's rendering, is the assumption of "bounded uncertainty."

Bounded uncertainty does not overturn the idea that there is a natural order of and in the world. What it does suggest is the difficulty in going from subjective, cognitive experience to knowledge and foresight about events. As with most modernist epistemologists, Shackle preserves the duality of a natural order and a knowing subject. Unlike them, however, he posits an incommensurability that stems from the subject's natural limitations and, more importantly, from the fact that in creative actions individuals make history (thus changing the world's order). Reason and time are forever out of synch because historical time—as subjective, lived experience—can exist only when creative acts take place. And, creative acts take place only when certain knowledge is impossible. Subjectivism is potentially destructive, in this way, of modernist epistemology, but can achieve that destruction by upholding other key elements of that epistemology, the subject-object distinction and the "centering" of the subject. Hence, in our view, the various elements of Shackle's antimodernism do not translate into postmodernism.

Uncertainty in Keynes

It is not with the modernist and antimodernist elements of the treatments by Knight and Shackle but, rather, with the work of Keynes that the more destabilizing or "nihilistic" effects of uncertainty in economics have been most closely associated.

Part of the reason for the "excesses" attributed to Keynes's approach is that he introduced the idea of uncertainty with respect to the long-term expectations of investors. These were supposed to be the "captains of industry" who, at least in much of existing mainstream economic discourse (if not in the wider culture), were the bearers of rational calculation and foresight. These were the "men" who were charged with the responsibility of making the "correct" decisions concerning current production and, especially, future fixed capital investment, which, in turn, would fulfill the conditions of Say's Law and create the possibility for full employment and stable long-term economic growth. Keynes, however, emphasized the "extreme precariousness of knowledge on which our estimates of prospective yield have to be made" (1964, 148). This precariousness is based on two elements: First, the knowledge about future events upon which expectations of prospective yields would otherwise be based is, in principle, uncertain; thus according to Keynes, they "can only be forecasted with more or less confidence" (147). Second, given the uncertainty that characterizes knowledge of future events, investors tend to make decisions on the basis of other facts "about which we feel somewhat confident" (148). The result is that, in Keynes's view, so-called rational investors end up forming long-term expectations based partly on uncertainty about the relevant future and partly on facts that are "less decisively relevant" (148).

So that the point of his work would not be missed, Keynes drew attention to the centrality of uncertainty in his recasting of economic theory and sharpened the characterization of what he meant by uncertainty in his now-famous article in the *Quarterly Journal of Economics*:

> By "uncertain" knowledge . . . I do not mean merely to distinguish what is known for certain from what is only probable. The game of roulette is not subject, in this sense, to uncertainty; nor is the prospect of a Victory bond being drawn. Or, again, the expectation of life is only slightly uncertain. Even the weather is moderately uncertain. The sense in which I am using the term is that in which the prospect of a European war is uncertain, or the price of copper and the rate of interest. . . . About these matters there is no scientific basis on which to form any calculable probability whatever. We simply do not know. (1973–79, 14:113–14)

What, then, lies beyond the limits imposed by uncertainty? In the *General Theory*, Keynes argued that, instead of rational calculation based on certain knowledge, investors are guided by "spontaneous optimism" and, even more noteworthy, "animal spirits," which he defines as a "spontaneous urge to action rather than inaction, and not as the outcome of a weighted average of quantitative benefits multiplied by quantitative probabilities" (1964, 161).[10] Later, in the *QJE* article, Keynes points to still other consequences of uncertainty:

> a practical theory of the future . . . has certain marked characteristics . . . [B]ased on so flimsy a foundation, it is subject to sudden and violent changes. The practice of calmness and immobility, of certainty and security, suddenly

---

[10] Roger Koppl (1991) explains nicely how Keynes's use of the idea of animal spirits was his solution to the problem of investment choice in the face of radical uncertainty, for which rational behavior and probabilistic calculations of expected asset values are impossible. Koppl goes on to argue that, for Keynes, animal spirits were necessary to explain why and how investors are not frozen into inaction when confronting radical uncertainty.

breaks down. New hopes will, without warning, take charge of human conduct. The forces of disillusion may suddenly impose a new conventional basis of valuation. All these pretty, polite techniques, made for a well-paneled Board Room and a nicely regulated market, are liable to collapse. At all times the vague panic fears and equally vague and reasoned hopes are not really lulled, and lie but a little way below the surface. (1973–79, 14:114–15)

Let us attempt to assess the implications of Keynes's ideas about the nature and role of uncertainty. In particular, does he, like Knight and even Shackle, merely extend the boundaries of modernist economics, in the process taming and mastering that which was thought to lie beyond the previous limits of the knowable? Or, alternatively, does Keynes succeed in moving beyond, thereby disrupting, the modernist conception of economic knowledge and knowing economic agents—and therefore in paving the way for postmodernism?

There is ample evidence, in both the *General Theory* and the *Quarterly Journal of Economics* article, that Keynes, having recognized the role of uncertainty in long-term investment decisions, held out the possibility that "rational selves" would eventually find a way to defeat the "dark forces of time and ignorance" (1964, 155). Where circumstances permitted, rational calculation would still be used to arrive at prospective yields; in other cases, individuals could be said to rely on "conventions," especially that of "assuming that the existing state of affairs will continue indefinitely" (152). In the article, Keynes admitted that

> the necessity for action and for decision compels us as practical men to do our best to overlook this awkward fact and to behave exactly as we should if we had behind us a good Benthamite calculation of a series of prospective advantages and disadvantages, each multiplied by its appropriate probability, waiting to be summed. (1973–79, 14:114)

There is little hint here of the "nihilism" that Coddington (1976, 1982), Tony Lawson (1985, 1988), and others (e.g., those whom Gerrard [1992] refers to as the "new Keynesian fundamentalists") have feared in adhering to Keynes's notion of uncertainty—and from which they have expended no little effort in distancing their own approach to economic theorizing. According to Coddington, for example, the traditional fundamentalist reading of Keynes's contribution "would have nihilistic implications for the entire corpus of theory and in particular for its applicability" (1976, 1261). In particular, it "does not provide any sort of determinate theory or model of how the economy functions at the aggregate level; it does not enable one to make any definite prediction about the likely effects of alternative policies or circumstances. On the contrary, it is a viewing point from which such constructions would appear as rather desperate makeshifts of transient applicability" (1262–63). Fundamentalism, then, is an economic modernist's nightmare. It defies the criteria for scientific knowledge because it resists the formalism of model-building and sees the limits to knowledge as constitutive of economic science itself. It builds uncertainty and its effects into the very structure of economic discourse.

As Coddington puts it, "to stress the basis of all economic activity in more or less uncertain expectations is precisely to emphasize the openness and incompleteness of economic theorizing and explanation. It does not itself provide any kind of fixed mechanism according to which the unfolding of events takes place; but it does show how one would set about constructing a narrative of events" (1976, 1263). Perhaps this is why some, like John Eatwell and Murray Milgate, have visceral reactions to the fundamentalist readings of Keynes. Much to their chagrin,

> the appeal to unknowable imperfection—uncertainty, disappointed expectations, "conjectures" and the like—serves to deprive economic analysis of all definite content, thus reducing the discussion of economic policy to the status of guesswork and negating the single most important achievement of economic theory during the past two hundred years—namely that the market mechanism is governed by systematic, objective forces. (Eatwell and Milgate 1983, 279)

Lawson, in turn, has sought to dispute Coddington's interpretation of the destructive effects of Keynes's writings, though he shares Coddington's concern to avoid the nihilistic implications of uncertainty. Lawson's alternative argument is that Keynes's integration of uncertainty into economic analysis "presupposes notions such as *intention* and *deliberation* and allows the assumption that individuals have the *power* to choose" (1985, 919). Thus, while uncertainty may constrain choices, people still use "good reasons" to choose. Therefore, Lawson concludes, "it is only in as far as knowledge and reason guide action that people are free to discern alternative possibilities and to frame purposes" (919).

Lawson tries to forestall comparisons with the neoclassicals. He asserts that the fact subjects come to knowledge through practice means that neither the knowing subject nor the social practices within which s/he is inscribed are the primary presupposition for knowledge and action. Keynes is no "subjectivist," since he sees the "good reasons" behind subjects' choices and locates these choices in the interaction between subjectivity and social institutions. However, Lawson's determination to find a place for rational behavior of unfragmented subjects in Keynes's discussions of uncertainty can be linked, if tentatively, to the modernist fear that without a specified and exalted place for rationality, economic theorizing is simply impossible.

Following on such interpretations of Keynes's writings on uncertainty, many economists have attempted to circumscribe the ambit of uncertainty, making it conform to the modernist protocols of mainstream economic theory. One approach has been to define the scope of uncertainty as other than all-embracing, such that it refers merely to long-term expectations ("particularly expectations of future yield from capital-assets"), and to posit the existence of psychological structures that make economic behavior, in the end, predictable (e.g., Winslow 1986). An alternative way of proceeding has been to recognize that investors do, in fact, form long-term expectations in the face of uncertainty and, therefore, although the rational decision-making processes of individual agents cannot be modeled using traditional methods, it is still possible to identify and analyze the behavior of economic "groups" (e.g., Dow and Dow 1985). Still another "solution" to the nihilistic implications of uncertainty has been to presume that, when confronted by uncertainty, economic agents still make "sensible" decisions to enter into nominal contractual commitments that, in turn, make it possible for them to form "sensible" expectations about future nominal cash flows (Davidson 1991). In all three cases, then, Keynes's writings on uncertainty have been interpreted as a positive addition—rather than a fundamental challenge—to the methods and procedures of economic modernism, although perhaps different from those laid down by neoclassical (and, later, new classical) economists.

Where, then, is the postmodernism in Keynes's approach? In what sense does his notion of uncertainty violate the strictures of modernist economics and, thus, point in the direction of an alternative, postmodern approach? From our perspective, there are at least four implications of Keynes's discussion that are missing from the above interpretations and that do, in fact, constitute the nihilism that Coddington and others seem intent on avoiding.

First, what Keynes accomplishes by defining uncertainty as ignorance (the idea that "we simply do not know") is to acknowledge that the barriers to knowledge may be and often are impenetrable. There is simply no way of knowing that which is, in principle, unknowable. Not only does this aspect of uncertainty accept the "reality" that the (modernist) chasm that separates the knowing subject from the knowable object is, in many cases, unbridgeable; it also threatens to eliminate the distinction between the "expert" knowledge of economic scientists and the forms of "everyday" knowledge on the part of economic agents. If the agents within economists' models and stories are faced with the prospect of confronting the limits to their knowledge—they can only know and act on what they already know—then, at least in principle there is no reason why economists should not be bound by the same limits to knowledge. The point here is that *both* everyday and expert knowledges may reach their limit in the already knowable.

Second, accepting the idea that there are impenetrable barriers to knowledge and, therefore, of the impossibility of rational calculation (at least in terms of future events), Keynes begins to sever the connection between knowledge and action. While individuals continue to act—to invest but also to save, consume, exchange, work, and so on—those actions may not be preceded by any form of calculation, whether "rational" or conventional. The idea of "animal spirits," for example, points not to the mind—and, thus, to processes of intellection, decisions to follow conventions, and the formation of conscious expectations or, alternatively, of subjective choices and desires—but, instead, to the body.[11] As Susan Bordo points out in her discussion of Cartesian epistemology:

> the body is not only the organ of the deceptive senses, and the site of disruption and "commotion" in the heart, blood, and animal spirits. It is also the most brute, pressing and ubiquitous reminder of how *located* and perspectival our experience and thought is [sic], how bounded in time and space. (1987, 94–95)

By invoking the bodily animal spirits instead of something associated with agents' minds, Keynes calls into question the (fundamentally modernist) idea that some form of mind-based rational and/or conscious intellection is a necessary antecedent to action.[12] In addition to the body's being the site of "nonrational" motives and inspirations, its "situatedness"—the extent to which the body is often conceived to respond to fundamentally local and specific stimuli—also serves to disrupt the presumed universality of the motivating causes and reasons that, at least in modernist thought, are often presumed to lend order to the outcomes of individual actions.[13]

---

[11] Koppl (1991) places Keynes's use of the term *animal spirits* within a long historical tradition in medicine and philosophy stemming from Galen down to Descartes. Descartes in particular, according to Koppl, envisioned a conflict within the body (specifically, within the pineal gland) between animal spirits, which were "brewed in the heart and filtered through the brain," and the soul, the site of correct judgment. Thus, for Descartes, like Keynes, animal spirits may lead people to act independently of reason or and even contrary to it. D. E. Moggridge (1992) confirms Keynes's allusion to Descartes's discussion of animal spirits, while Terutomo Ozawa (1992) adds that Marx used the term, in volume 1 of *Capital*, to refer to the increase in efficiency—"through the stimulation of the animal spirits"— brought about by the "cooperation" of labor.

[12] Here, we note that, in invoking the body as an alternative to mind-based rational intellection, Keynes (along with Bordo and others) may close at one level—by presuming a singular body underlying economic behavior—what he has disrupted at another level—in allowing for nonrational motives and forms of agency occasioned by uncertainty. In this sense, creating disorder in one realm (in deconstructing rationality, its ultimate lack of closure and indeterminacy) by reinstating order in another (in invoking the rule of *the* body) leaves the divide between modernism and postmodernism itself uncertain.

[13] E. G. Winslow (1986) convincingly argues that Keynes's emphasis on "animal spirits" and other "irrational" elements of economic agency—especially the love of money, the love of moneymaking, and a sadistic love of power—corresponds closely to Freud's psychoana-

Third, Keynes's reference to the role of "whim or sentiment or chance" (1964, 163), instead of certain knowledge, may make it impossible for economic theorists to connect an agent's actions—whether that agent is conceived to be a single individual or a group of individuals or, for that matter, an institution such as a firm or government agency—to a particular set of intentions or anticipations that, presumably, determine that agent's actions. In other words, whether or not processes of information gathering, rational deliberation, or the formation of expectations can be said to take place either preceding or in conjunction with agents' actions, their connection one to the other may be tenuous, at best. Thus, for example, even if surveys or questionnaires are capable of giving information about the "state of mind" of an individual, social group, or institution, that information may offer little in the way of knowledge about what economic agents will do in the future or why they acted the way they did in the past. It may therefore be necessary to have recourse to other notions of causality—such as Freud's notion of "overdetermination" in the interpretation of dreams—or even to develop entirely new causal or relational metaphors to link actions with prior states of mind and bodily sensibilities, not to mention the social contexts or conditions within which such actions take place.

Finally, and following on the preceding points, by placing uncertainty at the center of this theory of employment, Keynes calls into question the usefulness of many of the metaphors and "tools" that are often conceived to guarantee the certainty and scientificity, the clarity and rigor, associated with modernist economics. The idea of equilibrium, for example, is deprived of meaning (or, at least, its usual meanings) if individual actions or determinate states of the economy cannot be reduced to the rational— or, more generally, "weakly rational" or "sensible"—choices of economic agents. While it has fallen to others to explore the relationship between Keynes's method and the use of disequilibrium and other, not-necessarily-equilibrium concepts,[14] Keynes expressed his own reservations about the usefulness of mathematical formalism and econometrics on a number of occasions.[15]

---

lytic theory of the anal-sadistic character. While there is nothing inherently or uniformly postmodern in Freudian theory, it is important to recognize both that the psychoanalytic accounts of economic behavior disrupt modernist conceptions of the conscious, knowing agent in much economic analysis and that late-nineteenth- and twentieth-century economists have chosen not to explore the implications of psychoanalysis in accounting for agents' (let alone scientists' own) dispositions and behaviors.

[14] See, e.g., the quite different approaches of Leijonhufvud (1968), Shapiro (1978), and Bausor (1986).

[15] See, e.g., Keynes's criticisms of cause-and-effect logic (1973–79, 29:265), of Tinbergen's econometrics (1973–79, 14:306–18), and of mathematical modeling (1964, 305).

These are, in our view, some of the "disturbing" elements that are provoked by Keynes's notion of true or radical uncertainty, elements that spill over the limits imposed by much modern economic analysis. To avoid misunderstanding, our argument is *not* that Keynes set out, intentionally, to overturn the modernist protocols of "classical" economics (as he referred to the neoclassical economic theories of his time) or even that, regardless of his intentions, he was uniformly successful at doing so. Rather, what we have picked out as some of the nihilistic—from the perspective of Coddington, Lawson, and modernist economics more generally—or—now from our perspective—the postmodern moments of Keynesian uncertainty are precisely those "excesses" that modern economics (again, with the important exception of Shackle) have tended to deny or to contain and domesticate and that postmodernists seek to affirm and to build on. Because postmodernists do not see true uncertainty in the same way that modernist economists do—as fundamentally destructive of any economic discourse or as ultimately translatable into familiar, modernist terms—they are not faced with the "cruel choice" between these two alternatives. Instead, postmodernists are interested both in exploring the "disruptive" effects of uncertainty for existing economic discourses and in using uncertainty and related notions to produce new discourses in and about economics.

Uncertainty and Discourse

One of the distinguishing features of postmodernism is its conception of uncertainty as a discursive phenomenon. Uncertainty (and, by the same token, certainty and all other forms of knowledge) is understood to exist only in and through discourse, in the form of "texts" in which uncertainty is recognized as such. This emphasis on the discursivity or textuality of uncertainty leads away from the view that uncertainty is a "given," singular condition and toward the idea that uncertainty is a multiple notion: first, because "it" is constituted and acquires different meanings in different discourses; and second, because "it" literally exists, that is, makes sense, in some discourses and not in others (not unlike the situation of societies described by anthropologists for which there may be no concepts or experience of individuality, freedom, and so on).[16] Therefore, we can-

[16] It is interesting that Ian Hacking (1990b) reads Friedrich Nietzsche's writings on chance and necessity to involve Nietzsche's positing of a subject's fundamental experience facing an uncertain world. Yet, perhaps unwittingly, Hacking provides evidence that Nietzsche is less than decisive about the shared, universal human experience of uncertainty. Hacking notes that, for Nietzsche, chance is experienced by those who have "a sense of purpose," And this sense of purpose is itself, ironically, a result of "being in what looks like

not attribute any universality to the idea of uncertainty—either inside "academic" economic discourses or outside those discourses, in the discursive worlds inhabited and produced by economic agents, or between the discourses of economists and economic agents.[17] Uncertainty may or may not exist within different discourses, and, even if it does, the various senses of uncertainty may not be comparable. In other words, there may be a substantial amount of "misrecognition" among and between economists and economic agents where uncertainty is concerned.[18] Thus, for example, economic theories will differ according to whether or not they allow for the discursive constitution of uncertainty (i.e., the rules according to which their texts are constructed allow for the possibility of uncertainty); also, economic agents may not "see" or "experience" the fact that they are uncertain in the same instances or in the same ways that economists would "see" the uncertain predicaments and forms of knowledge of such agents.

A second implication of this discursive conception is that the terms in and through which uncertainty (and, by extension, certainty, confidence, and the like) is constituted may be ultimately undecidable or indeterminate. As we have remarked in the first chapter, from the perspective of postmodernism—especially its more Derridean or "deconstructive" currents—no discourse can claim to speak the truth of its own textual production. In particular, no text (or, for that matter, painting, building, piece of literature, musical composition, or clothing style) can be successful, no

---

an orderly world" (148). Hacking goes on, though, to state that Nietzsche also holds the view that there are "those who know that the universe is a matter of blind chance" and as a consequence "are untroubled by the simulacra of purpose." This unremarked detailing of Nietzsche's portrayal of the irreducible diversity in human experience—based on different "perspectives," one could say "discourses" on the world—contrasts with Hacking's earlier appreciation of Nietzsche, who along with Charles S. Peirce, "were the two great complementary philosophers of the end of the nineteenth century. Their conception of chance and creation and necessity was curiously similar. Both believed that our world, which others find orderly, is a product of chance. Neither thought that the presence of law in the universe makes it any less chancey" (147). We note that this conjunction of Nietzscheanism and pragmatism (Peirce being considered the "founder" of this philosophical tradition) foreshadows our discussion of these two traditions in chapter 5 on the role of values in economics. Suffice it to say that, in our view, similar postmodern moments occur in Nietzsche and pragmatism that are both instructive and potentially generative for a thoroughgoing transformation of contemporary economic theory.

[17] In contrast, e.g., to Peter Marris (1996, 1) who presumes universality in discussing uncertainty both as "a fundamental condition of human life" and as a condition that is always "uncomfortable" and that, therefore, "we try to master." Elsewhere, however, he admits that "uncertainty is created by our own preconceptions" (1996, 16).

[18] Vivienne Brown (1994b) makes the "polyphony of voices" a distinguishing characteristic both of the economy and of the discipline of economics, which can therefore generate "different interpretations and different processes of reading" (378).

matter how well designed and executed, at arranging its terms in such a watertight or complete fashion that all meaning is ultimately decided. Instead, through the operation of such textual features as "supplement" and "trace," writing can be said to involve a certain slippage or looseness of language such that there are always elements of undecidability. It is in this sense that no formal system succeeds in completeness; each is subject to a deconstruction. Therefore, the discourses according to which uncertainty can be said to exist and be experienced as such cannot ensure either that uncertainty be known to exist (either by observing economists or by the economic agents themselves) or that, if it is determined to exist, to conform to any particular standard or set of criteria.

The third implication that we wish to call attention to is that uncertainty, when viewed as a discursive phenomenon, is considered to be neither "subjective" nor "objective."[19] It is not subjective in the way that some (e.g., F. A. Hayek and other Austrian) economists seek to portray ideas such as imagination, preferences, knowledge, and the like.[20] According to this view, uncertainty is grounded in the subjective "consciousness" of individuals, in the sense that individuals are free to imagine states of the world and to attach weights of confidence and degrees of belief to them as they wish. While tending to relativize the knowledges, both certain and uncertain, that individuals may hold (much to the con-

[19] Or, to put the matter in more dialectical terms: the postmodern, discursive approach to uncertainty affirms what each, subjective and objective, denies—thereby superseding the terms of that dichotomy.

[20] The sobriquet of subjectivist—along with "idealist" and "mentalist"—has been attached to our own discursive treatment of uncertainty by Man-Seop Park and Serap Kayatekin (2002). Their argument rests on the presumption that, since we reject an objectivist notion of probability, i.e., the idea that uncertainty is a more or less adequate representation of something "out there," outside of discourse, we *must* accept the subjectivist notion. First, as we hope we have explained adequately in the first chapter, a discursive approach to such phenomena as uncertainty does not entail a denial of a world outside of discourse; as with Derrida's infamous phrase "il n'y a pas de hors-texte"—not to mention many other postmodern approaches rejected by critics as "relativist"—the point is to rethink the lines of causality that run between texts and the world beyond them, to question and develop alternatives to received notions of representation, not to reduce the world to discourse. Second—and this is the point we want to make with respect to Keynes and our own discursive approach to uncertainty in the remainder of this section—discursivity represents a challenge to both subjectivist and objectivist notions of uncertainty, i.e., it rejects and furnishes an alternative to the very terms with which that dichotomy is founded. In sum, our aim in emphasizing the discursivity of uncertainty here, no less than that of the body and much else in subsequent chapters, is not to deny the "materiality" of discourses. Instead, we want to denaturalize notions that are taken to be "correct"—and therefore "normal"—representations of such phenomena as uncertain knowledge and human bodies because they are taken to be extradiscursive givens. Indeed, it is precisely because of the material conditions and effects of economic discourses that we have focused attention on the diversity of (actual and potential) representations.

sternation of the majority of economists, who seek to hold on to some form of "objective" knowledge, if only of the present and past), this view ultimately refuses the postmodern idea that the consciousnesses of individuals are themselves discursively constituted.[21] That is, it refuses the notion that what individuals are "conscious of" is, at least in part, a product of the discourses in which they participate and which have formed, therefore, their individual consciousnesses.[22] Where subjectivists tend to locate the origin of uncertainty and so on in the autonomous individual, postmodernists reject any such originating moment and, instead, seek to examine both the discourses within which uncertainty is theoretically constituted and the social conditions in which such discourses arise and change over time.[23]

It follows that the subjectivist refusal of the discursivity of uncertainty also applies to ways agents are thought to respond to uncertainty. The notion of the autonomous individual who experiences, at least cognitively, a partly or wholly chaotic world is also a guiding premise of the types of probabilistic calculations that are thought to be "subjective," as

[21] Of course, the use of the term *knowledges* here is precisely what may be in dispute in discourses of uncertainty. Following the lead of Frank Ramsey, Richard Jeffrey states that when we shift from certain to possible knowledge, "the obvious move is to deny that the notion of knowledge has the importance generally attributed to it, and to try to make the concept of belief do the work that philosophers have generally assigned to the grander concept" (1988). Such a change in language permits partly the move from "objective" to "subjective" calculations that constitute action under varying conditions of perceived uncertainty—discursively constituted, that is.

[22] Ted Burczak (1994), though, makes the argument that the humanism of both Shackle and Hayek avoids the perils of modernist humanism, or at least of the approach according to which economists see the human subject as unified, centered, and essentially constituted prior to its participation in markets. In this regard, then, Burczak treats Shackle and Hayek as having postmodern conceptions of the economic subject. Burczak (2001a and 2001b) has debated Roger Koppl and William Butos (2001) on the similarities and differences between Keynes's approach to uncertainty and expectations and that of Friedrich von Hayek and other Austrian economists.

[23] Although we cannot pursue the argument here, the postmodern approach suggests that, if many individuals today are conscious of various degrees and types of uncertainty, this condition may itself be an effect of the modernist discourses—including, importantly, much of twentieth-century economics—which initially produced and then proceeded to elaborate and refine such notions. (Theodore Porter has written about one side of that relation, arguing that the history of statistical method is "inseparable from the history of politics and society" [1990, 69]; that is, Porter focuses on the impact of social analogies on the emergence and development of statistics. What remains to be undertaken, at least insofar as we are aware, is an analysis of the effects of new conceptions and methods of risk and uncertainty outside the academy, on "everyday" notions and experiences of uncertainty.) Similarly, the presence of postmodernism, both in economics and in the wider society, may both signal and contribute to changes in the existing consciousnesses of uncertainty—with consequent implications for the ways in which individuals are able to allow for or even to embrace different forms of uncertainty.

in Bayesianism. As Gärdenfors and Sahlin (1988) explain, "a central part of Bayesianism is the doctrine that the decision maker's knowledge in a given situation can be represented by a subjective probability measure defined over the possible states of the world" (313). Gärdenfors and Sahlin point to the problem involved in strict versions of Bayesianism—in which a subject is presumed to have a unique probability measure defined over all states of the world—by arguing, as numerous others have, that for many situations agents have only partial knowledge of such states (316). This criticism is, once again, familiar modernist territory, since it takes as the problem a "real" impossibility of knowledge on the part of the autonomous subject, and disregards the fundamental postmodern position that the cognitive experiences of all such impossibilities are, themselves, bounded by the discourses that give rise to them.

But neither, in the postmodern view, is uncertainty and the actions that are consequent to it understood to be objective (as many Keynesians, post-Keynesians, and, it seems, Knight and Shackle themselves believe) in the sense that it is not conceived to exist "out there," beyond or outside the particular discourses in and through which some individuals (but, of course, not others, who participate in other discourses in which uncertainty simply does not exist) "experience" it. In particular, postmodernists do not understand uncertainty to be a product of the "fundamental unknowability" of the future, where the future (and, by extension, other notions of time, such as the present and the past) is conceived to be a nondiscursive or transdiscursive condition. As we discuss in more detail below, from a postmodern perspective, time—including its passage through, and its division (or not) into, past, present, and future—is itself a discursive construction and, therefore, no more an objective, nondiscursive "cause" of uncertainty than any other concept or idea.

Probability in Keynes

We would be hard pressed to demonstrate that Keynes "reached" this discursive aspect of the postmodern view of uncertainty either in the *General Theory* or in any of his other "economic" writings.[24] However, Keynes's *Treatise on Probability*—published, however ironically, in the same year as Knight's text and now considered by many, beginning especially with the work of Anna Carabelli (1988), but also including that of Rod O'Don-

---

[24] Keynes does, however, refer to the "existence of a *variety* of opinion about what is uncertain" in his discussion of the future of the rate of interest (1964, 172), thus eschewing the idea that there is any nondiscursive "foundation" for forming knowledges about that which is unknown.

nell (1991), Lawson (1988), Athol Fitzgibbons (1988), and others, to be an important precursor to the elaboration of his subsequent views on uncertainty—contains important elements that complement what we have called the postmodern moments of Keynes's treatment of uncertainty.

For example, Keynes begins his discussion of probability by measuring the distance between his views and other—especially subjectivist—approaches to probability:

> in the sense important to logic, probability is not subjective. It is not, that is to say, subject to human caprice. A proposition is not probable because we think it so. When once the facts are given which determine our knowledge, what is probable or improbable in these circumstances has been fixed objectively, and is independent of our opinion. . . . What particular propositions we select as the premises of *our* argument naturally depends on subjective factors peculiar to ourselves; but the relations, in which other propositions stand to these, and which entitle us to probable beliefs, are objective and logical. (1921, 4)

Keynes acknowledges the influence of so-called subjective factors, a term that he also employs in the *General Theory* to refer to "those psychological characteristics of human nature and those social practices and institutions which, though not unalterable, are unlikely to undergo a material change over a short period of time except in abnormal or revolutionary circumstances" (1964, 91). Yet, Keynes is quick to sever the connection between his own notion of probability as referring to rational arguments—and thus the logical, "objective" relations that can be established between evidence and propositions—and the idea that probability is a construct of a person's mind—which refers to an individual degree of belief or confidence and, therefore, can vary from one person to another. In Keynes's view, what probabilities refer to are logical arguments, discursive connections between premises and arguments, not subjective states of mind.

But, having raised these criticisms, Keynes then assumes the subjective mantle for himself and uses it to oppose so-called objective interpretations of probability. Early on in the *Treatise*, Keynes clearly indicates that, in his view, probability refers to "*propositions* instead of the occurrence and the probability of *events*" (1921, 5). Later (e.g., in chaps. 8 and 24), he argues that the frequency interpretation of probability, and the general notion of induction to which it is often connected, cannot serve as the *basis* of the theory of probability; instead they are *dependent* on such a theory. Thus, Keynes interprets the probabilities with which initial evidence is connected to further propositions, not as referring to or being grounded in extradiscursive events and statistical frequencies (or even the "limiting values" of such frequencies) but, rather, to a priori conceptions of what it is rational or logical to believe based on the available evidence. This is precisely why Keynes is considered to be one of the first exponents of an "a priorist," "logicist," or what Hacking (1990a) prefers to call a "rationalist" understanding of probability.

If Keynes was successful in threading his way between the Scylla and Charybdis of subjectivist and objectivist—the twin pillars of modernist—understandings of probability, and thus in moving toward what we consider to be a discursive notion of probability, then we can begin to appreciate the extent to which there may be other postmodern moments in his treatment. There is, for example, Keynes's suspicion toward the presumption of a "discoverable system" amidst the "apparent disorder" based on the existence of stable statistical frequencies.[25] Such a view "complicates" the terms of discussion in which probability (and, by extension, uncertainty) are often presumed to exist *either* in the mind *or* in the world. In such discussions, either probability and uncertainty refer to our ignorance of an objectively certain world (i.e., we know that the world operates according to determinate rules but we have, as yet, only partial or imperfect knowledges of such rules), or they represent our certain knowledge about a "truly" uncertain, random, or nonergodic world. In both cases, probability and uncertainty are presumed to stand in a relation of adequacy between a knowing subject and the "external" world. Whence the usual posing of the argument: if one does not believe that the world is inherently uncertain (i.e., governed by a "hidden," if probabilistic, order), then one *must* believe that the world is certain (i.e., that it is possible, at least in principle, to discover or know that order). Keynes's "equivocation" on the issue of order and disorder can be interpreted as a refusal of both views, that the world "out there" is inherently either orderly or disorderly. Instead, order and disorder—and related ideas of determinism and randomness, certainty and uncertainty—are discursive constructions that cannot be said to "capture" (or not) the world "as it is."

Another moment that is potentially disruptive in Keynes's treatment of probability is what he later points to as an "arbitrary element in the situation" in a letter, dated 27 July 1938, to Hugh Townshend (1973–79, 29:289). As Carabelli and others have shown, Keynes allows for the possibility that the logical, probable connections between premises and arguments may not be measurable, numerical, or comparable. In such situations, individual probabilities may be "known"—that is, logical connections can be established between particular bodies of evidence and individual arguments—but they may not be subject to any ordering (whether binary, multiple, or continuous). In such cases (Keynes refers, in the same letter, to "millions of cases"), the formation of individual probabilities cannot serve as the basis of the kind of well-ordered, rational calculations that modern economists often attribute to economic agents.

---

[25] See, e.g., his discussion of Poisson in chapter 28.

Both these moments serve to problematize the connection between the existence of a "formal" discourse of probability and the idea that such a discourse can serve as "foundation" of a process of rational decision-making under uncertainty. However, what remains to be determined is the extent to which what we understand to be Keynes's "discursive" notion of probability is something "more" than a formalism of the sort that characterizes other philosophical and mathematical projects to which Keynes's is temporally related, such as Bertrand Russell and Alfred North Whitehead's *Principia Mathematica* (1910–13), G. E. Moore's *Principia Ethica* (1903), Ludwig Wittgenstein's *Tractatus Logico-Philosophicus* (1922), and Rudolph Carnap's (1950) own "logical" theory of probability, and that has been a defining feature of modernism in art, architecture, and literary criticism.[26] Such formalisms, which formed the basis of the project of analytic philosophy for the better part of the twentieth century, involved the construction of complete, logically perfect, foundational systems of representation or rational discourse starting only from certain— rational or empirical—premises. What is valuable to remember here is that, according to postmodernism, the rules of any discursive formation are incomplete. First, whatever meanings exist "within" a discourse refer to—by differing from and deferring to—the other elements of that particular discourse and those of still other discourses, in an endless chain of signifying elements. Second, the rules of discursive formation are always subject to interpretation and negotiation; thus, meanings, when they can be determined, are conceived to be purely local and contingent points of "stability," subject to reinterpretation and renegotiation. Therefore, from a postmodern perspective, the discourses according to which probabilities are formed cannot ensure either that the probabilities are "known" to exist (either by observing economists or by the economic agents themselves) or, if they are determined to exist within a specific discourse, that they conform to any particular standard or set of criteria. Probabilities are, in this sense, "undecidable."

In the case of Keynes's treatment of probability, a degree of undecidability appears to inhere in the role of evidence. Since probability is defined as a relation between an argument or hypothesis and the evidence that is brought to bear, the degree of rational belief depends on both the quality and amount of evidence. As Keynes points out in his critical discussion of the principle of indifference, "the rule that there must be no ground for preferring one alternative to another, involves . . . an appeal to judgements of *irrelevance*" (1921, 54–55). In order to apply the principle of indifference (and thus to set a priori equal probabilities), it is therefore

---

[26] See Weatherford 1982, especially chapter 3, for an insightful discussion of the relationship between Keynes's and Carnap's "a priori" notions of probability.

necessary to determine what parts of available evidence are relevant to the proposition about which a probable belief is to be formed. In addition, the amount of evidence, although not conceived by Keynes to determine the values of probabilities, does affect their "weight," and thus the degree of belief or confidence an individual can hold with respect to logical probability judgments.

If the quality and amount of evidence play such a crucial role in determining the probability and weight of an argument, and the evidence is neither obvious nor complete, that is, if the meaning of the evidence is not given by the "external" world, then Keynes's treatment would seem to rest on—or at least leave open the possibility for—an "internalist," discursive conception of testing. Both the formation of initial probabilities and the necessary judgments concerning evidence are, in this sense, internal to theory and therefore subject to the incompleteness of the rules of discursive formation.

Not surprisingly, other systems of probability, notwithstanding their own pretensions to completeness, are also beset by this "problem." As Mirowski (1997) has shown, the "classical" conception of equal probabilities—for example, in games of chance—rested on a prior judgment that the games themselves were fair. Therefore, the discourse of classical probabilities is incomplete in itself and must refer to another discourse: a discourse of "fairness."[27] Keynes, as we saw above, developed a similar argument in the case of frequentist notions of probability: the "discovery" of relative frequencies depends on a prior conception or discursive ordering of probabilities. Subjectivist interpretations of probability, such as that of Frank Ramsey (1978)—later extended by Bruno de Finetti (1964) and Leonard Savage (1954) and which has become the basis of contemporary expected-utility theory—are also incomplete systems: the "no book" criterion of consistency with which Ramsey sought to stabilize subjective probability calculations merely displaces the problem of indeterminacy onto another discourse of probability against which a particular agent's set of "subjective" probabilities can be declared rational or not. Determinacy is achieved only by dictating that one theory or discourse of probabilities is the standard, the "master" text, against which all others will be measured. In all three cases, then, the process of forming probabilities is

[27] And, as Judith Mehta (1993, 94–95) explains in the context of game theory, " 'fair' does not have some singular, objective meaning or exteriority such that we can assign a determinate value to 'the fair solution.' The meaning of 'fair' is not fixed and univocal, but is situational in so far as its precise meaning for two bargainers shifts according to its mutually recognized difference from 'unfair' in a particular bargaining situation, which may well differ from its meaning in some other bargaining situation. The meaning of 'unfair' must, then, be anterior to and leaves its trace in the meaning of 'fair'; and 'unfair' is itself marked by the possibility of further meanings."

caught up in an endless, and therefore not ultimately decidable, chain of references within and between discursive formations.

The discursive nature of probability judgments turns out to be quite significant. In the absence of an extradiscursive move designed to stop the play of signifying probabilities (e.g., the economic scientist's "legislating" that a particular set of criteria should serve as the ultimate foundation for the formation of probabilities), it is quite possible for there to be quite different—arbitrary and potentially incommensurable—probabilities produced according to the rules of formation of different discourses. In this sense, the discursivity of probability leads to a diverse, fragmented world in which there is no necessary common ground or foundation for probability "calculations," on the part of either economists or the agents whose actions they seek to account for and to "model" in their economic theories.

Uncertainty and Probability

At two quite different points in his life, and in two apparently different kinds of texts—one "philosophic," the other "economic"—Keynes addressed the issues surrounding chance, randomness, and the lack of certainty that seem to accompany the processes of decision making and knowledge production. In the *Treatise on Probability*, Keynes developed a theory of logical probability judgments; later, in the *General Theory*, Keynes discussed the role of uncertainty in investors' long-term decision-making and, following on that, in the *Quarterly Journal of Economics* article, he emphasized the centrality of uncertainty in his approach to economics and proceeded to define uncertainty as ignorance, as simply not knowing. In each of these cases, we have called attention to what we believe are some of the postmodern moments in Keynes's treatment, moments that others consider (again, we think, correctly) to be nihilistic with respect to the existing methods and procedures of modern economic science.

What, then, is the relationship among these different points in Keynes's attempt to grapple with probability and uncertainty? In particular, is there a sense in which the changes in his treatment constitute a progressive movement toward postmodernism, in the direction of an increasingly nihilistic position? On the basis of the evidence that we have examined and presented thus far, it is tempting to argue that Keynes did, indeed, move over time to what we consider to be a more postmodern position—that is, that the "late Keynes" is the more postmodern Keynes. From this perspective, the Keynes of the *Quarterly Journal* article ended up with a notion of radical uncertainty and, in the process, relinquished *both* a belief in rational rules of noncertain or probabilistic knowledge (the "early

Keynes" of the *Treatise*) *and* the idea that "animal spirits," conventions, and the like would allow investors to overcome uncertainty (the "middle Keynes" of the *General Theory*). Focusing solely on the issue of the possibility of knowledge—of certain knowledge or of some logical substitute for such knowledge, thus allowing for the possibility of rational or sensible decision-making—then, indeed, Keynes did move toward a more nihilistic or postmodern view of uncertainty over the course of his life.

This notion of a "progressive slide into nihilism" is, in turn, buttressed by Keynes's own view of the changes in his thinking over time. In the essay "My Early Beliefs" (which was prepared for and read to the Bloomsbury Group in the year following the publication of the *Quarterly Journal* article), Keynes admits the "flimsily based" and "pre-Freudian" cast of his earlier views of human nature. After noting the difficulties involved in his own attempts to break from the idea of rationality,[28] he puts forward the view that

> The attribution of rationality to human nature, instead of enriching it, now seems to me to have impoverished it. It ignored certain powerful and valuable springs of feeling. Some of the spontaneous, irrational outbursts of human nature can have a sort of value from which our schematism was cut off. Even some of the values associated with wickedness can have value. (1973–79, 10:448–49)

The "late Keynes" thus appears to be much more willing to reduce the scope of rationality, including the rules of logical belief, and to acknowledge the brute limits imposed by uncertainty. In this, Keynes appears to have moved increasingly toward, if not actually embraced, what others have taken to be a nihilistic view of the possibility of rational decision-making on the part of economic agents and, thus, of the knowledge of the rules and results of such decision making on the part of economic scientists.

However, there is another sense in which the chronology of texts (and of Keynes's own assessment of his changing beliefs) betrays an opposite movement. For if the Keynes of the *Treatise* focused on the rules of discursive formation of probability—and thus opened up the possibility of diverse and potentially undecidable and incommensurable notions of less-than-certain knowledge—the later Keynes seems to have stressed the "brute nature" of uncertainty—and therefore the idea that uncertainty is a given and singular phenomenon. In this sense, what Keynes *gains* in true or radical uncertainty he *loses* in discursivity or textuality.

----

[28] "I still suffer incurably from attributing an unreal rationality to other people's feelings and behaviour (and doubtless to my own, too). . . . I behave as if there really existed some authority or standard to which I can successfully appeal if I shout loud enough" (1973–79, 10:448).

Because these two conceptual moments of Keynes's treatment cannot be said to coexist or to succeed one another chronologically in the sequence of texts, we are led to a quite different view of the relationship between his work on uncertainty and that on probability. We find it difficult, for example, to accept the traditional view (held, perhaps, by a majority of contemporary philosophers and economists) that his theories of probability and uncertainty are simply unrelated.[29] The fact that, in both areas, Keynes's treatment produced what we have described as postmodern moments, and that others have taken to be nihilistic tendencies in his work, serves to create an important connection between his theories of probability and uncertainty. We thus find ourselves in sympathy with the more recent view, espoused by many post-Keynesians, that "Keynes the philosopher" and "Keynes the economist" cannot be so easily divorced one from the other. However, our interpretation of the different postmodern moments in Keynes's thinking does not coincide either with the "continuist" or with the "discontinuist" theories put forward in the literature—either the view that his theory of probability is simply a precursor to and a foundation for his theory of uncertainty (or, alternatively, that the two are governed by or expressions of the same "vision" or philosophy) or that Keynes's theory of uncertainty represents a sharp break from his earlier treatment of probability.[30]

Instead, we see the relationship between Keynes's theories of probability and uncertainty as an uneven, neither unrelated nor linear, development in which each can said to condition the existence of the other but in which neither can be deduced (or entirely separated) from the other. What serves to connect his treatment in these two areas is that, in both cases, Keynes's thinking ran up against and, at particular moments, actually succeeded in crossing the boundary between modernism and postmodernism.

Uncertainty and Postmodernism

We think that the postmodern moments represented by the introduction of radical uncertainty into economic analysis are bound up with key aspects of Keynes's treatment of both probability and uncertainty: on one

---

[29] The majority of modern economists would appear, then, to treat Keynes's writings in a manner much like they do Smith's: unaware of or even embarrassed by the methods and content of the "noneconomic" texts (the *Treatise on Probability* and the *Theory of Moral Sentiments*), they content themselves with referring to the achievements of the "economic" texts (the *General Theory* and the *Wealth of Nations*).

[30] John Davis (1994) emphasizes the discontinuity between the philosophical outlook of Keynes's early and later writings, while Ann Carabelli (1995), among others, argues in favor of a fundamental continuity.

hand, the idea that probabilistic knowledge (and, by extension, all other forms of knowledge, certain or otherwise) is a discursive phenomenon, and therefore that the discourses in and through which both economists and economic agents make sense of the world may be (and often are) incommensurable; and, on the other hand, the idea that there are situations (perhaps many) faced by economic agents in which we "simply do not know" in advance the range of probable or even possible outcomes and, therefore, have no reliable means at our disposal to make plans and predictions. The perceived nihilism of this conception of uncertainty can be attributed to the anxiety or dismay that without some notion of a "rational" process by which agents arrive at their decisions or undertake economic actions, any kind of economic theorizing may be impossible. This, at least, is the conclusion arrived at by Coddington, Lawson, and others who either reject Keynes's approach (as, alternatively, "innocuous" or fundamentally "disruptive") or seek to reformulate it so that it is more in accord with "recognizable" economic methods and procedures. The fear that uncertainty halts economic theory's progress—that it preempts economic analysis altogether—because it can neither make predictions about outcomes faced by economic agents under conditions of uncertainty nor, perhaps, even describe the processes by which these same agents may ultimately take actions has been met by most post-Keynesians (and those neoclassicals and traditional Keynesians who are, in one way or another, intrigued by the radicalness of uncertainty), as it was by Keynes himself (at least at significant points in both the *Treatise on Probability* and the *General Theory*), with an opposite reaction. In general, the response has been to hold on to some minimal, limited notion of rational behavior, that is, to maintain the dubious (and modernist) link between some form of cognition (now understood to be based on convention, past experience, and "muddling through") and individual economic action.

Note, then, what many of these recuperative reactions—on the part of Keynes, Knight, Shackle, and of many contemporary mainstream economists—keep in place. It is instructive to view these reformulations and replies because they suggest, by looking at what they seek to constrain and control, the degree to which uncertainty has the potential to disengage contemporary mainstream economics from its modernist moorings. Here, we focus on three implications of such reactions.

First, they retain a sense that uncertainty is a "fact of nature." That is to say, they see uncertainty, as Keynes himself seemed to in the *General Theory* and the *Quarterly Journal* article, as a "real force" in the world outside of the subject, and refuse to incorporate the other side of Keynes's approach—to understand and deploy it as a discursive construction. The implication of such a treatment is that the problem of uncertainty becomes one of the *limits to knowledge* imposed externally by given, external conditions upon otherwise rational subjects. But because the problem of knowledge is merely one of coming up against irremovable (and universal, because confronted by all economic agents) "natural" barriers, uncertainty, in this rendition, does not imply an epistemological break. What is left intact is the conception of knowledge production and acquisition from post-Enlightenment epistemological positions, such as empiricism and rationalism (or their offspring, positivism and realism). The possibility is never entertained, then, that "solving" the problem of choice under conditions of uncertainty may involve a shift in discursive structure, and may likewise include an epistemological rupture. If uncertainty is a discursive construction, and if some economic discourses "see" the radical aspects of uncertainty as nihilistic to their own premises (which, often, are pronounced as a more general threat to *any* economic theorizing), then it is unlikely that these radical aspects will be produced and developed consciously within those discourses. To put this otherwise, the introduction of uncertainty into mainstream economic theories has tended to destabilize those theories at least partly because the same discursive structures that allow for the perception and further elaboration of uncertainty also contain epistemological norms that may be violated by confronting the nihilistic implications of uncertainty.

Second, these attempts to take up the issue of uncertainty while, at the same time, neutralizing the more nihilistic aspects of uncertainty also retain the idea that, even when full and complete rationality (as implied, e.g., by prominent versions of both neoclassical and new classical or rational expectations theories) may not be possible, some form of rationality—and, importantly, some dichotomy between rationality and irrationality—can be preserved. The fear of action not governed by some sort of conscious, rule-driven, intellectual process involving knowledge and rational decision-making is so strong in modern economics as to make virtually impossible an alternative position, for example, one that understands rationality as being overdetermined by a plurality of causes, as much overlain with and constituted by contingent and specific social conventions and habits, psychological "drives," and "hidden" motivations and desires—and, thus as individual, arbitrary, unpredictable, and ultimately undiscoverable—as irrationality itself is often conceived to be. Our point is that, if the modernist distinction between rationality and irrationality is effaced then, as Keynes rightly pointed out, there is no single authority or standard that can be used to model and predict (and, as Foucault showed, to control) the behavior of economic agents. So-called irrational (or "weakly rational") elements of decision making and behavior could no longer be considered as a "residual," allowed into the analysis when the conditions for rationality (or "strong rationality") do not obtain. Economic agents would then be seen as fully "decentered," composed of a multiplicity of conscious and unconscious—conventional, rationalizing, "wicked," and so on—knowledges and forms of decision making. It takes some doing both to acknowledge this decentering in the case of uncertainty and then to assert that, when certain knowledge is possible, agents resort back to a singular and unified form of rational decision-making— as though agents were able at a moment's notice to recognize when they are faced with certain, probable, or uncertain outcomes, to flip the toggle switch, and to recuperate a centered stance. Thus, for the economic theorist, the complex question of determination is frustrated, at least for those who wish to link, in an essentialist or cause-and-effect fashion, certain states of rational intellection with specific actions and results. Let us say, then, that the nihilism of uncertainty may have as one effect a paving of the way for notions of the overdetermination and potential infinitude of simultaneous knowledges, forms of decision making, expectations, and of much else in the mainstream repertoire that is usually contained at the level of the singular and determinant.

Third, these reactions seek to maintain a conception of uncertainty as a "problem" in need of a "solution." Many post-Keynesians, faced with the potential nihilism of uncertainty, join with Keynes (and with the mainstream, "hydraulic" or "bastard" Keynesians from whom they otherwise wish to distance their approach) to assert that the instability or disorderliness of a capitalist ("noncooperative" or "entrepreneurial") economy is based on a volatility of expectations that, in turn, is tied to the existence of significant uncertainty on the part of economic agents. In the more radical versions of uncertainty, such as Shackle's, the impossibility of certain knowledge opens up new realms of "freedom" and "creative imagination." In this sense, the instability and disorder associated with uncertainty represent, at least for the case of economic agents, a condition to be embraced. Of course, it would be possible for economists to view the situation caused by uncertainty as one creating the conditions for their own "freedom," since they could now use their creativity and imagination to construct explanations and tell stories that are not circumscribed by the mechanistic (deterministic, equilibrium-based) models with which they usually work. For the "domesticators" of uncertainty, however, stability and order are preferred to their opposites. Therefore, either uncertainty has to be eliminated (e.g., by the application of the appropriate macroeconomic and industrial policies or the creation of "stabilizing" rules and institutions) or it has to be reconciled with the perceived regularities and continuity of the economic system (e.g., by finding arenas in which uncertainty does not obtain or institutional arrangements that serve to mitigate the effects of uncertainty). What appears to be expressed in such approaches is a fear that the economic systems "out there" may not be governed by some sort of order—however apparent or hidden, whether a "general equilibrium" of autonomous individual decisions and actions or a set of durable behavioral "laws" and institutions—that can be "captured" by the appropriate model and, therefore, fear that the potential nihilism of uncertainty might spill over and engulf the enterprise of economic theorizing itself. And this difficulty is compounded if we treat knowledges as discourses such that the terms *order* and *disorder* are constituted in different ways—according to different rules of formation, methods, epistemological norms, and so forth—according to different economic discourses. The "order" constructed by economists in the face of uncertainty would be no more preferable (indeed, in many instances, it may be "worse") than the "disorder" associated with the uncertainty to which economic agents are said to be confronted. The nihilism of uncertainty here—its postmodernism, if you will—is the breaking of the hierarchical couplet *order/disorder* such that there is no longer any privilege to be accorded to the "discovery" of a hidden order on the part of economists or the "creation" of such an order on the part of economic agents. With this rupture, a key part of the post-Enlightenment (and certainly modernist) philosophical outlook falls away. Here, the specter of the disorder that such a position suggests to most mainstream economists means that this implication of uncertainty, to this point, has not been embraced.

Modernism's Revenge: Rational Expectations

While uncertainty unleashes a postmodern reaction to knowledge, rationality, and order, modernist economists have sought consciously to counter this reaction and its effects. John Muth states, for example, that "it is sometimes argued that the assumption of rationality in economics leads to theories inconsistent with, or inadequate to explain, observed phenomena, especially changes over time (e.g., Simon). Our hypothesis is based on exactly the opposite point of view: that dynamic economic models do not assume enough rationality" (1961, 316). If a postmodern interpretation of uncertainty proposes the extension of its nihilistic effects on knowledge and so on to present behavior, modernists push back the other way by extending the traditional neoclassical understandings of these concepts to expectations about the future.

The "new classical economists" are well aware of the potential nihilism of the Shackle/Keynes view of uncertainty. What they have criticized is precisely the turn to modernism to which Austrian and Keynesian economists have been led in order to prevent the destruction of economic theory implicit in uncertainty. It is valid to ask why we would assume that unified subjectivity (which is necessary for a notion of "self-interest") and rational behavior regarding all "present" concerns are inapplicable to expected outcomes of future occurrences. Why would we expect subjectivity and rationality to fall apart in confronting the unknown? In accordance with the time-honored mainstream tradition in economics of positing the eternality and universality of rational choice, new classical economists have asked why we should discard this view in discussing expectations. As Rodney Maddock and Michael Carter write, "The rational expectations hypothesis, in itself, should not be provocative to economists. It merely brings expectations within the scope of individual maximizing behavior" and "provides a way of incorporating expectations which is inconsistent with the orthodox economic theorizing" (1982, 49). Perhaps the great modernist synthesizers, Samuelson and Hicks, and not Lucas and Sargent, should be the main targets of criticism.

The rational expectations approach shows that if economic agents are self-interested, then they will make every effort, over time, to acquire information that bears upon outcomes that can affect their economic well-being. According to Mark Wiles, "irrationality is unnecessarily expensive—it is more expensive than using the available information efficiently" (1981, 86). If markets are competitive, knowledge is transferable, and information is not withheld or hoarded, subjects will try to supply themselves with information that could make anticipated events less uncertain. As Arjo Klamer puts it, the idea of "rational expectations . . . assume[s] that individuals do not leave any opportunity unused to improve their decisions" (1983, 14). More importantly, there is no reason to believe that the information subjects acquire (through learning, purchase, or gift) is of a different consistency than the information economic scientists produce in their forecasts. If scientists' information is better at predicting future outcomes than subjective expectations independently formulated, economic agents will have the necessary incentive (since they fear being "fooled" and hope to make some pecuniary gain) to obtain information in forming their expectations. In particular, if policy rules and their effects are known by theorists, as long as these rules and knowledge of their effects are made available (through markets or otherwise), self-interested, rational subjects will have an interest in and should be able to use such information.

New classicals and their interpreters stress that the hypothesis of rational expectations does not imply the omniscience of either subjects or scientists. It does not imply that scientists and economic agents make no errors in their predictions and subjective anticipations. Indeed, one defense of rational expectations is that rationality, as new classicals define it, does not require either full or certain knowledge for forecasters or for expectant buyers and sellers. Rational expectations does imply, however, that if errors are systematically biased, then economic scientists *and* agents will have both mutually consistent perceptions about the environment and reasons to take this into account in their next forecast and formation of expectations. Uncertainty is understood, in this case, to be a matter of either predictable outcomes or complete randomness. If predictions can be made, tested, and adjusted through a probability calculus, then uncertainty can be faced by rational behavior. If, however, deviations from predictions (errors) are "random shocks," then uncertainty can be practically ignored in forming expectations and forecasting economic trends.

This defense, though adequate to some criticisms, is no response either to the nihilistic versions of uncertainty or to postmodern epistemology.[31] Postmodernism explodes the "specularity" of subjectivity and scientific knowledge not by preserving the pristine difference between the two, but by shattering the mirror. The mirror is destroyed by postmodernism's emphasis on the discursive constitution of subjects *and* knowledge and on irreducible differences, where they exist, among knowledges, rationalities, and so on.

For now, however, the modernism of rational expectations has prevailed in mainstream discussions of uncertainty and expectations. In the rational-expectations debates, only the post-Keynesians seem to have insisted on the more nihilistic senses of Shackle's and Keynes's discussions of uncertainty and expectations (this is especially true of the post-Keynesian notion of the "heterogeneity of expectations"). However, post-Keynesians' crude empiricism (see, for example, Eichner 1983), committed humanism, and defense of order are inscribed within modernist discourse and seem far away indeed from the postmodern implications of uncertainty.

Nevertheless, as our discussion in this chapter suggests, the elaboration of uncertainty within modernist economic discourse has produced changes in the concept of economic knowledge. As Mary Morgan (1987, 137) concludes in response to rational-expectations theory, "once again it appears that probability ideas have been used successfully to plug one gap in the system of economic theory only to find that uncertainty remains as considerable as ever." If Morgan is right, then as the meanings of knowledge and subjectivity change and the discursive production of the "unknown" continues, the effects of postmodernism will continue to be felt, even in the midst of economic modernism.

---

[31] Nor does Sargent's more recent treatment of "bounded rationality," which is provoked by the idea that the assumption of rational expectations presumes more knowledge than econometricians are usually assumed to have. Now, economic agents are understood to "theorize, estimate, and adapt in attempting to learn about probability distributions which, under rational expectations, they already know" (1993, 3). See Sent 1998 for a discussion of the problem of "symmetry" between economic agents and scientists in Sargent's writings.

3

The Body and Neoclassical Economics

We are and we are not our bodies.
—Jeanette Winterson, *Gut Symmetries: A Novel*

There is no such thing as *the* body.
—Jean-Luc Nancy, "Corpus"

THE HUMAN BODY plays a key role in contemporary economics—as it has throughout the history of modern economic thought. Different conceptions of the body have been central to a wide range of issues, from theories of economic value to conceptions of agency and subjectivity, and to the extensive debates that have taken place on these topics. Yet many economists—some with apparent approval, many others in evident reproach—argue that the body has largely disappeared from view in recent times. In this chapter, we explain how postmodernism can help make sense of the supposed disappearance of the body from the scene of current economic theorizing. Our discussion is focused on a particular reading of neoclassical economics (together with the comments of some of its staunchest critics) and develops the argument that not only has the body not vanished from neoclassical theory but, in an important sense, a fragmented, decentered—what many would consider to be a postmodern—conception of the body has been produced.

Our concern with the body stems from the fact that modern economics was created at least in part as a discourse about the capacities and functions of the human body and that the body has continued to exercise a decisive (albeit changing) influence across paradigms and throughout the history of economic thought. Adam Smith, for example, created a theory of value that was grounded in both the desiring and laboring dimensions of the human body. In particular, for Smith, human needs and wants stood at the beginning of the economic process, establishing the reason for production and exchange, but the amount of labor, the "toil and trouble" involved in acquiring goods, determined the amount of exchange-value. Smith's "labor theory of value" was complemented by his conception of economic agency according to which various corporeal dimensions—from basic needs, sexual drives, and the ability to engage in mental and manual labor through vision, sympathy, and trust to caring, imagination, and reason—were ordered in a hierarchical fashion and reconciled such that the "lower" orders could successfully be governed by the "higher" ones.[1]

It was this particular theory of value and agency—and, therefore, the conception of the human body—that was criticized by the neoclassical economists of the late nineteenth century and that they attempted to sweep aside. In their view, the combination of needs/desires and labor in classical political economy created a "paradox of value" that could only be resolved by focusing on utility (especially the extra or marginal utility derived from consuming goods and services) and therefore by reordering the body in terms of a calculus of pleasure and pain such that labor was reinterpreted not as a separate determinant of value but as a "disutility," and thus another dimension of the subject's needs and desires. In this fashion, the body was foreshortened in terms of its presence and effects in order to constitute what came to be known as specifically neoclassical theories of value and agency.

While Carl Menger is often considered to be one of the founders of the marginalist approach, twentieth-century Austrian economists increasingly distanced themselves from their neoclassical counterparts. The thoroughgoing "subjectivism" of the Austrian school of thought represents both a critique of and an alternative to the conceptions of equilibrium, time, and much else (except, significantly, the idea that value originates in the subjective, desiring order of the body) that has constituted the history of neoclassical economics. An important aspect of the Austrian emphasis on process and innovation is the idea that economic agents (and thus their diverse abilities to gather relevant information and make appropriate decisions) are bounded by and situated in terms of their bodies. Since Austrian economists argue that no one agent or set of agents—whether an individual entrepreneur or the members of a government institution within capitalism or even socialist planners—is capable of being everywhere, thereby making knowledge of all economic data impossible for any participant or observer, their approach concentrates on the emergence and effects of the partial and differentiated knowledges acquired and utilized by economic agents.

Nobel laureate Amartya Sen has long criticized the mainstream neoclassical tendency, especially within welfare economics, to focus on utility to the exclusion of a wide variety of other corporeal "functionings" and

---

[1] Michael Shapiro (1993) argues that Smith invokes two different sources of the hierarchical self-ordering of the body: the internal "vice-regent," which refers to an imagined observer whose viewpoint is such that it is engaged in the external appraisal of what is being viewed by the subject's body, and a "natural governor," which adjusts the passions so that they are expressed at a level "in balance with the degree of sympathy an observer could be expected to evince" (108).

"capabilities." For Sen (1985), the utility perceived or derived from the possession of commodities (and therefore the standard utility-maximizing choice) is not an adequate measure of the well-being of a person because it does not account for what a person succeeds in doing or being with the commodities at his or her command. His alternative approach —which is reflected in numerous applications, including investigations of poverty, famine, gender inequalities, and human development (Sen 1992)—represents an attempt to take into account the physical characteristics of individual bodies (e.g., whether one is able-bodied or disabled) as well as the bodily identities and circumstances that may constrain choice and enjoyment (such as those of the "destitute thrown into beggary" and the "subdued and subjugated housewife").[2] In Sen's view, focusing on the body's real and potential achievements makes it possible to assess both persons' well-being and the opportunities and obstacles they face for improving their well-being.

Our argument is that, in these four cases (and many more that comprise the history of modern economic thought, some of which we touch on during the course of this chapter), the body has played a decisive role. The debate between classical and early neoclassical theories of value reveals the fact that, notwithstanding their different approaches and conclusions, value is conceived in both cases as a relation of depth with respect to a particular "life force" that can be identified within the body. Similarly, neoclassical and Austrian theories of competitive markets can be compared according to the ways in which the ability of economic agents to carry out and to coordinate their decisions is determined by the limits (or not) imposed by their bodily "containers." Sen problematizes what he considers to be excessively narrow neoclassical conceptions of choice-theoretic agency by invoking orders and functions of the body that harken back to classical, especially, Smithian concerns. In our view, the modernism of economic thought is closely associated with these and related attempts to ground the concepts and schemes of the economy, particularly (but in very different ways, and with contrasting implications for) notions of economic subjectivity and individual identity, in an underlying reality about the human body.

Precisely because the body has been so central to modern economic thought—for which it has served as an underlying ontology, organized in a hierarchical manner, invoked as a unified entity—it serves an important

---

[2] Sen's capabilities approach became the basis of the United Nations Development Program's definition of "human development" (measured and presented annually in the *Human Development Report*) as distinct from the "opulence" approach adopted by the World Bank (and issued annually as the *World Development Report*). For a discussion of Sen's role in the intellectual origins of the concept of human development, see Desai 1991.

register both of the predominance of economic modernism and of the emergence of postmodern issues and concerns. We must admit, however, that, to many observers, much of economic discourse (especially, but not only, neoclassical economics) in the second half of the twentieth century can also be seen as a determined disavowal of the significance of the body for economic analysis, as a series of attempts to reduce, ignore, or eliminate any and all references to the body, in favor of what are considered to be the noncorporeal dimensions of economic agency, price determination, and market coordination. Not only does the body seem to have disappeared from economic thought; with few exceptions, economists today are largely "silent" on the question of the body.[3]

The (Dis)appearance of the Body?

Such is not, of course, the case outside of economics. The human body has recently emerged as a central and favored object, explicitly discussed and debated, in many different fields of discourse and practice. The human body suffers; the human body seeks pleasure; the human body is subjected to a variety of disciplinary regimes (including self-regulation, such as dieting, safe sex, and so on). The human body emerges in contemporary discourses as gendered, as reproducing and reproducible (increasingly by "artificial" means), as racialized, as infinitely differentiable, as transformable (e.g., sex change and cosmetic surgery), even as potentially replaceable, but also as immutable (as in some evolutionary biology and psychology, in which such phenomena as sexual preference, environmental adaptation, and more are considered "hard-wired" in the genes). Today, the human body is everywhere investigated and on display across different fields of thought and social action.

But—in the midst of this profusion of words and deeds—what if the body is "absent" from the scene of a particular discourse? What happens if the body, as an object that grounds a discursive practice, is nothing but a specter, haunting the site where, at least once upon a time, it was visible for all to see? How, and in what way, can "the body" be dematerialized to such a degree within a whole tradition of writing that many of its past inscribers cannot recognize "its" existence? That is, what if the existence of the human body within a theoretical tradition, due to its supposed absence, is called into question? Something resembling this situ-

---

[3] The title of Michael Ghiselin's "Economy of the Body" is deceptive, at least in terms of our concerns in this chapter: his primary concern is with forming a branch of knowledge called general economy by combining "natural economy" (biology) and "political economy" (economics).

ation—this transmutation or, perhaps, displacement of the body—is said to characterize modern economic thought in its most recent, high formal constitution.

Writing prophetically in 1947, Paul Samuelson seems to declare this very displacement. Samuelson's announcement takes the form of reflecting upon the legacy of utility—that seemingly quintessential corporeal concept—within the discipline of economics.

> There has been a shift in emphasis away from the physiological and psychological hedonistic, introspective aspects of utility. Originally great importance was attached to the ability of goods to fill basic biological needs; but in almost every case this view has undergone extreme modification. At the same time, there has been a similar movement away from the concept of utility as a sensation, as an introspective magnitude. (1983, 91)

How are we to understand Samuelson's remarks? Was Samuelson reporting a fait accompli, the human body's disappearance in economic discourse brought about by a shift in focus to the hegemonic formalism of axioms and lemmas? Had the desiring and/or laboring bodies of past economic thought become so embarrassing or irrelevant to economists that they could no longer be talked about or studied within the "core" of economic theory? In other words, had Samuelson simply stated both his observation and his will that the body was disappearing, thankfully, from economics?

Arjo Klamer is one contemporary thinker who believes that such a disappearance has all but been realized in "late modernist" economics. Though Klamer (2001) speaks more in terms of "subjects" than "bodies," it is clear that, in his view, the formalist revolution from the mid–twentieth century on has meant the disappearance of feeling, thinking, and morally dedicated subjects—or, in our terms, subjects with bodies that feel, think, and care. For Klamer, the "loss of character" he decries in the recent work of the new classical economists is well represented by a lifeless "man without qualities." No body, no self, inhabits the stick figure of "Max U," at least no body or self of human substance, with discernible "qualities." Thus, we think that Klamer would accede to the idea that, indeed, the "great disappearance acts," as he labels them, brought about by new classical economics involve the loss of the human body as well as other human characteristics in the "subject" that is barely described in the formal axioms and algorithms.

The body, then, could be said to have "disappeared" from the site of economic discourse. And, as we relate below, this disappearance could easily be demonstrated by means of a historical narrative in which the current absence of the body and its attributes and effects in the frame of discourse is linked, by critics, to the dematerialization of economics as a

Figure 3.1. Barnet Newman, *Vir Heroicus Sublimis* (1950–51). Oil on canvas, 7'11 3/8" x 17'9 1/4". Gift of Mr. and Mrs. Ben Heller. Museum of Modern Art, New York. (Credit: Digital Image (c) The Museum of Modern Art/Licensed by Scala/Art Resource, New York.)

whole, its increasing "unreality" and obliviousness to the real pains and pleasures, the real suffering and needs of the economic agents it purports to represent, as Klamer has argued (as have a whole host of heterodox economists for a good fifty years).

Yet, this is not our view. In fact, our argument in what follows is that no such disappearing has occurred. To the contrary, we believe that—perhaps unwittingly—the movement in the past forty years toward increasingly formal and axiomatic modes of presentation in economics has ushered in a different conception of the human body, one certainly cut off from its historical roots in classical political economy for sure, but one that still preserves the notion of human corporeality within the "core" of mainstream economic theorizing. If this is so, though, we are lead to wonder, what explains the view that the body has seemingly disappeared from economists' sight?

Hidden Bodies, Absent Bodies: What Are We Looking For?

The problem of the "disappearance" of bodies is, of course, one that both motivated and enlivened the work of Michel Foucault in his wide-ranging discussions of the ways in which modernity produced for itself a complexly "problematic" body, enmeshed in networks of power. We may think of fears that the body has disappeared from economics as an example of the fetishism of the body that, for Foucault and others, so engrossed nineteenth- (and, we would add, twentieth-) century Western societies, whose representations were produced in the tension between "repression" of, and the ubiquitous (and verbose) worrying about, the body (especially in its sexual aspects). There is a paradox, then, in speaking or worrying about the disappearance of the body. For, as Peter Brooks writes in *Body Works*, "when the body becomes more secret, hidden, covered, it becomes all the more intensely the object of curiosity" (1993, 15).

Are we then speaking here of a hidden body, one covered up by the formalism of economic discourse? Is the desiring or laboring body the "shame" that can no longer be spoken, but which always lurks in the background, within economic discourse? Is this the true sense of the "disappearance" of the body? (In which case, all that needs to be done is to "out" all those putative repressions and voluble "silences" that must have accompanied the supposed dematerialization of bodies in economics.) This, of course, is one way to read the famous sentences (cited above) in Paul Samuelson's *Foundations of Economic Analysis* that, for all intents and purposes, announced to the world that which had already transpired within the dominant neoclassical economic paradigm.

As is well known to historians of economic thought, Samuelson was both reacting to and building upon the work of prior economists, at least since Vilfredo Pareto, who sought to shift much of the marginalist revolution in economics onto nonutilitarian territory. Samuelson was preceded by almost a decade by John R. Hicks, whose *Value and Capital*, many thought, dealt a final blow to the hedonism undergirding the neoclassical project. Hicks reports in his great work of 1939 that the hedonistic assumptions of utility theory had in his day made "many people uncomfortable" (himself obviously included), and he went on to uphold "the right to an economics free of utilitarian assumptions" (18). Substituting "preference" for "utility" (and, thereby supposedly, delinking consumption choice from calculating degrees of physiologically experienced desire), Hicks proclaimed in his book that the necessary task was nothing less than "to undertake a purge, rejecting all concepts which are tainted by quantitative utility" (19). There is evidence in Hicks (as he reports) of an embarrassment shared by "many" economists—necessitating a "purge," no less—in retaining utility, and, perhaps, then, in grounding the neoclassical theoretical tradition so clumsily (because so visibly) in the desiring body.[4]

Samuelson's argument in the 1940s did not foretell of the absolute disappearance of utility—that magnificently dense concept which, in the his-

[4] Mark Blaug (1980) uses language similar to that of Hicks in describing the theoretical impetus for Samuelson's revealed preference theory: to wit, "Samuelson's revealed preference theory . . . proposed to purge the theory of consumer behavior of the last vestiges of utility by restricting it to operational comparisons between value (quantity times price) sums" (165–66).

tory of economics, has been rendered differently according to whether "the body" or "the mind" (either in separation or in combination) was in current favor as the privileged origin of all consequent economic behavior. The situation in some quarters of neoclassicism in economics at present goes beyond Samuelson's description:

> it is not merely that the modern economist replaces experienced sensations or satisfaction with anticipated sensation, desire, according to the now familiar distinction between ex post and ex ante analysis. But much more than this, many writers have ceased to believe in the existence of any introspective magnitude or quantity of a cardinal, numerical kind. (1983, 91)

Indeed, as Samuelson himself perhaps saw, Hicks's substitution of "ordinal" for "cardinal" utility was one step—but perhaps not the decisive one—in the move to the (presumably) complete denunciation of any recourse to the desiring body in producing economic analysis as a theory of choice.

Samuelson himself continued his own onslaught on utility theory through his "invention" of the weak axiom of revealed preference, which was meant to shift demand theory entirely from the realm of "unobservable" expected utility to the presumably demonstrable market behavior of actual consumers. Yet, as Stanley Wong (1978) was able to point out, Samuelson's own theoretical and methodological defenses of revealed preference theory were modified in successive formulations, and these subsequent defenses are seemingly inconsistent or even contradictory in regard to the ultimate disappearance of utility. Caldwell (1984) summarizes Wong's view nicely: according to Wong's critique, "Samuelson first claimed to be constructing a new theory of consumer behavior which dispenses with the need to refer to utility (ordinal or cardinal). He later switches to the claim that revealed preference theory provides an operational method for the construction of an indifference map. In his final commentary on the subject, Samuelson asserts that his theory is the observational equivalent of ordinal utility theory" (197).[5]

While many economists today deny entirely the effectivity of utility on their theoretical output, not unlike Samuelson's early defense of revealed preference, it still remains true that most textbooks written to introduce undergraduates to economics make utility a central concept, even if it is supposedly stripped of its nineteenth-century hedonism. Or, as Eugene

---

[5] Blaug (1980) makes a related point that "RPT [revealed preference theory] can be used to derive all the standard properties of demand curves that were earlier derived via cardinal and ordinal utility theory" (166), so that "RPT and the theory of utility are logically equivalent, and Samuelson's original claims on behalf of RPT as a new approach to the problem of consumer behavior must, therefore, be rejected as unwarranted" (166–67).

Rotwein (Hume 1970) sagely noted, "the concept 'preference' is equally open to a hedonistic construction, if one chooses to invoke it" (li). Perhaps, then, the disappearance or reappearance of the hedonistic body in economics may be primarily a question of invocation and discursive performance.

Feminist and other cultural theorists have done much to deepen our understanding of the effects of the discursive invocation and performance of this or that notion of the body—hedonistic, reproducing, or otherwise. In *Bodies That Matter*, Judith Butler discusses the idea that bodies are forces, sites, and events that *require* discourse for their ongoing appearance, but whose appearance and effects overflow discourse. In other words, claiming that the human body is, in essence, structured by hedonism or, alternatively, is ruled by more "neutral" preferences has a profound effect on what can be said about the body and much else "in theory"—as well as the "actual" ways "real" bodies are recognized and performed. (This is similar to the view expressed by Robert Frank and colleagues [Frank, Gilovich, and Regan 1993, 1996] that teaching economics students about "self-interest" tends to produce performances and self-definitions consistent with this "motive," as compared with other students who are not exposed to this basic "fact" of economic life.)

Perhaps more importantly for this chapter, Butler (together with Elizabeth Grosz and others) questions the singularity of the term *the body*. This, as we will see, is crucial to the argument we make below. As recent literature on bodies has exemplified, the unity and "fullness" of "the body" is a fiction—a productive fiction, no doubt—that has functioned to circumscribe alternative notions of bodies that exist in the interstices of discursive formations. A central problem for any discourse—economics included—then becomes how one *recognizes* bodies in their emergence or discursive performance within the confines of the field. For the purposes of this chapter, we leave aside the all-important questions concerning bodies that are "marginalized" in mainstream discourses within the field of economics. Lord knows that the history of economic thought is full of such marginalizations. Though it is also true that the pushing to the margins of raced and sexed bodies, to take one example, can call critical attention to the centrality of the distinction that permits one construction—the European male body capable of the utmost refinement and dexterity, for instance—to become the normative "body" of that discourse and that dictates to all other bodies their deviation from the norm.[6] Instead, we

---

[6] Permit us, however, one remarkably fertile example from the existing literature: Alfred Marshall's *Principles of Economics* (1961) is replete with corporeal references, including classed, raced, colonial, and gendered bodies that were pushed to (and perhaps beyond) the margins by later neoclassical economists. Still, as feminists and other heterodox economists

are concerned here more with the problem of this *recognition*, that is, the degree to which "the body" in any of its constructions and appearances is visible to practitioners of a field, such as economics, as well as to anyone else perusing the traditions of economic thought.

So, let us then state our thesis again: we reject the notion that "the body" has disappeared from contemporary neoclassical economic discourse. As we argue below, we prefer instead to think of what has transpired as a *change* in the conception of the human body (or a proliferation of such conceptions) as it is represented in economic discourse. We believe that the body has not disappeared, but has been reconceived and theoretically transformed from earlier conceptions.

The so-called dematerialization of the body—its disappearance from the scene of economic discourse—is a produced effect of particular stories (or performances, if you like) in which anything other than the "full" body, believed to "obviously" exist, is regarded as a lack, or absence, of corporeality in the discursive field. Below, we piece together such a story from the many comments on and criticisms of neoclassical economics we have heard over twenty-five years in the profession.

Our goal in presenting this cobbled-together story, and especially in presenting our critique of it, is to make central to contemporary economic discourse reevaluations of the experiences and distributions of pleasure and pain, work and desire, base and refined instincts, emotions and reason, passions and interests, sex, race, and class, and the like, many of which are fed by considerations of "the body." But, in so doing, we wish to avoid the view that the body is only recognizable and acceptable as a focus for theory and practice if it conforms to more "classical" and normative notions of the "full" human body.

The Fall from Grace: A Narrative Account of the Disappearance of the Body in Economic Thought

In a paragraph that nicely prefigures our story about the "disappearance" of the body in contemporary economic thought, Peter Brooks produces a succinct précis of such narratives as they pertain to the increasing "problematizing" of the body in modernity. Brooks writes that there is "a certain romanticized nostalgia typical of some recent views of early modern Europe as a period of more unified sensibility, where bodily functions, sexuality, and death were more full integrated in human consciousness as

---

have argued in recent years, the ghosts of such bodies continue to haunt the conception of subjectivity in neoclassical theory. For additional discussion of this theme, see chapter 4 below.

'natural' parts of life. We are prone to assume that we live after a Fall from a time of greater unity of consciousness, language, and being" (1993, 5).

Here, then, is a story—one we find compelling and yet disagree with fundamentally—about the body and its relation to the history of economic discourse. A story, no doubt, about the Fall.

From the early beginnings of modern economics in the late eighteenth century to the early decades of this century, economic theory was grounded in different but explicit theories of the body, its disposition, and its effects. The classical political economists, from Smith to Mill, were inclined to express the categories and concepts of economic analysis as dimensions of personal sensations and sensibilities, regardless of whether the individual thus constituted by the senses was perceived primarily as a entity whose body's unity could be organized and represented by his or her desires or, alternatively, by the capacity to labor. The birth of modern economics, therefore, saw the sensate body elevated to the privileged status of a first principle. The virtue of classical political economy, in this story, is that it was a coherent, centered discourse in which the "whole human," with all of his or her natural sentiments, emotions, affections, passions, and sensations (nowhere better presented than in Adam Smith's *Theory of Moral Sentiments*), became the organizing principle to understand, traverse the landscape of, and manipulate individual bodies within the social body.

As this story continues, in contrast to the period of the birth of modern economics, the formalization of economic thought during the present century, in conjunction with the predominance of the neoclassical school of thought, has subsequently pushed the question of the body to the margins, so to speak. While presumably originating from the idea of the desiring body—the body that seeks to minimize pain and to maximize pleasure—whose very hedonism and fluidity is controlled and channeled by the rational mind, neoclassical economic thought has increasingly obscured the nature and effects of bodily desire as it has moved in the direction of axiomatizing human behavior. As we saw for Klamer above, the human subject, the thinking, feeling, working organic individual—the individual whose body comprises chapter after chapter of Smith's *Moral Sentiments*—has simply disappeared in the contemporary neoclassical clamor for parsimony, simplicity, and elegance in high theoretical (read mathematical) expression.[7] In an interesting development, the aesthetics of high

---

[7] Susan Feiner (1999) questions the related view that the notion of "rational economic man"—the quintessential neoclassical notion of the economic agent—has been constructed as a depthless subject, lacking in substance. Feiner's psychopathological reading of "homo economicus as a young man" puts forward in place of this view the idea that the neoclassical subject "is a character with feelings, unexplored depths, and sensitivities" that can be mined

modernism—in economics, associated largely with the norms imposed by the application of advanced calculus, topology, set theory, and more recently, game theory—came to dominate the very constitution of scientific economic discourse itself, determining largely not only the form but also the content of economic concepts and categories.

In this narrative, the formalization of economics in this century thus has come at a cost. Human bodies are no longer recognizable as the site at which the various economic "functions" do their work. The full discussion in classical political economy of sensation and sentiment, passions and interests, which informed so much of the theoretical legacy handed down to today's economists, is not so much reduced in importance with the onset of axiomatization as it is ignored or even renounced as extraneous to the methods and procedures of contemporary economic discourse. The "scientizing" of economics in the twentieth century jettisoned the human body and its complicated excesses from the domain of legitimate economic discussion.

In seeking the origins of this displacement and even obliteration of the human body (and human subject) in contemporary economics, the narrative identifies especially the period after World War II during which economics reached its high modern, formalist stage (which has yet to pass). Following the lead of Samuelson, who, we might remark again, was cognizant of the fear and embarrassment of "the body" that neoclassical economists had demonstrated in their rush from cardinal utility, economists tried to bring to a close earlier attempts to displace "value theory" (theories of the origin and primary causes of economic value or price) from its prior importance in economic discourse. The move to "hide" the body took the form of resistance (expressed, for example, by John Hicks and R. G. D. Allen [1934]) to being inscribed within an economic discourse that had at the center of its analysis the desiring body or psyche as the initiating, first cause of economic value. Ironically, Samuelson's famous "revealed preference" theoretical approach to demand theory, and therefore his initial suggestion (but see our discussion of Wong's critique above) that the theoretical determination of price did not logically require utility as the premise from which all other concepts need derive, did remove for many economists the last remaining link to the more corporeal and psychological theories of their eighteenth- and nineteenth-century utilitarian and preutilitarian predecessors.[8] Increasingly, neoclassical

---

by a reading of his or her unconscious as it manifests itself even in the more formal and abstract methods of contemporary economic thought.

[8] One reviewer of this manuscript responded hilariously but insightfully to the narrative we have conjured up by stating that "there is a nice story to be told about the movement

economists since the 1940s have treated the question of the body's place in determining or even registering the effects of economic activities as "exogenous" to the main tasks of economic theory. Among other things, the claim that a theory of the body and its order did not need to be part and parcel of a properly "economic" analysis may explain the disdain some American economists expressed in encountering Keynes's investment theory of the 1930s and 1940s, which (as we saw in chapter 2) reduced the portfolio decisions of entrepreneurs, in the end, to "animal spirits" (and therefore to that which is most base because it suggests the power of the body to supersede rationality in cases where reason fails). Bluntly stated, the study of the body and its many effects has vanished from economic discourse.

The narrative of the disappearance of the body posits as the transitional moment the emergence in Europe in the 1860s and 1870s of the neoclassical paradigm. The neoclassical revolution, which instated a marginalist approach to all economic categories capable of being quantified, took over from the classicals the largely utilitarian premise regarding the centrality of the desiring body for economic theory. Indeed, the neoclassicals opted for the utilitarianism of Jeremy Bentham, for whom, as David Morris notes, "pain and pleasure stand as . . . rock-solid opposites" (1993, 237).[9] Yet it is also true that the different renditions of marginal utility or *rareté* that were put forward at the time by Menger, Jevons, Walras, and others were accompanied by at least two significant departures from the classicals, if not from Bentham.

First, utility was clearly raised to an exclusive initiating cause so that the inscription within economic theory of labor as a primary source of value (found to different degrees in Smith, Ricardo, Mill, and others) was mostly eschewed. It is interesting here to note that Jevons is known to have toyed with the idea of labor as a source of value (White 1994, 220), but in his landmark *Theory of Political Economy*, he moved instead to the view that labor and the decisions concerning its use, efficacy, and expenditure (its cost) could be reduced mostly to a question of bodily desire or feeling, in this case to the disutility (the pain) that a subject would endure in the time he or she allotted to work. In any event, the marginalist revolution was the occasion for a rupture with previous "objective" theories of value in which the laboring body was seen as the privileged origin (or at least, one of several prime causes) for the determination of value,

---

from hedonism (involving the body) to cardinal utility (less body) to ordinal (even less) to revealed preference (consistency suitable for a machine or a brain in a vat)"!

[9] Morris contrasts Bentham's treatment of pain and pleasure to that of his late-eighteenth-century contemporary the Marquis de Sade, for whom pleasure and pain were combined in chaotic relations resulting in uncanny forms of mixture and substitution (1993, 237).

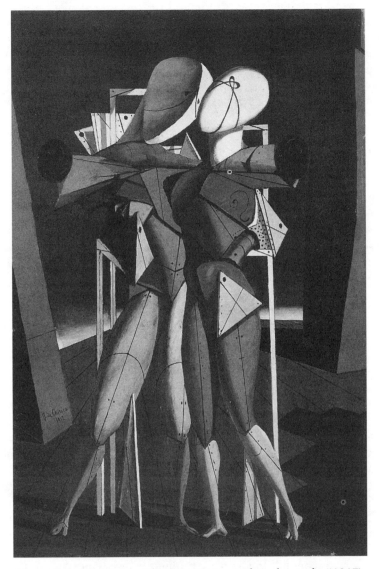

Figure 3.2. Giorgio de Chirico, *Hector and Andromache* (1917). Collection Mattioli, Milan. (Credit: Scala/Art Resource, New York.)

price, profit, and much else. Desire and the mental calculation of utility and disutility—in Jevons, of pleasure and pain—replaced energetics and labor expenditure as the body's determinant cause, at least in the context of the choices that were available to subjects regarding how to utilize their bodies to bring ultimate satisfaction in consumption and production.

Second, as Philip Mirowski (1989) has carefully shown, and for many critics this is the crux of the matter, the neoclassicals sought to model their new marginalist theoretical apparatus on nineteenth-century mechanics and energetics. In this regard, Jevons and Walras certainly stand out in proselytizing for a thoroughgoing mathematization of the field of economics in line with contemporaneous changes wrought in the studies of motion and energy. The notion of calculating most economic quantities at the margin, amenable to and best expressed in modern calculus, was joined to the concepts of equilibrium, and much else that was borrowed, in some cases wholesale, from nineteenth-century physics. The math and physics envy emboldened economists to think of reestablishing their discipline (or at least large parts of it) on a modern scientific basis. Such a move required the shift in deriving and expressing economic concepts in more "imprecise" notions of social and economic value—grounded in a discourse in which the body in its many aspects and appearances was present—to representing the changes in language and conceptual framework in more recent recognizable scientific trappings. This strong belief that science required quantifiable entities and formal analysis for its primary legitimacy was responsible, therefore, for a math craze that has since run amok in modern economics.

Yet, despite the insistence on employing mathematical formulations that worked primarily for and with objectively quantifiable entities, the founders of neoclassicism curiously insisted on the principle of utility, which they soon were forced to admit was anything but representable in "objective" terms. The subjective value theory that was enshrined with the neoclassical revolution was and continued to be a sore spot for those economists in subsequent years who were determined to rid economics of all concepts and terms that could not be scientifically established (read, empirically observable or verifiable). Nineteenth-century neoclassical economics, then, marked only a partial transition from the classicals insofar as it allowed economic theory to be thought of as having a point of origin in a theory of value and as it sought to ground this theory of value in some metaphysical discussion of the desiring body. Thus, for the early neoclassicals, the body was reduced and abridged, at least so far as value determination is concerned. Labor and all other actions and sensibilities relevant to economic theory largely became subcategories of utility, just as utility became less and less dependent on a full-blown physiological/ psychological theory for its expression. Desire became a primary cause, but it was tendentiously linked with the equally strong interest of neoclassical economists to organize the field of economic discourse into a modern scientific discipline. As the developments in the twentieth century demonstrate, the desiring body became oblique and extraneous to the scientific concepts and protocols of economic theory. While the early neoclassicals may have intended otherwise, the revolution they set off has led to the current state in which the body has, for the most part, disappeared in economic analysis.

Teleology and Humanism: The Body in Heterodox Economic Critique

While the preceding narrative of the disappearing body provides a compelling reading of the last two centuries of economic thinking, one of our goals is to recompose this story into something different. As we stated above, we believe that no such disappearing act has occurred in the passage through modern economics. To the contrary, our reading of the traditions discussed here indicate to us simply that mainstream and neoclassical economic discourse(s) have proffered distinct "orders" of the body in each of the three phases of modernism in economics. Or, to put this differently, we discern different conceptions or materializations of the body and perhaps different places within discourse that the body has appeared in the constitution of these phases. To help illuminate our view, we call attention first to several aspects of the above story that stand in contrast to our own reading.

First, the historical narrative offered above is constructed as a teleology. As we have re-presented it, the story's structure is familiar in that it proceeds like all historical narratives that seek or trace a progressive regression or, as we put it, a deepening "fall from grace." Historians of economic thought, regardless of their training and allegiance to whatever school of economics, are prone to tell their stories of changes in economic thinking or to trace movements in the discipline as either culmination or decline. The normative elements of the story of economics' decline in regard to the disappearance of the human body and also subjectivity are apparent in the narrative of regression. The differences among "leading" economists or between the parts of their work within each of the historical phases are swept away by the force-fitting of the "key developments" in economic discourse into the constraints of the descent from Eden. Modernity, in economics, emerges as a progressive nightmare, one in which the "whole subject" and his or her "real" self—a living, breathing, thinking subject—is replaced by theoretical and formal abstraction. Indeed, the teleology of this story gives rise to the view that the victory of "humanity" represented by the Enlightenment has been deconstructed to such a degree, at least in economics, that simultaneously precise but shapeless functions and forms are now hailed in preference to the messy but distinct corporeality and subjectivity that were the innovations of the birth of the modern age in the seventeenth and eighteenth centuries.

In our reading of the history of economic thought, such a teleology has no place. As we describe below, there is neither a simple (or complex) progression nor regression on questions of the body in economics over the past two hundred years. Measured according to a different scale, the passage of mainstream neoclassical economics through various discursive forms has not meant the displacement of the body, or of subjectivity. Nor, for that matter, has it meant the increasing unreality of representations of the body (as we discuss below, the fragmentation of the body and the body without center or origin that may be said to emerge in contemporary neoclassical thinking can be thought of, ironically, as more in tune with recent "postmodern" cultural representations of the body and subjectivity). Our reading suggests that relatively discrete views of the body, its order, and distribution have existed within mainstream economics, and each can be seen, from different vantage points, as a development or retrogression in theories of the body.

Let us put this last point differently. Since we do not have in mind a particular notion of the body and its order as "correct" or as corresponding to any specific historically determined objective reality, we have no interest in preserving the idea that contemporary neoclassicals have systematically misrepresented or displaced "the body." Based both upon our reading of several representative texts and our adherence to a Foucauldian notion of the constitution of bodies within particular discursive formations, we find no basis for the claim that one representation of the body in the history of economics is empirically grounded in preference to others. The view that allows critics of neoclassicism to detect the disappearance of the human body from economic discourse is one that often presumes that an observer would know the "real" body in its appearances in economic theory if he or she did in fact see it. As Althusser argued in relation to Marx's privileged "sight" regarding the errors of Smith and Ricardo, the ability to see or not to see a particular object (in this case, the human body) in discourse depends primarily on the discursive "problematic" that is employed. It is not a matter of discovering the always-already existing body by performing a magical act of conjuration. It is rather a matter of creating the possibility, of imagining, that there is no fixity to the body and its forms of appearances as we move from one discourse to another. Thus, the view that the human body must be presented as whole rather than dispersed, as sensual rather than ethereal, as congealed rather than fluid, as bounded rather than excessive, prevents the possibility of "seeing" the body's appearance in economic discourses, such as contemporary neoclassicism, in which previous conceptions of sense, sensibility, psychology, and much else are pushed to the background.

This brings us to a second observation and our second objection to the story of the disappearance of the body in modern economics. It must be remarked that this story is of course one that shapes many criticisms of neoclassical economic discourse. That is, it is a narrative that shows up in Austrian, institutionalist, radical, Marxian, feminist, post-Keynesian and other "alternative" discursive traditions within economics. Despite differences of emphasis and detail, the common thread in all such criticisms of mainstream theory is that economics has moved increasingly over the past century away from the observable and that which can be intuited about actual human beings. What we find usually in most of these critical traditions is the charge that neoclassicals, with their preference for formalization and abstraction, have lost the "real" human being as the agent of economic behavior. Small wonder, then, that the story of the neoclassical fall from grace is dependent on a nostalgia for a time, located roughly in the early days of classical political economy or in Marx or in the early institutionalists (such as Veblen) in which human beings and their corporeal bodies were the point of departure for economic analysis. From this standpoint, the debates over objective versus subjective theories of value in exchange or over the desiring body versus the laboring body (utility versus labor) as the origin of economic activities and institutions (and therefore of economic categories) are of greater pertinence and reality than today's axiomatizing would allow for. The classical economists, and certainly the Smith of the *Moral Sentiments*, are hailed for their respect for and understanding of the complex ways in which human bodies are constituted as economic agents.

This nostalgia for the true humanist beginnings of modern economics is one we do not share. In addition to our belief that the concept of the human body has no particular form of representation or performance that correctly captures the state of human existence, we think that the humanism that informs the critics of neoclassicism is troubling in numerous ways. We have registered our objections to humanism both within and outside of economics in the previous chapter. Here we note that the notion of the centered subject in which sense experience or rational control of the body or desire or affection or any other presumed attribute of human bodies is seen as the essential and often natural determinant of the unity of the body has a long and varied history. While some of that history is one of "liberation," it is also one—as Foucault, Althusser, Balibar, and others have rightly shown—in which the notion of the "true" human body is notorious for its complicity in some of the more heinous exercises of power and violence of the modern age. These include not only the forms of discipline and punishment that are recorded in much of Foucault's writings, but also the definitions of, and practices to seek out and control, deviance that have structured Western knowledge from the birth of modern psychology to theories of colonial administration. It is by now well established in the humanities and social sciences that the early modern notions of the normal and/or natural human body and its essentialized effects have played critical roles in the elaboration of gender, race, class, and sexual differences and their perversions.

Neoclassical Theory and the Dispersion of the Body

In any event, we do not find the views of the body proffered by classical political economists (or, for that matter, by early neoclassicals or Austrians) to be "fuller" or more descriptive of reality in any sense, and we certainly hold no hope for criticisms of the neoclassical school that chastise it for its possible abandonment of the idea of the "truly human." Indeed, there is a certain refreshing quality to recent neoclassical thinking in that it mostly displaces the question of the body as origin and proliferates, instead, a differentiated, fragmented body according to various functions that do not necessarily impinge upon or govern each other. To say this differently, we are interested and regard with some degree of approval the appearance of a body in high-level neoclassical theory (as, for example, in Gerard Debreu's *Theory of Value* [1959] or in Kenneth Arrow and Frank Hahn's *General Competitive Analysis* [1971]), of bodily functions and capabilities (of consumption, production, and distribution, not to mention, in subsequent works by them and other neoclassicals, the formation of institutions, strategic interaction, and so forth) that only obliquely relate to a central, unifying dimension.

In these theoretical formulations, consumption, production, and so on emerge as composites of various elements and, as separable realms, do not inform one another either in their respective determinations (the consuming body, or its functions, can be rendered independently of the producing body, or its functions) or in their respective effects (outcomes of these discrete functions imply nothing about the unity that may be presumed to hold them together). The dispersed map of the body that some contemporary neoclassical economists have produced is one that can lead to a distinctly nonessentialist view of the body and its inscription within both discourse and society. While it may still be true that there is often an obligatory nod to the "rational/desiring/maximizing subject" as the appropriate agent in contemporary neoclassical theory, it is also true, in our view, that the consequence of axiomatizing economic behavior has been to render as discrete and distributed the forms of behavior—and thus to attribute agency to these forms themselves—that are henceforth being modeled.[10]

This, we think, is precisely the importance of general equilibrium theory for neoclassical economists: it serves to coordinate (at least in principle) the various dimensions or behaviors of the body, and thus the different agencies attached to such bodily orders, at a level separate from any individual body. The insistent expressions of admiration for the "refinement" and "power" of the Arrow-Debreu model betray a certain nervousness that, once value is unhinged from the "deep" structure of the classical and early neoclassical laboring and/or desiring bodies, a set of prices and agent plans that would reconcile the economic agencies dispersed throughout the economic space—the space of the individual agent as well as that of the economy as a whole—might not (logically) exist. In this sense, contemporary neoclassicals' own narratives of theoretical continuity (not to mention improvement) from Smith's "invisible hand" through Walras's "equation counting" to the axiomatic logic of postwar general equilibrium theory are not only teleological but disingenuous: while all three systems can be said to demonstrate the existence of coherence and harmony within a market/capitalist economy (in contrast, for example, to the tension and conflict portrayed in Marxian and other approaches), the conception of the body for which each serves as the expression and "solution" is fundamentally different. In the case of contemporary neoclassicals, the attempt to break both from the complex, prereconciled individual agent of the classicals and from the hierarchically arranged "psychologistic" or "rational" subject portrayed by the early marginalists in order to create what they considered to be a mathematically sophisticated, more scientific conception of value, one that did not simply represent the "unobservable" internal order of the body, required a new approach. It is the search for this new approach, and then its refinement and further elaboration, that has dominated neoclassical theory in the postwar period.

One of the important conditions, as we have noted above, for this "problem" to emerge was the discomfiture occasioned by the seeming identification of value with an inner (physiological and/or psychological) pleasure-seeking drive on the part of market participants. The great merit

---

[10] Brian Rotman (1993) presents a fascinating and lucid account of the notions of subjectivity that are implicit in even the most formal mathematics. While Rotman takes aim at the ghostlike, godlike subject implied in the idea of infinity (or endless counting), his discussion of the three types of subjectivity (the Subject, the Subject's Agent, and the Person) that are interpellated (Althusser's term) or assumed in modern mathematics has great promise, and at the very least shares with this chapter the view that mathematical language is not necessarily antithetical to notions of embodiment.

of Samuelson's contribution, whether or not it can be judged ultimately successful on strictly behavioralist grounds,[11] was to focus attention on the conditions associated with or required by consumer choice rather than the extent to which the actions of economic agents could be said to be governed by, and thus to adequately represent, some set of underlying processes. Still, as Samuelson himself perhaps saw coming, the substitution of "ordinal" for "cardinal" utility was only one important step in the move to the eventual denunciation of any recourse to the desiring body in producing economic analysis as a theory of choice.

In our view, revealed preference theory (along with the proof of its weak or strong equivalence to ordinal utility scales or indifference curves) helped to create the conditions for invoking a "flat" body, one without depth. Subsequently, in many quarters of neoclassicism, there would be nothing but the surface, the (internally consistent) choices made in each particular context based on the feasible alternatives available and the relevant constraints. Or as Amartya Sen has formulated it, the binary relations that are the "stuff" of rational choice would come to be seen as *reflections* of choice rather than *determinants* of it (1990, 202).

One way of understanding the effects of the neoclassical axiomatization of economic behavior, then, is to see it as having turned the body inside out. Instead of attempting to discover the hidden, because internal, driving force or self-regulating principles of the body, it has derived the body from its externality. The focus of neoclassical value theory has, in this sense, moved to the outside, to the ways in which choices are displayed on, rather than emanating from deep within, the observable planes and superficies of the body. Departing both from the classicals, for whom what was interesting and important about the body was its ability to organize and order its various rational, emotional, and physical needs and impulses, and from the early neoclassicals, for whom the body was moved and directed by the intensity of its potential energy, later neoclassical economists focused on the diverse and separable behaviors and functions of the body as they are revealed in their interactions with external objects.

If this "second marginalist revolution" of Samuelson and company began the process of dissociating consumer demand (and economic decision-making more generally) from the "amount" of utility felt or envisioned by economic agents, it also created the problem of seemingly unhinging the determination of value itself from its original human(ist) origins. Value could no longer be said to be caused by or to represent the internal order or force of the body, whether labor (embodied or commanded) or desire; instead, it was conceived to be a consequence of the

---

[11] Wong (1978) declares Samuelson's approach to have been unsuccessful because it was not ultimately able to eliminate all nonobservational concepts from consumer theory.

consistency among otherwise uncoordinated actions and plans of different agents. The project taken up by Arrow, Debreu, and other neoclassical economists from the 1950s onward was how to fragment and distribute the body across the economic space, invoking one or another of the various bodily orders or functions where appropriate, and, at the same time, to determine the conditions under which a "competitive equilibrium" for such an economy could be said to exist.

The proposed (general equilibrium) solution has become the standard for all subsequent developments within neoclassical theory. In its simplest formulations, the economy is divided into two groups of agents: producers (or firms) and consumers (or households). Avoiding unnecessary detail (and purposely shunning the mathematical formalisms prevalent in this literature), we can see that the role of producers is to choose a production plan (quantities of inputs and outputs) from the feasible set of production plans (determined by the available technology) in order to maximize profits. Consumers, on the other hand, are characterized by a set of preference relations (defined over the entire set of available commodities); their goal is to choose a consumption plan to which none is preferred, subject to the constraint that their total expenditures not exceed their total wealth. Once the total resources are introduced, and under various sets of restrictions on technology and the choice criterion, it is possible to show that a set of prices exists according to which all agents can carry out their respective plans.

This relatively simple "economy" can be, and has been, refined and extended (becoming, we should add, a veritable neoclassical industry) to include a wide variety of additional dimensions: uncertainty, savings, capital, international trade, exchange, and so on. Our point is not to review the history or what are considered to be the respective successes and failures of general equilibrium theory.[12] Rather, we hope to explain the sense in which, if only in a preliminary fashion, the body has not only *not* disappeared from late neoclassical theory, in the form of the Arrow-Debreu model, but that the multiple ways in which bodies are implicitly assumed and explicitly summoned presage what we mean by a postmodern conception of the body. We should note that whatever body is presumed by or produced through this axiomatic treatment of value is likely not the unified, "natural" body that was invoked as the ground for economic discourse in earlier periods (and, as we show below, by other schools of thought today). To presume such a body is to misrecognize other discursive existences of the body, to rule out from the start the presence of other bodies.

---

[12] Comprehensive histories are provided by Ingrao and Israel (1990) and Weintraub (1979, 1985, 1991).

What we are interested in, then, is what happens to readers when they confront the theorems, equations, and verbal explanations in and through which the Arrow-Debreu model is presented. What do we see, what kind of narrative do we construct? In particular, what images of the body emerge from our engagement with the text? In many cases, as we have discussed above, readers do not see a body at all—or at least a body that conforms to their expectations. Therefore, in searching for a particular set of familiar images, they conclude that the body is missing. Our own reading is, as we have indicated, quite different: because we refuse to make assumptions about a "naturalized" or "full" body, and thus a body that *must* serve as a ground for representation in economic discourse, we come away with a diverse (although, as we explain below, not necessarily rich or imaginative) set of corporeal images. Therefore, in our view, neoclassical value theory does represent an extended allegory about the mechanisms and capabilities of the body.[13]

We can see this in the treatment of both the "producer" and the "consumer." As we follow the presentation of the nature and role of each in the texts of neoclassical theory, we are struck by the extent to which they are treated as distinct, "relatively autonomous" sites in which various and differentiated bodily orders reside and function.

Producers, for example, are often defined as operating within a commodity space in which inputs are transformed into outputs according to technological possibilities and the rule of profit maximization. Clearly—and this we grant to the critical stories concerning neoclassical theory we referred to above—this kind of "activity" analysis (and the "netput" vector conception of the location of the results of production in commodity space) rules out some of the most famous bodies that have populated the history of treatments of production. We do not find, for example, the value-creating laboring bodies of classical theory or the pain-avoiding bodies of the early neoclassicals—or, for that matter, the heroic entrepreneurs of the Austrian economists. Indeed, the familiar outlines of laboring, pleasure-seeking, and entrepreneurial bodies, along with the (legal, sectoral) boundaries of the enterprise itself, tend to fade into the background or disappear altogether. What does emerge, however, is a different set of bodily functions, for example, those associated with the meticulous bookkeeping necessary (if only implicitly) to choose, from among all the possible production sets, those that meet the criterion of

---

[13] Much of Judith Mehta's recent work has, at least in our view, focused on exploring the problems and possibilities that exist in the relationship between observation and representation in and around economic discourse. In "Look at Me Look at You" (1999) Mehta challenges the "arbitrary and unnecessary constraints on knowledge" imposed by modernist theoretical protocols and creates a text in which she invites the reader/viewer to participate in creating a new mode of seeing.

imagined to be in the plane of the page, the straight line 0, 1 to be perpendicular to the plane of the page and pointing toward the reader. The production set of the first (resp. second) producer is the closed half-line Y_1 (resp. Y_2) in the plane 1, 2 (resp. 2, 3). Then the total production set Y is the shaded angle.

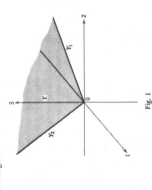

Fig. 1

In the language of the theory, this whole section is expressed as follows:

The number n of producers is a given positive integer. Each producer is indicated by an index $j = 1, \cdots, n$. The jth producer chooses a point, his production or his supply y_j, in a given non-empty subset of R^l, his production set Y_j. Given a production y_j for each producer, $y = \sum_{j=1}^{n} y_j$ is called the total production or the total supply; the set $Y = \sum_{j=1}^{n} Y_j$ is called the total production set.

3.3. Assumptions on Production Sets

All the assumptions on the sets Y_j, which are used at one point or another below, and others closely related, are discussed here. The order in which they are listed corresponds approximately to decreasing plausibility.

(a) *Y_j is closed* (continuity),

i.e., let (y_j^q) be a sequence of productions; if all the y_j^q are possible for the jth producer, and if $y_j^q \to y_j^0$, then y_j^0 is possible for the jth producer.

The rest of this section will study the continuity of γ_i. The definitions of 1.8.b–f apply only in the case where X_i is compact. It will be shown in 5.4, 5.7 how, under certain rather weak assumptions, the consumption set X_i can indeed be replaced by a certain non-empty *compact* subset of X_i. The following fundamental theorem will now be stated, discussed, and proved:

(1) *If X_i is compact, convex, and if (p^0, w^0) is a point of S, such that $w_i^0 \neq Min\ p^0 \cdot X_i$, then γ_i is continuous at (p^0, w^0).*

In other words, given a compact, convex consumption set X_i, and a price-wealth pair (p^0, w^0) in S_i, the correspondence γ_i is indeed continuous at the point (p^0, w^0) provided one rules out the exceptional case where $w_i^0 = Min\ p^0 \cdot X_i$, i.e., where the wealth w_i^0 is so small that for any smaller wealth there would be no possible consumption satisfying the wealth constraint.

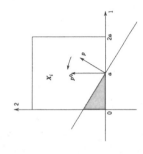

Fig. 5

Figure 5 shows how γ_i may not be continuous if $w_i^0 = Min\ p^0 \cdot X_i$. The set X_i is the closed square with edge 2. Consider $p^0 = (0, 1)$ and $w_i^0 = 0$; the corresponding wealth hyperplane is the straight line 0, 1. The exceptional case $w_i^0 = Min\ p^0 \cdot X_i$ occurs, i.e., there is no point of X_i below the wealth hyperplane. Let then a be the point $(1, 0)$, and let p, w, tend to p^0, w_i^0 in such a way that the corresponding wealth hyperplane rotates around a as indicated in the figure. As long as $p \neq p^0$, the set $\gamma_i(p, w)$ is the shaded region whose limit is the closed segment $[0, a]$. However $\gamma_i(p^0, w^0)$ is the closed segment $[0, 2a]$.

Figure 3.3. Gerard Debreu, *Theory of Value* (1959). Photo: Preston Thomas for Visual Ear. (Permission: Yale University Press.)

profit maximization. Without this practice of accounting, of keeping track of inputs and outputs (and their respective "given" prices), no choice of profit-maximizing production plans would be possible. Perhaps even more important (certainly in terms of explicit discussion), we see the bodily orders and capabilities associated with the assembly, transformation, repackaging, and so on of one set of objects (inputs) in order to end up with a different set of objects (outputs, including new potential inputs for the next round of production). Neoclassical production is thus rendered as a collection or assemblage of heterogeneous elements and materials, a set of operational linkages and external relations between things, machine connections (if not a "whole" machine), in which a discontinuous series of bodily organs, processes, and flows (for example, "the labor of a coal miner, of a truck driver, of a member of some category of teachers, of engineers, of draftsmen, of executives, etc." [Debreu 1959, 30–31]) come together with other things (the divisible "raw materials, semifinished products; land and equipment or their uses . . . at various dates and locations" [38]) according to the available codes, the technologies of production.

It is the characteristics of these codes that tend to receive the most attention in neoclassical theories of production. Here we find the ubiquitous discussions of the assumptions, conventions, and restrictions required to define a "closed, convex cone" of production possibilities. Technology, in this scheme, plays the dual role of being an extension of the body, the ability to coordinate the alignment of services and other inputs at particular points in space and time in order to produce outputs, and a way of writing on the body, to the extent that neoclassical economists have taken on the project of specifying the rules that these technologies must adhere to so that firms' output supply functions assume the appropriate forms. In the first case, then, the technical codes invoke a body or corporeal agency that determines the possible linkages among and between factor services and (produced and nonproduced) inputs. In the second case, the body operates as a surface on which the requirements proposed by the theorists can be inscribed. Both are central to the neoclassical theory of production.

What is apparent (at least to us) in this treatment is that production itself is deprived of any depth (in comparison to other, classical or early neoclassical theories, that is). It serves merely to determine a particular vector of outputs from the set of all possible outputs. Production is not conceived to be governed, for example, by the bodily imperative of reproduction (as it was for the classicals and still is for the Sraffians) or of the body's experience of pain or disutility (which could be compensated by a corresponding increase in utility in consumption for Jevons and the other early neoclassicals). Instead, the realm of production in contemporary neoclassical theory consists of a diverse set of bodily functions and activities—the calculations of profit-maximizing conditions, the flows and intensities of factor services, the ability to assemble or bring together disparate body movements and objects, and so on—which have no "underlying" purpose or "compensating" relief other than to move from one point to another through commodity space.

In our view, then, neoclassical economists' theory of production, in eschewing both the unity of a single "productive" or "entrepreneurial" body and any hierarchy of functions and requirements, creates an open-ended terrain in which distinct and separate bodily orders literally meet and engage in activities that result in the supply of new commodity outputs. Obviously, this horizontally (dis)integrated conception of the "producing" body is similar, in outline, to what some regard as a pure "machine." Yet, of course, this machinic conception of the body has a long history in Western thought, and, while subject to a humanist critique, it is, nonetheless, still one important way in which bodies have long been recognized, known, and performed in economics and elsewhere.[14]

What, then, on the consumer side? Here we encounter, once again, a diverse set of bodily surfaces that are written on and of bodily functions and orders that are invoked as economic agencies in their own right. We recall that the role of consumers in neoclassical theory is to choose, from the array of available commodities, a plan of consumption whose monetary value is less than or equal to their total wealth. That wealth derives from the sale of factor services and any other goods to, plus the receipt of profits (if and when they are shareholders) from, producers. Consumers' bodies therefore enact a variety of different agencies. For example, they are conceived to be endowed with, and thus are capable of performing, factor services. According to Arrow and Hahn (1971, 75), "among the endowments of the household, the most important in practice are the capacities to perform different types of labor." The kind and amount of labor that any consumer decides to demand and supply are seen to be constrained by such factors as the kinds of skills they possess, the amount of time of which they dispose, and their ability to withstand the "arduousness" of the tasks involved. Consumers are not only characterized by the ability to furnish and execute labor services; they also enjoy non-laboring time in the form of leisure. Thus, for example, if a consumer is capable of teaching for twelve hours, s/he can decide to teach for eight

---

[14] According to Anson Rabinbach (1990, 51), "the metaphor of the machine in physiology has roots in Aristotle's thought and was well established by the time Vesalius described the human organism as 'factory' in the mid–sixteenth century." Not surprisingly, the Industrial Revolution gave additional impetus to machinic conceptions of the body, the most famous of which is Julien Offray de La Mettrie's eighteenth-century treatise *Man a Machine* (1748). See also Cohen-Rosenfield 1968.

hours and enjoy "teaching leisure" for four hours (Arrow and Hahn (1971, 75). In addition, since consumption is assumed to take time, consumers are, in effect, conceived to pass through or enact different bodily orders during any given period of time (day, year, or lifetime): they can perform some or all of different kinds of labor, spend their time not working, and/or consume commodities. Each of these activities is based on qualitatively different and changing capabilities and orders of the body, various processes, intensities, and organs, as an individual passes through and experiences each of these ways of spending time. Presumably, the only thing that the different orders and combinations of laboring/not working/ consuming bodies have in common is that they have to endure or enjoy these activities within the constraints of the available time.

Not surprisingly—given the importance they attribute to consumer choice and, at the same time, their aversion to invoking the inner, "psychologistic" assumptions of early neoclassical theory—neoclassical economists devote the major part of their efforts in this area to discussing the conditions under which consumers decide how much and what kinds of (net) labor services to offer and what commodities to purchase. The focus here is on the nature of the preference (pre)orderings that are seen to guide and thus to be expressed in the choices that consumers make. Thus, "the preference ordering of the ith consumer completely expresses his tastes with regard to food, clothing, housing, . . . labor and also to consumption at some date or some location rather than another" (Debreu 1959, 54). As in the case of technology, consuming bodies are invoked in two different senses: on one hand, they consist of the specific and differentiated tastes or preferences, the particular consumption codes, whereby individuals express their interest in performing factor services and in consuming outputs over all possibilities; on the other hand, they represent the material on which neoclassical economists can write the appropriate codes (expressed, e.g., as insatiability, continuity, and convexity) such that the resulting demands and supplies are "well behaved." The importance of these codes is that it becomes unnecessary to peer inside, to invoke any kind of deep structure of "utility" that can be said to govern, the bodies of consumers. Instead, the utility functions that consumers are seen to "maximize" are merely the numerical representations of their stated (or revealed) preferences. In this sense, everything that consumers do (or are restricted to do) resides on the surface.

Of course, the focus on the choices that consumers make in the different domains of offering factor services and demanding commodities, constrained solely by wealth or budgetary considerations (along with restrictions on preference orderings), leaves open the possibility that the separable decision units, and hence the bodily functions to which they refer, may not cohere in any simple fashion. A similar issue arises in the case of production: even in the presence of technological codes that serve to align the bodies and inputs so that a profit-maximizing netput vector can be said to exist, the different bodily orders may operate with greater or lesser degrees of autonomy than a unified, fully machinelike, body would allow. In both cases, we may observe what Jon Elster (1986) has referred to as the "multiple self." Elster, who is far from being a critic of neoclassicism and its conception of methodological individualism and rational choice, and the other contributors to his important edited volume recognize that when the unified, singular body (as traditionally understood) is fragmented into different orders or functions and scattered within any individual sphere and throughout the economic space as a whole (as we have seen in general equilibrium theory), a wide variety of possible new agencies emerge. And when economists (and other rational-choice theorists) attempt to account for the interaction among these body parts, they begin to challenge the usual presumption of combination and coordination, leading to a proliferation of forms of disunity—from the "loosely integrated self" to an infinitely fragmented, "no self" conception of the body. In our view, it is precisely the attempt on the part of Samuelson, Arrow, Debreu, and others to displace the deep, hierarchical ordering of the body in favor of theories of consumption, production, and distribution based on the horizontal linkages among a wide variety of bodily functions that leads to the differentiated and dispersed (what we prefer to call a postmodern) body.[15]

One way of understanding the effects of the neoclassical axiomatization of economic behavior, then, is to see it as having turned the body inside out.[16] Instead of attempting to discover the hidden, because internal, driving force or self-regulating principles of the body, it has derived the body from its externality, from its surface fragmentation and dispersion.

The Organic Unity of the Body in Classical Political Economy

We compare this fragmentation and dispersion with the work of the classical political economists who, we believe, were able to produce a rich the-

[15] This is not to say that because we view with a great deal of interest the emergence of a postmodern treatment of the body in at least some of the "classic" texts by neoclassical economists, we simply applaud their efforts or the results of their work. Quite the contrary. The relative lack of interest on the part of neoclassicals in exploring the ways in which bodies are produced and inscribed in the discipline of economics and in "real" economies means that we will have to borrow and invent metaphors and languages beyond those of neoclassical economics in order to develop appropriate conceptions of the body.

[16] Notions of the "inside-out" body and other related respatializations of the body in philosophy and cultural theory can be found in such important poststructuralist and feminist works as Deleuze and Guattari 1983; Lyotard 1993; and Grosz 1994.

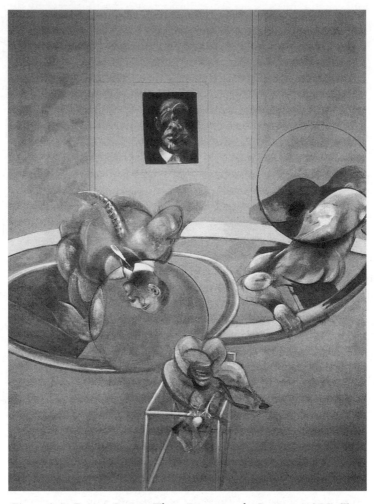

Figure 3.4. Francis Bacon, *Three Figures and a Portrait* (1975). Tate
Gallery, London. (Credit: Tate Gallery, London/Art Resource, New
York.)

ory of the differentiated body. In fact, reading Smith has led us to think
that economics has suffered a relative impoverishment in the language of
description of the body if not in its ultimate conception. While for Smith
and several of the others, the complexly differentiated human body—with
its imperatives, instincts, artifices, and constraints—is a site of mutual
effectivity, the body and subject find at the point of ultimate determination an organic totality in which all elements seem to cohere. One way of

seeing this in Smith, for example, is by noting how his vision of society and the body come to both mirror and determine one another. Just as the social body can be the harmonious outcome of the principle of the division of labor (and here, we note that the division of labor is the key to the material abundance for the satisfaction of individual bodies promised by industrial rule), so the body itself is divided into various components that are or can be harmoniously conjoined in the person of discretion and moral sensibility.[17]

The satisfying completeness with which classicals, such as Smith and his contemporary Hume, described the body and its component sensations and motives, especially in pursuit of moral refinement, has been remarked upon by literary theorists and economists alike. In *Sensibility*, Janet Todd regards Smith's *Theory of Moral Sentiments* as "the last major work of the period to admit the sentimental aim of trying systematically to link morality and emotion" (1986, 27). For Todd, the period of sentimental literature and moral tracts, stretching roughly from the 1740s to the 1770s in Europe, was one in which such emotions or sentiments as "sympathy," a key concept for both Hume and Smith, functioned not only to organize the social body, but individual bodies as well. Sympathy, as rendered in medical tracts of the time, allowed "organs to communicate with each other and to react and suffer together" (27). The notion of sentiment itself, dominant in the heyday of Hume and Smith, connected bodily sensibilities with moral concerns. Sentiment was understood as "thought, often an elevated one, influenced by emotion, a combining of heart with head or an emotional impulse leading to an opinion or principle" (7). The role of sentimental literature was the elicitation of an emotional response, perhaps the outpouring of "tears and trembling," through which the body registered its "sympathy" with the plight of others. The heightened sense of experience condensed in the notion of sympathy signified a "fullness" of the body, its ability to feel and express in

---

[17] It is impossible to leave this topic without some comment on Catherine Gallagher's (1987) work on Malthus. In her reading, Malthus emerges as the champion of the body, while Smith (at least in her interpretation of Malthus's position) is cast as an enemy of the body. Gallagher's argument depends upon her novel reading of Malthus's criticism of Smith's rendition of the labor theory of value, and Malthus's emendations to that theory via his rethinking of the Smithian distinction between productive and unproductive labor. Whatever the status of this argument, Gallagher raises important ideas regarding the seeming contradiction between the healthy body and the health of the social body in Malthus's theory of population. While Malthus may have focused on the contradiction by showing that the healthy and normal demands (for food and sex) of the body lead to an enfeeblement of the social body, Smith took up this contradiction too, but he looked at the overworked and fatigued body of the industrial worker as a condition of the general prosperity of society. For more on this point, see note 20 below.

intricate ways the relations among organs and the sentiments arising from them.[18]

The economist Eugene Rotwein (Hume 1970) also comments on the harmony of disparate bodily elements brought to unity in the rich descriptions of Hume, Smith, and others. Speaking of Hume, Rotwein states that his economic thought "displays an awareness of the complex interrelations between passions, or of the essentially organic character of human experience" (lii). Rotwein credits Hume with an analysis that "conveys an appreciation of the ineffable density of human behaviour and an understanding of the opposing forces on which it rests" (lii). Indeed, according to Rotwein, Hume's complicated treatment of human behavior and the body was far more advanced than the later "nineteenth century liaison with psychological hedonism" (li) found in Jevons and other neoclassical thinkers.

Hume's treatment, though, tends toward a theory of moderation and refinement (just as Smith in the *Moral Sentiments* stresses self-command and desire for approbation). The body that achieves balance—the morally and aesthetically refined body—is the one that avoids excess. As Hume states, "human happiness . . . seems to consist in three ingredients; action, pleasure, and indolence" (1970, 21). But while "these ingredients ought to be mixed in different proportions" so that "no one ingredient . . . be entirely wanting" (21), their combination can be pernicious when carried to degrees of excess. The healthy body, the norm for a prosperous society, is one in which the appropriate admixture of these ingredients achieves refinement. Overall, in Hume, the body's fullness—its "organic character"—is expressed by reference to a multitude of interwoven and even contradictory passions, affections, and thoughts that, properly directed, leads to beneficence and ultimately "industry, knowledge, and humanity" (23).

---

[18] The rise and fall of sentimental literature in the eighteenth century left in its wake a conception of the body that was particularly attached to women. Perhaps, then, we can see Smith's *Theory of Moral Sentiments* not just as the crowning moment of "bourgeois psychology," as Harvie Ferguson (1990, 188) would have it, but also as a text grappling with the problem of moral sensibilities in relation to gendered bodies. Todd, for example, tells us that "the female body became an organism peculiarly susceptible to influence. Women were thought to express emotions with their bodies more sincerely and spontaneously than men; hence their propensity to crying, blushing, and fainting. At the same time, such a susceptible organism could easily become erratic and deranged" (1986, 19). Thus, hysteria signified the limit condition of moral sentiments as it was understood to be "an exaggeration of very human susceptibility or physical sensibility" (19). Todd quotes from Foucault in this regard: "the entire female body is riddled by obscure but strangely direct paths of sympathy . . . [F]rom one extremity of its organic space to the other, it encloses a perpetual possibility of hysteria. The sympathetic sensibility of her organism . . . condemns a woman . . . to diseases of the nerves" (19).

Figure 3.5. Thomas Frye, *Henry Crispe of the Custom House* (1746). Oil on canvas, 124.3 x 101.6 cm., Tate Gallery, London. (Credit: Tate Gallery, London/Art Resource, New York.)

This fullness of the body was part of the larger movement to view the individual subject and his or her body as an organic unity. Or, to use Harvie Ferguson's phrase, the human body was now thought to be "a cosmos in its own right" (1990, 178). The body as organic unity is one that has depth (perhaps in contrast to the more horizontal or "flat" arrangement of body functions in the neoclassical version) because of the principles of utility (or labor, if one prefers a more Marxian reading of the classicals), sympathy, and affection.[19] The classical body can be viewed

[19] In the expansive literature on theories of value in economics, the divide is drawn so sharply that often labor and utility are viewed as incompatible principles, certainly in the determination of value. This divide has unfortunately also obscured the forms of determination between, and admixtures of, labor and utility that can be found in most traditions of

as an expressive totality in that it can always signify the essential determinants of its constitution and disposition. Hence, as we say above, despite its beautiful complexity, especially in the hands of Smith, the body in classical political economy is one in which difference is always sublated or resolved by subsumption into a higher unity. It is not a discontinuous body. Again, the mischief caused by such a notion of the organically unified, though internally differentiated body—a body with an ultimate center, and usually, therefore, signifying a particular "normal" gender, race, sexuality, and so forth—has been extensive.

It is striking, then, to see the extent to which the humanist bias gives rise to the view that mainstream economics has all but made the human body disappear, and the extent to which a return to the body, à la the classicals, is advocated. We conclude this chapter with a brief discussion of how the alternative outline we propose conflicts with the humanist purposes of some critics of neoclassical economics—here we concentrate on some parts of the Marxian and feminist enterprises in economics—that purportedly seek to reinscribe the "whole" human body within economic discourse.

Marxian Value Theory and the Laboring Body

As we have noted, one crucial element of classical political economy that was eventually displaced in the neoclassical revolution of the nineteenth century was the idea that labor was a primary or even exclusive determinant of value. Now, readings of Marx that posit him either as the last of the great classicals or as the leading left-wing critic of political economy often share in common the claim that Marx extracted from the classicals the view that labor is the sole source of value. Thus, as we

---

economic thought. While the neoclassical revolution certainly had room for a consideration of the intersection of these principles, most often it took the form of asserting the aversion for labor (disutility) that workers would experience after some point of exertion. Hume, in interesting contrast, based much of his economic thought on the idea that a main force guiding individual and therefore social prosperity was the desire for labor (and thereby gain). As he states it, "there is no craving or demand of the human mind more constant and insatiable than that for exercise and employment; and this desire seems the foundation of most of our passions and pursuits. Deprive a man of business and serious occupation, he runs restless from one amusement to another; and the weight and oppression, which he feels from idleness, is so great, that he forgets the ruin which must follow him from his immoderate expences. Give him a more harmless ways of employing his mind or body, he is satisfied, and feels no longer that insatiable thirst after pleasure. But if the employment you give him be lucrative, especially if the profit be attached to every particular exertion of industry, he has gain so often in his eye, that he acquires, by degrees, a passion for it, and knows no such pleasure as that of seeing the daily encrease of his fortune" (1970, 53).

get even in such a sophisticated reader of Marx and the classicals as Maurice Dobb (1973), Marx is applauded for his consistent formulation of a labor theory of value, and, therefore, for his adherence to the view that social relations of production, which are objective and observable, determine the distribution of social labor and the exchange-value of commodities. For Dobb, as for many other Marxists, the fact that individuals may be desiring beings and motivated in their behaviors by instinct, affection, emotion, and so forth is relegated to the status of secondary phenomena insofar as the determination of value, the social allocation of labor, and the distribution of income and wealth are involved. For many Marxists, the essential causes of economic activity are labor and production. Thus, the laboring body, rendered in some versions of this story as a truly transhistorical corporeal entity, is given pride of place in establishing the conditions for that which is uniquely human and thereby economic. As Jean Baudrillard (1975) and others—such as Georges Bataille (1991) and Gilles Deleuze and Felix Guattari (1983)—have pointed out, this "productionist" bias of Marxists has been the grounds by which Marxism has discursively excluded libido, excess, and true expenditure in economic theory.

Contemporary Marxian critics in the field of economics, then, often prefer to resurrect the nineteenth-century debates over the correct attribution of value to either desire or labor. Their critique of neoclassical theory devolves on the claim that the bourgeois individualism, naturalism, and arcane abstraction consequent upon the use of axiomatic formulations in neoclassicism obscure the true (because transhistorical) conditions under which economic activities and institutions arise. Whereas production is viewed as ubiquitous across epochs and geographical boundaries, desire and utility maximization are seen as limited in historical importance to capitalist societies and, even there, are more a consequence of a hegemonic false consciousness imposed by the self-promotion of the bourgeoisie (to hide the "fact" of exploitation) than the objective condition of life under capitalism. The modernism of much Marxism consists at least partly in its insistence in finding an ontological referent for the essential cause—labor—that emerges in Marxian theory as the source of value. The laboring body and the conditions of work, then, take precedence in everything from an estimation of the good life (the elimination of alienation in work) to the primacy of factory struggles in the movements to supersede capitalism.

It is interesting to note that one source of debate even within such a productionist terrain has been different readings on the exact connection Marx makes between labor and the condition and trajectory of the body. Rabinbach tells us, for example, that Marx moved in the course of his writings from an early view (in the *Economic and Philosophic Manu-*

Figure 3.6. Hugo Gellert, "Primary Accumulation" (1934). *Karl Marx' "Capital" in Lithographs* (New York: Ray Long and Richard R. Smith, 1934). (Permission: Reference Center for Marxist Studies, New York.)

scripts) that labor is invigorating and the wellspring of human freedom and liberation to a later view (in *Capital*) that labor is fatiguing and constraining of human freedom. For Rabinbach, then, Marx's discovery of "energy" as the abstract concept of productive force led him to redefine "human freedom from emancipation *through* labor to emancipation *from* labor" (1990, 80).

This view, incidentally, can be compared with Smith's paradoxical presentation of labor in *The Wealth of Nations*, where labor is first seen as the means by which human beings extend, represent, and augment their bodily powers by becoming more dexterous and efficient as the result of the division of social labor. When the division of labor is *not* developed,

Smith says, "a man commonly saunters a little in turning his hand from one sort of employment to another. . . . The habit of sauntering and of indolent careless application . . . renders him almost always slothful and lazy, and incapable of any vigorous application even on the most pressing occasions" (1965, 8–9). Smith states in making his initial case for the division of labor that "the certainty of being able to exchange all that surplus part of the produce of his own labour . . . for such parts of the produce of other men's labour . . . encourages every man to apply himself to a particular occupation, and to cultivate and bring to perfection whatever talent or genius he may possess" (15). This benevolent view of the division of labor contrasts with Smith's later depressing remarks, also in *The Wealth of Nations*, that labor divided by task and specialization becomes pure drudgery and leads to stupefaction and the reduction rather than the extension of the body's powers.[20]

In the tension between the augmenting power of labor and its diminution of the body's capabilities, we can see as well Bataille's point that

[20] In book 5 of *The Wealth of Nations*, in the fascinating section on the question of whether public expenditure on the education of youth is a necessary or even useful expense, Smith provides this dismal portrait, rivaling in its bleakness Engels's descriptions seventy years later of the depravity of industrialized labor: "The man whose whole life is spent in performing a few simple operations, of which the effects too are, perhaps, always the same, or very nearly the same, has no occasion to exert his understanding, or to exercise his invention in finding out expedients for removing difficulties which never occur. He naturally loses, therefore, his habit of such exertion, and generally becomes as stupid and ignorant as it is possible for a human creature to become. The torpor of his mind renders him, not only incapable of relishing or bearing a part in any rational conversation, but of conceiving any generous, noble, or tender sentiment, and consequently of forming any just judgment concerning many even of the ordinary duties of private life. . . . The uniformity of his stationary life naturally corrupts the courage of his mind . . . [I]t corrupts even the activity of his body, and renders him incapable of exerting his strength with vigour and perseverance, in any other employment than that to which he has been bred. His dexterity at his own particular trade seems, in this manner, to be acquired at the expence of his intellectual, social, and martial virtues" (1965, 734–35). As though this were not enough, Smith goes on to contrast the worker in the most advanced industrialized processes with those in "the barbarous societies." In this comparison, the noble savage clearly wins out because, as Smith puts it, "in such societies the varied occupations of every man oblige every man to exert his capacity, and to invent expedients for removing difficulties which are continually occurring. Invention is kept alive, and the mind is not suffered to fall into that drowsy stupidity, which, in a civilized society, seems to benumb the understanding of almost all the inferior ranks of people" (735). The sapping of the modern worker's vitality and strength developed into a main concern of social science, says Rabinbach in *The Human Motor*. Rabinbach dates this development, a century after Smith's comments, in late-nineteenth-century studies of energetics and especially of the problem of fatigue: "fatigue thus became the most apparent and distinctive sign of the external limits of body and mind, the most reliable indicator of the need to conserve and restrict the waste and misuse of the body's unique capital—its labor power" (1990, 6). For Rabinbach, fatigue's "ubiquity was evidence of the body's stubborn subversion of modernity" (6), a point, we see, anticipated a century earlier by Smith.

labor provides the basis for regulation and the expenditure of libidinal energy whose very excess threatens the order of social relations. In *Erotism*, Bataille tells us that taboos function in most societies to channel creative and destructive forces into work: "taboos are there to make work possible; work is productive" (1986, 68). Work is the means by which sexual exuberance and violence are blocked, and it also functions to alienate humans from their "animal nature," expressed precisely in the sexual excesses lurking within human bodies. In a wonderful twist on the "liberation" of humans from labor promised by Marxist visions of the utopia to come, Bataille sees the "underworld" or, as he connects it to Marx—the lumpenproletariat—as true performers of sexual freedom and violence. The lumpenproletariat is freed from the regimen of work and discipline; "extreme poverty releases men from the taboos that make human beings of them, not as transgression does, but in that a sort of hopelessness, not absolute perhaps, gives the animal impulses free rein" (135). Hence, the body's potential to realize libidinal surpluses is constrained by the body's potential to produce "surplus" commodities. The laboring class may be libidinally exhausted, while the "underclass" and those living off the worker's surplus, for whom leisure is the primary state of life and not a potential, are destined for sexual exuberance.

We leave for a later chapter the elaboration of the idea that, rather than codifying the classicals' laboring body as a first principle, Marx can be said to disrupt the order of the body established in classical political economy and in much of the Marxian tradition. On this view, Marx is not the inventor of a new anthropology (his work, Althusser argued, stands as a sharp rupture from the humanist anthropology that preceded him). Briefly stated, Marx's contributions can be viewed more along the lines of presenting the human body as a register of class and other capitalist economic and noneconomic processes, a place where the effects of capitalism are largely inscribed, rather than the site of the privileged origin (through labor) of socioeconomic relations. In other words, the body that Marx presents in his writings is overdetermined and has no center or essential unity other than that which is the effect of the historical conditions of production, circulation, distribution, consumption and so forth.[21] In this limited sense, Marx's body, in our view, may be closer to some

---

[21] Elaine Scarry's (1985, 243–77) extended reflection on Marx's materialism stresses the sense in which the body "makes" and "unmakes" itself while it makes and unmakes the world. In her reading of Marx, the body is at once an artifact and something that is employed in artificing. The body is not fixed in this view, and its relation to "the world" is in constant flux, just as the body itself is made, remade, and destroyed through its own actions, devices, and products. Scarry's discussion moves us part of the way toward our view that labor and bodies, for Marx, are constructed and deconstructed in the movement of history. They have no pride of place, for us, as the fixed starting point for this same movement.

current neoclassical renditions, at least insofar as the body is differentiated, dispersed, and brought to temporary unity by specific productions
rather than by the presumption of its essentiality.

The problem, then, for some of the Marxian critics of neoclassical
theory is that the story they prefer revives a view of the body and subjectivity that is fully part of the modernist project to promote an exhaustive
notion of "Man." In this regard, the postmodern moments of Marxism
are suppressed, and the affinity that Marxists may have with other developments within which the humanism of the classicals is finally displaced
is ignored. The retention of the laboring body as prime cause of social
and economic relations does little to undermine the humanist essentialism
that, purportedly, many Marxists have been at pains to attack over the
course of the last century. While recent neoclassicals and Marxists may
make absurd bedmates, there is a sense in which Marxists can supplement
rather than blunt their attacks on bourgeois economics and social order
by acknowledging the fragmentation of the human body and the dismemberment of theoretical humanism that may have been accomplished by
some neoclassicals.

Feminism and Gendering: Approaching or Departing from the Humanist Body?

The recent emergence of feminism in economics is partly responsible
for putting questions of bodies—gendered, sexualized, reproducible and
reproducing—on the agenda for economists. The brilliance of the feminist critique has been to show that the concepts of the body that have
characterized all of the schools of modern economic thought—from
the mainstream to the most radical—have been gendered and therefore
"partial" in their implications. The desiring body and its rational monitor
have been aptly shown to express degrees of maleness (and whiteness and
Europeanness and heterosexuality) that have henceforth been ignored
in economic discourse. For example, the pathbreaking article by Julie
Matthaei (1995) on gay and straight sexualities as they are socially and
economically constructed calls attention, among other things, to how
some forms of (hetero)sexuality have been considered so "normal"—for
economists, among others—as to require little commentary and no consequent analysis.

Yet, current discussions among some feminist economists bear witness
to a continuing tension, one in which the hierarchical model of subjectivity and "the body" represented by the nineteenth-century neoclassicals
is sometimes challenged and, at other times, upheld. For other feminist
economists, tired of being forced to state all "scientific" theses in the form

of rational-choice problems (including sexual "preference" itself, as both Matthaei and Lee Badgett [1998] have noted), the promise is held out that some suitably revised economic theory can indeed capture and express a view of the "total" and real human body. This, for example, can be seen in "additive" conceptions of the human body so as to now "include" female bodily functions, and affections that are thought to be mostly "feminine," in existing models of economic behavior.

Such a move may be seen, to take just one example, in Julie Nelson's important article (1993) on the predominant "masculinity" of mainstream economics. Nelson seeks to avoid the reinscription of the Cartesian duality in economics that simply distinguishes (and valorizes) masculine in contrast to feminine forms of subjectivity and economic behavior. But in eschewing "feminine" economics as the alternative to "masculine" economics, Nelson calls for economics to be a "human science in the pursuit of human ends" (33). This "human science" is built on combining—even in constructive relief or critique—those elements that are gender-distinguishing in character. Resorting to an unspoken presumption about human needs and a universal body (for what else does Nelson mean when she urges us to consider "focusing economics on the provisioning of human life, that is, on the commodities and processes necessary to human survival" [32]?), Nelson trumps the Cartesian split by a totalizing move characteristic of humanist discourse. In her incisive critique of Nelson, Rhonda Williams (1993) sees Nelson's solution to the Cartesian split as speaking from "unified and stable conceptualizations of masculinity, femininity, and humanity" (148), which, we might add, are directed toward normalizing some particular conception of the human body, one that now includes "both sides" of the gender divide. While feminists may be loathe to regard the classicals as the "fathers" of the discipline, there may be a tendency by some to find favor in the discussions of altruism, sympathy, emotion, and much else that had their discursive appearance with the classicals and have since faded from view.

An arresting alternative to the implicit humanism of some feminist economics is contributed by Gillian Hewitson, whose project to date (1999, 2001) has been to bring to bear feminist poststructuralist concepts and perspectives on both existing feminist economics and nonfeminist neoclassical theory.[22] As Hewitson notes (1999), various feminist approaches

---

[22] In addition to Hewitson's work, we also see much to gain in Richard Cornwall's (1997, 1998) call for and pursuit of "queer political economy." Cornwall has a great deal to say about identities and bodies with which we are in fundamental agreement: "[the] dependence of sexual identities on culturally inherited discursive structures also means that what is 'lesbian' and what is 'gay' are fluid and are historically contingent on other social constructions. This poses a danger for economists who are as mentally conditioned as any other market-players to seek discrete, firm identities which can be captured by yes/no decisions (zero/one

in economics (which she lumps under the common heading of "gender feminism") have come to rely on the sex/gender distinction, where sex refers to "natural," anatomical differences between the bodies of men and women while gender is a socially constructed (and acquired) phenomenon. In Hewitson's view, while the distinction between sex and gender may have served the feminist cause by providing a way of rejecting justifications or rationalizations of women's subordination that are premised on biological or naturalistic arguments, it also reproduces the modernist mind/body, culture/nature, and representation/real dichotomies that structure existing gender-biased laws and forms of knowledge within economics. The alternative that Hewitson outlines is based on the idea that both sexed bodies and gendered identities are products of culture—"its discourses and institutional forms"—and hence not natural.[23] Thus, for example, "a woman exhibiting the masculine trait of raising her voice during an argument may be labeled hysterical, whereas a man exhibiting the same trait would be seen as forceful. In each case, the gendered characteristic is produced as meaningful only in relation to the body" (1999, 117). Hewitson's feminist poststructuralist alternative consists of seeing the dominant neoclassical representation as a discourse that actively produces—instead of, as other feminists would have it, merely denying or misrepresenting—notions of subjectivity as embodied sexed subjectivities.

By taking such a poststructuralist tack, Hewitson is able to criticize neoclassical models of surrogate motherhood for their tendency to "disembody" pregnant women in positing the "womb as capital" and their conceptual separation of the fetus from the pregnant woman as a distinct, individual entity, owning its "own" body in the womb. As Hewitson points out, positing the womb as capital turns the surrogate mother into a "self-possessive individual," one who can rent out her capital in exchange for payment, but who therefore loses her particular identity as a sexed body and, instead, enters into neoclassical discourse as a "contracting liberal individual." In Hewitson's view, the surrogate mother "conceptually separate from the fetus, becomes a 'universal,' seemingly

---

dummy variables) across history" (1998, 77). Cornwall's statement can be read to include, as well, our view of the fluidity of notions of bodies (including their "sexuality") and also of how economists think about the question of whether or not, if, and when bodies do exist in some discursive space (if one "queers" the body, for example, would it be recognizable to those looking for the body of classical political economy, say?).

[23] According to Elizabeth Grosz (1994, 23), "the body must be regarded as the site of social, political, cultural, and geographic inscriptions, production, or constitution. The body is not opposed to culture, a resistant throw-back to a natural past; it is itself cultural, the cultural, product." Birke (2000), Shildrick and Price (1998), and Haraway (1991) offer explicit feminist engagements with, but different reconceptualizations of, the "biological" (and biomedical) body.

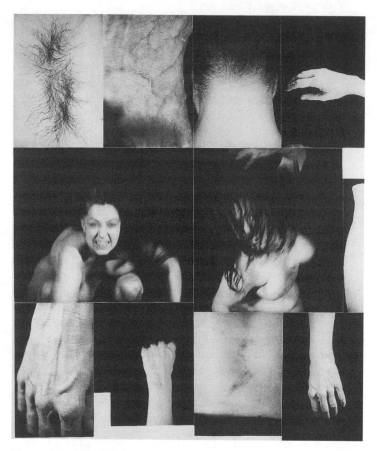

Figure 3.7. Kiki Smith, *Las Animas* (1997). Photogravure, 60 x 49 1/4″. (Credit: Collection Fred Jones Jr. Museum of Art, University of Oklahoma, Gift of the Jerome Westheimer Family, 1999; published by Universal Limited Art, Inc.)

disembodied, rational agent with the property rights of a citizen of the civil sphere, who is therefore able to undertake voluntary exchanges in that sphere." But Hewitson is careful in her analysis and critique of this form of disembodiment not to posit some other "natural," centered body—existing "out there"—as the ground for a truer conception of surrogacy. In Hewitson's work, therefore, the "real" sexed, female body is not so much missing from neoclassical discourse as it is simply discursively constructed out of existence (or, at best, in contradiction).

It is still uncertain, however, whether or not many feminists in economics will go the route of Hewitson and other critics of "modernism" in economics,[24] or will simply insist upon a more inclusive and complete view of the human body, as though the discursive constitution of different types and orders of the body could somehow resolve into a singular formulation.[25]

Postmodern Conceptions of the Body and Contemporary Economics

The postmodern body resists (and comprises an alternative to) the unified and centered representations of the body depicted and invoked by economic modernists. To choose but one example from the vast literature, the body that is presaged—if not, in our view, creatively explored and developed—by neoclassical general equilibrium theory leads in the direction of the body described by Shelley Jackson (1997):

> It's not what we wish it were.
>
> The real body, which we have denied representation, is completely inimical to our wishful thinking about the self. We would like to be unitary, controlled from on top, visible, self-contained. We represent ourselves that way, and define our failures to be so, if we cannot ignore them, as disease, hysteria, anomaly. However:
>
> The banished body is unhierarchical.
>
> It registers local intensities, not arguments. It is a field of sensations juxtaposed in space.
>
> It is vague about size and location, unclear on measurements of all kinds, bad at telling time (though good at keeping it).
>
> It is capacious, doesn't object to paradox, includes opposites—doesn't know what opposites are.

[24] But see Badgett's (1995b) balanced and thoughtful note on the possibility of taking "postmodernism" seriously in feminist economics.

[25] In her study of women's bodies and their alternative depiction in modern medical science and by women subjected to medical practices, Emily Martin mostly decries the "alienation" that she believes to be attendant upon the "fragmentation" of women's bodies in scientific consciousness. Drawing on the Marxian critique of alienation and the feminist assault on male domination in the history of medical science, Martin finds the metaphors of modern science—from the vision of women as "intake-outgo" vessels to more recent visions of women as "factories," and then beyond—to be largely suggestive of bodily dismemberment. As Martin says, "women . . . suffer the alienation of parts of the self much more acutely than men" (21), and she holds out the possibility of rearticulating these parts in a feminist reconstruction of women's bodies. While Martin does acknowledge the possibility that fragmentation can be a weapon in resistance to alienation and oppression, the weight of her argument is that fragmentation is a primary form of modernity's victimization of women, especially when "science treats the person as a machine and assumes the body can be fixed by mechanical manipulations" (19).

It is simultaneous.

It is unstable. It changes from moment to moment, in its experience both of itself and of the world.

It has no center, but a roving focus. (It "reads" itself.) It is neither clearly an object nor simply a thought, meaning or spirit; it is a hybrid of thing and thought, the monkey in the middle.

It is easily influenced; it is largely for being influenced, since its largest organs are sensing devices.

It is permeable; it is entered by the world, via the senses, and can only roughly define its boundaries.

It reports to us in stories, intensities, hallucinatory jolts of uninterpreted perceptions: smells, sights, pleasure, pain.

Its public image, its face is a collage of stories, borrowed images, superstitions, fantasies. We have no idea what it "really" looks like.[26]

Here, we find some of the key elements of a postmodern conception of the body. The "banished body" shares the qualities of decentering and discontinuity with the body that, at least on our reading, is produced within the Arrow-Debreu approach to general equilibrium theory. But because Jackson, in contrast to neoclassical economists of the past seventy or so years, is actively engaged in thinking and writing about the body, her description (here and in her novel, *The Patchwork Girl*) is, in our view, more elaborated and more suggestive of further attributes and assignations than anything we can find in either older or more recent versions of neoclassical theory. Our goal, therefore, is not to celebrate the particular conception of the body that emerges in some neoclassical texts. Nor do we have any interest in determining or representing what the body " 'really' looks like." But we do think that the postmodern approach to the body, precisely because it brackets and deconstructs humanist conceptions, has made it possible both to retrieve orders and functions of the body that characterize diverse moments in the history of economic thought (including bodies and body parts that have been marginalized or banished from economic discourse) and to invoke still other configurations (especially those that are being pioneered by Jackson and many others outside the discipline of economics).[27]

[26] These two paragraphs are from a section, entitled "The Banished Body," of the transcript of Jackson's presentation at the "Transformations of the Book" Conference held at the Massachusetts Institute of Technology on 24–25 October 1998. The reason they are relevant, in addition to her providing some of the key elements of what we consider to be a postmodern conception of the body, is that Jackson is the author of a hypertext novel, *The Patchwork Girl*, which is a postmodern rewriting—in both form and content—of Mary Shelley's *Frankenstein*.

[27] Including, significantly, the corporeal identities and capabilities identified by Regenia Gagnier and John Dupré (2001) within cultural history. Indeed, we applaud Gagnier and

In the end, however, we believe that the challenge to economic theory that the introduction of the postmodern body has suggested has yet to be picked up. So as not to be misunderstood, while we think it is plausible to entertain the idea that the body has not disappeared but has been re-composed in recent neoclassical thinking along lines of fragmentation and differentiation, we also think that the neoclassical rendition of the frag-mented body is stunted and meager at best. The richness of the classicals' approach (or, for that matter, the various dimensions of the human body emphasized by Marxists, Austrians, feminists, and others) has not been replicated by today's neoclassicals because of the latter's reluctance to treat directly the dispersion of the body and its effects as an object of economic theory.[28] That is, we contend that neoclassicals have been un-aware in the main of the changes in the concept of the body that their formal analyses have implied, and they remain uninterested in consider-ing, for example, how the processes of gendering and so forth may further alter the kinds of theoretical work that they are willing to recognize as "economics" proper. And we acknowledge as well that when pushed to defend the integrity and unity of their work, many neoclassicals still resort to homo economicus as the starting presupposition despite the fact that, as we see it, even this belabored idea has been reduced in scope and been given new meaning in the conglomeration of behavioral theorems and lemmas that now comprise the contours of economic agency for today's model builders.[29]

The challenge of introducing postmodern bodies for different economic schools of thought remains, not only for neoclassicals but for their critics, a largely unrealized project. While it may be the case that each school of thought has had its postmodern moments in the disruption of the eigh-

---

Dupré's interest in integrating into economic discourse a plurality of bodies in "diverse rela-tions of cooperation and opposition" (187). We are concerned, at the same time, that their insistence on identifying agency or subjectivity only with whole, human bodies represents a return to the humanist legislation of the "normal" appearance and functioning of the body.

[28] Thus, we can interpret the distance between classical and neoclassical theories as marked by the shifting rendering of the individual and the body. While an individual subjectivity has been the focus of both approaches, it has gone from being a problem to be solved (both in relation to itself and to the larger society) to being a presumption of the theory (i.e., contempo-rary neoclassical theory presumes that the world can be explained as if unitary individuals can and do make rational choices). The body has not disappeared during this transition, but it has acquired a certain neutrality or transparency, as a set of requirements (such that produc-tion and consumption can take place) and not the real or potential source of anything addi-tional to or disruptive of the individual subjectivity constituted by choice algorithms.

[29] We may therefore draw a parallel with the ironic point we made in the previous chap-ter: while Keynes was able to disrupt modernist notions of certainty by invoking the singular body, contemporary neoclassical economists have "saved" modernist notions of the rational subject by dispersing and fragmenting the body.

teenth- and nineteenth-century forms of modernism and humanism, the reliance on modernism and humanism to mourn the body's purported disappearance or to recompose and reconstitute the "full" human body reproduces a critical narrative that avoids rather than faces the innovations that are under way mostly outside the discipline of economics in refiguring the body of postmodernism.[30] Coming to terms with these innovations *within economics* is, in any event, the project we hope to have encouraged and begun in this chapter.

[30] We are thinking of the discussions of the body, in addition to those already mentioned during the course of this chapter, by Elkins (1999), Feher (1989), Frank (1990), Hillman and Mazzio (1997), Leder (1990), Stafford (1991), and the various authors in the collection edited by MacCannell and Zakarin (1994).

4

Feminist Economics: (Re)Gendering Knowledge and Subjectivity

But what if these "commodities" refused to go to
"market"? What if they maintained "another"
kind of commerce, among themselves?
  —Luce Irigaray, *This Sex Which Is Not One*

WHILE FEMINISM has been challenging and transforming the methods and procedures of a wide variety of academic disciplines (from literary criticism and legal studies to the history and philosophy of science) for the better part of the past three decades, it is only recently that it has come to occupy a prominent position within economics. Of course, women and feminist economists have sought to increase their representation within and to reframe the research questions and policies of the discipline of economics from early on.[1] But, in the last fifteen years or so, feminist approaches to economics have both expanded and taken a new turn, introducing the issues of gender into the very notions of knowledge and subjectivity that have served to undergird neoclassical theory (and, perhaps to a lesser extent, other schools of thought within modern economics).[2]

Actually, feminist attempts to question and move "beyond economic man" should be understood as involving a regendering or expanded gendering of modern economists' conceptions of *homo scientis* and *homo economicus*, since one of the key points of criticism is that these conceptions have been gendered from the very beginning. That is, contemporary

---

[1] Since the contributions of women and feminists within economics had long been ignored or buried in the "official" histories of thought, it has taken a project of rediscovery and excavation within the context of contemporary feminism to bring such contributions to light. See, e.g., the work of Mary Ann Dimand (Dimand, Dimand, and Forget 1995), Ulla Grapard (2001), and Michele Pujol (1992, 1995) and the special issue of *History of Political Economy* (1993). Randy Albelda's (1997) is the first full-length study of the history of representations of women in economics.

[2] Gillian Hewitson (1999) similarly distinguishes between two different feminist engagements with the discipline of economics: one in which the goal is to add women to neoclassical economics (which she also refers to as "add women and stir") and a second whose objective is to criticize the gender biases in the core assumptions of neoclassical economics.

feminist economists have identified and made visible the existence and consequences of the "masculinist" or male-biased forms of knowledge and subjectivity which, in their view, permeate the questions, methods of analysis, policy prescriptions, and pedagogy of economics—indeed, the very definitions of what economists can and should do. Thus, feminist economists have called attention to the ways in which the gendered nature of modern economics leads to such diverse features as a privileging of formal, mathematical modeling; the relative neglect of nonmarket relations such as the household and, when the household is examined, the presumption of benevolence on the part of the household "patriarch"; the view of the discipline of economics as a free market in ideas; the focus on rationality and self-interest to the exclusion of other forms of behaviors and motivations; economic policies that "forget about" gendered divisions of labor and other gender-differentiated economic and social roles; the few examples of, and the small number of pages devoted to, women and issues related to feminism in economics textbooks as well as a lecture-style format of teaching; and much, much more.[3]

In order to criticize and propose alternatives to these gender biases, feminist economists have focused their critical attention on the presumed objectivity and universality of the categories of knowledge and subjectivity associated with modern economics. And by showing how they can be regendered—for example, by including a "feminine" principle as one of the constituents of at least some forms of knowledge and some subjects—feminists have moved in the direction of fragmenting (or, alternatively, of recognizing the fragmentation implicit in) modern economists' conceptions of knowledge and subjectivity. The combination of gendering and fragmentation thus paves the way for more concrete and contingent notions of both knowledge and subjectivity and, ultimately, a decentering of economic theory. It is in this sense that feminist conceptions of knowledge and subjectivity help to bring to light additional postmodern moments within modern economics.

One way of highlighting and exploring the consequences of feminist challenges to the gendered concepts and protocols of modern economics is by analogy to the disruptions introduced by recent treatments of the gift, which itself has been considered by some a "feminine economy," opposed to the masculinist economy and economics of market exchange. For many commentators, from Marcel Mauss and Claude Lévi-Strauss to Hélène Cixous and Luce Irigaray, the gift has come to represent the "other" to the economics of market exchange: it has served as an alternative both to the universality of markets, as a social practice "outside ex-

---

[3] See, e.g., Feiner and Roberts 1990; Aerni et al. 1999; Hyman 1994; Strassman 1993; Strassman and Polanyi 1995; and Nelson 1993.

change," and to a large part of the discipline of economics for which the exchange of commodities is everywhere, and therefore "outside economics." The problem is, such treatments of the gift often leave the existing conceptions of exchange in place, thereby allowing some notion of equivalence classes—something implicitly calculable—to creep back in. As a result, the gift becomes impossible and dissolves back into exchange. From a postmodern perspective, it is only when the "otherness" of the gift makes exchange itself impossible, when the ambiguity and social embeddedness associated with the gift are used to rethink the activity of market exchange, that the decentering effects of the gift on modern economy theory will be felt.

The situation is similar with contemporary feminist economics. If the consequences of the fragmentation and decentering of knowledge and subjectivity are followed through, modernist conceptions of knowledge and of the originating subject are made both unavailable and unnecessary for economic theory. However, as with many recent approaches to the gift, the postmodern implications of feminist economics can be muted or contained, for example, by invoking empiricism to "prove" alternative notions of subjectivity or by reunifying the subject or reconstituting it as the center of economic discourse. Such treatments retain key aspects of economic modernism. An alternative approach, one that draws from recent developments within postmodern feminism, explodes and displaces the notion of the originating subject. Such an approach therefore points toward the possibility of viewing the economy and economic theorizing itself not in terms of an origin or essential cause but, rather, as "processes without a subject."

Knowledge and Agency in Modern Economics

The main target of criticism for feminist economists has been neoclassical theory, especially neoclassical economists' conceptions of knowledge and subjectivity.[4] Indeed, one way that neoclassicals have often defended the scientificity of their approach is by reference to their use of general, formal, analytical models and methods in order to arrive at objective, value-

---

[4] While feminist criticisms have mostly been aimed at one or another version of neoclassical theory, the gender biases inherent in heterodox economic theories have not been overlooked. See, e.g., Nancy Folbre's critical discussions of Marxism (1988, 1993). Still, most of the existing literature notes the affinities between feminism and nonneoclassical schools of thought, including institutional (Waller 1999; Waller and Jennings 1990; Peterson and Brown 1994), Austrian (Horwitz 1995), post-Keynesian (Levin 1995), nondeterminist Marxian (Fraad, Resnick, and Wolff 1994; Gibson-Graham 1996), and radical (Matthaei 1992) economic theories.

free conclusions concerning the economic world. Another way has been the necessary grounding of economic theory in a conception of the subject as the inevitable wellspring of economic decision-making and, thereby, of economic arrangements among and between subjects (including market transactions and all other institutions, from firms to families). That is, neoclassical economic theory is based on a methodological position in which the motive force of both economic knowledge and economic processes and institutions is self-activating atoms, "individuals."

These individuals, as economic subjects, are thought to be guided in their actions by two quite different forces: desire and rationality. One of the most interesting questions in the history of economic thought—dating from the early utilitarians through Adam Smith and, later, to the marginalists and those who followed—is the precise rapprochement between these two heroic subjective attributes or essential categories, one representing the passions that emanate from the human body, the other representing the distinguishing feature of human beings in mastering nature, both within and outside their corporeal containers. In this struggle, passions and interests, the signs of desire, are domesticated by reason, by the capacity of humans to resist, withstand, and finally overcome the irrational and random actions to which desire might drive them. This is precisely the struggle of Robinson Crusoe (within himself and with the servant Friday) that Daniel Defoe so perceptively depicts and that, in turn, is taken up and made the overarching narrative of the work of classical and neoclassical economists.[5] Neoclassical theory, built as it is on a view in which human nature reflects this dramatic and historic struggle, takes the stance characteristic of much post-Enlightenment thought in which the outcome of this tension is mostly beneficent and "useful" to human beings and is, therefore, the only secure basis for civil society (just as is for Crusoe and the new "civilization" he founds on the island). Desire, the menacing, more primitive side of human nature, to which all outbreaks of madness and excess can be attributed, is not abolished but, rather, tamed and directed in such a way as to achieve salutary ends.

The taming of desire involves the mind's exercising monumental control not only over the body's "baseness" but, more importantly, over the multiplicity of excessive behaviors that seem to have no rhyme or reason other than the necessity of release. Indeed, it is precisely the ultimate reduction of this multiplicity of unfathomable desires that marks the great achievement of the rational mind in invading and directing the body's passions and in showing that one can arrive, through knowledge, at particular ends that encompass the pleasures (or pains) for which the body yearns. Devel-

---

[5] See Hewitson 1994, 1999; Grapard 1995; and Samson 1995 for feminist readings of the Robinson Crusoe fable and its use in economic thought.

oping in an era announcing itself philosophically as being predicated on the rule of reason, distinguished entirely from the blend of ephemerality and faith that constituted what was considered medieval (and later) Western religion, the post-Enlightenment concepts of modern subjectivity that entered economic thought increasingly were presented as the hallmarks of progressive civilization. On one hand, the *modern* subject is, of course, grounded in the earthy facticity of desire, passion, and interest. Civilization does not represent the elimination of these forces so much as their domestication.[6] On the other hand, the modern subject is conceived progressively as the historic outcome of a period in which it is finally possible for an extended, mass rationality to emerge (for, in prior ages, the ability to arrive at enlightened, knowledge-based decisions is conceived to be restricted only to the privileged few who could, by virtue of economic, gender, racial, and individual distinctions, rise above pagan and religious dogmas that obstructed rational ways of appropriating the world). The apogee of human subjective development coincides nicely, then, with the progress of civilization and, of course, with its realization in the forms of bourgeois society that were depicted, by Smith and the utilitarians, as the natural outcome of freely interacting, rational individuals.

This story proceeds by introducing the supposedly abstract and universal subject. Feminists outside of economics (e.g., Benhabib et al. 1995) have pointed out that this abstraction is hardly universal but summarizes, in a condensed form, a very male subject (seen in its historical self-consciousness as the triumphant "subject of history" and, therefore, as the object of discourse). But there is an additional issue. The very idea that the mind comes ultimately to achieve mastery, however limited, over the body may be read as an allegory for the suppression of "femininity" and its unimportance as a basis for socioeconomic and historical analysis. It is remarkable that, starting from Smith and lasting to this day, the desires and emotions that are said to emanate from the body are seen as impossible sources for the more or less orderly actions that comprise economic decision-making. To put this otherwise, desire and the body are allowed subordinate efficacy in determining economic and social behavior. The degree to which, historically, women were seen in post-Enlightenment, Western thought as pure body (or, alternatively, as the site of a rationality

---

[6] At various points, Defoe's Crusoe implies that one of the important conditions for his ability to insulate himself from the desires of the body (and, thus, for reason to take hold) is that the conditions of scarcity normally assumed in neoclassical models did not obtain. For example: "In the first place, I was removed from all the wickedness of the world, here. *I had neither the lust of the flesh, the lust of the eye, or the pride of life.* I had nothing to covet; for I had all that I was now capable of enjoying; I was lord of the whole manor; or if I pleased, I might call my self king or emperor over the whole country which I had possession of" (1965, 139).

subordinated to desire), makes the story of the mind's taming of the body—as the appropriate basis for individual behavior, civilization as a whole (a version of the story in which man is cast as culture and woman as nature), and much else—to be simultaneously a tale of the progressive victory of "maleness" over "femaleness" in human history.[7]

But, to be a bit more careful here, there is a sense in which the classical story (transported into the present by neoclassical economists) is, in fact, one of the subservience of the mind and reason to the essential dictates of the body. "Feed and clothe me," says the body to the mind, and the mind obeys—or, more formally, given an individual's nonsatiable preferences for food and shelter and the scarcity of means to satisfy them, his or her rational faculty is required to formulate the appropriate (consistent, utility-maximizing) choices. In this understanding, however, the fact that the body is not allowed to speak on its own (it has no immanence or control), but must be channeled through the mind that it ultimately controls by the unrelenting and unlimited nature of its desires, gives rise to a more ambiguously gendered story (that is, at least, within the restricted gender terms of this classical tradition). The blunting of the pure immediacy of the body can be read as a metaphor for the denial, in the space of classical theory, of the feminine. But it can also be argued that the allegory allows for the feminizing of economic subjects and civil society—a major worry of post-Enlightenment thinkers, inside and outside economics—insofar as the body comes to determine, if only in the last instance, the actions of the economic subject, again abstractly conceived.[8]

In any event, we must be clear about the force of neoclassical theory. One of its most powerful ideas—which makes up its self-identity, justification, and defense against alternatives—is the sophisticated story in which desire and reason (and their interactions) are brought into play as the foundation of a theory of economic relations and institutions. Neoclassical theory's view of the subjective basis of economic analysis is simultaneously a form of naturalism and humanism or, rather, a combina-

---

[7] Sherry Ortner published one of the earliest texts (1972) in which women's subordination was tied to, and explained in terms of, a universal tendency to distinguish between nature and culture, to associate woman with nature and man with culture, and to privilege the latter over the former. In a later essay (1995), she reiterates that conclusion, with two caveats: *(a)* that male dominance was better explained by "some complex interaction of functional arrangements, power dynamics, and bodily effects," not just the linkage of female/nature and male/culture and *(b)* that the nature/culture distinction, in its Western sense, is not universal. (Both essays are reprinted in Ortner 1996.)

[8] Indeed, Stewart Justman (1993) argues that Smith invokes the Stoic virtue of self-command in order to fortify the manhood of (male) subjects who are otherwise "feminized" by the vanity, corruption, and propriety that are encouraged by commercial society. McCloskey (1996), for her part, defends the market for encouraging and supporting "feminine" virtues that encompass, partly, care, responsibility, and perhaps even love.

tion of the two. Since the nature of human beings is taken to be twofold, both desiring and reasoning, neoclassical economists often regard their perspective as closer to nature (both human and nonhuman) than alternative views. Unlimited bodily needs and desires are forced to confront, and obey the dictates imposed by, the brute reality of scarce resources. But the neoclassical story of the subject is also progressivist and, therefore, optimistic. The humanist optimism stems from the idea that the subject, as it succeeds in overcoming the multiplicity and wildness of bodily desires and emotions (often rendered, historically, as "femaleness") through the application of reason and the use of knowledge in guiding behavior, will achieve beneficial ends, both individual and social. And neoclassical theorists historically have defended their discourses precisely on the grounds that only they have ascertained the sanguine facts; study neoclassical theory, it is repeatedly announced, and you too can discover the salubrious results that are occasioned by the bridling of passion by reason, of insatiable desire by rational calculation. These results, if formulated and studied properly, can lead not only to correct policy prescriptions (mostly involving "hands off") but also to clear ethical and political positions.

It should be noted that the victory of reason over desire belies, as well, a preference for the well-behaved rules and codes of conduct for that which is publicly or universally shared—encapsulated in the modalities of rational calculation (which, as we saw in chapter 3, are written on the body) and the actions based on such calculations—over the unruliness associated with the inner life of subjective preferences. In this sense, reason can be said to succeed in harnessing, subduing, and projecting into the exterior world of economic and social interaction the excessive demands and drives experienced in the internal world of private desire. The governing of desire by reason thus enacts and maintains a strict (and natural) division between the public and private spheres as a necessary condition for carrying out the economic decisions that promise maximum individual and social benefits. The public world in which calm, sober decisions are made and enacted—the marketplace, above all—is thereby protected from the uncontrolled and incessant needs and desires experienced by and in the private sphere, best exemplified in the domestic household.[9]

This particular way of harmonizing reason and desire is, in turn, promoted on economic, ethical, and political grounds as preferable to any attempt to control the human body through the exercise of power by "other" bodies. That is, individual desire is not best controlled and directed by the manipulation of one individual's body by another individ-

---

[9] William James Booth (1993) contrasts the liberal, contractarian separation or disembedding of economic activity from the household to what he considers to be the two alternatives: the ancient *oikos* and a Marxist socialist household economy.

ual, class, or state. The manipulation of an individual's body—the restriction or self-legislation, of the mind's "freedom" to exercise control over one's own body—is a maneuver of power. And power, of course, is the result of a will that is it itself a manifestation of desire. Freedom from externally imposed control allows the mind to practice the only power permissible: the rule of reason. Additionally, power and reason only coincide with forms of political rule (democracy, for example) that are built upon—and, in turn, serve to reinforce—the civil society of free and self-regulated subjects. These individuals cannot be subjected to an alien will, to someone else's desire. They can, however, come to rule themselves by the application of reason to societal concerns, using similar forms of rational calculation and maximizing behavior. In such a state, power is transformed from an expression of desire's will into a conduit of enlightened knowledge. Thus, the neoclassical view of the modern subject is not only powerful for its "economic" content, but also plays an important role in demonstrating that only particular political and social arrangements are truly consonant with the successful rule of reason over bodily desire.

The power exercised by the mind over the body is also crucial to the constitution of the knowing subject as a condition of the objectivity claimed by neoclassical economists. Neoclassical theory is often thought to be objective in at least two distinct but related senses.[10] First, the idea of objectivity is bound up with notions of absolute truth and the representational character of economic analysis, that is, with the view that neoclassical economic scientists are able to accurately describe the economy and/or predict its movement over time. In this sense, neoclassical economics is taken to represent a "mirror of nature." The second sense of objectivity refers to the methods and procedures for analyzing the economy. Here, the claim to objectivity is based on the view that the axiomatic logic, formal models, stylized facts, and tools of empirical estimation of neoclassical economics constitute rigorous, universal, and nonsubjective means for formulating and testing hypotheses about the economy.

This neoclassical "flight to objectivity" (Bordo 1987) is predicated on the ability of the mind to separate itself from and to avoid being misled by the prejudices and passions, the desires and deceptive sensations, associated with the body. The knowing subject must therefore overcome and relinquish its corporeal identity—in order to achieve, first, a distanced, detached, cognitive relation of self to the external world and, second, the ability to distinguish clear, certain thought from subjective emotion and belief. The process of formation of the identity of the modern knowing

---

[10] Sandra Harding (1995) notes still other senses of objectivity, including its attribution to certain individuals and social groups (and its incapacity to others) and to certain knowledge-seeking communities (e.g., those that maximize ideal speech conditions).

subject therefore parallels that of the modern economic subject. The claim, in this case, is that the mind's attempt to subordinate to its will and thereby transcend the unruly and untrustworthy drives of the body will have the beneficent outcome, perhaps for the first time in history, of making possible objective knowledge concerning economic processes that are seen to exist "out there," independently of the economic scientist.

Feminist philosophers and historians of science have argued that the mastery of mind over the body represents a masculinization of thought, as the forms and procedures of imperfect and subjective knowledge that are associated with the body (such as sympathy and intuition) are precisely those attributes that have long been attributed to "feminine" engagements with the world. In this sense, the gendered conception of science that emerged over the course of post-Enlightenment philosophy and science and that has been appropriated and reinforced by neoclassical economics refers not to the discrimination against women or so-called women's issues within the practices and institutions of science (although those, too, certainly) but to the privileging of masculinist conceptions of objectivity and the "othering" of all other notions, including those traditionally defined as feminine.[11]

A second way in which the knowing subject has been gendered refers to the purported goal of objective knowledge: mastery and control over the world. The refashioning of nature—and, later, society—in mechanistic terms can be understood as eliminating from the depiction of the lifeworld the "female" (passive but receptive and fertile) principles that had previously been taken to animate it. The birth and development of modern economics, from the classicals through the neoclassicals, are certainly consistent with this story. The purpose of studying and modeling economic processes and events is to discover the laws governing the economic body in order to master and control it. When the economy is viewed as a machine, the goal is to fix it; as a living organism, the aim is to identify the economy's diseases and to cure them.[12] In both cases, economic scientists express their rational power in constructing the appropriate (formal, mathematical, and/or empirical) model and then devising the policies that will guide the economic body to the desired ends.

However, it must also be admitted that the hierarchical relationship of mind over body is neither fixed nor permanent. The classical and, espe-

[11] This argument is made by, among others, Harding (1986, 1991), Helen Longino (1990), and Dorothy Smith (1990).

[12] Gibson-Graham (1996, 92–119) discusses the various metaphors within neoclassical and Marxian economics that are used to depict the "body economic." Emma Spary (1996) explores, for the eighteenth century, the changing use of economic metaphors in natural history and of natural (especially body) metaphors in depictions of the economy and economic policy.

cially, neoclassical story has also often been one in which the relationship is reversed and man's body is forced to submit to the rational dictates of the economy. Some economic and social policies (often involving the freeing up of national and international markets) are required while others (just as often those which call for extramarket, especially government, interventions) are ruled out because, otherwise, the "normal" functioning or equilibrium state of the economy will be disturbed. When this occurs, the economy becomes the site of reason, a self-regulating and orderly mechanism that must not be disrupted by the weaknesses and irrational desires (often expressed as "populism" or "protectionism") represented by or contained within the social body.[13] But, ultimately, man is able to reassert his sovereignty and scientific rule: it is only in the economists' models that the economy reveals its secrets and its logic can be studied, mastered, and lorded over the world.

Even in the context of doing science, the economist's own body doesn't simply disappear; it may be allowed a limited role in the context of discovering and disseminating knowledge. Thus, the emotional commitments and subjective values that reside in and are said to characterize the body's engagement with the world may exercise decisive influence in posing questions and formulating hypotheses. But, once that first stage is accomplished, the mind is taken to operate independently of the body so that the justification (or falsification) of nonarbitrary and nonsubjective knowledge can be achieved. The body may also "speak" and play an important role in reporting the results of scientific investigation. However, once again, the body is rendered irrelevant to the actual process of assessing and adjudicating among knowledge claims since corporeal means of persuasion—what are taken to be rhetorical devices as distinct from rational, formal representations—are considered to be independent of (or inimical to) the scientists' ability to arrive at objective knowledge.[14]

The bracketing of the effectivity of the body is therefore a decisive moment in creating the possibility not only of individual economic knowledge but also of the progress of objective knowledge. The rational self-mastery of the knowing subject, its ability to rise above and to transcend its own subjective passions and prejudices, allows it to exchange knowledges with other such subjects on a free and equal footing. The result is a conception of the interactions within the community of scientists as a "marketplace of ideas," in which the only self-interest that is recognized

[13] The irony, of course, is that such a view entails protecting the economy from protectionism.

[14] Even McCloskey (1985a), who in many ways is responsible for putting rhetoric (including, significantly, the metaphorical status of mathematical models) on the economic map, has largely maintained the distinction between the rational content of economic theory and the "talk" that concerns such theorizing.

is the mind's will to objective knowledge (and in which other perceived or announced interests are barred as either nonexistent or illegitimate). The competitive incentives and pressures that characterize the relations among participants are then taken as a guarantee that only objective knowledges will be accepted (enshrined henceforth in the textbooks that are used to train future economists and the general citizenry), and all other ideas will be set aside (the detritus that is relegated to the purview of nonneoclassical economists and historians of economic thought). Thus, the neoclassical view of the knowing subject, the anxious and dramatic struggle of mind over body, plays an important role in establishing the objectivity and universal validity of the ideas that are predominant at any point in time as well as the steady growth of the stock of objective knowledge over time.

Feminist Criticisms of Modern Subjectivity

It is precisely the presumed unity and universality of objective knowledge and rational economic agency—of the knowing and acting subjects—that neoclassicals consider to be the necessary underpinnings of economic theory that have attracted the attention and critical scrutiny of feminist economists. The use of a feminist approach serves both to reveal the masculinist biases and exclusions that are "hidden by the invisible hand" (Feiner and Roberts 1990) and to prepare the theoretical terrain for alternative—gendered and fragmented—notions of subjectivity for economic discourse.

Questions and criticisms pertaining to the masculinist view of economic agency presumed by neoclassical theory have taken numerous forms within feminist economics. The most common concern the "separative self," the sense that neoclassical economic subjects are cast as individuals who are—with one, key exception—emotionally detached or separated from each other. Paula England (1992), for example, focuses attention on what she considers to be three distinctive features of the neoclassical rational decision-making individual: the ruling out of interpersonal utility comparisons, the presumed exogeneity of tastes and preferences, and the assumption of self-interested market behavior (the idea that individuals' utilities are independent of one another). She notes, however, that when it comes to the neoclassical analysis of the household, the third assumption is relinquished and replaced by altruism. England's conclusion is that "taken together, this view glorifies men's autonomy outside the family while giving them credit for altruism within the family" (1993, 49).

England's critique does not mean that she disagrees with the idea that altruism exists inside or outside the family. What she objects to is that, within much neoclassical theory, economic agents' identities are bifurcated between the two realms. Her alternative conception of economic subjectivity would resolve this "inconsistency," by allowing for altruism within markets (e.g., as a way of analyzing promale discrimination) and selfishness within households (e.g., when unequal power is used to create or reinforce income disparities).

Nancy Folbre and Heidi Hartmann (1988) have also been concerned to undo the "conceptual segregation" of self-interest and altruism (and the binary oppositions to which those characteristics are often related: public/private, market/household, economic/noneconomic, male/female). They argue that the notion of the self-interested subject may have emerged as the result of male economists' projection of putatively male "aggressive" and often antisocial behavior onto all forms of subjectivity. In opposition to this masculinist bias of neoclassical theories of "rational economic man" (and, we should note, a similar masculinist bias in Marxian theory, which stresses, for example, production over reproduction in defining and privileging the subjective "class" interests of laboring men), Folbre and Hartmann promote a feminized view of subjectivity—but one that encompasses *all* subjects, male and female—that emphasizes cooperation, loyalty, reciprocity, and caring feelings for others as human motivations at least as important as self-interest in undertaking economic actions.

A similar approach is adopted by Julie Nelson (1996), who uses a "gender-value compass" to suggest that the oppositional hierarchy of separative and connected selves invoked by neoclassical theory can be reinterpreted in order to identify the negative dimensions of the masculine pole and the positive dimensions of the feminine one.[15]

According to Nelson's scheme, separative turns out to represent the lack of related and the perversion of individual (thus becoming a negative masculine attribute) while related (now seen as positive feminine characteristic) can be contrasted with its own perverse form, soluble. Nelson's conclusion is that the perverse or extreme forms of the separation/connection dualism (separative and soluble) should be rejected in favor of the complementarity of the positive dimensions of the separation-connection dualism (individual and related), thus leading to a "conception of humans as differentiated individuals who are also interdependent and connected" (1996, 16).

---

[15] As Nelson explains elsewhere (1993, 29), "if gender and value are thought of as orthogonal dimensions, then it becomes possible to think about good and bad aspects of characteristics cognitively associated with masculinity in our culture, and good and bad characteristics of what we think of as feminine."

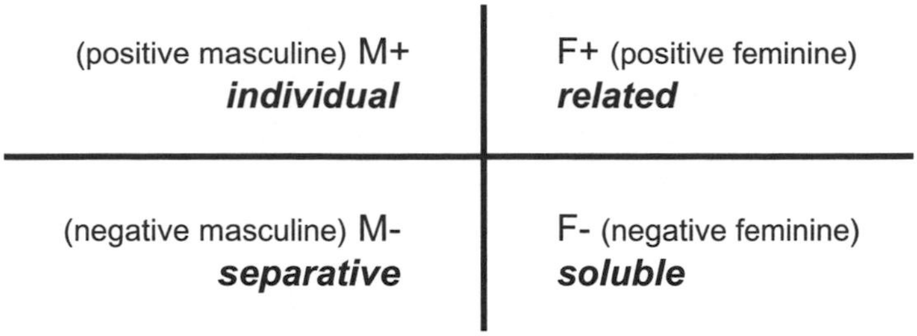

(positive masculine) M+ *individual*	F+ (positive feminine) *related*
(negative masculine) M- *separative*	F- (negative feminine) *soluble*

Figure 4.1. Gender-value compass. Source: Nelson (1996, 16).

For Susan Feiner (1994), rational economic man does not entail a denial of all social ties. She argues that, in fact, specific forms of community and femininity characterize the symbolic content of the neoclassical conception of market exchange. Using the insights of psychoanalytic theory, Feiner discovers that the theory of the perfectly competitive, free market in equilibrium produced by neoclassical economists represents a shared group fantasy of the mother/child relation: because it satisfies all needs, completely and instantaneously, it is a "substitute for the perfect mother who is unfailing in her capacity (and willingness) to meet all needs" (1994, 57). From this perspective, the autonomy and separation of homo economicus represents a gendered defense against scarcity, the fear of being separated from the market-as-mother. The celebration of rational choice and individual self-interest is therefore an attempt to undo the (unconscious) anxiety associated with the possibility of frustrated desire and infantile dependence on others. Feiner contrasts this masculine form of desire with an approach that is focused on exploring the emotional and material pleasures of sharing within and between diverse social communities.

Feminists have also raised questions about the rationality that is attributed to economic subjects within neoclassical theory. While England expresses her ambivalence about whether or not the usual assumption of rationality is gender-biased (it may be, she argues, when combined with the assumption of exogenous tastes), both Nelson (1996) and Folbre (1994) have shown that neoclassical economists tend to deploy a narrow, gendered conception of decision making. Nelson, for example, looks to overcome the simple equation of rationality with strict logic and precision by including other dimensions and conditions of decision making, such as the emotional acknowledgment of need as a prerequisite of good judgment. Folbre, for her part, argues that rational choice is a gendered term, one that leads to a privileging of an objective, dispassionate, masculine approach in contrast to a subjective, emotional, feminine approach. Even imperfect or institutionalist rationality—which allows for uncertainty, imperfect information, and interdependent utilities—suffers from a gender bias, by taking individual self-interest as a given. The alternative suggested by Folbre shifts the focus from narrowly defined interests to social identities, combining "purposeful choice" (which "encourages us to ask how people define and pursue their desires" [1994, 28]), with a theory of the social structures that serve to influence and constrain individual choices.

The preceding criticisms of rational economic man have, in their different ways, focused on the radically individualist, separative, and narrowly rational conception of agency within neoclassical theory. Together, they demonstrate both that the neoclassical economic subject includes significant masculinist biases and that it is possible to regender the subject by incorporating nonmasculine—related, caring, altruistic, eroticized, purposefully rational, and other—traits and characteristics. Introducing alternative, feminized notions of agency disrupts the presumed unity and universality of the subject that serves as one of the cornerstones of the modernism that characterizes much neoclassical economic theorizing. Such work thus creates the space for more fragmented and diverse notions of economic subjectivity, including not only newly gendered identities but also those of race, queerness, and much else.[16] In this sense, feminist criticisms of the gendered economic subject have identified and promoted the further development of an important postmodern theme within contemporary economic discourse.

Feminist criticisms of the modernist knowing subject have followed related paths and have had similarly postmodern implications. The project of examining the gender biases that are inherent in the rule of reason invoked and imposed by neoclassical and other economic scientists has led to a regendering and fragmenting of the knowing subject and, with it, of the meaning of objectivity, science, and the general process of constructing economic knowledges.

Once again, there are many different questions and concerns raised by feminist treatments of the knowing subject of the sort that predominates within and is presumed by mainstream economics. But it is the idea that the rule of reason accords little or no relevance to a knower's embodiment that has been signaled as the major source of masculinist bias and point of contention in the existing literature.

For some, the idea that the knowing subject is constituted by the victory of reason over the body leads to a privileging of certain methods

---

[16] See, especially, the work of Williams (1993), Matthaei (1998), Cornwall (1998), and Badgett (1995a).

of economic analysis and the downplaying or ignoring of many others, considered unrelated and even detrimental to true reason. Thus, in Nelson's (1996) view, economics has come to be identified with a particular way of knowing—formal, logical, especially mathematical, reasoning—which is contrasted to and elevated over intuition, verbal reasoning, and other ways of acquiring knowledge that are considered to be "soft," illogical, and feminine. It is possible, Nelson suggests, to undo the gendered dualism that reduces scientificity, objectivity, and precision to mathematical modeling by recognizing both the negative dimensions of masculine-associated knowledge (what she, following Nicholas Georgescu-Roegen, refers to as "arithmomania") and the positive attributes of different-than-logical methods (such as the use of concrete examples, carefully constructed analogies, and rich descriptions, all leading to a more "humanistic" orientation). Such a revaluing of the gendered ways of knowing opens up a space for a wide variety of alternatives, including "conjective" (McCloskey 1993) and "interpretative" (Klamer 1995) approaches, that are excluded by the rule of reason.

Nelson also takes issue with a second implication of disembodiment: the presumed detachment of the knowing subject. An exclusive focus on the power of reason tends to make the isolated individual the sole origin of objective and certain knowledge. Building on the work of feminist philosophers and historians of science such as Harding (1986, 1991), Longino (1990), Donna Haraway (1991), and Evelyn Fox Keller (1985), Nelson argues that the masculinist ideal of detachment operates on at least five levels:

Social influences (the impact of cultural conceptions on scientific analogies and assumptions)

The object of study (the position of the scientist with respect to the phenomenon to be investigated)

Other researchers (the relations among the members of the community of scientists)

Practical or immediate concerns (the relation of science to practical problem-solving and pressing social questions)

Partisan ties (the preconceptions and biases held by a particular community of practitioners)

In each case, the official or approved position for the scientist is one of distance or separation. Nelson's alternative suggests not only that such factors have played an important role in the actual conduct of economic inquiry, such that detachment has merely been an elaborate illusion within mainstream economics, but that the practice of economics would be improved precisely by recognizing "one's own various attachments" and the "partiality this location lends to one's views" (1996, 48).

Sandra Harding (1995) makes a similar case against the positivist view that economics is—or even can or should be—neutral with respect to values and interests. For Harding, the situation within economics is similar to that of the social and natural sciences (especially biology): external or contextual values and interests "intrude" into scientific research and, at the same time, internal or constitutive values and interests "take sides" with external value/interest positions. Thus, feminists can't be blamed for introducing political assumptions into economics; they've been there all along. But Harding also wants to argue something more— that the objectivity of economics is *weakened* by the assumption of neutrality and that *stronger* standards of objectivity can be created precisely by allowing values and interests to operate within the practice of science. The key step comes from "standpoint theory," the idea that different bodily places in and engagements with the world give rise to different ways of knowing the world. In Harding's view, the values and interests associated with feminist and other "politically disadvantaged positions" can assist in identifying and eliminating unwarranted cultural assumptions; perhaps even more important, they can positively affect the growth of economic knowledge, for example, by resisting the occlusion of evidence that, once revealed, will lead to new critical discourses concerning dominant institutions.[17]

The two major implications of feminist treatments of the embodied knowing subject—the appreciation of ways of knowing other than logical reasoning and the social "situatedness" of scientific knowledges—can be combined in order to reconceptualize modern economic practice. A powerful example is provided by Diana Strassman and Livia Polanyi (1995), who argue against the "stance of detached objectivity claimed by the predominant practitioners" of economics (143) and thus against the idea that mainstream accounts of, for example, the household are authoritative, dispassionate, and independent of the interests of those practitioners. Their alternative approach focuses, first, on the ways in which standard economic models (specifically, the application of neoclassical utility theory to household production) are not formulated on the basis of pure reasoning but, rather, the narrative elements of storytelling. They then demonstrate how the assumptions that are built into such stories correspond to the interests of the (white, Western, male) model-builders and, at the same time, serve to exclude the situated perspectives and knowl-

---

[17] Alison Jaggar formulates a similar argument with respect to the exclusion of feminist and other "outlaw emotions" from the process of inquiry: "I would claim that the emotional responses of oppressed people in general, and often of women in particular, are more likely to be appropriate than the emotional responses of the dominant class. That is, they are more likely to incorporate reliable appraisals of situations" (1997, 398).

edges of "potential economists who might tell other stories, stories perhaps more resonant with the experiences of groups currently underrepresented in the ranks of the profession" (144).[18]

Together, feminist criticisms of the rule of reason lead to a regendering or expanded gendering of modernist conceptions of science, objectivity, and, in general, the ways in which economic knowledges are produced. What is particularly important is that, in establishing the relevance of corporeal attachments and ways of knowing, feminists have succeeding in disrupting the unity and universality usually attributed to the knowing subject within mainstream economics. Reimagining the subject of knowledge in terms of fragmentation and difference therefore represents another postmodern moment within feminist economics.

In the foregoing discussion, we hope to have demonstrated that the project of recognizing, criticizing, and formulating alternatives to the masculinist biases in the notions of subjectivity that predominate within much standard economics has led feminists to challenge key aspects of economic modernism. Regendering and fragmenting existing conceptions of knowing and acting subjects—making them more concrete and contingent, acknowledging existing differences and introducing still other forms of difference, expanding the range of possible subjectivities of and for economic discourse—are precisely the effects of the postmodern turn that, in our view, has been identified and fruitfully deployed by recent feminist approaches to economics.

But we also think it significant that other feminist economists have expressed the worry that the promise and distinctness of feminist economics with respect to mainstream economics (especially the dominant neoclassical theory) may be elided and even erased by maintaining the view that the primary problem with existing conceptions of the knowing and acting subjects is their abstractness or unreality. In these cases, the goal is to introduce a more adequate (empirically or experientially grounded) notion in order to fill the lacunae or solve the difficulties of existing economic theory. However, criticisms of this sort tend to invoke modernist protocols, often a combination of empiricism and humanism. This is most evident in the work of those critics who wish to argue that what is lacking in neoclassical theory is a view of the "whole" human being, one

---

[18] There is a burgeoning literature on the "male biases" inherent in the structural adjustment programs that have promulgated in the third world during the course of the past twenty years. The work of Diane Elson (1995) and Lourdes Benería (1995) has been central to the effort to demonstrate that such programs presume unlimited supplies of female labor, inside and outside the household, and may cause and/or reinforce many other forms of gender discrimination. Suzanne Bergeron (2002) analyzes the gender biases involved in the construction of "women" in recent World Bank literature.

in which the attributes of separateness and disembodied reasoning are only part (and perhaps a small part) of subjectivity. While such treatments can be credited with having successfully called into question the masculinist biases inherent in neoclassical conceptions of the subject, they do not imply a change in the general role of the subject either as the origin of economic knowledge or as the starting point for economic theory. In this, they may overlook an additional source of gender bias in the mind/body relationship constitutive of neoclassical theory or, indeed, any modernist economics.

We can draw a parallel here between some feminists' partial or incomplete break with the masculinist biases in modernist economic discourse and recent treatments of the gift. Gift economies have often been perceived and theorized, by feminists and many others, as "outside economics," as an alternative to both market exchanges and the economic discourses that celebrate such forms of exchange. The problem is, the radical otherness of the gift has been difficult to sustain, often collapsing back into some form of equivalent exchange. In our view, this problem emerges not because of the impossibility of types of transactions different from market exchange but, rather, because exchange—like the subject in economic discourse—remains for the most part trapped within modernist premises, unchallenged in terms of its own possibility.

Feminist Economics and the Gift

Theories of the gift have an extended lineage—stretching back to the pioneering and oft-cited work of Marcel Mauss (1950)—within anthropology and sociology and, more recently, within philosophy and literary and cultural theory.[19] Throughout that history, the gift has attracted attention as a form of economy that represents an alternative to monetary, market exchange: markets are often taken to be self-regulating, largely independent of the society within which they exist, and to involve the immediate and equivalent exchange of goods; while gift giving is seen to be embedded within the wider society, an expression of a wide range of noneconomic social relations, and to be characterized by extended (and thus ambiguously defined) reciprocity. The contrast between gift and exchange—and between economic and social theories that privilege one over the other as the basis of sociality—could not be starker.

---

[19] The enormous literature on the gift continues to expand. Some recent contributions, in addition to those referred to below, are Godelier 1999; Komter 1996c; Schrift 1997b; and Vandevelde 2000.

But the gift has also been haunted by its "impossibility." If, as Jacques Derrida (1992) argues (following Mauss), the offer of a gift creates a debt, a demand to be repaid with a countergift, then perhaps the gift annuls itself in the very act of giving. Some commentators, such as Antonio Callari (forthcoming), strive to keep this impossibility in play, as a moment of undecidability that implies a space for—indeed, the very existence of—ethics and politics. Others, however, conclude that the distinction between gift and exchange simply cannot be sustained. Philip Mirowski (2001), for example, argues that, because reciprocity involves some notion of intentionality related to equivalence, the master code underlying exchange, the gift can only operate within a network of exchange. In other words, while gift giving may represent an attempt to circumvent or transcend the value-invariant institutions of exchange, it only acquires meaning in the context of exchange. Therefore, in Mirowski's hands, the gift dissolves into a form of market exchange.

The tendency to see every act in which things change hands as one of exchange is the product of an economic discourse in which the construction of the circle of value starts from a world populated by separate and separable individuals. Stephen Gudeman (2001) has been most adept in showing that reconstructing the economic field as one whose initial premise is, instead, community (and the extension of its boundaries) can provide the impetus for reciprocity to be once again enshrined as a leading concept into all theories of transaction activities. This alternative starting point gives rise to views that impel us to see the practices in which things change hands as stemming from solidifying or dissolving social ties (and, often, both). It further implies the need to see economic activity as necessarily "embedded" within community practices.

The view that the field of value begins with an individualistic conceit, and that therefore demonstrations of the impossibility of the gift retain such a conceit, has precisely been the concern of feminist economists.[20] From this perspective, the debate over the gift concerns the role of such notions as caring, affection, and responsibility, all of which point historically and at present mostly to the activities of and ties forged by women (at least in the West). If a discourse of value is retained, then one part of the feminist contribution is to suggest that generosity, sharing, and emotional labor cannot be reducible to self-interest and need to be accounted for in such places as economic statistics indicating the money value of gross domestic product. In our view, this is one of the crucial contributions that such writers as England, Folbre and Hartmann, Nel-

[20] Indeed, Alan Schrift (1997a) makes the point that the renewed interest in the theory of the gift during the past two decades has had as one of its prime components feminist investigations of the relation between gender and the gift.

son, and Feiner provide in distancing themselves from neoclassical value theory—and, by implication, Mirowski's alternative social theory of value—since, in similar ways, both these approaches subsume the affective realm to other master codes that are more pertinent to masculinist notions of economy. The problem of the economic value of such activities that involve caring or generosity has led some, like Irene van Staveren (1999), to imaginatively attempt to specify different economic value spheres (for van Staveren, these are the spheres of freedom, justice, and care, implying respectively exchange, rules, and the gift). But, of course, van Staveren and others note that any particular transaction can and often does involve all three value considerations, thus making the value (if measured in money terms) quite difficult to specify.

The tensions and difficulties that arise in the attempt to theorize reciprocity as both of and other than the regime of exchange give rise to a different desire for gift theory. And that desire is based on the view that economic discourse is so inextricably bound up with masculinist discourses of value that it is impossible—starting with nearly any value theory—to refound consequent notions of economy that would presume responsibility and caring as two connected foundational moments. Hélène Cixous (1997, 159) raises just this problem in discussing the "return" that is expected of the gift:

> Really, there is no "free" gift. You never give something for nothing. But all the difference lies in the why and how of the gift, in the values that the gesture of giving affirms, causes to circulate; in the type of profit the giver draws from the gift and the use to which he or she puts it.

For Cixous, masculinist economies of value are based on the direct return of revenues and profit—and the fear of loss and expense. The alternative, feminine economy she theorizes "doesn't try to recover its expenses"; it is defined as the affirmation of generosity, a giving of gifts that promotes the establishing of relationships, the continued circulation of giving. Perhaps, then, a truly feminist economics can refashion the gift as a way of giving voice to these other foundational principles.

Yet, there is also a sense in which traditional gift theory, from Mauss to the French poststructuralists, retains a masculinist edge as well. This can be seen in the view that the gift is not just about "generosity" but also involves all kinds of political and social acts that can be seen to be constraining and aggressive, even violent, in the construction of community (as with potlatch).[21] In fact, looking for the "glue" that holds society to-

---

[21] Maurice Godelier (1999) notes that the "madness" of the potlatch that Franz Boas had documented (and that so fascinated Mauss, George Bataille, and others) was a version that had been profoundly altered by the effects of colonialism: "Mauss probably did not take

gether in these acts of prestation and status is, of course, to focus largely on the activities of men in societies in which these acts are said to occur.[22] Additionally, such gift transactions often include the "exchange" of women themselves, and this fact surely raises suspicions that perhaps gift theory is less than amenable to an "alternative" reading of the possibilities of a different economic life. Feminist economists, perhaps like van Staveren then, prefer instead to focus on the activities in which care and responsibility are socially binding, thus suggesting (at least by implication) that the concentration on power, status, and impressed obligation found in much gift theory only differs from traditional economic value theory in choosing masculinist "community" over masculinist "individuals."[23]

Perhaps the most influential and exhaustive treatment of the problem of discerning the gendering that is represented, and/or constituted, and/or performed in gift exchange is that by the social anthropologist Marilyn Strathern (1990). In her wide-ranging discussion of Melanesian gift networks and the difficulties encountered by anthropological, economistic, Marxist, and especially feminist approaches to the issue of the gift, Strathern warns that there is no place from which the Western theorist can speak of the gift that is not always/already occupied by discourses and concepts of previous colonialists, anthropologists, "natives," and so forth. The warning includes the instruction—gently given—that "one cannot read gender ascriptions off in advance, not even when women appear to be the very items which are gifted" (xi). This is because, as Strathern details in

---

this historical context into account when analyzing the potlatch. Because he focused on the agonistic character of the potlatch, he probably privileged a historically late and pathological form of the institution" (77–78).

[22] Bronislaw Malinowski's original fieldwork in the Trobriand Islands has focused almost exclusive attention within gift theory, from Mauss onward, on the role of men in the famous *kula* rings. Annette Weiner's pathbreaking research (1976, 1988), fifty-six years after Malinowski, uncovered the significance for Trobriand economic and social dynamics of the wealth and participation of women in equally important prestational activities (such as those associated with mortuary and marriage rituals). In a more general vein, Weiner explains that "since the ethnographic examples from which traditional exchange theories are formulated rely almost exclusively on examples of men's production and men's exchanges, the reproductive energies in such things as women's bones, sacred cloth, hair strings, banana-leaf bundles, weaving poles, and birthing houses, are largely unrecognized or, when recorded, are reduced by anthropologists to prosaic categories lacking economic or political provenience" (1992, 155).

[23] Aafke Komter (1996a), though, explores the active role women may take in gifting in terms of their acquisition of social and political power. Thus, Komter states that in modern Western societies, where women are more likely to engage in gift giving than men, it is "improbable" that this is due to a greater degree of altruism than men, and that power considerations are often chief motivators. Additionally, among other reasons to give, Komter notes that "women seem to be no exception when painful, hurting, or offending gifts are given" (130).

page after page of her monumental study, "it does not follow that 'women' only carry with them a 'female' identity. The basis for classification does not inhere in the objects themselves but in how they are transacted and to what ends. The action is the gendered activity" (xi).

In her attempt to reinscribe that which she takes to be in accordance with Melanesian talk and practice (in opposition to what she refers to as "Western orthodoxy"), Strathern goes on to demonstrate that in Melanesian gift exchange, "at certain moments male and female persons may be opposed, as discrete reference points for the relationship between them. In itself being neither, the relationship is different from them and may be imagined as embodied in its product. The (androgynous) entity so produced, the object of the relationship, literally evinces their cross-sex relationship within itself" (184). Thus, this formulation "cuts across the commodity-derived view that it is as (figuratively conceived) individuals with intrinsic ('biological') attributes that male and female persons are in a perpetual relation of difference. We therefore have to avoid any presupposition that takes the differentiated single sex state as a 'natural' reference point. If there were such a reference point in Melanesian society, it would have to be drawn from the root metaphor—the multiple person produced as the object of multiple relationships" (185). It is problematic, then, in Strathern's view to produce a straightforward gendering of gift economies, at least without consideration of the "orthodoxy" of whatever culture is the locus for its appearance.

In light of such ambiguities, there would then seem to be two tasks for contemporary feminist economists in this area. One consists in recreating the possibility of the gift, by eliminating the masculinist biases in gift theory and regendering reciprocity and transactional activities other than exchange, including the gift. The other is to relinquish any claim to "foundations"—whether community or the individual, reciprocity or exchange—and to leave indeterminacy (of both transactional activities and the boundaries of economic discourse concerning such activities) in play by using the various attributes of the gift to interrogate the possibility of exchange itself.

Indeed, we can follow Callari's lead here in seeing traditional conceptions of exchange as producing a rather pale figure compared to the robustness of the gift, since the latter connotes forms of social practice that exchange is thought to either be independent of or to transcend, like ethics and politics. There is therefore just as much benefit to thinking about exchange as simply "impossible" since, as it is discursively constructed by most practicing economists, it occupies the perhaps ridiculous space of "self-reproduction" and thus self-determination. This is the claim that the realm of markets, or for that matter any act of exchange, contains within itself most if not all of its subjective and social conditions of existence.

What is so fascinating, to us at least, is that any conception of the economy as self-reproducing could be so naturalized as to require great effort to demonstrate, in contrast, its ideological/discursive constituents and determinations. For it should be by no means obvious that "things" exist as "others"; that these things should therefore enter the realm of that which can be alienated from self or community (or other entities); that these things should be seen to possess something in common (even if the quality "in common" is that they maximize utility, satisfy needs, or that they are the results of a labor process); and that these things can and should be numbered and calculated. The world in which these are all encountered—as Callari calls it, the "world of goods"—is, of course, a world that must constantly be produced and reproduced precisely because there is nothing more or less "natural" about this set of practices than any other different or even opposing way of thinking about selves and others, some things and "other" things, and so on. Or, to put this otherwise, the production and reproduction of such a world of goods require all sorts of cultural, ideological, political, moral, and other practices for the events (such as exchange) that constitute its supposed manifestations to occur in time and space.

Still, there is also a sense in which exchange approximates more closely than gifts a transaction involving goods since exchange, it is often thought, is less symbolic, less constitutive of subjectivity, and more regulated by considerations of equality and/or realized preferences.[24] For many economists, as well as many advocates of gift theory, monetary or market exchange is somehow seen as more transparent, more able to represent already given value considerations, including the meeting of trading partners' needs, and already constituted subjectivities. This, we think, is mistaken. For there is nothing at all "certain" about any act of exchange, and nothing less symbolic and/or less "about" power, responsibility, meaning, and so forth. Likewise, there is something fundamentally "constitutive" about identities and subjectivities in every act of market exchange. Buying and selling are overloaded activities: trading partners not only may be and are of several different minds about transactions; they are also often uncertain as to what exactly such transactions "mean"

[24] A related point is that, for some, gifts represent or even produce "identity" to a greater degree than does exchange. Komter (1996b, 6) summarizes this point: "gifts reveal something about the identity of the giver . . . but a gift also imposes an identity on the recipient, in the sense that the ideas which the other person's needs and desires evoke in our imagination—ideas about his or her typical characteristics and peculiarities—are exposed to a certain extent in our gift." Advertising, marketing strategies, focus groups, and many other devices found in contemporary market culture should at least suggest the possibility that a subject's "presence" and identity may, likewise, be just as much at stake in the realm of exchange.

in terms of their own and others' wealth and property, the effects on their well-being, who or what subject positions they occupy, and what exactly is being traded.

And even though it seems to be the special province of the gift to leave the issue of time and the return in doubt (hence the vaunted indeterminacy of the gift), there are countless occasions in which what we normally consider exchange has exactly this kind of unclarity and question of time's passage attached. Market exchange is also a difficult action to pin down, since it is never clear which part of the activity—is it the talk or gestures involved? the determination of the nature of the good? the calculation of the price? the physical changing of hands of things? the symbolic offer and receipt or the actual transfer of the means of purchase? the moments before, during, or after the change in ownership money and goods takes place?—is considered its essence and defining moment.

Exchange, then, is privy, just as is the gift, to a whole host of perturbations and undecidables. Why not view every event of exchange, for example, as in doubt, as uncertain, as requiring so many different determinations for its constitution? Why not posit the fundamental uncertainty and indeterminacy of every act of exchange, including those that seem to involve such a high degree of routine and habit as to obliterate from economic discourse the precise fragility (in the sense of the need to stand on "others' " legs) of the social practices of exchange? Why not, in this sense, view market exchanges just as "impossible" (although thinkable) as the transactions of things through the gift?

Marking the impossibility of exchange is not intended to erase the real differences between gift and market exchange (or, for that matter, the range of other transactional activities), whether in terms of "actual" economies or economic discourse. It does, however, represent a movement away from the modernist—and masculinist—attempt, first, to inscribe some foundational moment of sociality (in either exchange or the gift) and, second, to establish an origin or essential condition of exchange and the gift (in, respectively, the individual and community). In this, it also parallels and prefigures a feminist decentering of economics from subjectivity.

Feminist Challenges to Subjectivity

Some feminists in economics argue that it is necessary to go beyond the view that neoclassical theory presents only partial, albeit highly gendered, views of knowing and acting subjects—as if human subjectivity were "out there," waiting to be more or less adequately represented within economic discourse, and as if an appropriately regendered, "socially and materially situated human being" eliminated all masculinist bias in economics. Such a view not only invokes the modernist protocols of empiricism and humanism in order to remedy the gender biases inherent in neoclassical conceptions of the subject; it leaves intact the place of subjectivity as a necessary starting point of and within economics.

An alternative approach is to make the subject itself "impossible," unavailable and unnecessary for economic theory and the analysis of economic events. This is the path suggested by the work of, among others, Lee Levin (1995), Gillian Hewitson (1999), J. K. Gibson-Graham (1996), and Suzanne Bergeron (2001), which, in different ways, focuses on the social and discursive construction of subjectivity.

Levin's contribution represents both a thoroughgoing critique of what he considers to be the modernist and masculinist conception of agent knowledge deployed by neoclassical capital theory and the elaboration of an alternative theory of investment, one that "understands the knowledge of agents to be constituted by social and emotional influences" (1995, 108). Instead of presuming that economic agents are "unified, sovereign, and constant" and, as a result, possess access to knowledge (for example, of the expected rate of return on real capital assets and the marginal cost of financial capital) that is objective or transcendent, Levin argues that investment decisions can be theorized in terms of the social and emotional constituents of agents and their knowledges. Thus, he presents various social elements—such as conventions, rumors, social comparisons, fads, and fashions—and emotional processes—including cognitive dissonance, contagion and suggestibility, anguish, and turmoil—as components of an alternative theory of capital investment. The result is to shift the focus of analytical attention away from given, individual economic subjects and their more or less objective knowledges and toward the conditions whereby, on one hand, economic agents are constituted and, on the other hand, the shifting, unstable, even contradictory knowledges, thoughts, and perceptions concerning the economy are formed.

If Levin demonstrates the possibility of carrying out economic analysis while decentering such analysis from always-already given forms of subjectivity, Hewitson shows that economic discourse is itself productive of particular notions of subjectivity. Her starting point is the idea that a distinction can be made

> between a person, say a woman, who undertakes economic activities such as work and other exchanges, and the subject position which is constructed for women in such exchanges by the discourse of neoclassical economics. This is the distinction between economics as literal, although abstract, representation of women's activities, and economics as a productive discourse which constructs the meaning of these activities in particular ways. (1999, 190)

In Hewitson's view, such a distinction is crucial because it marks the difference between understanding neoclassical economics (or any economic theory, for that matter) as *reflecting* only a partial view of society—ignoring the experiences of women, for example—that can be "fixed" by adding regendered forms of subjectivity, and seeing how neoclassical and other economic theories *construct* embodied subject positions—relying, for example, on the exclusion of the feminine for its truth effects, an approach that does not presume an empirically "correct" conception of the subject.

In the course of her analysis, Hewitson reveals the ways in which the masculinity of economic agency is constructed, in such diverse forms as the figure of Robinson Crusoe and the neoclassical interpretation of surrogate motherhood exchange, in and through the binary opposition of man/not-man. In both cases, a supposedly universal subject is inscribed in terms of a masculine body, a textual move that "works" only by first producing and then excluding a feminine body. As Hewitson explains, "the male body and masculinity are constructed discursively in opposition to, and valued at the expense of, the feminine, which is understood as irrational, dependent, passive, vulnerable, and self-sacrificing" (163). The key point is that excluded femininity is not something that exists prior to or independent of neoclassical economic theory (such that it can be more or less adequately represented within theory); rather, it is produced within that theory, as its foundation.

Hewitson also explains that the process of constituting gendered subjects within neoclassical theory also pertains to the economic scientists themselves. Phallocentrism or excluded femininity operates in structuring knowledge production and the subject position of the knower—determining the presence of the knowing subject, mind, and reason and the absence of the known object, the body, and emotions. In her view, "it is these absences which structure knowledge and enable the production of knowledge as unbiased representations of the 'real world' " (124).

Hewitson's solution is not to attempt to give the acting and knowing subjects of neoclassical theory truly feminine bodies (which, in her view, would simply reproduce the binary oppositions on which their masculine bodies have already been constructed). Her alternative approach insists, instead, that femininity and masculinity necessarily refer to sexed bodies and that such bodies are both textually produced and constitutive of subjectivity. The result is both to retrieve the body as the basis for a feminist intervention into economics and, at the same time, to open the body to multiple readings, thereby creating the possibility for nonmasculinist constructions of embodied subjectivity within and for economic analysis.

The project of focusing on and writing gendered bodies in new ways is taken up by Gibson-Graham. In contrast to Levin and Hewitson, who focus on the masculinist constructions of subjectivity in neoclassical theory, the immediate goal of Gibson-Graham's work is to produce a feminist rethinking of the categories of Marxian political economy.[25] In particular, in a chapter titled "How Do We Get Out of This Capitalist Place?" she is concerned that, while certain feminist knowledges of space (e.g., the city) that seek to reverse gender hierarchies and to uncover and then celebrate the "hidden" roles and spaces of women (including shopping, giving birth, and so on), contribute to changes in the livability of urban space for women, they do so at the cost of remaining within the limits set by masculinist categories (such as unified and totalizing visions of capitalism). Gibson-Graham therefore employs an alternative approach, one that challenges the familiar spatial language of the body—inside/outside, surface/depth, emptiness/fullness—in order to rewrite the body in terms of alternative metaphors. One example she deploys is "chora," the term Plato used to denote the movement between being and becoming, which becomes a way of conceiving of space in terms of air and openness, a place resplendent with positive immanence and potentiality.

Rewriting feminine space and agency in this manner is not a reference to an original ground, a representation of the way that feminine bodies "really" experience the world. Gibson-Graham makes no such claim. Her argument, instead, is that different ways of spatializing the body have different theoretical effects, such that respatializing female sexual space, "as surface, as active, as full and changing, as many, as depth," can contribute to new agencies for women in the city and larger political economy.

Gibson-Graham, like Hewitson, extends her rewriting of the body to include the role of economic scientists who, in the gendered hierarchy of reason and the body (presumed in a wide range of discourses, from neoclassical to Marxian), relate to the economy as both servant and master:

> In all these conceptions, the economy is both the master of Man and the site of his mastery, whether that mastery be gained through knowledge or through action. This paradox reflects Man's dual existence: as mind and as embodied Reason, he governs and controls; but as mere and mortal body, he looks to the economy, the perfect face of Reason, and submits to it as to his god. This back and forth is the signature of the binary and hierarchical regime of gender. Man cannot escape it, for it is his creator. Instead he plays it out in his discourse and practice of economic intervention. (1996, 104)

The role of the knowing subject is constituted, in part, by the conception of the economy. Thus, for example, viewing the economy as an organic totality—"centered, internally connected, hierarchically ordered, and governed by laws of motion" (106)—which can be replicated by reason, suggests that the economic scientist need only identify the right place to

[25] See also Biewener 1999 on the relation between Marxism and postmodern feminism.

repair whatever is not functioning correctly or to advocate that nothing at all should be done (since the organism will operate better without any outside intervention). However, using an alternative metaphor, such as that of an "intereffective social totality," in which economic and noneconomic processes—diverse households and other sites of production, capitalist and noncapitalist practices and institutions—are seen to "overdetermine" one another and in which there is no origin or center, deprives the economy of its unifying rationale and thus undermines the "ecstasy of rationalism and the arrogant security of determinate effects" (119). Instead, the economic totality—and, with it, the role of subjectivity—depends on how that totality is discursively constructed.

An incisive use of Gibson-Graham's critique of the masculinist discursive bias of conceptions of "the economy" (and certainly of a self-reproducing capitalism) and subsequent subjectivities can be viewed in Bergeron's (2001) important discussion of the intersection of discourses of globalization and feminist political economy. Bergeron notes the ways in which many feminist political economists tend toward hegemonic notions of global capital that then can only be responded to by a to-be-constructed mammoth global women's movement—"global sisterhood" (the parallel to the Marxist tradition of the absolute necessity of an "international workers' movement" to combat capitalist imperialism should be apparent). While Bergeron supports some of what such a movement might promise and even achieve (as do we), she also points out, following Gibson-Graham and others, that this vision of a global sisterhood is, itself, determined in its necessity by the presumed global logic of Big Capitalism. In this way, the discourses of global capitalism "derive rhetorical staying power from their reliance on conventional patriarchal gendered meanings," such as the idea that capitalism violently "penetrates" the societies that it encounters, thus constructing fundamental identities and subjectivities as essentially "victims" of this violence. Bergeron goes on to support the idea that replacing such masculinist discourses/metaphors of globalization may be what is required to tackle the differential and contradictory ways in which, here and there, capitalist firms interact—or not—with such societies and produce a plethora of subject positions, even ones in which "resistance" is not only possible, but routinely practiced. In Gibson-Graham's terms, this discursive replacement would open up the space of contestation—also the space of immanent life—for subjects and social formations alike.

Together, the contributions of Levin, Hewitson, Gibson-Graham, and Bergeron begin to chart a new path for gendering and fragmenting the subject by and within discourse. What are the consequences for economic theory of this "discursive turn"? First, we think that the idea that knowing and acting subjects are always discursive constructions, and thus have no "reality" outside of determinate discourses, makes difficult a reconcilia-tion of neoclassical and other such views of subjectivity. Here, we wish to stress the irreducible incommensurability of concepts of subjectivity and individuality. This means that our investigation of any alternative notions of the gendered and fragmented subject, such as we explore below, is not meant to claim that such notions are "empirically" better or more adequate. Likewise, we do not regard as decisive neoclassicals' (or other modernist economists') retorts to their critics that they alone have captured the essence of economic actions through, for example, their portrayal of the intentional and rational subject.

Second, if subjectivity is textually produced in distinct and different ways in diverse economic discourses, then the question of the role of sub-jectivity in economic theory is likewise specifically and variously deter-mined. Thus, there can be no transdiscursive criterion or imperative that requires that "economics" be grounded, either ontologically or epistemo-logically, in a theory of the subject. While it may be the case that neoclassi-cals and many of their critics (including some feminist economists) find it crucial to establish the correct nature of intentional action or objective method, it may also be true that the importance of this question applies only to those discourses in which subjectivity is conceived as the founda-tion for all consequent social relations and knowledges. The question re-mains, however, whether or not feminist economics requires such a foun-dation. If not, the question of establishing the "correct" nature of the subject in and for economics may be of little or no importance, at least in terms of establishing the possibility of concrete economic analysis.

Third, some feminist conceptions of agency and knowledge may be unsettling for modernist discourses, and their insertion into these discur-sive formations can lead to a deconstruction and transformation of main-stream economic theory. Although many neoclassicals claim, for example, that there may be no a priori imperative to use the concepts of "rational economic man" and "rational economic scientist" as presumptions for economic theory (as long as *some* notion of subjectivity is included in the initial assumptions concerning the economy and economic knowledge), introducing feminist notions of fragmented subjects may be disruptive or "nihilistic" in constituting the consequent economic theories. On this point, we believe it can be shown that, when faced with such deconstruc-tive effects, neoclassicals (and others) retreat to the mostly abstract (but masculinist) notions of subjectivity that allow their theory to remain more or less consistent and coherent.[26] In other words, we think that, for politi-

---

[26] Rebecca Blank (1993, 138–41), for one, defends the "mainstream economic model of human behavior" on the grounds that it is a "wonderful" null hypothesis (because widely accepted), it can be easily translated into familiar mathematical forms, and because it repre-

cal and theoretical reasons, neoclassical economists may refuse to construct their economic explanations in relation to such postmodern ideas
as the "decentered subject," one of the products of recent feminist work
in and around economics. Postmodern notions of subjectivity may destabilize neoclassical theorizing to such a degree that their introduction may
compromise the dominance of neoclassicism in the discipline of economics. This possibility, to our mind, distinguishes the critical effects of postmodern feminism from the critiques that aim simply at regendering knowing and acting subjects and that, as a result, remain within the bounds of
economic modernism.

The issue of discursivity is only one way in which the methodological
and epistemological premises of subjectivity are undermined by some
variants of feminism, especially those that pursue their affinities with postmodernism. Additional problems arise with the notion of the decentered
or fragmented subject; the consequent idea that subjectivity, therefore, is
never "closed" but remains open because it is "overdetermined"; and,
finally, the possibility that there may be no such general categories as "the
economic agent" and "the subject of knowledge," or at least the conceit
of general, universal types may be called into question on grounds simultaneously of their ahistoricity and historically determined biases.

One difficulty in discussing postmodern subjectivities is that we wish
to avoid the empiricism we noted above. Such avoidance, ironically, cannot be said to characterize some of the more important presentations of
postmodern subjects and knowledges. Therefore, some advocates of postmodern thought and culture prefer to conceive of subjects as fragmented
because, in their view, this is the way subjects truly are in the present.
Similarly, some feminists criticize the universalizing aspects of modernist
concepts of the subject. The criticisms often presume, however, that the
crucial problem with such universality is that the resulting constructions
leave out the particular subjectivities of women. Thus, in opposition, a
concrete multiplicity of subjectivities—structured according to gender,
race, ethnicity, class, and other forms of social differentiation—is conceived to derive from differential experiences and resulting epistemological "standpoints." The problem with this "bounded universality" (insofar
as it is limited to the "universal" of women, for example) is that it purports to capture what is truly human (or female) but does so by negating
the specificity of concrete subjectivities and the distinctness of experience,
often by privileging even in critique the particular gestalt of one subgroup

---

sents a "very good approximation of reality" for "white, middle-income persons in a democratic, industrialized, and Westernized society." (She also notes that the neoclassical model
of rational subjectivity serves to attract some, usually male, students into economics and to
exclude many others.)

(men, for example) as the "human condition" sui generis. Thus, a "better" set of explanations of social events would arise as a resulting of substituting multiple subjects, with their empirically based standpoints, for the universal and eternal individual, most often some version of the Cartesian subject.

Keeping in mind our view that subjectivities are always discursively constructed and that there can be no epistemological privilege granted to this or that alternative conception, we turn to discuss the three points adumbrated above. On the issue of the decentered subject, some postmodernists and feminists (most notably Judith Butler [1990], Denise Riley [1988], and Jane Flax [1987]) challenge the idea that subjects exist as singular and unique "I's." This challenge involves several related ideas. First, the idea of the decentered subject presumes that no permanent totality of cognitive traits characterizes the psyche or identity of either knowing or acting subjects. Here, the argument is both one of transitoriness (the idea, for example, that, even if a totality called "the mind" exists, it is constantly being formed and reformed, in new and different ways) and of totality itself. Central to the idea of the Cartesian subject is the view that "I" come to know and act in the world. This "I" is total or uniformly constituted, as it comes to know itself as an entity rather than distinct and perhaps discrete entities. In the postmodern notion of the decentered subject, the "I" is fragmented and dispersed into many component psychical and cognitive parts, with no necessity of their congealing or cohering at any given moment into a unity or essential identity. Add to this the idea that the fragments comprising the "I" may be in contradiction and of different composition, and the view that rational thought or even identity stands as the guide for objective knowledge or purposive action is confounded. We note the possible difficulty that both neoclassical utility theory, where a single set of determinate preferences is rationally acted on by a unified "I" in the pursuit of knowable ends, and neoclassical conceptions of scientific knowledge, where a singular standard of reason serves to guide the unified "I" to discover objective truth, may have with such a view.

The second point, that of the problem of the closure of subjectivity, is related to the issue of the decentered subject. Here, however, subjectivity is seen to be "undetermined" in its overdetermination. The multiplicity of fragments and causes may make it impossible to conceive of the subject as "complete" or "whole." And this problem is not restricted to a historical epoch (say, postindustrial society) or economic form (for example, the market). It reflects, as well, the conditions that may occur at any moment in time or type of economy. Once again, the lack of closure of subjects means that no complete "I" may guide its actions toward particular ends, whether in the realm of knowledge or the economy. The "open" subject is one whose subjectivity is constituted in the very acts in which he or she is engaged. Following no necessary prescribed paths, operating on perhaps multiple and diverse impulses and forms of rationality, and having these impulses and rationalities constructed and transformed in the process of knowing and/or acting, the open subject comes to particular ends that can be conceived as the overdetermined result of perhaps an infinity of causes and conditions and not the single result of a closed, totalizing "I."

The third point is the issue of a universal form of subjectivity, something akin to establishing the character of *the* human essence. On this point, feminists (and others, especially institutionalists and Marxists) have been quite successful in showing that universality almost always proceeds by privileging the subjective status of some groups in the determination of the supposedly all-embracing concept. Universality goes hand in hand with positing both the timelessness and consistency of the essential qualities of the subject, thereby adding the dimensions of eternality and uniformity as well. Recent work by feminists outside of economics is noteworthy for exploding the universality of modernist notions of subjectivity. From the standpoint theory of Sandra Harding (1998), Donna Haraway (1991), and Dorothy Smith (1990) to the postmodern feminism of Butler, Riley, and Flax, this project has been particularly fecund. Of special interest to us is the groundbreaking work of certain French feminists, such as Monique Wittig (1992) and Luce Irigaray (1985), which raises the concern that all universalistic conceptions are necessarily masculinist. For Irigaray, for example, the problem with the notion of the rational subject is not that it leaves no room for nonmasculine forms of discourse, thought, and action. Rather, in her view, all forms of universalizing, including the distinction between the rational "I" and its "others" (in which "otherness" may include such "feminine" subjective attributes as altruism, empathy, connectedness, and so forth) involves a soliloquy by men about men. This is so because all of men's "otherness" depicted in alternative views of subjectivity is simply a side of men that they repress (but define themselves against) when asserting their presumably dominant, masculine side. Thus, both the subject and its other are wholly masculine. Attempts to characterize "otherness," in this view, remain inscribed within the universalizing, totalizing tendencies of men to (perhaps unconsciously) presume that *their* concrete subjective determinations—of all their "sides"—adequately capture the essences of both themselves and their others.

Beyond Subjectivity

The postmodern alternatives to the neoclassical view of the subject—the economic subject as well as the subject of knowledge—are only just beginning to be expressed. In this context, it is important to return to our point in the beginning of the chapter. Gendering and fragmenting the subject do not on their own lead to a new place for subjectivity in conceiving economic discourse or the events constructed by that discourse. Thus, for example, we see in feminist economists' penetrating criticisms of both *homo economicus* and *homo scientis* a concerted attempt to regender the masculinist subject and making that subject more "whole" by introducing various forms of connectedness, especially with other acting and knowing agents. Such work raises the important question of how neoclassical theory might be changed by incorporating the gendered (and, perhaps, fragmented) subject.

On one hand, the work of England et al. shows that the fundamental structure of neoclassical theory need not be changed insofar as subjective preferences (now refurbished to include altruistic calculations as well as strictly "selfish" ones) and the scientific method (appropriately reconfigured to incorporate "dialectical" concepts and other ways of appropriating knowledge) remain the starting points for economic theory. We must ask the question of whether or not, in this sense, there might exist a "feminine" preference ordering and standard of objectivity that, in their basic structure, exhibit themselves in a different way from the masculine conception. If so, what is being suggested is that any subject, regardless of biological sex, can be gendered in different ways by the degree to which they possess and act on such distinct and mutually exclusive preference orderings and ways of knowing. We must also consider the possibility that even the notions of "rational" choice and knowledge are now changed so that the ordinary "rules" of utility and knowledge production are altered. Of course, it is possible, as well, that a feminist economics, starting from the premise of a gendered and even fragmented subject, may eschew entirely the role of rational choice and objective knowledge. But we should add that, if this is done, while breaking in a most significant way from neoclassical thought, it would still be the case that alternative views of acting and knowing subjects could more or less easily supplant traditional views of the subject without displacing subjectivity from its essential role in determining the conception and order of economic discourse.

Such cases are common, we think, in economics. A recent example may be some interpretations of game theory (especially concerning the household) where the previous notions of rationality and preference have been scaled down and replaced by notions of unequal bargaining power, coalition formation, and "ethically driven" behavior attributed to the economic actors.[27] In this case, a modified view of the economic agent may replace the earlier view of the origin and role of preferences, even to the point of allowing for the introduction of the endogenous determination

[27] See, e.g., Agarwal 1997; Bergstrom 1996; Folbre 1997; and Nelson 1994.

of preferences. And the nature of the economic scientist may be similarly altered, for example, by focusing on the causes and conditions (often assumed to be given in game-theoretic models) that give rise to different gendered choices and forms of behavior in the first place.

Yet, and this is our point, the change in the concept of the subject does not, by itself, imply a change in the exalted role of the subject in and of economic theory. To do so would mean pushing the connotations of gendering and fragmenting to their limits by seeing the holism and masculinity of economic theory not only in the concept of the unified subject (as both economic agent and producer of knowledge) but also, as Irigaray and Wittig argue, in the very notion of "theory" itself in which universalistic, essentialist, and therefore abstract reasoning predominates. This is the path suggested by the feminist writings of Levin, Hewitson, Gibson-Graham, Bergeron, and others, which promises a more sweeping decentering of economic theory precisely by focusing on the role of textuality or discourse in producing particular notions of subjectivity, of economic agents as well as of economic scientists. Such work implies that there is no central aspect of the economy or of knowledge production, including the subject however fragmented and regendered, that serves as the ultimate determinant of all other aspects. They thus break from the modernist history of the mind/body relationship and establish the possibility of conceiving of both the economy and knowledge in postmodern terms, as "processes without a subject."

5

Values and Institutional Economics

We can never be entirely separate from the question
of value, never fully escape its gravitational pull,
nor ever fully inhabit it as our home, or *ethos*.
—Steven Connor, "The Necessity of Value"

"VALUE IS, as Nietzsche said, *the* modern problem." This sentence, with
its original emphasis included, occurs in a now-neglected collection from
1949, entitled *Value: A Comparative Inquiry*. The writer was Edwin
Thomas Mitchell, a philosopher trained in the 1920s at the University of
Chicago—the hotbed of American pragmatism during that period—who
spent the majority of his career teaching at the University of Texas at Austin, known as well for its connection to institutionalist economics. The
occasion of Mitchell's observation about Nietzsche is a compilation of
original articles and rejoinders, edited by Ray Lepley, organizedaround the
brief but influential essay "Some Questions about Value," by John Dewey.[1]
Dewey's essay initially appeared in 1944 in the *Journal of Philosophy* and
is reproduced as part of Lepley's introduction to this edited text. The authors contributing to this collection include some of the leading lights of
American institutionalist thought in economics, such as C. E. Ayres, as
well such distinguished philosophers of the time as Henry David Aiken and
Steven Pepper. Nietzsche is mentioned only once in this text, but Mitchell's
attribution speaks loudly of Nietzsche's significance in defining the key
theoretical issue, and in the context of *modernity*, that needed to be addressed by mid-twentieth-century ethicists and moral philosophers.[2]

In a sense, our chapter can be understood as largely about the past
and potential legacy bequeathed to economics of these two great modern

[1] Lepley followed up this collection with a sequel in 1957 entitled *The Language of Value*.
The focus of this later text is the linguistic, semantic, and semiotic dimensions that are both
exemplified in and give rise to value discourse and valuation practices in general.

[2] Edward Andrew (1995) claims that it is customary to cite Nietzsche as "the person most
responsible for introducing values into philosophy" (5). Yet, according to Andrew, "values-
discourse existed in American philosophy from the time of the translation of Rudolph Hermann Lotze's works into English in the 1880s" (5). A consequence of this translation was
that "William James, George Santayana, and John Dewey began to use values-discourse in
the 1890s when they were at best imperfectly acquainted with Nietzsche's work" (5).

figures in the philosophy of values: Nietzsche and Dewey. These names stand out as monuments for what have become curiously intersecting tendencies (and ones that also remain worlds apart) in the litany of critiques of "modernist" positivist and utilitarian epistemological and moral theory, including within the field of economics. Indeed, in the writings of Richard Rorty (1979, 1991), to take just one example, Dewey and Nietzsche closely cohabitate in a sweeping postmodern assault on modernist philosophy and science. That is, Dewey and Nietzsche are recurring references in different attempts by postmodernists and their friends to establish the moments of rupture, often decisive, between the pursuit of knowledge as a "mirror of nature" and the mostly concomitant displacement of "values" from the sphere of legitimate knowledge to a distinct and well-defined (and well-behaved, it is hoped) normative realm.

Institutionalist economics is the focus of this chapter. A version of Deweyan pragmatism has been one of the key ingredients in the institutionalist assault, almost from its inception, on the positive/normative split in mainstream economics. In contrast, Nietzsche's influence upon institutionalism is fleeting at best, and in our experience, institutionalists express deep hostility towards and mistrust of Nietzsche's "transvaluation of all values." Yet, as we show, there are elements of the institutionalist value theory that come remarkably close to Nietzsche's perspectivist view of values and scientific knowledge. These elements comprise the postmodern moments of institutionalist economics, though they remain largely suppressed by a more "absolutist," instrumentalist approach that institutionalists have long claimed derives from Deweyan pragmatism.

Institutionalists undoubtedly can trace their lineage on questions of value to diverse traditions in moral philosophy. For example, Aristotelian approaches—pertaining to household provisioning and the behavior appropriate to it—also inspire institutionalist value discourse. The institutionalist dimensions of Arjo Klamer's work (2001), to take one instance, is predicated on a unique blend of Aristotle and Adam Smith on the notion of "the good life." In a book devoted to Karl Polanyi, J. Ron Stanfield (1986), a leading American institutionalist, attributes Polanyi's economic perspective and his institutionalist leanings primarily to Aristotle, and still others have found resources, if not solace, in the moral and ethical stances of classical economic theory, most certainly Smith.[3]

---

[3] Charles Griswold (1999) upholds Smith as a "resource" for a partial defense of "the Enlightenment" against those antimodernist critics—among these he names Nietzsche, Heidegger, and Rorty—who link Enlightenment ideals with Platonic moral theory and consequently call for the "death of philosophy." In Griswold's comprehensive study, Smith's moral philosophy, above all else, is held to provide a rich and nuanced defense of both Enlightenment political philosophy and moral tenets as well as "a profound appreciation of the ironies and dissatisfactions associated with them" (25–26).

But Dewey is a touchstone for a large number of institutionalists, and the recent popularity of Dewey in discussions of economic methodology have made even more evident his contributions to the ways in which institutionalism has developed over the past century.[4] Deweyan pragmatism, though, is not now nor ever has been interpreted in a singular fashion. To the contrary, as Lucas Wilson (1996) has perceptively pointed out, the readings and uses of Dewey in economics and in other disciplines range from "cognitive modernism" and epistemological essentialism to postmodern relativism and antifoundationalism. In economics, Dewey is most often used to defend modernist premises about values and science, but Dewey affords a different reading as well, one that Wilson has done much to champion. We return to the different Deweyan pragmatisms later in the chapter to indicate the possibility that Dewey can be employed to critique modernism, even in its institutionalist guises. Even so, we develop a different possible postmodern trajectory for the role of values in economic discourse, one owing more to Nietzsche than to Dewey.

Institutionalist Economics and the Problem of Value

The postmodern turn in philosophy and social theory is often associated—credited or blamed, depending on the perspective of the commentator—with the disappearance of values. The "absence" of values is thought to undermine the grounds for formulating and adopting "principled positions" in the arenas of culture and politics (see, e.g., Squires 1993). Postmodern challenges to the traditional canons of taste and categories of high and low art have called into question absolutist or foundational notions of aesthetic value, while the critique of humanism and the focus on difference have made problematic the metanarratives of social justice conventionally used to formulate and legitimate ethical positions and political activity.

---

[4] In his entry "Institutionalism" for *The Handbook of Economic Methodology*, Malcolm Rutherford (1998) states that "the methodological principles of most importance in the institutionalist tradition are to be found in the evolutionary and holistic ... view of the social and economic world, combined with the instrumentalist theory of knowledge taken from the work of John Dewey" (249). Rutherford goes on to say that "the instrumentalist theory of knowledge as developed in the work of John Dewey quickly became incorporated within the institutionalist tradition" (251). Rutherford presents a common reading of Deweyan instrumentalism: "Dewey's version of instrumentalism views theories as instruments or tools for the betterment of human life. Theories are both developed and judged as tools, they arise out of attempts to modify the world and are judged on the basis of the consequences of their implementation. What is sought is not truth or certainty, but effectiveness in application. For most institutionalists, then, the test of their ideas is to be found in their application to the solution of social problems" (251). As we argue below, following Wilson (1996), this reading turns Dewey into a "cognitive modernist" and, ironically, ends up evacuating values in many of the protocols of scientific practice.

Whether or not one accepts the idea that postmodernism has occasioned or created a "values vacuum" (and we have our doubts),[5] it would seem that economics should be able to offer a solution. Value in its many senses has a long and honorable history in economic thought, dating at least as far back as Aristotle and, later, scholastic notions of the "just price."[6] The irony, however, is that economists, especially those in the mainstream of the discipline, spent the better part of the twentieth century distancing themselves and their work from anything that hints of values and value theory. Certainly, if what we mean by *economic* value is a category that lies before, behind, or beyond and that serves to determine market prices, then contemporary neoclassical economists have mostly relinquished (as either embarrassing to or unnecessary for their enterprise) the attempt to explain prices in terms of an antecedent value of the sort that motivated much of classical political economy, early neoclassical theory, and other schools of thought.[7] Value, as it turns out, is not a major area of concern within mainstream economists.[8]

[5] In Ruccio, Graham, and Amariglio 1996 we have presented our own views on the postmodern—what we consider to be a discursive—approach to value.

[6] A brief note on terminology. There are numerous meanings and uses of the term *value*. It is customary among many economists, for example, to reserve the term for questions that pertain to the determination of prices in markets. Value, then, is used to refer to *economic value* or to the older term *exchange-value*, which is often distinguished from the notion of utility or *use-value*. The debates over value in the history of economic thought have been largely about the question of a meaningful distinction, or not, between price and value, and of course about the determinants and composition of economic value, however defined. This general usage is now most often differentiated from the notion of "values," especially when this second term is associated with the ethical stances or moral judgments of economic scientists and/or the agents they describe. The generic term *value*, though, is also used in a variety of realms other than economics, such as in art and culture, where the concept of aesthetic value is meant to designate the aesthetic effect and worth that a cultural artifact either deposits (or embodies), or that is granted by one who is enjoying an aesthetic experience or who exercises aesthetic judgment. Again, there are many other uses and registers for the term *value*. But to return to economics, while there is a common difference drawn between *economic value* and *values*, the distinction is one that is blurred considerably in the institutionalist tradition, the subject of this chapter. As we discuss below, treating markets as "institutions" with unique cultural and historical constituents at different moments in time means treating the prices that arise therein as affected and comprised of a variety of elements, including that of "values." Thus, "value theory" in its usual sense within economics cannot, for institutionalists, be separated entirely, if at all, from "values theory." In our effort to respect this view, we move from "economic value" to "values" throughout this chapter in a manner, we hope, that does justice to institutionalist usage.

[7] It is no wonder, then, that John Guillory (1993) views (and criticizes) Barbara Herrnstein Smith's (1988) conception of "contingent values"—especially her reliance on the idea that individuals existing in "valuing communities" are the ultimate source of value judgments—as closely related to neoclassical economists' refusal of a theory of economic value.

[8] Robert Garnett (1999a) arrives at a different conclusion, arguing that value theory is central not only to neoclassical theory but much of what constitutes the modern discipline

Aside from Marxist economists, for whom value is still an important (albeit controversial) area of inquiry, it is institutional economists who can be credited with keeping the discussion of value(s) alive within the discipline. Following in a tradition associated with the pioneering contributions of such critics as Thorstein Veblen, John R. Commons, Clarence Ayres, and Karl Polanyi, contemporary institutionalists (including such diverse figures as Warren Samuels, Marc Tool, Yngve Ramstad, John Elliott, Anne Mayhew, and William Dugger) argue that orthodox economists' preoccupation with and celebration of the "competitive" model are fundamentally flawed: in place of the abstract theorizing, methodological individualism, and equilibrium method that lie at the core of neoclassical economics, institutionalism is concerned with the effects of "real" economic and social institutions, the cultural embeddedness of economic agents and their activities, and the movement over time of economic processes within an evolving social order. Institutional economists have sought to develop a far-reaching alternative to mainstream economics, oriented by a fundamentally different approach to economic policy (often favoring various forms of democratic planning and social reform over the safeguarding and/or creation of free markets) as well as to the goal of economic inquiry (focusing on "social provisioning" versus the efficient allocation of scarce resources) and to the process of economic theorizing itself (where priority is given to case studies and narratives of institutional change instead of the formulation of mathematical models of the decisions of rational individual economic agents).[9]

Perhaps the central element of institutional economics—both its critique of the mainstream and its alternative approach—concerns the "value problem." Institutional economists reject the neoclassical approach to market prices, in which prices are determined via supply and demand, once endowments, technology, and preferences are taken as given. In contrast, institutionalists prefer to focus attention on the process of economic valuation and, especially, on the institutional, including the legal and power-based, causes and consequences of "administered"

---

of economics, because he sees value theories "as paradigmatic exemplars ... whereby schools of thought seek to formalize their a priori visions of a market economy" (820). Value theory, in this sense, refers to any attempt to find an order within or underlying the apparent disorder of markets and exchange.

[9] Clear and comprehensive introductions to the basic concepts of and the diverse perspectives encompassed by institutional economics include Gruchy 1987; Dugger 1989; and Tool 1993b, as well as the "official" journal of U.S. institutional economics, the *Journal of Economic Issues*. The essays in the recent volume edited by Samuels (1998) explore the roots of institutional economics in Veblen's *Theory of the Leisure Class* and Ayres's *Sociological View of Sovereignty*.

prices.[10] They also take issue with the claims to "value-free" scientific inquiry on the part of mainstream economics and the positivist underpinnings of such claims. In the view of many institutionalists, both past and present, economic analysis is necessarily value-laden to the extent that it is guided—implicitly or explicitly—by an approach to economic and social problems that combines issues of "what is" and "what ought to be." All economists, regardless of their paradigmatic orientation, are seen to be engaged in a normative enterprise that involves the question of appraisals relating to the future—the possible future states of the economy as well as the knowledges produced by economic scientists. The difference between institutionalists and their mainstream counterparts, it is argued, is that the former recognize the normative nature of their activity while the latter do not.

Institutionalism represents, on one hand, a far-reaching and penetrating critique of the positivist dichotomy between facts and values that has been (and, in many ways, remains) so central to economic modernism. In arguing that values permeate the process of scientific inquiry, institutionalists deconstruct the fact-value dichotomy and, in the process, identify and induce an important postmodern moment within contemporary economics. The institutionalist focus on values serves, inter alia, to focus attention on the social embeddedness of markets, to identify modes of social provisioning outside of or beyond markets, and to recognize the existence of a plurality of value discourses in and around economics. The work of (at least some) institutionalist economists therefore points in the direction of a more socially contingent and pragmatist approach to economic discourse, one that points beyond modernism.

At the same time, institutionalists seem to presume that the only alternative to the positivist tradition—of distinguishing between facts and values and then emphasizing the former over the latter—is to reverse that hierarchy and to privilege values as being of a higher order than so-called value-free statements. In our view, such an approach, while providing valuable criticisms of the modernist scientific claims made by many main-

---

[10] While often noting the affinities between institutional and Marxian economic theories (e.g., Tool 1986, 135–78 and Stanfield 1989), especially "overdeterminist" approaches to Marxism (see, e.g., Ramstad 1989, 771), institutional economists also make clear their rejection of a Marxian theory of labor value (see, e.g., Dugger 1989, 2–4). Mirowski (1990), for one, has made much of Marx's "blunder" in attempting to reconcile two different—"substance" and "real-cost"—approaches to labor value. We should note that one source of misunderstanding may be institutionalist economists' acceptance of the idea that there is a single Marxian value theory (or, in Mirowski's case, two different versions of such a theory) rather than a diversity of—modernist and postmodernist—approaches to economic analysis, including value theory, within the Marxian tradition. Wolff, Roberts, and Callari (1982), for example, have challenged and provided an alternative to the modernist framing of Marxian value theory presumed by Mirowski and other institutionalist critics.

stream (and, we should add, not a few heterodox) economists, ends up borrowing its conception of values from the same positivist story of the post-Enlightenment separation of reason from ethics and values. It thus sidesteps an alternative way of proceeding, one that we associate with Nietzsche's "perspectivist" critique of values, which can be used to establish a different (postmodern) terrain in order to take seriously and, at the same time, to "devalue" the place of values in contemporary economics.

Social Value Theory

Marc Tool's theory of "social value" stands at the center of the contemporary institutionalist debate concerning the role of values in economic theory. In an extended series of essays (especially 1986 and 1993b), Tool both elaborated what he considers to be the distinctive institutionalist approach to value and defended his interpretation of that approach against critics from within the institutionalist tradition.[11]

Throughout his work, Tool has held firmly to the view that institutional economic theory represents a radical departure from other economic discourses by virtue of its treatment of the social value problem, which "may well be its most significant contribution" (1986, 8). That treatment combines a focus on the status of values in all forms of economic inquiry, as well as the role played by values in "real" economic and social institutions, and the formulation of a specific set of values that informs (or should inform) institutional economic theory. Most contemporary institutionalists appear to share Tool's view that values permeate all economic discourses and that the attempt to identify and critically examine such values (in the realm of economic theory as well as the evolution of economic institutions) is one of the distinguishing characteristics of a specifically institutionalist approach to economics. Yet there are some who take issue with the position that institutionalism can be defined by a single, overarching value position. Mayhew and Wendell Gordon are leading spokespersons for the view that Tool (like others who share his position) has gone too far—that the set of values he proposes for institutional economics is, in some important sense, "absolutist" or "universal"—and that institutionalism should avoid upholding any such set of values. Tool, in defense of his views, notes that institutionalists who refuse to invoke an all-encompassing, "instrumental" value principle—embraced by many pragmatists—are forced either to defend the fact-value dichotomy associ-

---

[11] Tool (2000) has restated his interpretation of the theory of instrumental or social value in a recent summary of J. Fagg Foster's seminal contribution to the formation of institutionalist economic theory.

ated with a positivist conception of economic science or to succumb to "moral agnosticism" or "relativism."

In posing the problem as he does, Tool chooses to reproduce the terms of debate and disagreement—the common terrain—of his theoretical adversaries, both inside and outside institutional economics. This common terrain involves a shared and modernist conception of the meaning of values and, more indirectly, a shared and modernist conception of the scientific. Let us examine how this might occur.

The question of the status of values in economic inquiry begins with the idea that choices are continually being made in the course of economic analysis. Tool, along with other institutionalists such as Allan Gruchy (1987), William Waller Jr. (1989), and Samuels (1988), argues that normative premises and criteria of judgment permeate all stages of economic investigation—from the choosing of the problems to be addressed, the objects of inquiry, and the means and methodologies that are employed to the conclusions drawn from such investigations concerning the advocating of specific policies and assessments of the consequences of such policies. All such choices are determined, at least in part, by a judgment of "what ought to be," and therefore "*all* compel recourse to social value theory" (Tool 1986, 57).

Economic analysis is, from Tool's perspective, replete with value-laden choices—and thus intrinsically normative—because it is understood in terms of an instrumental approach to knowledge. Borrowing from a particular reading of the pragmatist philosophy of Dewey (1938, 1939), Tool argues that all forms of economic theorizing and empirical investigation are purposive activities in which the ends in view (e.g., the conclusions) can be evaluated as to their worth only on the basis of their ability to solve the problems presented by the conditions under investigation. In this sense, there are no general, a priori warrants for knowledge—for example, what Rorty refers to as the "mirror of nature"—because then any such knowledge would be devoid of instrumental value.[12] All economic (and, more generally, social scientific) knowledges are seen to be produced and validated according to the specific purposes that motivated the process of scientific inquiry in the first place.

From this, institutionalists emphasize the fallibilist character of economic knowledges and the evolving nature of economic inquiry. In the context of economic analysis, provisional knowledges are advanced that are presumed to be modified and improved according to successive investigations, thus ensuring the continuity of inquiry. As Tool explains, "the *process* of conducting inquiry fosters the uncovering and correcting of un-

---

[12] See Bush 1993 for an insightful discussion of the relation between Rorty's critique of epistemology and the pragmatist sources of institutionalism.

warranted assumptions, illogical constructs, disjunctions in coherence, or flawed connections (1993a, 130). An important dimension of this instrumental notion of continuity is that the means of investigation determine the consequences or conclusions that, in turn, become the means for further investigations.[13] And, for the institutionalist, valuational premises cannot but be present throughout this means-end continuum or interdependence.

The general scheme of value-laden, instrumental knowledge is clearly meant to challenge the positive-normative dichotomy associated with mainstream economics and, more generally, positivist and neopositivist approaches to scientific knowledge. This dimension of the institutionalist critique is the shared project of a wide variety of postpositivist conceptions of knowledge and science, including, in current economic philosophy, critical realism, constructivism, rhetoric, and overdeterminist Marxism. Most adherents of such otherwise diverse approaches would agree that the presumption on the part of neoclassical and other orthodox economists that there is a realm of positive, falsifiable economic knowledge that is unaffected by normative concerns and value judgments is contradicted by the adherence to such normative ideals as the competitive model, methodological individualism, and much else that serves as a criterion of judgment and standard of truth within modern mainstream economics.[14] While many mainstream economists may explicitly deny the relevance of values (or ethics, according to Sen 1987, or morality) to their theoretical enterprise, their work is necessarily (if only implicitly) informed by value judgments and normative concerns.

Tool and other institutionalists add that the specific neoclassical value principle suffers from being an ethically relativist one. In the institutionalist view, individual utility (the earlier cardinal conception as well as the later ordinalist approach) serves as the value referent, the key determinant of equilibrium prices, for both the theoretical work and the policies advocated by the majority of neoclassical economists. And since individual preferences are generally taken as given or exogenous, set outside the economic process and therefore beyond the purview of economic analysis, then, from the institutionalist viewpoint, the "what is" that is dictated by subjective preferences is made to serve as the indicator of "what ought to be." Since there is no criterion established independent of the preferences held by each individual and expressed in equilibrium prices—such that axiomatic choice theory does not afford the possibility of examining the origin, nor of judg-

---

[13] Institutionalists therefore reject the divorce between the realism of initial assumptions and predictive ability—and thus between means and ends—inherent in Milton Friedman's (1953) reference to "merely instrumental" knowledge claims.

[14] Tool discusses the ways in which the competitive model "sets the conceptual frame for inquiry and becomes an idealized standard of what is normal, right, and proper" in chapter 5 of his *Essays in Social Value Theory* (1986).

ing the "goodness" or "badness," of preferences or the actions and results based on such preferences—neoclassical economics is seen to lapse into an ethically ambivalent, fundamentally relativist position.[15]

Marxian economics is subjected to a somewhat different critique on the part of Tool and other institutionalist commentators. Marxists can be credited with rejecting the positivist dichotomy of facts and values; in this sense, they are commended for being practicing normativists. While Marx and Engels may not have formulated a single, coherent theory of ethics or moral principles, both they and later Marxists are recognized as taking seriously the role of values in economic and social inquiry and as applying social value concepts continuously in their work.[16] Institutionalists such as J. Ron Stanfeld (1989), John Elliott (1986), Steve Shuklian (1995), and Tool himself (1986, 135–78) have noted the explicit value dimensions of Marxian theory and the important affinities, at least on this issue, between Marxian and institutional economics. They are said to share, for example, a rejection of absolutist conceptions of values (in which the "good" is fixed, given, and final) and an interest in understanding the ways values are produced (and continue to change) socially and historically.[17]

Where Marxism comes under institutionalist criticism, however, is in the incompleteness of its distancing from ethically relativist positions. First, some forms of Marxism are charged with holding to class-based (and, therefore, class-relative) forms of morality in which either the dominant values that exist at any point in time are reduced to those of the "ruling class" and/or the moral standpoint from which value judgments can be made is that of the "exploited class." In the view of Tool and others, Marxism rests on a moral relativism if and when arguments are put forward to the effect that, in the case of capitalism, the proletariat

---

[15] In contrast to the institutionalists, Alasdair MacIntyre (1984) is concerned to show that it is the *failure* of the utilitarian project that explains the rise to prominence of the moral position he calls "emotivism," the doctrine according to which "all evaluative judgments and more specifically all moral judgments are nothing but expressions of preference, expressions of attitude or feeling, insofar as they are moral or evaluative in character" (11–12). MacIntyre goes further, still, to charge that pragmatism itself has served in the United States the role played by intuitionism in Britain in preparing the ground for the twentieth-century "decline into emotivism" (65–66).

[16] Whether or not Marx's (and, more generally, Marxists') critique of capitalism and support for socialism is based, at least in part, on a moral standpoint has been debated throughout the Marxian tradition. John Elliott (1986), E. K. Hunt (1979, 1982), Allan Buchanan (1982), Norman Geras (1985), and R. G. Peffer (1990) have defended the claim that Marxism does involve a moral stance, while Alan Wood (1972, 1984), Richard Miller (1984), and others have argued that Marxism explicitly rejects a moral basis for economic and social criticisms against capitalism and for socialism. More recently, Lawrence Wilde (1998) has attempted to defend and elaborate the ethical claims of Marxism against its "radical" critics.

[17] See Garnett 1999a for a discussion of additional affinities between institutional and Marxian economics.

creates historically its *own* notions of rights and justice and that there exist no criteria outside of the historical experience of the proletariat to evaluate those notions. Second, Marxism is linked to moral relativism to the extent that it fails to discriminate among wants and needs, to analytically rank or choose those forms of satisfaction or enjoyment that should be accorded priority from those that should be placed lower on the scale or abandoned altogether. Even the distinction between culturally determined, "artificial" wants and original, "true" needs (which, as we show in chapter 6 below, is part of a modernist approach to Marxian economics) fails to provide a convincing criterion for an institutionalism in which all such wants and needs are conceived to be "substantially shaped by culture" (Tool 1986, 166).[18] Finally, institutionalists are skeptical of Marxist arguments that refer to the "fulfillment of human potential" as the appropriate criterion in criticizing capitalism and arguing for socialism because, once again, no principle or criterion is given for choosing between good fulfillment and bad, between those dimensions of human potential that deserve to be fulfilled from those that do not. In all three of these cases, Marxism is seen to lack an adequate criterion of social value and, from Tool's perspective, "in the absence of such a criterion, the ambivalent wandering in the realm of ethical relativism must be presumed to continue" (168).

As we can see, the perspective of Tool and other institutionalists on the value position of institutional economics is substantially shaped by a general aversion to what they consider to be the ethical relativism of neoclassical *and* Marxian theories as well as the general "moral agnosticism" or "mores nihilism" characteristic of modern society.[19] What then

---

[18] Yuval Yonay (1998) discusses the institutionalist insistence on the sociocultural determination of all "human needs." This insistence arises mostly in the struggle with neoclassical theorists over their privileging of individual preferences and rational choice in explanations of consumer and producer market behavior. Interestingly, institutionalists borrowed heavily in conducting their attack from philosophical pragmatism, and certainly from Dewey. As Yonay states, "alongside the evidence of irrationality . . . institutionalists recruited the view of human beings held by pragmatists and symbolic interactionists to strengthen the validity of their argument. The pragmatists and symbolic interactionists emphasized the susceptibility of men and women to many influences from the surrounding community. The rationality of the 'economic man' means that one behaves according to one's real desires; not the 'false' desires society inculcates in us. The assumption is that human needs and desires are universal and constant and cannot be manipulated by others. The institutionalists, following pragmatists and symbolic interactionists, refused to accept this assumption and thought that human beings' basic needs and wants were determined by social forces" (104).

[19] They also state their rejection of ethical absolutism. According to Tool, the instrumental value principle he espouses "does not elevate an 'Absolute Truth' (e.g., Divine Right or power retention) to the status of exclusive judgmental premise. It provides no eternal verity" (1993a, 126). However, their critique of the value principles of other economic discourses focuses almost exclusively on the problem of ethical relativism.

is the social value principle that allows for judgments to be made and that avoids the problem of relativist values?

According to Tool, the appropriate criterion is to act or judge in a manner to "provide for the continuity of human life and [the] noninvidious re-creation of community through the instrumental use of knowledge" (1986, 10). Continuity refers to the preservation and fostering of human lives, ranging from such "obvious" principles as the condemnation of murder and warfare to a prominent concern for human rights in foreign policy and the role of education in developing critical and coherent thinking. The idea of recreating community begins with the notion that individuals are born into communities—defined by languages, customs, and order—and concludes that a key task is to renew that cultural, social order by modifying and transforming existing institutions. The use of the existing stock of reliable ("evidentially grounded, logically evolved") human knowledge to identify and solve the problems that prevent the continuity of life and the renewal of community is considered to be a specifically instrumental approach.

Finally, and perhaps most importantly, noninvidiousness is the criterion that seeks to reduce or remove forms of discrimination and disenfranchisement that operate on the basis of rank and prestige—that assess the relative worth of individuals according to race, gender, class, and so on— as well as all forms of ceremonial behavior—such as attempts to retain the privileges of power and adherence to what are considered to be outmoded work rules. Instead, the goal is to promote attitudes, behaviors, and institutions that foster the creation or extension of instrumental processes relating to the industrial or technological continuum, that is, the raising of technical efficiency in the service of overall social provisioning.[20] According to Tool and a wide range of other contemporary institutionalists, this instrumental value principle establishes the appropriate normative criterion for identifying, analyzing, and devising policies to solve the problems that arise not only in the economic arena but also in politics, human relations, and the environment.

Relative and Universal Values

While generally acknowledged to be one of the most developed formulations of an institutionalist social value theory, Tool's approach has been widely debated and criticized by other institutional economists.

---

[20] The ceremonial-instrumental distinction is generally taken to be the key "Veblenian dichotomy." Waller (1982) discusses the evolution of Veblen's specific usage into the contemporary ceremonial-instrumental dichotomy.

Ramstad (1989, 1995), for example, takes issue with Tool's position that there is a single value theory that derives from and is appropriate for institutional economics. Instead, he argues that Commons developed a concept of "reasonable value" that is fundamentally inconsistent with the notion of instrumental value that Tool and others have distilled from the tradition of Veblen (and his version of Deweyan pragmatism), Ayres, and J. Fagg Foster.[21]

Gordon and Mayhew also attempt to distance institutional economics from the instrumental social value principle adumbrated above. In their view, the particular value principle put forward by Tool (and endorsed by others, such as Tilman 1974) is neither necessary for, nor consistent with, what they understand to be the institutionalist treatment of values. Gordon (1984, 1990) questions the definition of specific terms (e.g., what does it mean to continue human life in the abstract? should all lives be continued? if not, which ones?), the criteria of choice of other terms (e.g., why noninvidiousness and not compassion, tolerance, or generosity?), and the applicability of the social value principle (e.g., is less inequality in the distribution of income the product of an antecedent or independent value judgment or, as Tool seems to argue, is it a direct consequence of instrumental valuation?). Perhaps most importantly, Gordon challenges the compatibility between the seemingly unchanging, universal status of Tool's principle and institutionalism's attention, in other areas, to the cultural situatedness of human knowledges (including value judgments) and the continual reappraisal and interdependence of tools and goals, means and ends.[22] According to Gordon, instrumentalism may explain how value judgments arise, but it does not validate or invalidate them.

[21] Although Commons was aware of the "Veblenian dichotomy" of the ceremonial and the instrumental, he did not consider it to be a valid principle either of analytical inquiry or of normative judgment. Instead, in Ramstad's view, Commons held to a view of "bargained justice" that begins with individual purposes and desires as they are revealed, however imperfectly, in competitive market transactions. Commons's goal was not to judge or supplant competitive economic institutions, according to an overarching social value principle, but to make the use of power by the bargaining parties (e.g., in labor-management relations) as balanced as possible. In that way, differences in the ends pursued by the contending parties could be ironed out, compromises reached, such that "reasonable" decisions could be arrived at. According to Ramstad, "whether or not the values underlying those ends were 'instrumental' or 'ceremonial' was of no apparent concern to [Commons]. Significantly, he strongly rejected the idea that 'intellectuals' or 'scientists' were better qualified to identify what goals people should pursue than they were themselves" (1989, 769). Mirowski (1987) adds to this interpretation the idea that Commons took over a theory of semiotics from the work of the pragmatist Charles Peirce in order to understand the actors' interpretations of the meaning of legitimate transactions, leading not only to conflicts of interest but also of interpretation. This makes the notion of reasonable value historical and contingent upon the evolution of the relevant interpretative community.

[22] Gordon is worth quoting at length: "The criteria of judgment applied in dealing with a problem are going to be whatever the individual, or the race, or the institution

Mayhew builds on Gordon's criticisms, accepting the notion that value judgments emerge from an ongoing social process and are therefore tentative, and similarly interprets Tool's value principle as a statement of "universal human goals . . . that can serve as standards against which performance can be measured" (1987, 598). In her view, the attempt to identify a set of "continuous human functions" that, once formulated, can serve as "objective" and "non-culturally specific" criteria for analysis and for judgment violates the key role of culture within institutional economics. For Mayhew, instrumental valuation *is* an aspect of all human behavior, but when it is elevated to the status of the criterion of judging institutions, the analysis of actual cultural patterns receives less emphasis. Even more important, the idea that instrumental valuation is considered to be an "elemental human strategy" means that cultures (and, perforce, the institutions in which they are embodied) are treated as either the products of reasonable choices or as obstacles to or constraints on instrumental processes. The specifically institutionalist conception of cultural relativism—in Mayhew's usage, the understanding of different forms of human behavior as the *consequence* of different cultures—is thereby rejected.[23]

It is this socially contextualist approach to value theory that, in the view of Robert Garnett (1999a), creates a distance from modernist approaches and moves in the direction of a postmodern treatment of value. First, the emphasis on the social embeddedness or contextualization of value implies that "there is no general form—hence no general laws or principles—of 'market economy' " (824). Instead, each market or collection of markets (whether art auctions, peasant marketplaces, or shopping

---

making the decision chooses to apply in a given situation at a given time and place. And those criteria that are actually applied, are going to reflect evolving technology, institutionalized behavior norms, the biology of the decisionmakers, and the availability of appropriate resources. . . . The relevant institutionalized behavior norms may include belief in the desirability of noninvidiousness in people's attitudes, or they may include a lot of other considerations. And all these attitudes and conditions are in a state of flux" (1990, 885).

[23] Walter Neale (1990) also defends what he calls "absolute cultural relativism" as the appropriate value for institutional economics. An earlier appeal can be found in the pragmatist George R. Geiger's contribution to the Lepley collection (1949). Geiger is not particularly intimidated by the bogeyman of moral relativism that results from attention to distinct cultural influences on values and knowledge. He writes, "But moral relativity cannot be avoided by an appeal to some abstract standard which, however noble, stands outside the system it is expected to judge. Such a criterion would require either a super-culture—and glorious as that would be, it has not yet appeared; or some intuition or revelation of the *right* values" (103). While Geiger proceeds then to abandon his own insight (or so it seems to us), nevertheless, he points in the direction of the "intradiscursivity" of value judgments and not their "extradiscursive" objectivity, an issue we take up more fully below.

malls or market systems in the United States or eastern Europe), and thus each manner in which market value is determined, must be understood as the product of a particular and changing set of cultural, political, and economic circumstances and conditions. In other words, each market is conceived to be a particular social institution, with its own modalities and effects; it cannot be reduced to a single essential cause (such as rational choice) or representation (like the familiar supply-and-demand schemes of mainstream economists). In this, institutionalist economists find themselves much closer to recent literatures in sociology, anthropology, and cultural studies in which markets (along with market values, money, and so on) are understood as contingently formed in and through different discursive and social contexts.[24]

A second postmodern moment in the institutionalists' approach emerges from their concern to include nonmarket forms of economy. Value is conceived to arise in the context of social provisioning. Yet markets are only one among many institutions for allocating goods and services to achieve such provisioning (including such diverse forms as production for use, "gleaning," an entire continuum of nonmarket exchanges, and government planning)—and, according to Polanyi (1957), a relatively recent and "artificial" construction at that. Therefore, institutionalist economics represents a way of "rethinking value beyond markets" while avoiding the peril of reducing all economic activities, market and nonmarket, to a single, overarching principle or rule.

Finally, Garnett argues that the postmodern moments within institutionalist economics have prompted at least some of its practitioners "to rediscover the still-active role of value theories in economic discourse and to reconceive and decenter this role" (1999a, 826). From an institutionalist perspective, specific values are embedded and expressed in any economic discourse; each carries a vision or set of commitments, a view both of what the economy is (where the boundary between the economy and the rest of society is drawn) and of what kinds of utterances are possible or permissible (and, thus, in what economic analysis consists and what is not economics and/or not science). At the same time, the contextualist or nonabsolutist strands of institutionalism raise the possibility that the role of value theory can be reinscribed, making it less central or foundational for the functioning of economic institutions and for carrying out economic analysis. This approach also creates the prospect of seeing and imagining spheres of nonvalue, theoretical and social spaces in which

---

[24] We are thinking of the work of, among others, Abolafia (1989), Appadurai (1986a), Kopytoff (1986), Watkins (1998), and Zelizer (1994). This parallel is not surprising given institutional economists' interest, from Veblen on, in anthropology. See, e.g., Mayhew 1998.

events occur that are usually regarded as the preserve of value but are not regulated or governed by value, discourses and activities (whether in Western or other cultures) in which value plays no role whatsoever.

It is precisely this last implication that other institutionalist economists appear to see and to keep at bay. Tool (together with F. Gregory Hayden 1989 and others) is quite critical of any attempt to divorce institutional economics from an instrumental value principle according to which judgments concerning the goodness or badness of economic policies and practices can be formulated.[25] Tool interprets Gordon's and Mayhew's approaches as depriving institutionalism of a principle of social value judgment, of attempting to make the institutional approach value-free but, for all that, lapsing into ethical relativism.

Gordon, in particular, is charged with upholding an individualistic, subjective conception of values because he emphasizes the importance of examining how value judgments are *actually* made by economic and social actors. Tool defends his own candidate for the instrumental value principle against criticisms of its purported universality by arguing that, while perhaps not universal ("there are, no doubt, areas of human experience to which it does not apply"), it "is a widely shared judgmental principle among those in the community who wish, through causal analysis and consequent appraisal, to understand and remove the institutional determinants of obstructions and impairments in the provisioning process and in the discretionary mechanism through which policy is determined" (1993a, 142).

In his response to Mayhew, Tool reiterates his belief that the various dimensions encapsulated in his instrumental value principle, especially the preservation of human life and the recreation of community, *are* pan-cultural obligations; therefore, they do not violate the institutionalist concern with cultural differences. Thus, Tool sees the instrumental value principle as the only valid principle for judging the goodness or badness, the instrumental or ceremonial character, of institutional arrangements and policies in *all* cultural settings. The alternative is to preclude the possibility of judgment, to restore the positive-normative dichotomy, and to fall back into ethical relativism.

---

[25] In response to Ramstad, for example, Tool argues for the necessity of being able to judge the resulting settlement, of distinguishing between a good compromise and a bad one. Instrumental justice differs from equational justice (of which Commons's notion of bargained justice is considered a special case) in that the former allows for judgments to be made concerning the extent to which flows of income contribute to "continuity, maintenance, or restoration of community, and noninvidious access" (1986, 132), while the latter may justify agreements between parties that have a negative impact on the community as a whole. Tool uses the example of "sweetheart" contracts, where labor and management are seen to conspire against the larger community.

Instrumentalism and Deweyan Pragmatisms

The instrumental value principle adumbrated by Tool and both embraced and criticized by Mayhew, Gordon, and others derives much of its philosophical grounding from the version of pragmatism developed by John Dewey. That is, Tool and many other institutionalists hold positions regarding the role of values in society and scientific inquiry that they attribute to the "instrumentalism" of Dewey's brand of pragmatism. While instrumentalist approaches are rife today in the philosophy of economics (and more broadly, in the philosophy of science), institutionalists can claim a long tradition of arguing for instrumentality—Dewey-style—in discussing the processes and goals of scientific reasoning and practice.

Yet as the discursive dispersion of instrumentalism itself implies, Dewey's pragmatism cannot be rendered univocally. As Wilson (1996) points out, Dewey has recently been the poster child for different "pragmatist" (read: instrumentalist) approaches within economic methodology. Uskali Mäki (1998) states that while "in economics, the label of instrumentalism has been used when characterizing the methodological positions of Milton Friedman and Fritz Machlup . . . it is also not uncommon to see the whole or a major part of neoclassical economics described in these terms. On the other hand, one tradition hostile to conventional neoclassical theory identifies itself as holding an institutionalist position. This is a major strand of North American institutionalism, inspired by John Dewey's pragmatist instrumentalism" (253).

What Mäki fails to note is that Dewey has been seen not only as the inspiration for institutionalists, but for Friedman himself. Indeed, there is now a considerable literature in the philosophy of economics that reads Friedman as either a nascent or a mature "Deweyan pragmatist." Nor is Dewey's golden touch restricted just to Friedman and institutionalism. Various other heterodox thinkers in economics have turned to Dewey in order to scan an alternative philosophical position to that of positivism on questions of value and knowledge.

Wilson (1996) is emphatic that these plural readings of Dewey cannot be resolved by reference to the "real" Dewey. Instead, he puts forward the notion that there are competing and often incommensurate readings of Dewey and, therefore, that pragmatism enters into economic discourse in a variety of ways and at a multiplicity of sites. Wilson's extensive discussion of Deweyan pragmatisms in economics is, for us, the single, best work on the subject. This is not only because of his useful and exhaustive limning of the different traditions in economic philosophy that have mined the depths of Dewey's work. It is also because Wilson places the discussion of Deweyan pragmatism in the context of modernism and postmodernism. That is, Wilson locates the different readings of Dewey according to whether or not the modernist or postmodern implications of Dewey's pragmatist philosophy are picked up or even noticed. For Wilson, both Friedman (and most Chicago-school and neoclassical economists) and institutionalists (he focuses his discussion on Veblen) tend to produce a modernist reading of Dewey, one that we think is consonant with Marc Tool's interpretation of instrumentalism and an absolutist social value principle. If there have been institutionalist criticisms of Tool's absolutism, some of them have sought philosophical refuge in more postmodern presentations of Deweyan pragmatism, such as that of Richard Rorty and Cornel West (1989).

Wilson traces Dewey's influence in institutionalism in relation to Veblen. This is a conflicted choice since, as David Riesman (1960) points out, while Veblen was indebted to Dewey for his own "renewed sense of man as an active being, one who selects his environment as well as is shaped by it" (19), he was at times critical in a sarcastic vein of Dewey, James, Peirce and the entire pragmatist movement.[26] Yet, if not a matter of derivation, there are still similarities in the institutionalism of Veblen and the pragmatism of Dewey. For Wilson, these similarities were themselves discursively constructed by later institutionalists who saw no significant difference between Veblen's treatment of the process of knowledge production and the role of culture (and thereby "values") and Dewey's "instrumentalist notion of inquiry."

The institutionalist version of pragmatism, according to Wilson, was "based on (*a*) an uncritical faith in science and the scientific method, and (*b*) a naturalist belief that human beings individually and society as a whole 'mirrored' the biological properties of lower organisms" (100). Wilson asserts that "these two elements define the nature of institutionalism's naïve empiricism and its vulnerability to cognitive modernism" (100). It is this second element that accounts, in Wilson's view, for the heavy reliance by Veblen and other institutionalists on Darwinian notions of evolution to describe the "process" of social inquiry, as well as that of society itself. But the first element places institutionalists, from Veblen and Wesley Mitchell to their contemporary descendants, squarely in the camp of scientific essentialists and modernists, if Wilson is correct. And this may help to explain consequently the absolutist strain in such notions as the "instrumental value principle."

This is so because, as Dewey himself insisted, there is no appreciable epistemological or methodological difference between moral discourse and scientific inquiry, and certainly not where issues of "truth" are in-

---

[26] Riesman (1960) adds that Veblen's sarcasm did not mean dismissal. Veblen "could hardly have believed he was being extra rough on thinkers who were, in many respects, his

volved. Dewey (1949) is emphatic about this point. He writes, "there is nothing whatever that methodologically (*qua* judgment) marks off 'value-judgments' from conclusions reached in astronomical, chemical, or biological inquiries. Specifically, it follows that the problem of 'the relation of value to fact' is wholly factitious, since it rests upon and proceeds from assumptions that have no factual foundation. The connection of value-*facts* with other facts forms a problem that is legitimate-plus. It is indispensable" (77). Dewey also makes it nearly impossible to distinguish "persuasion" and "should be's" from the normal procedures of scientific inquiry. In fact, he states that "both the morale and the technique of effective valuing are more highly developed at present in 'scientific' subjects than in those conventionally allotted to the field of 'value.' The function of persuasion and of producing conviction is so far from being peculiar to judgments conventionally recognised to be in the value-field that it is now better exemplified in 'scientific' inquiry and the propositions that result from it" (77).

This notion of the current or prospective unity of fields of discourse—from axiology to astronomy—means that instrumentalism is largely trans-discursive. Instrumentalism, then, is an approach in all realms in which goals direct active thinking (and thoughtful action). Therefore, much depends for Deweyans and their offspring on the particular notion of instrumentalism to which one adheres. There are absolutist notions of instrumentalism, just as there are ones that lead to pluralism and even relativism. If one can be an absolutist, for example, in the realm of science, and therefore eschew the epistemologically "relativist" notion that there can or even must be multiple "truths" as a consequence of the indefiniteness, culturally situated, and transitoriness of instrumentalist valuings, then one may also resist a similar approach to value discourse, in which case values are not, in any meaningful sense, "relative" in their "truth content." As we discuss below, there is a striking similarity in the absolutism that appears in institutionalist value theory and the notions of science that many institutionalists espouse, including the nonabsolutist critics of Tool.

Wilson argues that the institutionalists read Dewey as the source for their overwhelming commitment to "the scientific method." For example, "as Mitchell understood him, Dewey had advocated the wide application of the scientific method as a way of gauging 'how men think' " (103). Dewey, in many of his writings, certainly lauded what he called the scientific method, and just as often "the scientific habit of mind." Yet for many institutionalists, these references do not translate into positivism, but

---

intellectual allies—the notion of an alliance would have meant taking seriously the weight he himself could throw" (25).

rather to a nonpositivist instrumentalism in which, as we see in Tool, values are forever part and parcel of the epistemological and social process.

Cornel West (1989) is useful here:

> The distinction between scientific attitude and scientific method is crucial for Dewey; those who overlook it view him as a vulgar positivist, one who makes a fetish of scientific method . . . [For Dewey] the aims of critical intelligence are to overcome obstacles, resolve problems, and project realizable possibilities in pressing predicaments. A scientific attitude is indispensable for achieving these aims; the scientific method is usually the best means by which they are achieved. The first important point here is that critical intelligence is available to all peoples; it is neither the birthright of the highbrow nor the property of the professional. . . . The second crucial point is that though critical intelligence deploys the scientific method, the results of science do not constitute the disclosure of the real. Dewey is not an epistemological realist or ontological positivist, but rather a pragmatist with great faith in the power of critical intelligence. The cultural implication here is that Dewey's acceptance of the authority of science is itself instrumental—science is simply the best tool we conscious organisms have to cope with our environment. (97–98)

Valuation comes in through this instrumentality. The judgment about "best tools" is determined by "values" at many different levels, from epistemological norms to the practical aims of inquiry as well. This version of Dewey's instrumentalism leads thinkers like West to conclude that Dewey was, in many ways, an antiepistemologist, that is, someone who "evades" the issue of the foundations for knowledge, even in the refuge to values themselves as the arbiter of ultimate truth content in morality as well as science. In West's view, "For Dewey, philosophy is a mode not of knowledge but of wisdom. And wisdom is conviction about values, a choice to do something, a preference for this rather than that form of living. Wisdom involves discriminating judgments and a desired future. It presupposes some grasp of conditions and consequences, yet it has no special access to them" (86).

West, like Wilson, sees no necessity in interpreting Dewey here as a cognitive modernist, and certainly not one who thinks of science and method simply in the singular. Yet in Wilson's view, institutionalists have turned Dewey's pragmatist instrumentalism into just such a privileged procedure. Whether Wilson's arguments are accepted or not, it is our view that in refusing ethical and epistemological relativism, absolutist institutionalists and not a few of their critics recoil from the implications of West's reading, in which Dewey emerges as believing "that there are a variety of knowledges, each regulated by procedures that take seriously the role of hypothesis, evidence, and inference; that this epistemic pluralism gives no procedure privileged access to Truth and Reality; that science, though it posits unobservable entities, is the most reliable procedure regarding control of phenomena; and that commonsense reasoning is continuous with scientific method" (1989, 98).

After establishing the pragmatist (yet modernist) credentials of Veblen and like-minded institutionalists and Friedman and his Chicago and neoclassical admirers, Wilson discusses the postmodern reading of Dewey and its present and future in economic discourse. The key figure is Richard Rorty. Rorty is in fact the linchpin to much postmodern value discourse, as he reads Dewey mostly through Nietzsche and the French poststructuralists, and likewise reads Nietzsche and the others through Dewey. If there is to be a development of Deweyan pragmatism away from absolutism and a scientistic understanding of instrumentalism and toward something "different," then it is likely to come from an engagement with Rorty.

Wilson summarizes Rorty's mostly postmodern version of Deweyan pragmatism in three points. First, "pragmatism is 'antiessentialism' applied to notions like 'truth,' 'knowledge,' 'language,' 'morality,' and similar objects of philosophical theorizing. Antiessentialism applied to such notions opens inquiry to the activity of doing and demotes the activity of deciding whether a picture is true or false. The stress is placed on the usefulness and the consequences of usefulness" (1996, 230–31). Rorty himself states that "pragmatists recommend that we worry only about the choice between two hypotheses, rather than about whether there is something which 'makes' either true. To take this stance would rid us of questions about the objectivity of value, the rationality of science, and the causes of the viability of our language games. All such theoretical questions would be replaced with practical questions about whether we ought to keep our present values, theories, and practices or try to replace them with others" (1991, 41). Even more strongly, Rorty writes that "from a Wittgensteinian, or Davidsonian, or Deweyan angle, there is no such thing as 'the best explanation' of anything; there is just the explanation which best suits the purpose of some given explainer. . . . There is no description which is somehow 'closer' to the causal transactions being explained than the others" (1991, 60). Which is also to say that even if there are common purposes (and this surely doesn't imply the necessity of a universalist set of values), there will be explanations (in the plural) that will arise and flourish in any scientific or moral community

The second point is the by now familiar claim about the absence of any epistemological difference between "truth about what ought to be" and "truth about what is." Nor is there "any metaphysical difference between facts and values, nor any methodological difference between morality and science" (Wilson 1996, 231, quoting Rorty 1982, 163), which is a position we've met before in Dewey. In a similar vein, Rorty asserts that the need to establish epistemological differences between modes of thinking led to "the thesis, common to Nietzsche and Dewey, that the attempt to distinguish practical deliberation from an impersonal and nonperspectival search for truth (the sort of search of which natural science is thought to be paradigmatic) is an attempt at 'metaphysical comfort,' the sort of comfort that was once provided by religion" (1991, 60).

Wilson summarizes the third point as "there are no preset limits or rules for the process of inquiry, except those rules that facilitate the conversation . . . a postmodern pragmatism suggests that we are better off if we live without the 'metaphysical comfort' of guidance from rules. This exciting aspect of letting go of metaphysical hope is that 'our identification with our community—our society, our political tradition, our intellectual heritage—is heightened when we see this community as ours rather than nature's, shaped rather than found, one among many which men have made' " (1996, 231, quoting Rorty 1982, 166). This identification does not imply transvaluation per se. To the contrary, it implies that even the virtues of instrumentalism must, once again, be constantly placed within a determinate community. Though we don't much share Rorty's (or Dewey's) "Americanism,"[27] it is worth repeating Rorty's explanation for this aspect of Dewey's (and his own) pragmatism: "Dewey was accused of blowing up the optimism and flexibility of a parochial and jejune way of life (the American) into a philosophical system. So he did, but his reply was that any philosophical system is going to be an attempt to express the ideas of some community's way of life. He was quite willing to admit that the virtue of his philosophy was, indeed, nothing more than the virtue of a way of life that it commended. On his view, philosophy does not justify affiliation with a community in the light of something ahistorical called 'reason' or 'transcultural principles.' It simply expiates on the special advantages of that community over other communities" (1991, 43).

Rorty's reading of Dewey produces the kind of postmodern alternative for which perhaps Tool's critics and others may be striving as they consider the frailties of an absolutist pragmatism. Yet, as we argue, key aspects of this postmodern pragmatism are neglected by both Tool and his critics in favor of taking refuge in some form of modernism.

Value as an Objective Standard

As we noted above, a significant difference does exist between Tool and other instrumental value theorists, on one hand, and the critics of Tool's social value principle (such as Ramstad, Gordon, and Mayhew), on the

---

[27] Both West (1989) and Wilson (1996) make this "Americanism" a primary object of critical scrutiny, while also one of appreciation.

other. However, a closer look may help to reveal their shared terrain. What all these commentators share is the (mostly unspoken) view that a value principle and the set of standards of valuation are *extradiscursive*. From their shared terrain, it makes no sense to talk about a distinct discursive—whether institutionalist, neoclassical, or Marxian—notion of value and value judgments since any such notion would be considered internal, and thus *relative*, to the conceptual framework in and through which it is produced and deployed. Neither Tool nor his critics entertain the postmodern Deweyan idea that institutionalist thought might give rise to a particular concept of values, one whose regularity and use is restricted to an institutionalist discursive formation. Instead, they carry on their dispute based on the alternatives contained within an *objectivist* conception of value: either there is a single, pancultural approach to value judgment, or there is a variety of culturally specific values.[28] In both cases, values are considered to have an objective foundation.

In Tool's view, an adequate social value principle cannot be rooted either in absolute first principles, such as those of religious faith, or in the subjective preferences and desires of individuals. Instead, the instrumental approach to value he advocates is grounded in the idea that there is a "widely shared judgmental principle among those in any community who wish, through causal analysis and consequent appraisal, to understand and remove the institutional determinants of obstructions and impairments in the provisioning process and in the discretionary mechanisms through which public policy is determined" (1993a, 142). It is because the process of instrumental valuation is viewed both as existing "out there," beyond any particular discourse, as the "*critical aspect* in the analysis and resolution of social and economic problems" (150), and as the mode of valuation that is warranted, in the sense that it serves to "advance and facilitate the inquiry process" (129), that the instrumental value principle (and, with it, the judgments offered by institutional economists) is conceived to be objectively grounded.

---

[28] It is interesting in this regard to recall a response by Dewey to a question raised by one of the contributors to Lepley's 1949 collection. Dewey writes, "It follows that since selection-rejection as life-processes always take in something—some *thing*—which is selected or rejected, the answer to the preliminary question raised by Lee 'Is there any such thing as value which is not the value of some particular thing, event, or situation?' is definitely negative" (1949, 66). Now, in what sense is "some thing" restricted to "objects" or "events" but not discourses as well? Note that if we think of discourse as being such a "particular thing" or event, it follows that any value must be the value of a particular discourse, and that its transcendence of that discourse's boundaries is only a matter of what can be brought about by persuasion, force, or some other method leading to or compelling "agreement." Of course, this "perception" of intradiscursivity might also fall into the category of "objective"—that is, as a statement of the way things really are "out there." This is not our position, as we have argued throughout this book.

Tool's critics do not dispute the objective nature of the instrumental value principle. Gordon, for example, argues that, in the context of the historical evolution of the relationship between technology and institutionalized behavioral norms (in which, as technology changes, prevailing institutions, those that are inappropriate to the new technologies, are replaced by new institutions and behavioral patterns),[29] a self-correcting, instrumental value judgment process is responsible for posing and solving the recurring problems. During the course of this process, techniques and values are evaluated and revised accordingly. But, and this is the critical point for Gordon, both the instrumental efficiency of the techniques and the validity of the values are relative to "a given time and under given circumstances" (1984, 375). Therefore, while Gordon parts company with Tool on the question of the seeming universality of a single social value principle, they share the idea that the instrumental value judgment process is an objective fact of human existence (in Gordon's words, "it is self-evident that this is the way we actually behave" [1984, 376]). Gordon is also quick to add that, in common with Tool, his contextual approach to instrumental valuation should not be interpreted as "anything goes."

The specter of ethical relativism haunts these debates. It is also to a large degree responsible for agreement between the two sides. For all contestants, there is an unspoken fear that to argue for an *intradiscursive* value principle, one that is constituted *within* institutional economics—which is therefore not grounded in an objective, transhistorical, or pancultural valuational premise or process—would commit one to accept as ethically or morally defensible the worst effects and consequences of existing theories and/or institutional structures. If one accepts that institutionalist social value is so unlike other, contending notions of value so as to be incommensurate with them, then there can be no objective standpoint from which to criticize the negative consequences of other economic discourses or the "inhumane" dimensions of U.S. or any other country's institutions or economic and social policies. According to George DeMartino,

> defenders of moral objectivism are right to claim that it has much to recommend it. . . . Not least of its virtues is the fact that it provides a firm basis for its advocates to engage equally in intra- and cross-cultural critique. . . . Absent an objective code, after all, what basis is there to speak out against oppressive social practices in societies other than one's own? (2000, 133–34)[30]

---

[29] We can't help but notice that this scheme of technological and institutional change is remarkably similar to modernist Marxist conceptions of the correspondence (with a lag) between the mode of production and the political and ideological superstructure.

[30] While recognizing the attraction of an objectivist approach to morals and values, DeMartino then points to some of the major problems attendant upon such a conception. He notes, in particular, that moral objectivism rests merely on a *presumption* that a solid

In response to this fear of ethical relativism, a general, extradiscursive concept of values is necessary so as to have a higher order set of precepts to which we can appeal when evaluating any policy or institutional arrangement. The specific value principles of institutionalist, neoclassical, Marxian, or other economic discourses must be evaluated in terms of a general concept of value or process of valuation that is discursively privileged. And such a privileging of general, interdiscursive concepts or processes derives from an implicit epistemological value. This value presumes that general concepts, especially those that are objectively grounded and thus validated, have a truth content that is not restricted to a particular discourse or social situation. Hence, a general value principle is of a higher order than specific applications of, or deductions from, this concept or process since it represents a more objective and general truth.

The question of the priority of valuational statements vis-à-vis strictly scientific ones most often takes the form of a discussion of epistemological privilege of such statements. Where scientific statements may be local and contingent, moral or valuational statements, because of their interdiscursivity and generality, may represent even higher truths. In any event, ethical relativism must be rejected since it presumes a leveling of the truth content of different value positions and prevents higher-order ethical truths from being recognized.

This, we take it, is the view of valuational principles shared by Tool, Gordon, and other participants in the institutionalist value debate. Such as view is operative not just in the attempt to propose a general, extradiscursive concept of value or valuational processes but can be seen as well in the common attempts to define the character of valuational propositions.

The Humanist Bias: Values and the Good of Man

There is a humanist bias in these attempts. Valuational propositions are said to be ones that concern the "good" *of* and *for* humanity. Tool's argument that social value principles have to do with such notions as the "preservation of human life" and the "recreation of community" are prototypical of humanist approaches. According to such approaches, it is inconceivable that any properly valuational stance could "value" destruction, randomness, disorderliness, incoherence, decadence, and so forth. This is because these acts or states of existence are seen as antipathetic to the good of "man." (Since Nietzsche is the name most closely associated

___

foundation exists and is undermined by the possibility that different cultures might reach "different conclusions about the origins, substantive nature and practical implications of this objective basis" (2000, 132).

with such alternative "values," it is evident, in our view, that absolutist institutionalism is fundamentally non- or anti-Nietzschean.) Any such value in institutionalist thought, or in other economic discourses, must be regarded as either immoral or nonmoral.

DeMartino, who recognizes the political implications of such a humanism, is worth quoting at length:

> In a world marked by fundamental inequalities both within and across national borders, within which some groups have substantially greater ability to impose their normative accounts on others, moral objectivism is prone to the problem of cultural imperialism. This is because, first, moral objectivism does not lend itself to negotiation or compromise, given that it is taken by its adherents to be uniquely true. Second, and as a consequence, it is likely to be imposed by its advocates on others with alternative normative accounts on grounds that those on whom it is imposed will ultimately benefit from receiving the correct word. (2000, 132)

It is interesting to note that even Mayhew, who is an advocate of cultural relativism and quite critical of Tool's use of instrumental valuation as an overarching criterion to judge the validity of economic and social institutions, is still concerned to assert that instrumental valuation *is* an elemental human aspect and, as such, is the source (as the early institutionalists are credited with recognizing) of economic progress. In this sense, whatever forms of instrumental valuation that can be said to exist within diverse cultures are considered to make "positive" contributions to human well-being.

Notwithstanding their profound differences in terms of specific value premises, what Tool, Mayhew, and other institutionalists agree on is that the "life process of mankind" is enhanced by the "instrumental efficiency of the social and economic process"—that which does away with ceremonial behaviors and institutions and promotes the industrial or technological continuum. What institutionalists cannot allow is the possibility that these same values might bring with them violence, hierarchy, and domination or that ceremonial excess, expenditure, and the like might be positively valued within a different scheme. Any theorist or society whose actions and forces are perceived, from the point of view of a humanist valuational process, as "nihilistic" and perverse would be judged to fall outside the bounds of acceptable social value principles.

Institutionalism and Science

In our view, what is at stake in the debates over the status of social values in institutional economics is a more general attempt to claim for values an epistemological privilege vis-à-vis science. The attempt to establish this claim is primarily responsible for a shared, objectivist conception of valuational principles and processes. But it is also responsible for a shared conception of the scientific.

Tool and his theoretical opponents invariably portray institutional economics as different from other economic discourses because of its focus on values and its use of the instrumental value principle. Based on such a distinctive treatment of the role of values in economic inquiry, the next step that one would expect is the elaboration of a specifically value-oriented, institutionalist conception of science. However, when institutionalists do take up the issue of science, they end up elaborating a methodology in which values have a curiously ambiguous status or are absent altogether.

In their highly influential (and oft-cited) explication of the methodological orientation of institutional economics, Wilber and Harrison (1978) take great pains in defining, and identifying the shortfalls of, the "covering law" model of explanation of much mainstream economics and in contrasting it to the "pattern" model that they find implicit in institutional economics. The differences between the two models are, without a doubt, profound: whereas the covering law model presumes detachment and is designed to generate accurate predictions, pattern modeling focuses on participant observation with the goal of understanding. Among the other distinguishing characteristics of the institutionalist "investigatory mode," Wilber and Harrison focus on the various dimensions of "holism," which include the primacy of the subject matter (versus, e.g., the use of general scientific principles), the role of low-level descriptions and generalizations (as against abstract laws of behavior), the fitting of parts into a unified whole (instead of presuming separate, atomistic elements), and the view of the whole as a system of interrelations and connections (with the goal of looking for patterns and not cause-effect relations). But, aside from one brief mention (in a checklist of elements for verifying an institutionalist story, quoted from Benjamin Ward), values play no significant role in Wilber and Harrison's interpretation of institutionalist methodology. Instead, in their account, it is accurate, factual description—without any mention of the influence of values, moral concerns, or ethics—that serves as the key element in determining the scientific nature of institutional economics.

Paul Bush (1993) offers a quite different perspective on the modes and procedures of an institutionalist conception of science. In his view, valuational judgments not only are endemic to economic and social inquiry (they are involved in every step of the process) but they do not compromise the "objectivity," and hence scientific validity, of the process. This is especially true when, borrowing from Rorty's interpretation of Deweyan pragmatism, Bush repeats Rorty's claim that there is no epistemological difference between truth about what ought to be and truth about what is, nor any metaphysical differences between facts and values, nor any methodological difference between morality and science. (81)

It is on this basis that Bush argues that valuations are critical to the determination of what the relevant facts are: that all facts are, in this sense, theory-laden.[31] However, Bush is also quick to add that some values need to be "excluded from inquiry"—those that are considered to "take the form of absolutistic moral injunctions or some sort of 'subjectivist' set of preferences" (85)—and that the only relevant values are those that arise within the process of inquiry itself, namely, instrumental values. The result, it seems, is that only scientific values—those that generally govern the work of the scientific community and therefore, from an institutionalist perspective, that promote the continuity of scientific inquiry—are admissible. Objectivity is safeguarded by asserting a methodology in which instrumentally warranted values are posited as the necessary standards by which, during the course of inquiry, from the identification of problems to the application of monitoring standards, the correct (or, at least, self-correcting) choices are made.

Mirowski (1987) notes just this tendency by twentieth-century institutionalists to embrace a scientistic conception of economic and social inquiry—which, as he describes it, closes the distance to a positivist (Popperian) version of science. From Ayres onward, institutional economists have come to refer to science (and such related terms as *scientific verification*, the *scientific method*, and so on) in the singular. Absent is the idea that there may be different sciences, different scientific discourses, involving different syntheses of facts and values, scientific and moral statements, explanatory and evaluatory modes of inquiry. Mirowski, for his part, looks to an alternative side of the institutionalist tradition, one that builds on Peircean semiotics and culminates in a "hermeneutic" conception of science.[32] Such an approach would focus on the interpretative dimensions

---

[31] Another well-known institutionalist, Geoffrey Hodgson, takes Bush to task precisely on this point: in his view, "the idea of the epistemological equivalence of fact and value has highly damaging results" (1993, 115).

[32] Institutionalists have often split in their allegiance to one or another of the "founders" of pragmatism. As we mentioned above (note 21), Mirowski cites Commons approvingly because of the latter's tendency to employ some version of Peircean semiotic pragmatism. Yonay (1998), following Mirowski, states that "Commons was alone among major institutionalists in following this Peircean view. Veblen adopted a naïve belief in science, which was later taken to extremes by Mitchell and Ayres" (232). And what was the alternative, non-Peircean tendency in institutionalism based upon? Yonay answers, "It is not an accident that pragmatism entered the American scene through the works of Dewey, Veblen, and Mitchell, who shared the pervasive belief in science" (232). Rutherford (1998), though, has a somewhat different reading of who was on which side: "The exception to the [Deweyan instrumentalist] approach is Veblen, who was perhaps more influenced by Charles Peirce

of both the economic agent and of the economic researcher. Despite his promising criticisms of institutionalists' notion of a singular science, Mirowski quickly abandons the attempt to develop a specifically institutionalist conception of science, an intradiscursive notion of science—and, with it, of values. Instead, he derives the warrant for an institutionalist hermeneutics, together with his candidate for an institutionalist "social theory of value," from recent innovations within the physical sciences. And, to the extent that he mentions valuational issues at all (e.g., in the logics of choice of economic actors), they are invoked as "positive" terms, however ironically, in the spirit of modern positivism.

Reason and Values as Separate Realms: A Positivist Story

The idea that there exist separate realms of positive and normative inquiry is the hallmark of modern positivism. One aspect of the debate between positivists and their humanist critics is a disagreement over whether these realms are antagonistic or complementary. Another aspect of the debate concerns the epistemological status of these realms. Positivists may insist that valuational statements produce no objective knowledge, while humanist critics may assert either that values can be given an "objective" basis comparable to the sciences or that values inform all scientific statements such that, in a critical way, values stand as the "first principles" from which the meaning of scientific statements derive. The positivist story of the historical separation of Reason and morality leads to the consequent view that distinctive realms of positive science and normative values exist.

A typical positivist story describes the origin of modern economic science in the growing separation, since the Scottish Enlightenment, of moral thinking and economic scientific reason. The self-consciousness of this progressive separation is finally achieved with the advent of positivism, especially with positivism's enunciation of a radical separation of facts and values as they pertain to judgments of the veracity of economic statements. According to this story, beginning with the Enlightenment and reaching fruition in the positivist and neopositivist (we have Popper in mind here) movements of the twentieth century, Reason successfully and completely disengages itself from ethical ruminations. This separation of Reason and values is portrayed as the constitution of (potentially) mutually exclusive realms of experience. However, it is from the standpoint of Reason that such a separation is perceived in the first place; Reason announces its sepa-

---

than by Dewey" (251). In Rutherford's eyes, "Peirce was deeply opposed to the use of science for social engineering purposes. Although Veblen's detachment is sometimes exaggerated, he did see science as something to provide critical insight into the course of social evolution rather than as a tool to be used to control it" (251).

ration from morality on its own terms (since only Reason can perceive and judge the likeness and difference of discourses, especially in regard to the type of statements of which each discourse is comprised).

With the dominance of positivism, Reason sees itself "in-itself." That is, Reason announces itself as wholly distinct from moral discourse, and more importantly, it announces itself as exclusively competent to distinguish and judge all statements (at least insofar as their "truth claims" are concerned). Moral discourse, in contrast, is seen from the standpoint of the sciences created by Reason to have no particular claim to objective truths. The "logic" of moral discourse and its objects are categorized not by that discourse but, instead, by Reason.

Moral pronouncements—the discourse of values—do not enjoy the independence of science, since they are judged by Reason to operate according to different procedures and to utilize logics different from those of the sciences. Economic science is not simply disjoint from values; economic science is the standpoint from which economists must judge and label the types of moral statements and valuations that can be made and then discarded, at least as far as "objective" knowledge is concerned. It is the scientist—the person of Reason—who says, scientific statements are about "what is" and value judgments are about "what ought to be."

This positivist story, then, has a twofold purpose: First, it is intended to establish the decisive rupture that, with the growth of positivism, has occurred between Reason and morality. But second, it is also intended to establish Reason as the arbiter of morality (or, at least, of morality's "sense") and to make moral statements subordinate to scientific ones.

It is this positivist story that has penetrated so deeply into the consciousness of both positivist philosophers *and* their critics. Many critics of positivism accept the story of the progressive separation of Reason from moral thinking since the Enlightenment, often told in terms of the growth and independence of the natural sciences but not necessarily the social sciences. Further, the call for the "revaluing" of economics—making economic thought more "humane" and "morally sound"—proceeds most often on the unspoken assumption that Reason can and must be brought to bear on morality ("proving" the scientific or "objective" basis of value judgments, in opposition to positivism).

There also exists a further position, one which asserts that all Reason is derived from some basic, underlying valuational principles and that there is an unrecognized and unspoken moral foundation (often referred to by institutionalists as a social value principle and by Marxists as an ideology) for economic and all scientific discourse.

This last position has two important variants. The first variant, and the most common, argues that economic science can never be value-free and is, instead, overwhelmed by its (explicitly articulated or implicit) moral foundations. The impossibility of creating a value-free science is explained either by the "fact" that it is humanly impossible for scientists to leave their moral or ethical presumptions outside their practice or by the "fact" that, especially with the human sciences, the knowledge of human behavior requires some "inner" searching—a search for intentions, motives, and goals—in order to establish the "intersubjective" truth of these sciences, or, finally, by the fact that social problems can be correctly analyzed and solved only when the value judgments in the "real" social world are mirrored in the valuational premises of the scientists. In all three of these cases, morality and values stand at the beginning of the process of knowledge. All statements and practices of scientists are thus derived in some way from moral premises, whether or not practitioners are aware of them.

Borrowing from institutionalists, we call this variant the "holistic" approach, with the added proviso that, although this approach stresses the necessary unity of values and factual statements, it usually grants an epistemological and methodological primacy to values. This primacy is granted in the sense that, although values and facts may be inseparable, they can only be understood through an interpretative (or, for some, "hermeneutic") strategy. Such a strategy attempts to ground all statements in the intentions, desires, and motivations of human actors. In some versions of this interpretative stance, the "rules" of interpretation are themselves the expressions of intentions, motives, and so forth. It is not so much that Reason is made subservient to values. It is more that Reason is rendered wholly value-laden.

The second variant differs radically from the first in that it rejects the moral monism, the holism, and the humanism of the first variant. We attribute this second type to Nietzsche. This second variant can be brought to bear on the issue of the role of values in economics in a manner entirely contrary to the holistic and humanist view. In the remainder of this chapter, we show that Nietzsche opposes not only the post-Enlightenment story of the victory of Reason over morality but also the humanist criticisms of that story. His narrative of the historical relation between Reason and morality seeks refuge neither in the call for the "rationalizing" of moral discourse nor in a humanism that sees instrumental or interpretative strategies as a way to establish the discursive priority of value judgments.

Reason and Values: Nietzsche's Genealogy of Morals

In opposition to the positivist story presented above, we may ask the question: what if the division between moral and scientific discourses (and, with it, such notions as fact-value distinction) is not the story of the victory of progressive Reason separating itself from an inert and debilitating morality but is, rather, a story of the dominance of morality? What if we can tell a different story of the separation of Reason from morality, one that shows that, since the time of Socrates, particular moralities, as expressions of their "wills," have been the source of all narratives hailing the separation of Reason from morality?

While Dewey and his followers give one answer to these questions, we find a different presentation of the historical relation between Reason and morality in Nietzsche, especially *On the Genealogy of Morals* (1956) and *Beyond Good and Evil* (1966). Yet Nietzsche's story is not a simple reversal of the positivist one, as is mostly true with the holistic institutionalist position (though perhaps not the postmodern Dewey). Contrary to those critics of positivism who advocate the founding of modern thought on a morality of the "good" or "humanness," Nietzsche's story is not one of the victory or higher authority, in the realm of heavenly phrases, of good over evil or of the inhumane over the humane. The criticism of a positivist economics that the Nietzschean story permits is not founded on the reinterpretation and revaluation of the Enlightenment as a truly "dark age," in which all that is good and holy in life and thought—all that is whole and unified in God, Spirit, or in the customs and traditions of a premodern, "organic," human community—is destroyed mercilessly in the accession of the modern. Nor is it predicated on the idea, most closely linked to Veblen, that truly forward-looking, modern (e.g., technological) values are blocked or deflected by remnants of premodern ceremonies and institutions that only need to be displaced for human life to flourish. Nietzsche's story is not that of the coming-to-our-senses, the rediscovery, of the values we have lost or not yet fully grasped.

Many current critics of positivism and modernism, like Alasdair MacIntyre (1984), do wish to tell the story—not Nietzsche's—of the post-Enlightenment loss of moral sensibility, that most precious feature of the premodern or, alternatively, future-modern world. In contrast, Nietzsche's story, as MacIntyre himself points out, rejects a call to reclaim the primacy of *the* moral realm, a call for its reinstatement (whatever the source) as the origin of all statements and sentiments. There are two reasons for Nietzsche's rejection of such a call.

First, Nietzsche's writings are meant to problematize the notion of a universal moral realm. The idea of talking of morality rather than moralities, value or value principle instead of values and value principles, is utterly un-Nietzschean. Second, Nietzsche discusses morality not because he wishes to reach, in thought and practice, the universally good. He does not accept either the passing of many of the past moralities or the absence of an overarching present value principle as something to be mourned.

In sharp contrast to contemporary humanist (and Christian) critics of science, Nietzsche sees the moral world that has supposedly been lost (in fact, he denies that is has been lost—it is the subject of his indictment of the modern world) as the source of all that is stupid, vile, cowardly, and boring in our modern thought and action, including the sciences. And this is not because past moralities have been false; it is not that they have failed in achieving *their* good and avoiding *their* evil. To the contrary, it is precisely because of the continued predominance of Christian, Buddhist, Judaic, secular humanist, and other notions of good and evil—because of the success of these moralities in establishing and reproducing the conditions of contemporary thought and action—that modernism is stupid, vile, cowardly, and boring.

To avoid being misunderstood, let us emphasize that Nietzsche *is* a critic of modern science. He does not criticize moralities and values from the point of view of "scientific reason." Nietzsche's indictment of moral and ethical positions[33]—those present in his age and ours—is, at the same

---

[33] While we may transit in our discussion at times between "morals" and "ethics," Deleuze (1988) cautions us to restrict a Nietzschean critique to moral values, but not ethics. Deleuze derives his view from a seemingly simultaneous (or at least harmonious) reading of Nietzsche and Spinoza. He quotes Nietzsche writing to a friend, describing his path to Spinoza, "I am really amazed, really delighted . . . I hardly knew Spinoza" (129). Deleuze, in fact, credits Spinoza with first establishing an irreparable split between morality, as written and practiced, and ethics. For Spinoza, "there is no Good or Evil, but there is a good and bad" (22). Deleuze then quotes Nietzsche to much the same effect: "Beyond Good and Evil, at least this *does not* mean: beyond good and bad" (22). Deleuze explains how this position leads to the radical distinction between ethics and morality first for Spinoza and then for Nietzsche: "the good is when a body directly compounds its relation with ours, and with all or part of its power, increases ours. A food, for example. For us, the bad is when a body decomposes our body's relation, although it still combines with our parts, but in ways that do not correspond to our essence" (22). The crux of the matter is that "hence good and bad have a primary objective meaning, but one that is relative and partial: that which agrees with our nature or does not agree with it. And consequently, good and bad have a secondary meaning, which is subjective and modal, qualifying two types, two modes of man's existence. That individual will be called *good* (or free or rational, or strong) who strives, insofar as he is able, to organize his encounters, to join with whatever agrees with his nature. . . . That individual will be called *bad*, or servile, or weak, or foolish, who lives haphazardly, who is content to undergo the effects of his encounters, but wails and accuses every time the effect undergone does not agree with him and reveals his own impotence" (22–23). Deleuze continues: "Ethics, which is to say, a typology of immanent modes of existence, replaces Morality, which always refers existence to transcendent values. Morality is the judgment of God, the *system of Judgment*. But Ethics overthrows the system of judgement. The opposition of values (Good-Evil) is supplanted by the qualitative difference of modes of existence (good-bad)" (23). This type of Spinozan-Nietzschean distinction is employed best perhaps in Michel Foucault's explorations of "the care of the self" (1988). For what is ethically "good" for Foucault is that which, too, agrees with the body in a mode of self-care and replenishment, and, in contrast to many moralists, may often involve the free release of libidinal pleasure as an extension of the body's power.

time, an indictment of the sciences. In his story, the sciences, far from marking the separation of Reason from morals, have arisen and exist on a moral basis.

The Mask of Reason and the Ascetic Ideal

Nietzsche discerns, with disgust and amusement, the ruse that lies behind the enunciation of the victory of pure, disinterested Reason. The ruse consists of a supposedly disinterested Reason hiding its "will to nothingness" in the form of a celebration of intellect. Reason celebrates the victory of detached intellect—of "spectatorship"—over all other such wills and all values. Thus, Reason claims that by the concentration of pure intellect, it has freed itself from morality. Freed from morality, Reason announces morality as a distinct realm, one that requires more faith than instinct.

In order to reveal the particular masking strategy of modern Reason's will to nothingness, Nietzsche produces a "natural history" or "genealogy" of morals. In *Modern French Philosophy*, Vincent Descombes (1980) neatly summarizes Nietzsche's genealogical achievement as follows: "He demonstrates 'with a hammer' that science as such—the desire for truth—originates in morality, in the 'ascetic ideal,' and that morality as such is the result of resentment against life" (156). Nietzsche's genealogical procedure consists of tracing, since Socrates, the emergence of a "will to truth," of a will that seeks to establish the priority of Reason over morality in the production of objective knowledge. Nietzsche discovers the source of the will to truth in a highly celebrated moral virtue, the "ascetic ideal."

The emergence of the will to truth can be located in the "ancient theological problem of 'faith' and 'knowledge'—or, more clearly, of instinct and reason—in other words, the question whether, in the valuation of things, instinct deserves more authority than rationality, which wants us to evaluate and act in accordance with reasons, with a 'why'?" (1966, 103–4). Nietzsche continues, "this is still the ancient moral problem that first emerged in the person of Socrates and divided thinking people long before Christianity" (104). The fateful moment of Socrates consists in his having "initially sided with reason and, in fact, what did he do his life long but laugh at the awkward incapacity of noble Athenians who, like all noble men, were men of instinct and never could give sufficient information about the reasons for their action?" (104).

In Nietzsche's view, Socrates set philosophy and society down a path in which the dualism of knowledge and faith is seen as the uneasy coexistence of two related but distinct realms. Historically, then, a battle takes place, fought over more than two thousand years, in which either this or that moral outlook or this or that claim to knowledge thinks itself to have the upper hand. But, the Socratic moment of the enunciation of a distinct will to truth has monumental consequences for both morality and knowledge.

For in the realm of morality, the Socratic-Platonic tradition marks the ultimate victory of "slave moralities," while in the realm of knowledge, all attempts are made to hide the origin of a "disinterested" Reason in this victory. The weakening of "noble" values—their ridicule from the standpoint of Reason—permits the growth in influence of Judaism, Buddhism, Christianity, and other such religions. In Nietzsche's view, these religions are all slave moralities.[34]

What these (and all) slave moralities have in common is a hatred—a resentment—of the world and a consequent hostility to life.[35] During the "Christian era," this *ressentiment* is valorized in the "ascetic ideal." This ideal, Nietzsche claims, is the progenitor of modern Western moralities *and* of the modern sciences. The ascetic ideal expresses a negative will, a

[34] We entertain no doubts that Nietzsche's condemnation of "slave moralities" was not simply metaphorical. We regard as quite intentional Nietzsche's constant concretizing of his terms *slave* and *master* in particular religions, races, ethnic groupings, genders, and classes. Thought we do not share his elitism, sexism, racism, anti-Semitism, and so forth, and though we don't think much of reducing all conceptual categories to a typology of power, we do think that Nietzsche's terms succeed, in a necessary way, in "politicizing" supposedly neutral terms.

[35] Economists may be interested to learn that Nietzsche traces the notions of "guilt" and "bad conscience"—exemplary of a hatred of the world and life—to primitive trade and contract. In his second essay in *The Genealogy of Morals* (1956), Nietzsche expounds an economistic interpretation of the original history of guilt and punishment. He writes, "It is in the sphere of contracts and legal obligations that the moral universe of guilt, conscience, and duty . . . took its inception" (197). Nietzsche hypothesizes that from the earliest times, being unable to repay a debt warranted some form of punishment and the infliction of pain. While for "primitive" societies, this punishment was meted out by ripped-off creditors, or the community as a whole, with great pleasure and unfettered brutality, its codification within a moral code of obligations eventually led to the sublimation of pleasure and the evisceration of naked, vicious power in the practice of cruelty. And, this sublimation, based no longer on "eye for an eye"—or better yet, in Nietzsche's revelry, the ancient law of "a pound of flesh"—required that the defaulting debtor experience guilt and remorse: "pangs of conscience." In this way, guilt and bad conscience were taken on as defining aspects of an evolving, life-denying "civilization," thus leading to the most despicable (for Nietzsche) forms of human sickness. In *The Genealogy of Values* (1995), Edward Andrew subjects Nietzsche's "economics" to critical scrutiny. He does so by comparing and contrasting Nietzsche's aristocratic disdain for market economy and his related quasi- or pseudo-economics with the neoclassical revolution, that occurred at much the same time as Nietzsche's philosophizing. Interestingly, Andrew accuses Nietzsche (and Marcel Proust) of taking flight from economics towards aesthetics in order to ground his own approach to value discourse. This move, Andrew argues, is characteristic, even paradigmatic, of many elitist but anticapitalist value-theorists.

will to nothingness. Ascetics remove themselves from the world and deny the instincts and forces that affirm life. In their place, ascetic individuals discipline themselves, teach themselves how to control desire and to regulate pleasure. As the highest expression of this ideal, ascetics seek suffering as a way to transcend the world.

In Nietzsche's view, ascetics express resentment of the world by finding virtue in succumbing to life's harshness, by suffering. They will themselves to be subjected to the wills of others, if only to achieve a "higher" state of consciousness and purpose. They seek peace in suffering, pleasure in detachment, affirmation in subjection. The ascetic ideal is nothing but a "slave" consciousness of the world. For Nietzsche, it does not matter whether this ideal results in active and seething hatred of the world, a revengeful outlook seeking final redemption in the most terrible of Judgment Days (as with his "Judaic priest"), or leads to the serene realm of universal and everlasting love (his "Christian priest"). In terms of morality, the ascetic ideal is the purest expression of the will to nothingness. It affirms only the end of the world, whether in apocalypse or eternal beatitude.

The claim of the independence of Reason from morality is given an enormous boost by the ascetic ideal. That ideal—a moral precept—perfects Reason's will to nothingness by valorizing the act of removal from the world. Reason celebrates the ascetic act as its inaugural moment without naming it as such. Separation from the world is not hatred of the world. To the contrary, Reason explains that separation is a requirement for rational thought because it is only this separation that makes it possible to "disinterestedly" observe and contemplate the world. In its drive to be disinterested—to be the expression of no will, no value—Reason masks perfectly the will to nothingness of the ascetic ideal.

Wills and Values: A Nonhumanist Reading

In Nietzsche's view, all observations and concepts born out of the ascetic ideal express, in some way or other, the "value" that gives them their particular life. Modern Reason and the sciences join modern moralities in expressing resentment of the world and a will to nothingness. The active and noble will, the "will to power" of the "masters," has been in retreat since Socrates.[36] It is not "high" values that breathe life and strength into

---

[36] Heidegger (1991) identifies the will to power as the essence, for Nietzsche, of "will" in general. He states, "For in [Nietzsche's] view will is nothing else than will to power, and power nothing else than the essence of will" (37). And again, "Will to power is never the willing of a particular actual entity. It involves the Being and essence of beings: it is this

modern thought. Rather, the "base" and "low" values of a slave morality and outlook have been, until now, successful in holding sway.

In Nietzsche's work (especially *The Will to Power* [1967]), value is considered the expression of a will. Wills, however, should not be identified with "subjectivity." Values do not express the state of mind or feeling of the "subject." Nietzsche explains that the will to power or will to truth does not originate in subjectivity. On the contrary, subjectivities are, themselves, constituted by such wills. Readers of Nietzsche often miss his rejection of the notion of subject, certainly of the omnipotent and knowing subject, the "epistemological subject." Nietzsche discards the notion of the subject in several important ways.

First, he refuses to employ the humanist notion of man as the subject of knowledge and history. Nietzsche's entire philosophy stands as a stinging condemnation of a unified concept of man. Instead, Nietzsche affirms difference and hierarchy between humans such that any notion of a shared nature, existence, or experience is out of the question. As he proudly proclaims, "*My* hypothesis: The subject as multiplicity" (1967, 270).

In regard to knowledge, as Gilles Deleuze (1983) points out, the Nietzschean question is never "What is. . . ?" but "Which one. . . ?" In the epistemologies of the Enlightenment, the universal subject, the predicate of knowledge, is always the *one* who asks, "What is. . . ?" The existence of such a subject makes impossible the notion of *different* knowledges. For Nietzsche, knowledge is plural since it is always related to the values and wills that give it life. To ask the question "Which one. . . ?" is to ask which wills or which values breathe life into this or that knowledge. In contrast, since the Enlightenment there is, for us, *the* problem of knowledge (or epistemology). *The* problem of knowledge consists of establishing the conditions of knowledge such that *the* subject (or any subject, since we are all the same in regard to the possibility of knowledge) appropriates knowledge of *the* object. Epistemology is interdiscursive since it transcends particular wills, particular values. Hence, we ask "What is. . . ?" as though it were settled that "Which one. . . ?" is a question that has no bearing on knowledge.

---

itself. Therefore, we can say that will to power is always essential will" (61). Heidegger goes on to state that while Nietzsche never devises this formulation, it must be so: "otherwise we could not understand what he always refers to in connection with his emphasis on the character of enhancement in will, of the 'increase in power,' namely, the fact that will to power is something creative" (61). Heidegger cautions, though, that creativity here should not be read purely as "production." Rather, "what is decisive is not production in the sense of manufacturing but taking up and transforming, making something other than. . . , other in an essential way. For that reason the need to destroy belongs essentially to creation. In destruction, the contrary, the ugly, and the evil are posited: they are of necessity proper to creation, i.e., will to power, and thus to Being itself" (61).

In regard to history, Nietzsche rejects all "teleologies and determinisms" (1967, 297). Although this certainly means a rejection of the teleologies and determinisms of religious thought, Nietzsche makes it clear that he equally rejects the secular humanist story of the impending liberation or coming to self-consciousness of man. In modern philosophy, Nietzsche is one of the severest critics of a "dialectic of history" through which the "subject of history" comes to "realize" itself. Nietzsche's critique of the dialectic applies to either Hegelian or Marxian or institutionalist versions of it. That is, Nietzsche is critical of the historical dialectic whether it identifies the subject of history as Spirit or man. To Nietzsche, all such teleologies smack of the will to nothingness or slave mentalities since they envision an end to history. So, for example, Nietzsche would find the holistic institutionalism that affirms the preservation of life through instrumental knowledge, the organic union of Man with the industrial or technological continuum, as abhorrent and decadent—the working of a "negative will." He would be no less critical of a humanist Marxism that looks to the destruction of capitalism and the coming of socialism as the final liberation of Man.

Second, Nietzsche regards wills, and not subjects, as the active forces in nature. Or rather, particular subjectivities are produced by the conflict of wills that contend to possess us. The will to power may reside in us all. It may express itself in our ways of being in the world. However, this will does not have its origin in our "essential" subjectivity. As Deleuze points out, to ask the question of "which one . . . ?" is, for Nietzsche, a question of which will is operative, which will is dominant in the constitution of subjectivity.

If there is an essentialism in Nietzsche's work, it is an essentialism of the will. But it is a mistake to conflate this essentialism with one that sees the will as an expression or reflection of some "inner" human characteristic. Nietzsche's rejection of this humanist essentialism is one that has led many commentators to see in his work the anticipation of Freudian psychology, with its conception of the *construction* of the "ego" and the "unconscious," as opposed to those views that see the ego or the unconscious as the essential origin of our wills, desires, and so forth.

Facts, Values, Wills, and Interpretations:
The Importance of Difference

The idea that wills take possession of a subjectivity leads us back to the idea that values express wills. The crucial notion here is that of "taking possession," for wills are active forces,[37] affirming themselves in the act of possessing. This is even true of negative wills, such as the "will to nothingness." However, what distinguishes wills from one another, for they are not of the same type—they are *different*—is that some are always "active" or affirmative, while others are "reactive" or negative. Values thus express a contest of wills. Differences in values can be traced back to *which* will is dominant in *which* body (biological, social, and so on) at any moment in time.

Nietzsche replicates this view of the constitution of values as the differential affirmation of different wills in his discussion of the relation between facts and values. In Nietzsche's philosophy, facts are constituted in a manner similar to values. Facts are the site of contestation of values, each attempting to give sense to a thing. Thus, to produce a "fact" is nothing more than to say which values have taken possession of it, which values are dominant in its constitution. Facts are, therefore, always subject to change, always subject to a new interpretation, since the values that constitute its sense are likewise subject to change.

But not on their own accord. Facts are nothing more than interpretations, and each interpretation expresses the will that seeks to possess it. To say that values take hold of facts is to say that a particular interpretation, expressing the activity of some will, emerges in a particular way. To say, therefore, that facts are subject to change, as the values that possess it and give it sense or meaning change, is to say that a different will is expressing itself in a different interpretation.

Nietzsche's view that facts are interpretations and to interpret facts is to interpret an interpretation is the basis for seeing him as a philosopher of hermeneutics. However, Nietzsche differs from much of contemporary hermeneutics (within and outside institutional economics) in two important ways. First, Nietzsche parts company with those who think of interpretation as a contemplative act, an application of pure Reason to

---

[37] Deleuze (1983) develops a sophisticated reading of Nietzsche in which bodies are comprised of active and reactive *forces* (Deleuze, once again, finds this first in Spinoza). Active forces include such things as the "will to power" or "wills" more generally. Though Heidegger's reading of Nietzsche is not one to which Deleuze subscribes, Heidegger (1991) too renders some notion of force as foundational to Nietzsche's notion of power. Heidegger states, "Nietzsche often identifies power with force, without defining the latter more closely. Force, the capacity to be gathered in itself and prepared to work effects, to be in a position to do something, is what the Greeks (above all Aristotle) denoted as *dynamis*. But power is every bit as much a being empowered, in the sense of the process of dominance, the being-at-work-of-force, in Greek, *energeia*. Power is will as willing out beyond itself, precisely in that way to come to itself, to find and assert itself in the circumscribed simplicity of its essence, in Greek, *entelecheia*. For Nietzsche, power means all this at once: *dynamis, energeia, entelecheia*" (67).

an existing problem or "text." Interpretation is neither passive nor contemplative. These other, "reactive," ways of conceiving of interpretation are expressions, once again, of the resentment of the world that finds its manifestation in the ascetic ideal. Interpretation is a forceful act, an act of affirmation, and not an act of disinterested observation and commentary in the service of Reason.

Second, unlike many contemporary phenomenologists, Nietzsche's concept of interpretation is not anthropocentric. Nietzsche does not wed phenomenology and humanism, as do many current advocates of an interpretative economic or social science. Interpretation is not an act of discovering the essential motives and intentions of a subject (whether individual or collective). Interpretation is the affirmation of will, not the contemplative rediscovery of oneself on the part of the subject of history. In Nietzsche's words, "'Everything is subjective,' you say; but even this is interpretation. The 'subject' is not something given, it is something added and invented and projected behind what there is.—Finally, is it necessary to posit an interpreter behind the interpretation? Even this is invention, hypothesis" (1967, 267).

Perspectivism and Relativism: The Rejection of Epistemological Privilege

Nietzsche's "perspectivism" follows from this conception of the relation among facts, values, and interpretations. Nietzsche asserts that, as there are different wills and values, there are different ways to take hold of a fact. Hence, there are different interpretations that can constitute a fact. Which interpretation prevails determines the perspective from which facts are perceived. "In so far as the word 'knowledge' has any meaning, the world is knowable; but it is interpretable otherwise, it has no meaning behind it, but countless meanings.—Perspectivism" (1967, 267).

Though there are countless meanings, Nietzsche does not regard all meanings as equal. He does not identify difference with an equality of meanings. Thus, although he acknowledges the irreducibility of interpretations, he does not adhere to the familiar relativist position that a plurality of meanings establishes no means to distinguish among them. Quite to the contrary, Nietzsche both identifies and is interested in upholding only those interpretations that are active in affirming life. He regards such interpretations as noble, as ones worth holding and affirming against those that are reactive and negative. Since interpretations find their origin in the contest of wills, the commitment to one or another interpretation is an expression of one or another will.

In Nietzsche's view, there exist slave consciousnesses that interpret the world in a reactive and negative way. So, for example, interpretations that are generated by a Hegelian perspective are characterized by the dominance of the conception of the negative. The will that such a perspective expresses is an exhausted or decadent will, a will that affirms only nothingness.

Where slave moralities generate slave interpretations, noble moralities generate noble interpretations. All interpretations that express resentment of the world must be destroyed. For Nietzsche, such interpretations are identified by their adherence to the ascetic ideal and to the masking of the difference in wills and moralities from which this and all ideals come. One of the reasons that Nietzsche rails against democracy, egalitarianism, humanism, and other "leveling" doctrines is because they mask the consequential differences that give rise to an acceptance of one or another perspective on the world. Only a slave morality could give rise to egalitarianism and moral relativism since it is only the slaves' envy and hatred of their masters that could lead to a denial of the differential wills at work (in Nietzsche's view, a denial of life itself) in constituting the master and the slave.[38]

Nietzsche's Critique of the Sciences

Moralities or values, as expressions of wills, stand at the beginning of all attitudes toward the world. This includes attitudes to the "natural" and "social" worlds. Nietzsche carries his criticism of slave moralities, the ascetic ideal, egalitarianism, and the like into his discussion of the sciences. Nietzsche provides a twofold critique of the contemporary natural and social sciences.

First, Nietzsche criticizes modern science for its reliance on concepts of quantitative equality. He sees the operation of these concepts as the effects of utilitarian philosophy and egalitarianism. As Deleuze puts it,

> Nietzsche believes that science, in the way it handles quantities always tends to equalize them, to make up for the inequalities. Nietzsche, as critic of science, never invokes the rights of difference in quantity against quality, of inequality

---

[38] Permit us the following analogy with the situation in economics: whereas the "slave morality" of some heterodox economists remains inscribed within the protocols of mainstream economics, expressing both a resentment of the dominance of neoclassical and other orthodox theories and a requirement that all utterances be expressed in the terms defined by those theories, a "noble morality" celebrates the differences among these traditions and pursues the life-affirming project of elaborating specifically nonmainstream (institutionalist but also Marxian, feminist, and so on) economic knowledges.

against equalisation of quantities. Nietzsche imagines a "numerical and quantitative scale," but one in which the divisions are not multiples or factors of one another. What he attacks in science is precisely the scientific mania for seeking balances, the utilitarianism and egalitarianism proper to science. This is why his whole critique operates on three levels: against logical identity, against mathematical equality and against physical equilibrium. Against the three forms of the undifferentiated. (1983, 45)

Second, Nietzsche sees in the reduction of quantitative differences the denial of difference and, hence, the denial of life, the will to nothingness. Deleuze explains: "It is in this sense that Nietzsche shows that science is part of the ascetic ideal and serves it in its own way" (1983, 45). Science, "by inclination, understands phenomena in terms of reactive forces and interprets them from this standpoint" (45). Thus, the sciences contribute mightily to the "nihilism" of modern thought. The modern sciences advance interpretations of facts that are expressions of resentment, of bad conscience. They express moralities that deny rather than affirm life.

From Nietzsche's standpoint, the modern sciences must be revamped through the affirmation of "values." But not by the affirmation of negative values. It is the current operation of these negative values that accounts for the failings of modern science to begin with. Nietzsche's perspectivism does not make him indifferent to the values he believes the sciences should affirm.

Fact versus Value as a Nonepistemological Issue

We have tried to show that Nietzsche's story of the origin of Reason in morality differs radically from the positivist story of the separation of Reason from morality. Nietzsche's story is significant not only because it finds the origin of an autonomous Reason through the genealogy of morality but also because it leads to a "revaluation" of the sciences and modern moralities. Nietzsche's is not a critique of contemporary science from the point of view of contemporary morality. Nor is the reverse true. Nietzsche does not seek to privilege facts over values, but neither does he grant values a priori epistemological status.

Nietzsche's discussion of values makes it clear that their "truth" has little to do with epistemology but, rather, with whether they express an affirmative or negative will. To put this otherwise, Nietzsche's theory of facts, values, and interpretations—his perspectivism—is a theory of the *creation* of these elements and the *consequences* of their differential origins. Perspectivism is not a theory of knowledge in the sense of modernist (empiricist or rationalist) epistemology. His discussion of facts and values takes place in the context of an investigation into which life forces "take possession" of these elements and not in the context of solving the "problem of knowledge."

Nietzsche's perspectivism is thus radically different from positivism in its assertion of a multitude of nonreducible meanings. But it is not a passive observation on the state of modern knowledge. Nietzsche intends to use perspectivism to show that it matters *for life itself* which interpretations, which facts and values, take hold and are dominant at a particular historical moment. His elitist sentiments aside, his discussion of the relation between knowledges and moralities brings out quite clearly what institutionalists call the social value conditions and consequences of theory choice (and what Marxists, for their part, often refer to as the "political" or "ideological" implications of adopting one theory rather than another). For Nietzsche, perspectivism is not a kind of relativism in which the differential determinations of multiple interpretations or the differential effects of these interpretations are "equalized." Instead, he implores us to see and to value differently the *different* consequences of each interpretation.

The "New Nietzsche" and Institutional Economics

Nietzsche's critique of both Reason and modern morality resonates well with institutional economics, especially with the nonabsolutist tradition exemplified by Samuels, Mayhew, Gordon, Waller, Mirowski, and others. As Rorty suggests and goes far to demonstrate, perhaps it resonates well because of or through a postmodern reading of Dewey's pragmatism. We also think it poses a challenge to the nonabsolutist tradition, a way of engaging with value differences that avoids the problems or difficulties associated with relativism. Therefore, in addition to noting the similarities between the "new Nietzsche" and nonabsolutist institutionalism, we want to show briefly what, specifically, a reading of Nietzsche adds to the institutionalist treatment of values.

Nietzsche's critique touches on the nonabsolutist institutionalist tradition in several ways. First, as we have already shown in their critique of both the positive-normative dichotomy and Tool's absolutist social value principle, the institutionalist recognition of different values and cultures (whether in the realm of economic theory or in "the world") leads to a rejection of interdiscursive standards for epistemology, science, morality, and so forth. Indeed, Samuels recognizes that Veblen's "forté is precisely to puncture the balloons of . . . belief and pretense" (1990, 712) associated with presuming that there are absolute grounds of judgment. In other words, like Nietzsche, the nonabsolutist approaches to institutional economics are characterized by a willingness to recognize the often irreducible and incommensurable differences among epistemologies, sciences, values, and moralities. In this regard, of course, Nietzsche is similar to postmodern Deweyan pragmatism, à la Rorty, West, and Wilson.

But, second, like Nietzsche, this emphasis on the irreducibility of differences does not amount to a simple relativism. From Veblen and Commons to Samuels and others, nonabsolutist institutionalist economics focuses on the constitution of differences and their "effects." That is, as in Nietzsche, there is always a standpoint from which to judge difference, although this standpoint is itself "within" a particular discourse rather than universal. For Nietzsche, as we have argued, the interpretation of interpretations is not a passive act, since life itself is at stake. Both the differential outcomes of interpretations and the ways of being in the world that such interpretations reflect are matters of great importance, for the discipline of economics as well as for the world as a whole. The wills and values that are embedded in and expressed by the agonistic field of disciplinary protocols within economics (and, of course, the academy as a whole) affects not only which theories are predominant at any point in time but also which people are hired, given tenure, published, awarded grants, and so on—and which are not.

Similarly, the configurations of power relations that are embedded within economic and social institutions within and across societies—and therefore the groups and forms of development that are enhanced, created, and destroyed over time—are expressions of the different wills and values within society. And as Samuels explains with respect to Veblen's approach to judging "which institutions are and are not imbecile": "these judgments are in fact judgments and do not rest on 'a criterion which itself is not comprised of institutional forms or content' " (1990, 712). Here, Samuels captures the nonabsolutist institutionalists' acceptance that judgment is necessary (some institutions are imbecile while others are not) and, at the same time, their willingness to admit that there are no universal or absolute foundations for such judgments (since judgments about institutions are self-referential). Thus, in contrast to relativism, both Nietzsche and nonabsolutist institutionalists provide grounds for adhering to one or another interpretation which are neither absolute nor immutable. Another way of putting this is, the grounds for interpretative choice are socially contingent and partisan; they are, in this sense, political and not epistemological or moral (or, at least, not according to universal or interdiscursive, higher-order epistemologies or moral principles).

The rejection of interdiscursive, higher-order principles would appear, then, to commit the contemporary reading of the "new Nietzsche" and the nonabsolutist rendering of institutionalism to a common assault on humanism. "Man": neither his Reason nor his essential humanity transcends the particularity of difference. As Foucault (1973) argues, "man" and the "subject" are the dominant universals of modern thought, but they do not comprise the only possible horizon through which to produce knowledge and action. Mayhew (1987) shows, in her turn, that some institutionalists' focus on the universality of human reasoning and, with it, an insistence upon the universality and centrality of a rational strategy of human behavior threaten the recognition (and study) of cultural differences. The humanist criticisms of positivism, especially those that place universal "human values" at the beginning of all knowledge and action, are denounced alike by the "new Nietzscheans" and nonabsolutist institutionalists.

Nietzsche's contribution to institutionalism on this last point is that it is not sufficient to denounce humanism only from the standpoint of science, but that it is possible—in fact, necessary—to denounce humanism from the standpoint of an antihumanist morality. Here, we suspect, even the postmodern Deweyans will wish to part company. Nietzsche is the philosopher par excellence of an antihumanist morality. Despite the fact that Samuels, Mayhew, and other institutionalists have tried to detach the term *science* from its positivist moorings, it has remained true that none of the nonabsolutist institutionalists (to our knowledge) has sought to criticize humanism from the point of view of a distinct institutionalist set of values or morality, whatever that may be. The reluctance to so criticize humanism appears to be based on the fear that to make a value judgment is to undermine the principle of cultural relativism or that such a criticism would merely grant epistemological privilege to moral as opposed to nonmoral sentiments. Though we do not think this fear is valid, it has not been our purpose in this chapter to formulate a distinctly institutionalist moral position.

However, short of producing such a position, we may note that the "Nietzscheanizing" of institutionalism makes it possible to build on the postmodern moments of its treatment of value and, thus, to move beyond the current impasse over the status of values in institutionalist economics. If our previous discussion is accepted, then it follows that institutionalist economics need *not* place an overwhelming importance, as do both positivist economists and their humanist critics, on the issue of values in economic theory. Once institutionalist economics is disengaged from concerns over the epistemological privilege of values versus science, once this problem is "devalued," the issue of values takes on a different relevance. What this means is that the significance of values for institutionalist economics remains *to be produced* in attempts to establish the particularity of an institutionalist morality. Institutionalist economists can thus resist the temptation to assume, from the outset, that the issue of values is *in itself* a privileged one.

6

Capitalism, Socialism, and Marxian Economics

> We have arrived at an orderly destination, but it
> looks increasingly likely that we cannot rest there.
> —Frank Hahn, "General Equilibrium Theory"

FOR THE PAST one hundred years or more, Marxist economists have produced and disseminated a particular set of stories about capitalism and socialism. According to these well-known accounts, capitalism is depicted as a singularly destructive, crisis-prone system governed by the "logic of capital," which is often expressed in terms of economic "laws of motion" and the "drive to accumulate" on the part of capitalists. Socialism, in contrast, represents the suppression or elimination of such a logic, and its underlying laws and drives, and thus creates the possibility of a rational, planned way of organizing economic and social life.

When Marxist economists criticize capitalism, they often take aim at what they understand to be the fundamental instability and irrational consequences attendant upon a system based on private property and markets, especially one in which capitalists and wage-laborers operate. Thus, for example, Marxist economists have long pointed out the devastating economic and social consequences of capitalist institutions: economic anarchy (e.g., sales rarely match actual or anticipated levels of production, or the total amount of savings the projected investments, thus provoking business cycles and crises); inefficient outcomes and wasteful expenditures (unemployment, starvation, and ecological deterioration, not to mention luxury consumption for the few and military escalation); social fragmentation and disintegration (since they generate unequal distributions of wealth and power and encourage private, individual interests over public, social interests); alienation (e.g., through commodity fetishism, as the creation of "false" needs is promoted over the satisfaction of the "true" needs, and by denying individuals a "genuine" knowledge of themselves and of the society around them); and so on. Socialism, by eliminating—or, at least, circumscribing the scope of—private property and markets and through the institution of planning, is often portrayed as a system that exhibits a basic stability and rationality. The results, therefore, are quite different: economic balance and coordination (as formulated by a central planning board and followed by ministries and enterprises); efficiency and socially beneficial expenditures (based on rational calculation and the elimination of the profit motive); social harmony and unification (once relative equality is established and private and social interests are allowed to converge); and self-realization (since "true" needs can be expressed and the nature of social relations is made "immediate" and "transparent").

The contrasts between the two systems (and, of course, between these conceptions of capitalism and socialism and those put forward by mainstream economists) could not be more straightforward. We should add that these are not the only distinctions that are made by Marxist economists. In particular, attention is often directed at the extent to which capitalism is based on individual exploitation (the extraction of surplus value), whereas, under socialism, some if not all of the surplus is appropriated socially or communally.[1] Still, we find that, in a good deal of Marxist economic literature, either alongside or in place of the issue of surplus labor, the distinction between capitalism and socialism comes down to the difference—often posed as the key ethical or political choice—between one socioeconomic system (capitalism) in which anarchy, fragmentation, alienation, and unpredictability are the rule and another (socialism) in which social stability and unification, rational planning, unalienated and self-conscious subjects, fulfilled expectations, and true knowledge are key constituents.

A growing number of contemporary Marxian economists consider that these kinds of distinctions, however convincing they may have been (and still may be, to some), have carried with them dubious theoretical and political consequences.[2] They believe, for example, that past Marxist economists have exaggerated both the degree to which socialist planning involves, or is capable of generating, more stability and rationality than capitalist markets and, especially, the extent to which stability and rationality are always preferable to instability and nonrationality. Their view is that the focus on these oppositions has hindered Marxists both in their criticisms of capitalism and in imagining and constructing noncapitalist alternatives.

---

[1] Stephen Resnick and Richard Wolff (1988, 1993, 2001) and Stephen Cullenberg (1992) discuss the role of class and nonclass conceptions of socialism and communism. See also Ruccio 1992.

[2] Such distinctions have also been invoked by Marxist thinkers in disciplines outside of economics. It is interesting to note that while some Marxist economists and social theorists are questioning and rethinking traditional conceptions of the economy, including the contrasts between capitalism and socialism, Marxist literary critics (such as Fredric Jameson and Terry Eagleton) and others continue to rely on the distinctions between order and disorder, rationality and irrationality, and so on in theorizing capitalism, socialism, and the differences between the two systems.

Our own view is that, while Marxist economics differs quite substantially from neoclassical, Keynesian, and other economic discourses, it has shared with them certain foundational axes central to economic modernism. This shared modernist approach has often led Marxist economists to focus on the contrasts between capitalism and socialism that we saw above, and to prefer one set of characteristics over the other. The modernist Marxist preference is for stability, rationality, and, especially, order.

Order from Disorder: The "Invisible Hand"

Neoclassical economic thought, while arriving at conclusions that are quite at odds with those of Marxian theory (and other heterodox approaches), does tell at least one compelling story that shows nicely the possibility of the emergence of order from disorder. Often told by employing the trope of irony (perhaps modernism's characteristic literary strategy), the story of the "invisible hand" begins with the initial positing of disorder and then involves deriving a set of consequences that seems to be remote—an unexpected and unlikely possibility—in the stipulation of the initial conditions.[3]

Drawing upon Adam Smith, neoclassical economists begin with the premise that civil society, rather than being governed by an overarching religious authority or state, is fractured into competing human atoms who take actions without knowing in advance either the actions of others or the potential consequences of their own.[4] The chaos suggested by the interaction of the teeming mass of individual actors is shown to converge toward a well-ordered, "general equilibrium" solution—in which social welfare is maximized—by virtue of decentralized markets. Thus, the modernist paradox is solved by showing that *(a)* economic coordination can be achieved (market transactions are mostly orderly processes) as the outcome of *(b)* the unintended (or not necessarily intended) actions of self-interested, rational agents. Thus, the initial premise of apparent disorder is overcome by the order that is taken to be both an essential attribute and the necessary effect of market processes. The unfolding of this story gives rise to the characteristic optimism and progressivism—the utopian

[3] For a discussion of how irony emerged as the prevalent trope of historical writing by the end of the 1880s, see White 1975. In White's view, the "crisis of historicism" that emerged in historical writing toward the end of the nineteenth century was a function of the dominance by then of the "ironic condition of mind." In our view, White correctly links the emergence and dominance of irony with both the development of modernist historiography and the ultramodernist rebellions against it in this century.

[4] For a related critical discussion of the Smithian/neoclassical story, see Amariglio, Resnick, and Wolff 1990.

vision—of mainstream economic modernism, since it confirms post-Enlightenment beliefs in the efficacy and social beneficence of rationally directed, free, and individual choice.

Even within the confines of mainstream economic theories, however, the duality of order/disorder is unstable and often begins to unravel and/or to deconstruct itself. Thus, in the ceaseless pursuit to update the kind of market story we have just presented, economists of the twentieth century embraced disorder—including indeterminism, disequilibria, and chaos—as part and parcel of modern market processes.[5] But these elements—these discursive methods and conceptual concerns—also comprise postmodern moments whose disruptive potential calls into question the coherence and consistency of such narratives.

These postmodern moments also serve as an organizing point for a critique of neoclassical (and, for that matter, mainstream Keynesian) theory insofar as they allow critics to discern the "weak links" in the totalizing stories of these theories. They beckon toward alternative, oppositional theoretical stances. While to date these postmodern moments have been mostly domesticated and contained by the modernizing aspects of economic theory—for example, as we have seen, uncertainty is shown to be about degrees of either objective or subjective rational belief, thus keeping alive empiricist notions of objective reality beyond the subject—they are often picked up and pushed toward their deconstructive limits by critics and opponents of the mainstream. With post-Keynesian and Austrian economics (to cite but two examples), concepts of disorder play a key role in criticisms of mainstream neoclassical and Keynesian theories.

Post-Keynesian economists, as we saw in chapter 2, often court charges of nihilism in pursuing the disorganization of a monetary system and the ever-present disequilibria that arise in market situations. The entire apparatus of general equilibrium, often considered to be the hallmark of modern economic theorizing, is called into question by the claim that transactions made "outside equilibrium" are not only common but constitute the norm. In this view, the disorderly nature of decentralized markets is

---

[5] What we have in mind are various economists' attempts to extend the range of earlier general equilibrium models or to develop alternatives to such models. The result, in many cases, has been the "discovery" of situations in which the existence, uniqueness, and stability of general equilibrium solutions for a wide variety of economic models cannot be guaranteed. This has been the case, especially, in the use of game theory in economics—thus leading to a considerable degree of disenchantment among mainstream economists with the ability of game-theoretic methods to "save" the story of the invisible hand. See, for example, the "problems of game theory" discussed by David Kreps (1990). For Shaun Hargreaves Heap and Yanis Varoufakis, the "failure . . . to generate determinate predictions of what 'rational' agents would, or should, do in important social interactions" (1995, 260) calls into question the conception of individual agency on which much game theory is based.

stressed, although it is true that explanations are often given in which some order is indeed uncovered to explain the ever-present tendencies outside and away from equilibrium. Often this approach leads to the demand that institutional analysis be included in a theory of markets so as to reveal the underlying structural constraints or determinants that account for the existence of permanent disequilibria. By giving credence to institutional analysis, these post-Keynesians bring the wrath of other economists down on themselves by appearing to appeal to what are considered to be "ad hoc" explanations, that is, explanations that have no universal theoretical application or validity because they focus on the conjunctural and, therefore, disorderly nature of institutions and their effects. In addition, these post-Keynesian views are often dismissed as atheoretical because they lack the appropriate "microfoundations"—the idea that all economic behavior should be explained at the level of individual, rationally formulated actions—which are presumed to be a necessary condition for economic theory proper.[6] Although even post-Keynesians resort to concepts of institutional structures (such as collective bargaining and oligopolistic pricing) and mass psychology (e.g., the rush to liquidity) to bring order to their economic analyses, the mainstream reactions against their work on the issue of microfoundations indicate the degree to which they can be read as having displaced "economic man" as the founding element of economic theory and, thus, as having "destabilized," if not their conception of the macroeconomy, at least their explanations of causality and economic order.[7]

[6] For a philosophically informed discussion and critique of the charges of ad hoc explanations directed against Keynesian thinkers and the consequent appeal to "microfoundations" in much recent macroeconomic theorizing, see DeMartino 1993. DeMartino sees the charges and countercharges that have characterized the debates over microfoundations to have their origin in a mostly unspoken ontological commitment of both critics and defenders to a "necessity/ contingency" dualism.

[7] The issue of microfoundations has also arisen within the Marxian tradition. See the contrasting responses by Amariglio, Callari, and Cullenberg (1989), E. K. Hunt (1992), and Herbert Gintis (1992) to the attempt by so-called analytical Marxists to create an appropriate foundation for Marxian theory based on the constrained-maximization scheme usually associated with neoclassical economics. While the analytical Marxists, such as John Roemer, envision their work as a necessary "modernizing" of Marxian theory (and, therefore, an approach that eschews the postmodern moments that are our focus in this chapter), we suggest an additional interpretation: their use of many of the "tools" of neoclassical economics to "prove" the existence of exploitation is a way of showing that neoclassical theory does not logically exclude an analysis of power, exploitation, and much else that has traditionally been the province of Marxism and, thus, that neoclassical economists have "chosen" not to discuss such issues. That is, such an interpretation allows the deconstructive (or postmodern) insight that neoclassical economics (like any theory) is not as determined or complete a discourse as its modernist interpreters (both proponents and critics) are inclined to suggest or presume.

Austrian economics, although very close to neoclassical theory in other respects (especially its defense of free markets), also calls into question the conception of economic and social order associated with the story of the invisible hand by drawing out some of the postmodern aspects of contemporary economic theory. For Austrians influenced by the work of G. L. S. Shackle, "true uncertainty," seen as diametrically opposed to certain or even probable knowledge, is touted as the basis of a thorough-going reconsideration of any economic theory that is based on notions of equilibrium or order (including aggregate notions of allocational efficiency and social welfare) at the level of the economy as a whole. Instead, Austrian economists focus on the fragmentation of knowledge, the making of individual plans (for many, the only level at which it makes sense to speak of equilibrium), the equilibrating and disequilibrating tendencies associated with market processes, and the nature and significance of entrepreneurial discovery in historical time.[8] While their work (like that of Shackle) is embedded in a form of subjectivism and, therefore, preserves the humanist centering characteristic of neoclassical and other forms of economic modernism, the radicality of their view of the impossibility of either individual agents' or economists' obtaining knowledge of the economy-wide allocation of resources (because market prices at any given time are disequilibrium prices or because of the interpersonal incommensurability created by subjective senses of well-being) is sufficient to summon up the charge of nihilism.[9] Austrians regard their work otherwise; that is, it establishes a different economic theory, one that emphasizes the dynamic forces of competition (unfettered by government regulation or, worse, government planning), in contrast to the static view of competition that has been prevalent in mainstream neoclassical theory. According to the Austrian view, the disorder associated with markets—at least insofar as equilibrating tendencies cannot be said to outweigh the disequilibrating movements attendant upon "surprises" and the making of new individual plans—represents precisely their vitality and social usefulness. These conceptions contrast with the static view of competition that has been prevalent in mainstream neoclassical theory.[10]

---

[8] As Peter Boettke (1996, 29) explains, in distinguishing the Austrian conception of the world from that of neoclassical economics, "our general situation is one filled with imperfections, misperceptions, costly transactions, and utter ignorance of lurking opportunities."

[9] Including concerns expressed by some Austrian economists, such as Israel Kirzner: "to see the world as characterized by such extreme volatility is not only to deny the possibility of equilibrating tendencies; it is also to render economic science non-existent" (1994, 40).

[10] Austrian economists continue to debate the significance of spontaneous ordering versus nonequilibrating tendencies within their view of the market process. See, e.g., the contrasting views of Kirzner (1998) and Lachmann (1998).

Marxian Theory and Economic Modernism

Marxist economists have, of course, been at least as critical as post-Keynesians and Austrians of the neoclassical story of free markets and of the policies designed to maintain or create such markets throughout the world. They consider the story to be a pure fiction: capitalism cannot possibly achieve the harmonious coordination or produce the socially beneficial outcomes foretold by most mainstream economists. We hasten to add, however, that the contrast between order and disorder contained within the neoclassical master narrative also helps to constitute much of the alternative Marxian crisis theory; "in the last instance," the emphasis of modernist Marxism, too, is on forms of order (and, with it, centering, and uncertainty, and much else that constitutes economic modernism). In this chapter, we point out the central role this contrast has played and how the postmodern moments of Marxian economics have begun to be exploited and developed in order to undo this contrast and, thus, to accomplish a "rupture" with key elements of modernist Marxian discourse.[11]

The dialectical tensions in the order/disorder contrast get played out in a variety of ways in the Marxian tradition. To name just a few here, these tensions constitute the differentiations and oppositions between the realms of production and circulation, between markets and planning, and

[11] In the pages that follow, we present a view of modernist Marxism that we do not wish to attribute to any one thinker—though we are utterly convinced in our view that part of what we present here can be found in a wide range of texts from the past century. To our way of thinking, most Marxian economic thought during this period of time has been structured by the discursive framework that constitutes for us economic modernism. Allow us, then, to mention ten "classic" texts, of relatively recent vintage (primarily since the 1960s), most of them originally in English, that have been frequently cited. These texts differ radically in their views, so that it may seem perverse to lump them together. While we acknowledge that no one of these texts reproduces word for word the modernist Marxism we summarize below, and while some of them put forward alternatives on discrete points that can be likened to what we consider to be the more postmodern moments of Marxian theory, we believe that all these texts are similar in their abiding, prevailing constitution by economic modernism. We encourage readers to consult the following texts to satisfy themselves, we hope, of our reading: Paul Baran and Paul Sweezy, *Monopoly Capital* (1968); Ernest Mandel, *Marxist Economic Theory* (1970); Paul Sweezy, *The Theory of Capitalist Development* (1970); M. Howard and J. E. King, *The Political Economy of Marx* (1975); Michel Aglietta, *A Theory of Capitalist Regulation* (1979); John Weeks, *Capital and Exploitation* (1981); David Harvey, *The Limits to Capital* (1984); Jon Elster, *Making Sense of Marx* (1985); Duncan Foley, *Understanding Capital* (1986); and John Roemer, *Free to Lose* (1988). More recent formulations, which follow similarly modernist lines, include G. A. Caravale, *Marx and Modern Economic Analysis* (1991); Simon Clarke, *Marx's Theory of Crises* (1994); Robert Albritton, *Dialectics and Deconstruction in Political Economy* (1999); and Bob Milward, *Marxian Political Economy* (2000).

ultimately between capitalism and socialism. Indeed, there is a sense in which modernist Marxism's critique of the "invisible hand" as a story of capitalist social formations comes down to the contrast between one socioeconomic system (capitalism) in which anarchy, fragmentation, alienation, and uncertainty are the rule and a different one (socialism) in which social order and unification, rational planning, unalienated and self-conscious subjects, and fulfilled expectations and true knowledge are key constituents. That is, modernist Marxian theory makes clear that, at least at the level of "objective" and historically determined reality, the choice between capitalism and socialism is equivalent to the preference that one may have for living *either* in a society in which modernity—here identified with a rationally and communally planned "progressive" socioeconomic order—has truly succeeded (by coming to complete fruition) *or* one in which, depending on one's viewpoint, either the remnants of "premodernity" hold sway ("barbarism," ethnic, national, and racial hostilities, underdevelopment, and the like) or the "underside" of modernity (for some, postmodernity), in which for example social fragmentation is created but never resolved, is dominant.[12]

We return below to a more extended discussion of the role that the dichotomy between order and disorder plays in the endgame distinction between capitalism and socialism. In order to make clear what is at stake in retaining such a distinction, however, we now turn our attention to the specific approaches developed within modernist Marxism concerning the contrasts between production and circulation, the conception of competition, the opposition of markets and planning, and the role of subjectivity.

Production and Circulation

The distinction between the spheres of production and circulation is often conceptualized in modernist Marxism as the difference between the production of value, on one hand, and the realization of that value, on the other. In many versions, production is seen as structured and stable, at least to the extent that the production of value (including surplus value) is organized and controlled—ordered in a despotic fashion—by capitalists.[13]

---

[12] J. K. Gibson-Graham (1996) puts forward a powerful challenge to the modernist Marxian notions in which capitalism is presented as "unitary," "singular," and "totalizing." Readers will recognize in these discursive elements the notions of order (along with centering and certainty) we are likewise discussing.

[13] In their provocative attempt to overhaul much of Marxian political economy in terms of a probabilistic calculus, Farjoun and Machover (1983) make the argument that, at the level of the economy as a whole, the movements of capital and the consequent differences and fluctuations in profit in response to market conditions can be understood in terms of

Yet, although surplus value may be produced within the confines of capitalist enterprises, the realization of that surplus value (and therefore of money profits) depends upon the existence of demand for the commodities adequate to allow them to be sold at or near their production values. Numerous Marxists economists have found in Marx's discussions of the realization problem in volume 2 of *Capital* (1977) the general form of crisis within capitalism.[14] That is, because of the absence of foreknowledge of demand, and because demand is decentralized and is attendant upon the decisions of countless individuals and firms, the problem for capitalists in realizing the surplus value created in their enterprises and under their control is that the realm of circulation is quixotic at best and anarchic at worst. For example, some capitalists may face a problem of "underconsumption" if the sum total of wages that they, along with other capitalists, pay to their workers is insufficient to meet their initial output decisions. Similarly, capitalists may be victims of the absence of appropriate "proportionalities" between "departments" of production, such as the possible disproportionality that can occur between wage goods and capital goods sectors, which is the result of the lack of conscious coordination between these sectors. Each firm here makes calculations about its needed rates of input and consequent rates of output on the basis of its own estimates, but it lacks the foreknowledge of other firms' plans. One consequence, then, is that individual firms and even whole sectors can "miscalculate" the needs of other firms and households, resulting in the observed disproportionality.

Since uncertainty reigns in the sphere of circulation, individual capitalists suffer from the unplanned character of markets, and some are unable to appropriate (in the form of money) the surplus value that, in their view, they have worked hard to bring forth. Capitalists who are unable to sell their commodities at their value (price diverges from value by falling below it) or who are unable to sell them at all (the labor embodied in the commodities is deemed, by circumstances beyond their control, socially unnecessary) thus find themselves in the predicament of not being able to achieve the expected rate of profit. They respond, in turn, by making decisions to cut back on production and, if realization problems persist, to forestall new purchases (of labor power, machinery, raw materials).

---

randomness. However, they conceive of production as a fundamentally orderly sphere because of the control capitalists exercise over the conditions of production. Thus, while their move to indeterminism and probability is a way of developing an alternative to traditional forms of determinism in Marxian value theory, their argument reproduces some of the same modernist biases that we find elsewhere in Marxian economics.

[14] As Marx explains in his critique of Ricardo's theory of accumulation, "the possibility of crisis . . . lies solely in the separation of sale from purchase" (1968, 508). See Arthur and Reuten 1998 for a collection of essays on volume 2 of *Capital*.

The crisis of accumulation that the problem of realization sets off is one that therefore stems from the original distinction between production and circulation under capitalism insofar as the disorder of the market is blamed for eventually disrupting production and throwing the entire economic system into crisis.

We should note, however, that there is a different but related story often told in modernist Marxian economic thought that focuses alternatively on the "anarchy of production." Here, the sphere of capitalist production as a whole is viewed as disorderly. Although capitalists may exhibit class solidarity and coordination—for example, in their influence on the state or in relation to demands from contending classes (such as workers, bankers, or landowners)—no such coordination exists in the realm of production. The very fragmentation of capitalist firms, the competition among them, and the necessity to make individual production decisions that are guaranteed by the possession of private property rights over means of production create a situation in which each capitalist is forced to make decisions that, for the capitalist class as a whole, lead to a lower rate of profit. Such a situation may obtain if, for example, in order to expand production, capitalists' demand for laborers exceeds the available supply, thus depleting the "industrial reserve army." When workers' bargaining power is strengthened, wages will be bid up and the rate of profit will decline. The rate of profit may also exhibit a "tendency" to fall if, in order to stem the distribution of some of their surplus value to other, more productive firms in their sector, capitalists are forced to increase the "organic composition of capital" (the ratio of dead to living labor, of the value of means of production to the value of labor power), thereby decreasing the source of surplus value. Once again, the diagnosis is that the problem stems essentially from disorder in the capitalist market system, even though here the problem begins in the sphere of production and is the result of the "anarchy" that reigns because of the division of total social capital among numerous private capitalist firms.

Both cases are governed, as in the story of the invisible hand, by the master trope of irony. In these instances, however, rational capitalists who appear to be in control are forced, by virtue of their position in a disorderly, uncertain, and anarchic system of unplanned markets and individual competition, to make decisions that, rather than creating a general equilibrium, more or less inevitably lead to economic crises.[15]

---

[15] Stephen Cullenberg (1994) shows that the history of Marxian discourse concerning the tendency of the rate of profit to fall can be generally viewed as having two variants, Cartesian and Hegelian, that rely on treating the capitalist economy as a totality whose ability to reproduce itself is threatened by a fall in the rate of profit. The Cartesian notion is based on the premise that its constituent parts exist prior to and independently of the totality (hence its association with methodological individualism), while the Hegelian ap-

Competition

Marx's theory of competition plays a key role in this theoretical project. According to modern Marxist economists, the existence of instability and irrationality in capitalism (and, thus, of their negative consequences) can largely be traced to the activities of individual capitalists and capitalist enterprises. To choose but one example, the "law" of the tendency of the rate of profit to fall, a prime cause of economic crises in many Marxist analyses, is attributed to the aforementioned rising organic composition of capital, which, in turn, is explained by the concerted attempts on the part of capitalist enterprises within an industry to innovate in order to capture the largest possible share of surplus value.

Here, a key theoretical problem arises. The issue for Marxist economists in developing these explanations is that, while the *differentia specifica* of Marxist economics is often understood to be its theory of value and surplus value, the behavior of capitalist enterprises is said to occur at the level of prices and profits. The reason that volume 3 of *Capital* is so important for Marxist economists (and, not coincidentally, so contentious for them as for others) is that it serves both as a theory of what occurs on the "surface" of capitalism—prices, profits, and individual capitalist enterprises—and as a conceptual bridge to the "underlying" realm of capitalist production—of value, surplus value, and "capital as whole" (which is initially elaborated in volume 1 of *Capital*).

We do not want to enter here into the debate concerning the so-called transformation problem—which, at least upon some views, is a nonproblem.[16] The relevant issue here is a different one: how should one make sense of what is considered to be the unruly, anarchic, even chaotic realm in which prices are formed, profits calculated, and capitalist enterprises operate? For modernist economists, mainstream and radical alike, the validity of their science (and of their resulting stories about capitalism and its consequences) is predicated on finding the order that emerges from, or explains, the apparent disorder. For neoclassicals, who begin with a conception of individual economic agents, each pursuing his or her own self-interest, that order is "found," as we explained above, in market equi-

---

proach begins with the idea that the whole is a pregiven, structured totality (a form of social explanation known as holism). In our view, both concepts of totality reproduce—in older and more contemporary versions of Marxist theory—many of the aspects of ordering, centering, and so forth that are characteristic of economic modernism. Cullenberg (1996) presents an alternative to both approaches, which he refers to as a "decentered totality."

[16] For example, Wolff, Roberts, and Callari (1982, 1998) argue that the "transformation problem" has been created by imposing a Ricardian problematic on the categories and concerns of Marxian value theory.

librium: at the level both of individual markets (where excess demands are equal to zero) and of the economy as a whole (based on the idea of Pareto efficiency, where are all agents are able to realize their appropriately constrained plans). Not surprisingly, modern Marxist economists reject this particular story of partial and general equilibrium, of an "invisible hand" that is capable of creating order out of apparent disorder. They turn, instead, to a different approach, one that locates the motivating force and underlying structure of capitalism in the activities of "capital." In their view, the formation of prices and profits—and the resulting instabilities and irrationalities associated with capitalism—can be tied to the orderly laws and drives associated with the decisions and behaviors of capitalists (or of their institutional embodiment, capitalist enterprises).[17] One way of counterposing these two economic theories, then, is the following: while both construct their conceptions around the modernist opposition between order and disorder, neoclassicals tend to focus on the emergence of order from disorder, while Marxists move in the opposite direction, emphasizing the disorder that is created and reproduced by the underlying order.

It is this attempt to find the order "hidden within" the apparent disorder that seems to motivate modernist Marxist economists' theories of capitalist enterprises and of capitalist competition. Consider, for example, the usual treatment of the formation of a general rate of profit. Capitalist enterprises, in search of the highest rate of profit, are said to distribute and redistribute their capital investments (they choose to enter and exit different "industries") according as the actual or potential rate of profit is high or low, until "prices of production" are established that allow the emergence of a single, uniform rate of profit across all industries. The actions of firms also account for the "tendencies" of movement of the general rate of profit. In cases where capitalists innovate by increasing the organic composition of capital—in order, for example, to obtain "superprofits" (excesses of realized profits over the amounts of surplus value obtained from workers within those firms)—the rate of profit will have a tendency to fall. A similar outcome obtains when, together, capitalists

---

[17] Norton describes the method of traditional Marxian crisis theory in the following way: "On the one hand, capitalism must have an essential core of an abstractly determined sort, adequate to structure 'the accumulation process' in an epochally fixed way. On the other hand, the important phenomena of economic life, the growth rates of various macroeconomic variables (productivity, profit rates, fixed capital investment, etc.) must be regarded as responding to and expressing that core" (1992, 184). What Norton finds missing from the "logic of necessity" imposed by such a method are the contingencies of spatial definition, finance, culture, and much else. David Levine (1992), in contrast, argues that the very possibility of economy theory is predicated on a view of the economy as expressing an abstractly conceived inner logic.

increase their demand for labor power, thereby outstripping the available supply, and bid up the price of labor power. In other cases—for instance, when enterprises are successful at increasing the rate of exploitation (e.g., by increasing the intensity of labor), in depressing wages (either directly or through increases in the labor force, whether as a result of demographic growth, changes in the labor force participation rate, or the availability of immigrant labor), or in cheapening the elements of constant capital (via more efficient production or finding cheaper sources of raw materials)—the rate of profit will exhibit an opposite tendency.

These stories, and others (e.g., concerning the concentration and centralization of capital and the expansion of capital on a global scale), are too well known to require extensive discussion here. What is important for our purposes is the manner in which these results are obtained. Throughout the analysis, a particular notion of competition is invoked to explain the emergence of prices, profits, and their tendencies and countertendencies. Individual capitalist enterprises compete against other enterprises—in their own industry and in other industries—thereby compelling both themselves and the others to make particular decisions and to take specific actions: to shift capital from one industry to another, to increase the ratio of "dead labor" to "living labor," and so on. Once the "system" is set into motion, then, each firm is forced to make the appropriate calculations and to engage in the activities that ensure its own survival and growth over time.

Now, the actual starting point for setting the competitive process into motion varies depending on the particular theoretical strategy. In some approaches, firms are seen to be but individual manifestations of "capital as a whole"—and, since the central characteristic of capital is the self-expansion of value, they exhibit an essential drive to accumulate. All enterprises therefore devote the largest possible share of their profits (realized surplus value) to the accumulation of productive capital, capital that is productive of more surplus value. This "inner" drive, in turn, forces each enterprise into a competitive battle with all other enterprises. A second set of approaches begins with individual capitalist enterprises themselves. These firms are guided not by the general drive to accumulate (although they *do* accumulate, as part of their own competitive strategies) but, rather, by a form of rational decision-making with the aim of maximizing profits (and/or minimizing costs). Here, because all enterprises are conceived to be governed by the same form of capitalist rationality, and because the success of some can and often does come at the expense of others, they are compelled by "outside" pressures to compete with one another. Notwithstanding the wide differences between these two approaches, then, the result is that the competitive process in which capitalist enterprises are engaged serves as the basic element in explaining developments on the "surface" of capitalist economies.

What stands out in both sets of stories is the idea that capitalist competition is a fundamentally predictable, unified, and orderly process. All enterprises are characterized by a single, stable, "centered" identity: they allocate their profits to the accumulation of capital in order to maximize the amount of surplus value they can realize by outcompeting other enterprises in producing and selling capitalist commodities. And they know, with certainty, what their profits are and how best to maximize them (and, equivalently, their costs and how best to minimize them). It is precisely this ordering that allows modernist Marxist economists to demonstrate what are considered to be some of the fundamental propositions of Marxian value theory: that a general rate of profit can be established on the basis of prices of production (and therefore that prices and profits can be linked to values and surplus value); that the rate of profit exhibits regular "tendencies" (both downward and upward); and that instability and irrationality are part of the "normal" workings of the capitalist economy.

Planning versus Markets

In this analysis, the diagnosis suggests the cure: planned production and coordination among firms. This remedy, so the story goes, can be practiced only within the bounds of socialism, since the elimination of competitive market forces and private productive property serves as the necessary condition of existence for the emergence of coordination and planning. A more orderly form of economic organization is possible in socialism as long as a central planning board is able to calculate accurately the needed balance between inputs and outputs within and between different industries and branches of production. The fact that enterprises would no longer be motivated to engage in individual attempts at increasing, or at least maintaining, maximum rates of profit through strategies of increasing the rate of exploitation on workers means that these same enterprises can rationally plan—with social goals in mind, and with the foreknowledge of the plans of other firms—not only their output levels but also even the amount of "surplus" that they will be able to retain in order to expand production through additional capital formation.

Markets, on the other hand, preclude such centralized, orderly coordination. Market activity is predicated precisely on the separate (whether rational or irrational, it does not matter) decisions of enterprises and individuals without any ex ante or ex post reconciliation of privately formulated plans. Even the forms of planning that do exist—for example, among different units of the same enterprise, government monetary and fiscal policy, regulatory agencies, or indicative planning at the national and supranational level—cannot ultimately forestall (although they can mitigate some of the immediate effects of) the cycles and crises associated with capitalist production.

Therefore, many modernist Marxists are quite critical not only of capitalist markets but also of the various forms of market socialism that have been promulgated in recent years.[18] David McNally (1993), for example, argues that the "fundamental choice is . . . *socialism or the market*" (2), not in the sense either that markets can be eliminated overnight or that socialism might not contain "some market mechanisms," but that Marxist conceptions of socialism must be defined in terms of an unrelenting struggle against "the market" as a regulator of economic life. That is because, in McNally's view, capitalist relations and imperatives, especially the competitive "drive to accumulate for the sake of further accumulation" (183), are "built into an economy regulated by commodity production and exchange" (181). The alternative, therefore, is to reduce the scope of the market and to establish "social planning of production" (187).

The superiority of socialist production derives from the elimination of the disorder, uncertainty, and irrationality that characterize capitalist markets and competition. The order that is made possible by planning is presumed to be preferable to the anarchy of capitalist production since the former eliminates the tendency for crises (most importantly, by eradicating the crucial conditions for the existence of exploitation, and therefore the necessity for producers to sell their commodities at their values) while the latter always tends toward systemwide crises. Capitalist production, circulation, and distribution are thus seen to be fundamentally predicated on the absence of social and economic order while socialist production, circulation, and distribution are seen to be governed by the real possibility of such order.

Subjectivity

As we have seen, the modernist conception of the distinction between production and circulation, the nature and role of competition, and the differences between markets and planning are made to serve the ultimate distinction between capitalism and socialism. But this last distinction rests as well on other key modernist premises, such as the centrality of subjectivity in constructing an ethics of system choice. At first sight, this privileging of subjectivity would seem to be an object of Marxist scorn. After all,

---

[18] But modernist formulations of Marxian economics also include numerous outlines and strong defenses of market socialism. See, e.g., Roemer 1996 and Bardhan and Roemer 1993.

one of Marxism's strong points has always been the critique of bourgeois individualism. Marxists have in the past argued not only that any form of subjectivity—including individuality—is a product of historical circumstances and is therefore contingent and conjunctural (and not universal or eternal) but also that the appropriate agent of history is never the abstractly conceived individual but, instead, the masses or classes. In this sense, the Marxian tradition, even when thoroughly modernist, has been able to resist the Cartesian idea of the centered subject and its use in the hands of Adam Smith and others as the starting point for economic and social analysis. Yet we think it would be a mistake to conclude that this resistance has meant the complete displacement or elimination of the centered individual subject from Marxian theory.[19]

In place of the Cartesian concept of the individual subject, many Western Marxists seized upon Marx's early writings, in opposition to mechanistic and economic determinist Marxism, to "reintroduce" a subject whose essential nature is indeed alienated in the historical process. Such Marxists resurrected Marx's idea that class societies produce a rupture between the individual's species-nature and the conditions for its realization. Thus, the history of class societies is, at least in part, the history of the emergence of stunted, one-sided, and increasingly disaffected forms of subjectivity. In pursuit of this idea Lukács and the Frankfurt critical theorists alike were careful not to reinstitute the Feuerbachian notion of an abstractly conceived "man," but they read Marx as postulating an essential species-being that, in the process of its becoming—that is, its coming to self-consciousness—was capable in alienating circumstances of arriving at self-consciousness and, eventually, of realizing itself. Thus, the basic potential wholeness of the human subject was asserted, though now as the end to some teleological process of historical development rather than as an ever-present essence.[20]

In this way, although Western Marxists challenged the idea of the eternal, self-motivated individual whose every action reaffirms its essence, their reading of the "early Marx" and the consequent interpretation of

[19] Of course, class itself has often been conceived as a fundamentally orderly—centered and centering—subject in the Marxian tradition. See Gibson-Graham, Resnick, and Wolff 2001a for an innovative attempt to reconfigure, from a poststructuralist perspective, the nature and role of class in Marxian economic and social theory. The essays in Gibson-Graham, Resnick, and Wolff 2000 and 2001b offer a wide variety of specific examples of class analyses inflected with postmodern themes and concerns. In a related manner, focusing especially on the implications of indeterminacy, William Corlett (2000) raises "the possibility of a rethinking and a practicing of Marxism from a poststructural perspective that relies on the self-activity of working people, all the while insisting upon a Marxist understanding of capital as the possession of Labor's stolen goods" (158).

[20] A recent version of this argument has been put forward by Wilson (1991); see Ruccio 1995 for a critical review.

commodity fetishism and reification reinscribed the notion of the centered subject, perhaps as the historical origin (as in the state of primitive communism, with its putatively "organic" individuals) or the agent of history (embodied, e.g., in the working class or its political party), and certainly as the attainable goal of the "end of history." Thus, modernist Marxism breaks with its non-Marxist counterparts over the possibility of the realization of the centered subject in socialist rather than capitalist social formations.[21] The modernist Marxist criticism of postmodernism is that postmodernists deny the historical possibility of the centered subject (whether now, in the past, or at some distant point in the future) and therefore see decentered subjectivities everywhere and at all times. Modernist Marxists often see the decentered subject as the unfortunate historical product of capitalism and, thus, not to be treated as a universal, abstract, and historically transcendent form of subjectivity.[22] For contemporary modernist Marxists, the decentered subject is a deformation of capitalism whose eradication under socialism, where "wholeness" and true self-consciousness are at least historically feasible, is to be desired. The reification of the decentered subject by postmodern thinkers, according to such modernist critics, speaks volumes about the ineffective—or, even worse, irreducibly reactionary—political project of postmodernism.[23]

In Marxian economic theory this question of the form of subjectivity is best rendered in the debates over the meaning of Marx's discussion of commodity fetishism. The typical reading is that generalized commodity relations distort the subjects and their consciousnesses to the degree that they come to attribute the qualitative relations among themselves to the commodities that they possess and exchange. This "false consciousness" is a misperception, but it is also the "true" expression of the one-sidedness and alienation that is the lot of subjects in a totally commodified social formation. The consequences for the economy of this fetishism of commodities—this perversion of economic subjectivity—are several:

---

[21] Of course, what such subjectivity comprises—e.g., individual rationality versus class consciousness and human liberation—is also different in these traditions.

[22] E.g., Eagleton: "If the postmodern subject is determined, however, it is also strangely free-floating, contingent, aleatory, and so a kind of caricatured version of the negative liberty of the liberal self. . . . There is much of the Nietzschean will to power in this vision; but it also corresponds pretty well to the experience of advanced capitalist societies" (1996, 89–90).

[23] E.g., Christopher Norris: "their [referring to "post-structuralists, post-modernists, and other fashionable figures on the current intellectual scene"] 'radicalism' has now passed over into a species of disguised apologetics for the socio-political status quo, a persuasion that 'reality' is constituted through and through by the meanings, values or discourses that presently compose it, so that nothing could count as effective counter-argument, much less a critique of existing institutions on valid theoretical grounds" (1990, 3–4).

capital is treated as a "thing" and not a social relation; money, not surplus labor, is understood to be the source of self-expanding value; surplus value is viewed as arising in exchange rather than production; technology replaces the capitalist drive for profits as the key determinant of the forms of the labor process; profit is attributed to some quality of the means of production or the risk-taking activities of capitalists instead of exploitation; and much else.

The overthrow of capitalism, once again, promises a solution to all of this. In socialism, commodity fetishism is banished, as production no longer is for exchange but for use, thus eliminating the crucial condition for fetishism to arise. In the modernist Marxist tradition, then, socialism is additionally preferred to capitalism in that the crippling and distorting forms of subjectivity that reflect general market relations under capitalism are replaced by those forms of subjectivity in which agents are now able to "see" clearly (since these relations are now transparent) the social relations behind their interdependent economic links. As a result, as Marxists purport to show, socialism creates the conditions for true knowledge of economic processes and disallows the "errors" about capital, money, profit, and the like that were caused primarily by reification. There is no discrepancy now among the socioeconomic totality, knowledge, and subjectivity, and this finally leads to the true centering of the now "total" subject.

We have argued that the modernist contrast of order/disorder shows up in crucial places in traditional Marxian economic thought. The conventional distinctions between production and circulation, market and plan, centered and decentered subjectivities, and capitalism and socialism are in fact built upon these contrasts. As we have contended, modernism in Marxian economic theory has given preference (but not exclusivity) to order. In the remainder of this chapter, using a few examples, we present the objections that have been raised to this modernism and sketch the postmodern Marxism that, in our view, is suggested by the postmodern moments in Marx's texts and subsequent Marxisms.

Postmodern Moments in Marxian Economics

To be clear, the new kinds of Marxian economic analysis that we see emerging need not diminish the significant achievements associated with the utopian imaginary created by the order/disorder and other oppositions characteristic of modernist Marxism. Indeed, postmodern Marxists continue to advocate alternatives to capitalism (including various forms of socialism) and may even prefer planning to markets. The challenge, as we see it, is to acknowledge the dubitable theoretical and political consequences of the modernist configuration of Marxian economic discourse and to reconfigure Marxian economic categories along postmodern lines. Thus, for example, some Marxian economists and social theorists argue that the modernist tendency has overemphasized both the existence of disorder in capitalism and the negative consequences of the types of disorder that arise there. Likewise, it has exaggerated the orderly nature of socialism, and especially of planning, and has viewed as unduly positive the consequences of such order.

Plans and Markets

To take just the last point, there is little evidence that planning means stability and order or that it implies a "better" method to get at the "true" needs of individuals and/or enterprises. Planning, both in theory and as it has been practiced historically, is a process into which contention, conflict, and difference enter at every stage. Like all other social practices, it not only is the result of many determinations, but its effects are always multiple and are played out in a variety of often contradictory ways. Planning differs from markets in the degree to which some people's desires and plans are calculated and realized more heavily than others, but it does not diverge from markets either in the ability to forecast accurately the effects of the decisions taken nor in the controversies and potential imbalances and disproportionalities that may result. Planning, like markets, is always the site of social conflicts insofar as planners must make decisions on how to allocate among many different classes the surpluses that are produced. Indeed, it is precisely because planning under socialism often presumes the end of class conflict and announces itself as the establishment of socially rational order that, ironically for Marxists, class discourse may be neglected.[24] This neglect shows up in the inability of planners to account for the conflicts and difficulties that arise in the course of planning other than as "mistakes" in calculation and technical inefficiencies. The determinants and outcomes of plans are thus often as unpredictable as market solutions are said to be.

But this comment should not be taken to be one of criticism. According to postmodern Marxists, if planning announced itself purely as an activity in and through which the desires of "exploited classes" would be given priority, this would suffice to give it credence. But, as we know, this has generally not been the case. Instead, the defense of planning has included its promise to mediate different demands and to make rational choices

[24] See, e.g., the analysis of the conditions and effects of socialist planning by Ruccio (1986a, 1986b).

from the standpoint of society as a whole, thus eliminating the social uncertainty that previously stemmed from market conditions. Where mistakes arise, then, the promise to correct them always follows since the possibility of getting it right—of ordering the process accurately and acquiring and employing correct information about needs and so on—is implicit in the very (modernist) idea of the plan. Since planning is advertised as preferable to markets precisely because of this possibility, it is no accident that the political consequences of its presumed historic "failures" have led not only to the abandonment of socialism but to a rejection of planning *tout court*.[25]

Markets, of course, do not do much better. Yet, in the view of Barry Hindess and others, markets are stereotyped by modernist Marxism in that they are always seen as disorderly and incapable of meeting social needs. Marxists have tended to exaggerate the negative consequences of market disorder, to see only one side of the disharmonies that are characteristic of markets. Hindess (1987), for example, discusses and criticizes the "essentialism of the market" (and, from there, of planning) that can be found not only in Marxian thought but also in the Austrian economics of Hayek and others. We quote at length:

> To write of essentialism in this context is to say that the market is analyzed in terms of an essence or inner principle that produces necessary effects by the mere facts of its presence. In this case certain consequences are thought to follow merely from the fact that goods and services are provided through market exchanges rather than in some other ways. Precisely what those consequences are supposed to be, of course, will vary from one of these positions [Marxism or Hayekian liberalism] to another: they are anarchic and wasteful, they leave too much power in private hands, they generate indefensible inequalities; they are a realm of freedom and efficiency; they foster a spirit of egoism which undermines the altruism of social policy; under conditions of wage-labor they are the means of capitalist exploitation; and so on. The diversity of markets themselves and of the consequences that are alleged to follow from their existence may be obscured by reference to "the market"—as if what is at issue is an institutional structure of interactions with roughly similar properties in all significant cases. (149–50)

Hindess concludes that such essentialisms "mask extremely complex and heterogeneous sets of conditions" (150). As a result, "liberalism, Marxism, socialism, and many positions in between, treat market provision and public control as if they represented distinct and incompatible principles of social organization" (151).

---

[25] See Ruccio 1992 for a more extensive discussion of the connection between the "failure" of socialism and the turn away from planning and toward markets.

But just as critically, the degree of disorder has, we think, been over-stated by modernist Marxists. In their rush to criticize and to distance themselves from economic discourses (such as neoclassical theory) that celebrate the existence of markets and generally express a preference for markets over all other forms of social exchange and distribution of pro-duced goods and services, modernist Marxists (ironically, like their neo-classical counterparts) have tended to neglect the implications of an in-sight long ago provided by the Marxian tradition: that economic institutions and identities are socially and historically constituted in a cap-italist social formation. One possible implication of this social constitu-tion of institutions and identities is that the activities of capitalist ex-change mostly take place on a regular and orderly basis.

Consider, for example, the "normal" activity of consumers in an econ-omy characterized by markets. They often shop in the same locations, purchasing many of the same goods, even when prices vary (sometimes considerably) from one location to another and new products are placed on the shelves. In this sense, the participation of individual consumers in markets is a much more stylized and ritualistic activity than is usually presumed (by Marxist and neoclassical economists alike). Similarly, firms often negotiate long-term contracts with other firms (both suppliers of inputs and distributors of outputs) precisely in order to "stabilize" deliv-eries and to avoid the "disorder" attendant upon the continual recon-tracting and renegotiating that would be necessary every time the price and/or quality of a commodity changes.[26] In neither case—and these may be the norm rather than the exception—do markets exhibit the disorder frequently emphasized by modernist Marxists or, for that matter, implicit in those neoclassical stories that portray the instantaneous reactions of consumers and producers through the metaphors of supply and demand, "fish auctions," and *tâtonnement*. Instead, markets can be seen as sites (historically, symbolically, and culturally constituted) in which consumers and firms are often guided by tradition and habit, set prices, make con-tractual commitments, and otherwise "arrange" their transactions to con-tain or eliminate disorder.

This "anthropological" approach to markets is consistent with those views found in other heterodox economic discourses that focus on condi-

---

[26] William Milberg (2001) has challenged the central role of the "market metaphor" in the international economy: "Today's international economic relations are characterized by considerable amounts of non-arm's-length transactions. These take the form of intra-firm trade, inter-corporate joint ventures and alliances, special arrangements between buyers and sellers (supplies), and state-negotiated trade. The scope of this array of forms of non-arm's-length is so broad that the relevance of the market cum locus of arm's-length transactions is greatly diminished" (416).

tions of stability in capitalist exchange.[27] In most modernist versions of economic analysis, these conditions themselves are essentialized so as to find the "origin" or essence of market stability in some unique subjective attribute or institutional arrangement. For example, while neoclassical economists may have no particular recourse to "institutions" as ultimate explanatory variables, they do have the possibility of explaining the recourse to consumer and producer habit and ritual through such concepts as "risk averse" behavior, "impatience" with respect to the choice between present and future consumption, and "lack of foresight."[28] In these cases, habit and ritual are reduced to and are said to originate in an individual's preference for acting habitually. Yet, in our view, rationality itself can be seen as habitual and routine. That is, so-called rational behavior must be learned (and thereby turned into a "habit" of mind and action), requires repetition (at least if consistency is to be achieved), and, of course, is itself a matter of culture (that is, it only arises within certain social situations and discourses and varies accordingly). The ritualistic nature of rationality is usually ignored by most neoclassical economists who wish to use rationality as a term opposite to habit and convention and to essentialize them, in fact, as an alternative—and nonrational—origin for economic and social behavior. Many Marxists (as well as institutionalists and post-Keynesians), on the other hand, see social convention and habit in market behavior as stemming essentially from sociocultural norms (usually conceived as "outside" of markets and "historically determined"), as dictated by an individual's class position and interests, or as a rational economic strategy in the face of fundamental uncertainty.[29] In all three of these cases, once again, habit and ritual have an essential time and place of origin, do not arise for the most part in the process of exchange itself, and are not "overdetermined" in their constitution.

[27] Here we note (but cannot develop in any detail) the issues raised in the growing anthropological and cultural studies literature, following Jean Baudrillard (1975, 1981) and Marshall Sahlins (1976), regarding the symbolic or significatory order that is enacted and reenacted in exchange and consumption, constituting subjects and social structures (including markets) alike. Baudrillard and Sahlins have contributed especially to a rejection of classical Marxist "productionism" (the subsumption of consumption to production, or of exchange-value to use-value). Readers can also consult Douglas and Isherwood 1979; Appadurai 1986b; Miller 1992; Dilley 1992; Howes 1996; and Carrier 1997 for further elaborations of an "anthropology" of consumption and markets.

[28] An alternative approach serves as the foundation for the new institutional economics of neoclassical theory in which "institutions" (including "informal constraints" such as customs and traditions) are seen to be efficient solutions to problems of cooperation and organization in a competitive framework. Here, too, the goals of the agents (consumers or producers) are taken as given. See, e.g., the work of Ekkehart Schlicht (1998), Douglas North (1990), and Oliver Williamson (1985).

[29] See Crotty 1993 for a discussion of Keynes's notion of convention as the primary determinant of investment behavior under conditions of uncertainty.

We stress this last point since it bears as well on the concepts of habit and ritual that are especially appropriate to a postmodern Marxian approach to economic analysis. There is no reason to view habit and ritual as necessarily "orderly" because there is no reason to view the constitution of habitual or ritualistic behavior as other than always contingently and discursively constituted. In this regard, we note that there are, of course, many forms of habitual economic behavior that are normally viewed as disorderly. The "exuberant" attitudes and behavior of commodity traders and their markets—indeed, most forward markets and forms of speculation, which proceed according to well-defined rules—provide one such example.[30] While the habit and ritual of market transactions may permit the discursive introduction of more order than that which is found in the atomistic view of instantaneous markets—the view that comprises both the self-consciousness of neoclassical theory and the critique of the same by modernist Marxists—the conjunctural and overdetermined nature of habit and ritual (and thus their intrinsic disorderliness, because they may or may not be reconstituted from one moment to the next) makes it impossible to treat these as mere synonyms for socioeconomic order.

Even with the introduction of habit and ritual, capitalist markets cannot be see as uniformly orderly processes. In addition to the provisos we note above, there is no guarantee that a particular market will come into existence when it is called for (i.e., when either side of a potential transaction or some outside observer finds it "necessary") or that a market, once it exists, will continue to exist over time (e.g., that an object, once produced, will successfully complete the process of circulation). Markets, in this sense, are not self-organizing or self-regulating activities; they are always being broken up and need to be created anew. And this formation and re-formation of the activity of market exchange is predicated on the existence of processes and institutions throughout society in and through which the means and identities of such transactions are continually being created and destroyed. When markets are understood in this manner, they are seen to be "socially embedded" (indeed, socially constructed) institutions that are disorderly precisely because they are not the expressions of any underlying essence—whether a given economic rationality (as presumed by classical and, more recently, neoclassical economists) or a universal law of value (as often put forward by modernist Marxists). As with habit and ritual, markets are disorderly at least to the extent that their continued existence must be reproduced in each moment, and this reproduction requires its determination by myriad institutions and subjects,

[30] See, e.g., the work of Robert Shiller (1981, 1990) and Richard Thaler (1994) on the role of investor overreaction or exuberance in financial markets.

themselves requiring such reproduction. Change and dislocation, therefore, may be the rules rather than the exceptions. Similar characteristics apply to capitalist competition.

Disorderly Competition

If modernist Marxist economists have succeeded in extracting from volume 3 of *Capital* an orderly conception of capitalist competition, we think that there is ample warrant in the text for having done so. In various places, Marx does indeed refer to laws and tendencies, driving forces and determinate results, in order both to counter the claims of the classicals and to construct his own view of capitalism. However, it is also possible to detect in Marx's text other aspects of a theory of competition that have been ignored or downplayed by modernist Marxists. These other dimensions run counter to the modernist interpretations that have become the shared terms of debate and lead to a more decentered, unpredictable, and disorderly conception of competition.

To begin with, we are struck by the large number of references Marx makes to "averages" in his discussions in volume 3. In grappling with the tension between order and disorder—the problem of whether to order the apparent disorderliness of capitalism or to avoid altogether privileging one over the other, whether order or disorder—Marx often invokes the idea of averaging and emphasizes movement, random fluctuations, and even chance. The general rate of profit, for example, is taken to be an *average* rate of profit, "the average of all these different rates" (1977, 3:257), "an average of perpetual fluctuations which can never be firmly fixed" (3:261). Similarly, in discussing the movement of the general rate of profit, Marx emphasizes "the uninterrupted and all-round character of this movement" (3:269). We take these and other such references as a warning against too deterministic, ordered or unified, an interpretation of the notions of profit, price, and so on in the context of "capitalist production as a whole."

It is this concern with multiplicity and randomness that appears to show up in Marx's discussions of capitalist competition and that is largely absent from modernist conceptions of the competitive activities of capitalist enterprises.[31] According to modernist Marxists, as we have seen, firms distribute profits (or realized surplus value) to the accumulation of capital in order to compete with other enterprises. The problem is, this conception recognizes only some of the forms of competition that Marx discusses

---

[31] With one notable exception: Farjoun and Machover's (1983) use of notions of randomness to depict the movements of capital and the consequent differences and fluctuations in the rate of profit.

in volume 3. As Bruce Norton (1986, 1988, 1992), Cullenberg (1994), Gibson-Graham and O'Neill (2001), and others have noted, it is possible to expand the discussion by focusing on some of the other forms of competition, both outside and inside the enterprise.

As they see it, capitalist enterprises *do* compete with other enterprises, both within and between industries. In the context of individual industries, enterprises compete over the conditions in which they can realize, in the form of profit, the surplus value that they and other firms within the same industry have appropriated from their productive laborers. This process of competition leads to the formation of average market-values, which represent the extent to which any one enterprise will be able to realize its particular share of surplus value. Similarly, firms compete across industries, leading to capital flows and the reconfiguring of the structures of capital within and between those industries. This means that firms within one industry can, on the basis of an average rate of profit and corresponding prices of production, realize surplus value appropriated from laborers not only by their own firms and industries but also by firms within other industries. What emerges, as Bruce Roberts (1988) has pointed out, is a complex pattern of distributions and redistributions of surplus value among capitalist enterprises within and between industries.

Equally important, however, are other forms of competition over shares of realized surplus value. Marx goes to great lengths in volume 3 to point out that industrial capitalist enterprises compete with many other entities—enterprises, institutions, and individuals—that exist separately from those enterprises. Examples include financial capital, merchant capital, owners of equity shares, landowners, and the state. In each case, industrial (or functioning) capitalists are subject to competitive pressures to distribute a portion of the surplus value appropriated from productive laborers ("theirs" as well as those of other capitalists) to the occupants of "subsumed class" positions located outside industrial capitalist enterprises.[32] And in each case, not unlike the more traditional types of competition over surplus value focused on by others (involving market values, prices of production, and enterprise profits), the distribution leads to the formation of particular "prices" and "rates of profit": interest rates, commercial discounts, stock dividends, rents, and taxes.

These distributions of surplus value comprise types of competition because they represent, no less than the struggles amongst industrial capital-

---

[32] Resnick and Wolff (1987, especially chap. 3) have interpreted Marx's discussions of initial distributions of surplus labor (for both capitalist and noncapitalist class processes) in terms of "subsumed" class processes, which they distinguish from the "fundamental" class processes that define the performance and appropriation of surplus labor. Gibson-Graham (1996), for her part, refers to these as "distributive" and "appropriative" class processes, respectively.

ist enterprises within and between industries, different patterns of rivalry over the quantities and forms of realization of the surplus value appropriated from productive laborers. The existence of banks, merchants, stock owners, landowners, and the state depends (at least in part) on their ability to compete with one another and with industrial capitalist enterprises over shares of surplus value. Similarly, in order for industrial capitalist enterprises to successfully compete among themselves, they often find it necessary to "give up" portions of surplus value to entities other than commodity-producing capitalist firms.

In addition to these "external" forms of competition and related transfers of surplus value, Marx refers to other struggles over distributions of surplus value that take place *inside* industrial capitalist enterprises. These represent "internal" forms of competition. The accumulation of capital is one example: a specific portion of the surplus value realized by firms is earmarked for purchases of additional means of production and labor power. But, as Norton (1986, 1988) warns us, the accumulation of capital is only one of many distributions of surplus value that take place within the firm. Typical industrial capitalist enterprises also contain other units, departments, and individuals—such as management, supervision, training and education, public relations, advertising, research and development, bookkeeping, and so on—that compete with the accumulators of capital (as well as with each other) over shares of surplus value. While the accounting conventions may differ (salaries and departmental budgets instead of prices and interest rates), these, no less than distributions of surplus value to units outside the firm, represent ways in which surplus value is realized by entities other than industrial capitalists.

In addition to pointing out the multiple forms of competition that can exist both internal to the enterprise and externally, between it and other entities, we should add that there is no fixed boundary between the inside and the outside. Thus, for example, activities (and their corresponding flows of surplus value) that are, in one situation, located outside the enterprise can be and often are, under other conditions, brought inside the firm. Through a variety of mechanisms (such as mergers, acquisitions, and the setting up of new departments and units), enterprises can engage in their own financing of purchases, the selling of their commodities, ownership of stock, security, legal adjudication, and so on. An equivalent movement can and often does take place in the opposite direction: enterprises lose or give over to other entities such diverse activities as management consulting, personnel (through temporary employee agencies), bookkeeping and accounting, ownership of some or all of the means of production, and the like. Each of these moves leads to a new pattern of flows of, and thus competitive battles over, surplus value both inside and outside the enterprise.

The existence of these various and changing forms of competition calls into question the idea that there is such a thing that modernist Marxists often refer to as the "capitalist enterprise," with a given, stable, singular identity and corresponding competitive strategy—what is often taken to be the basis of an orderly process of competition. Indeed, Marx extensively grappled with the problem of the enterprise throughout volume 3 of *Capital*. And, in the course of his discussion, he provided some of the elements of a quite different conception of capitalist enterprises, whose identities are multiple and shifting, and therefore of competition itself, which we can now begin to conceive of as a disjoined, unpredictable, disorderly process.

Industrial capitalist enterprises will exhibit a wide variety of competitive strategies, themselves the products of the competitive pressures exercised both inside and outside those enterprises. What strategy any individual enterprise "chooses" will depend on the results of the array of both internal competitive battles (e.g., among various units such as accounting, purchasing, and management) and external forms of competition (not only with other industrial capitalist enterprises but also with banks, the state, and other such entities throughout the economy and society). The actual strategy, in other words, is a result of the way in which the specific identity of the enterprise is constructed, negotiated and produced, out of the complex interaction of these various forms of competition.[33] And since we can expect the identities of capitalist enterprises to vary across space (within and between industries) and time (as activities move inside and outside any one firm, and new competitive pressures are encountered), we will observe a wide variety of specific, changing competitive strategies on their part.

One of the implications of this approach is that competition loses its status as a lawlike, deterministic process in favor a much more random, fluctuating set of activities carried out by capitalist enterprises and to which they are, in turn, subject. Connected to this disorderly conception of competition is the idea that a certain ambiguity—and, at the same time, concreteness—is introduced into the value categories associated with the identity of enterprises. Profit, for example, can no longer refer to a single magnitude or thing but, instead, is a composite notion, a changing category that is constructed out of the competitive pressures to which each enterprise is subject and to which it responds. What profits are—the particular inclusions and exclusions that result in an excess of revenues over costs—is produced discursively in and through the accounting schemes that result from the complex struggles and negotiations that take place

---

[33] See, also, the discussion in Grahame Thompson 1982 and Cullenberg 1994, especially chap. 4, and 1998.

both inside and outside enterprises.[34] Profits are thus rendered ambiguous because there is no necessary set of value flows that, when added together, make up enterprise profits. The meaning of profits for a particular enterprise will depend on where the boundaries—legal, financial, state-regulated, and so on—between the inside and the outside are drawn. Hence, profits also become more concrete, to the extent that they are tied to the particular goals and procedures—and hence multiple identities—that are fought over and conjuncturally resolved in and around each enterprise.

The result is that the capitalist enterprise—understood as the site of certain necessary functions (such as the accumulation of capital), with a given identity (and therefore competitive strategy)—begins to fall apart and, ultimately, disappear. In its place we will find a variety of different capitalist enterprises, each the specific (and changing) site of appropriations or distributions of surplus value.[35] None of these processes can be considered the center or origin, the motive or goal that defines the identity, of the enterprise.[36] Instead, each enterprise will act out one or more of its many possible identities as the competitive battles that take place both inside and outside erupt, become resolved, and emerge once again—thereby leading to the formation of new identities.[37]

Focusing on the "decentering" of the enterprise, the "uncertainty" about profits, and especially the "disorder" of competition leads to an interpretation of the Marxist approach to economics that is quite different from modernist Marxist renderings. Instead of (or, perhaps, alongside the promise of) determining an equilibrium rate of profit and corresponding

[34] Marxist economists often distinguish between existing, bourgeois systems of national income accounting and national income accounts constructed on the basis of Marxian, labor-value categories (Shaikh and Tonak 1994; Moseley 1991). However, they have tended to overlook the role of accounting in the construction of calculable spaces, agencies, and categories—within enterprises, science, and elsewhere—that has been the focus of the "critical accounting" literature. See, e.g., Hopwood and Miller 1994 and Power 1994.

[35] And, we should add, noncapitalist enterprises, sites where production or other economic activities take place but in conjunction with noncapitalist—ancient, communal, and other—class processes.

[36] There is an interesting parallel here to recent developments in the theory of the firm within mainstream economics in which the blurring of the boundary between the inside and the outside—between transactions made within the firm and those made in the marketplace—calls into the question the idea of a single "owner" of the firm (see, e.g., Klein, Crawford, and Alchian 1986). The crucial remaining difference, of course, is that Marxist economists, even if they allow for a decentering of the identity of the enterprise, will still focus on the existence of such nonmarket phenomena as the extraction of surplus labor, property ownership, the exercise of power, and much else that distinguishes what occurs inside the enterprise from the transactions that take place in markets.

[37] The approach to the enterprise we outline here finds parallels in the literature on postmodern approaches to organizations, especially the concern to analyze "the production of organization rather than the organization of production" (Cooper and Burrell 1988, 106).

laws of motion, what Marx does is to call into question the integrity of the capitalist enterprise, the unity, singularity, and knowability of profits, and the orderliness of competition as presumed by mainstream economists. Such a postmodern Marxian critique of political economy shifts attention away from a general "logic of capital" toward more local, negotiated and articulated, actions of specific capitalist enterprises. It makes it possible to analyze (and, for that matter, to change) the particular composition, strategies, and effects of capitalist enterprises as they are constituted in and through the competitive rivalries over distributions of surplus value.[38]

But it is the same disorderliness that characterizes the activity of planning. Any act of planning requires, and differs according to the particular constitution of, a whole host of economic and social conditions: from forms of accounting and calculation to legal entitlements, social identities (of the planners as well as of those who execute or undermine and are involved in or resist the plans), and so on. And, as with markets, the conditions that overdetermine the activity of planning cannot but produce particular kinds of disorder—both in the activity itself and in its effects. Nor can disorder be considered uniquely unfortunate in its effects. The new possibilities and tensions that both give rise to and are consequences of an economic plan may be viewed by important segments of the populace (and even the planners themselves) to be preferable to stable or routine outcomes. Indeed, the disorder brought about by conflicting claims and struggles over the distribution of the economic surplus, for example, may give rise to future plans in which the concerns of marginalized groups and classes are now included. Therefore, it may be a mistake to focus primarily, as modernist Marxism has done, on the negative consequences of disorder, whether of markets or of planning.

Social Needs

The postmodern Marxian conception of the relationship of social needs to markets and planning also runs counter to the usual modernist story that sees planning as promising to satisfy the range of social needs that markets are incapable of meeting.[39] Frequently this story is supplemented

---

[38] As Gibson-Graham and O'Neill explain in their reconceptualization of the steel division of Broken Hill Proprietary, the largest industrial corporation in Australia: "The goal is to create an imaginative space within which a different and expanded (class) politics of the enterprise might emerge, and especially to enable new claims on the social wealth that flows through the corporation" (2001, 56).

[39] Richard McIntyre (1992) provides a valuable analysis of what he calls the "conventional Left critique of 'consumer society' " (40) that combines elements of Marx's and Ve-

by the argument (often said to be drawn from the manuscripts of the "young Marx") that there are two sets of needs: one "true," the other "artificial." So-called true needs are considered to be universal and authentic; they are seen as "basic" to humanity and therefore would continue to exist (and would finally be met) under socialism. Socialist planners are seen as possessing the unique ability to accurately calculate and arrange production to satisfy these authentic needs. On the other hand, there are "false" needs and desires, the "distorted" results of market manipulation, "created" (by advertising, the media, and so on) merely for the purpose of satisfying the capitalists' drive to produce and realize surplus value—needs that would, therefore, be reduced or eliminated altogether under socialism. From this perspective, what socialism represents is the transcendence of use-value over exchange-value inasmuch as the latter is seen to represent, among other things, the transitory and mostly artificial needs created purely by the market.

The problem is that, while modernist Marxists have distanced themselves from the neoclassical presumption that consumer preferences are given or exogenous—and, therefore, from the idea that human needs exist prior to and independent of the economic and social situation in which they are expressed—they continue to hold onto a distinction between two sets of needs: one that is "constructed" (in and by markets) and another that is "intrinsic" and "true" (and therefore transcends markets). Like Veblen, who distinguished between the "conspicuous" consumption of the elite and the "normal" consumption of seemingly everyone else (and who failed to understand, as both Mary Douglas [Douglas and Isherwood 1979] and Pierre Bourdieu [1984] have argued, that all patterns of consumption, from working-class to capitalist, involve diverse forms of "mimicry" and "differentiation" within and across social groups), modernist Marxists have exaggerated both the extent to which markets create needs and the extent to which planning merely responds to and thereby satisfies existing needs. From a postmodern perspective, there is no origin

---

blen's views of consumption and human needs under capitalist markets. The common thread that links modernist interpretations of Marx's views with those of Veblen is that "capitalism distorts humanity's natural development" (51), as represented in the manipulation and alienation of what are considered to be authentic human needs. McIntyre opposes this shared institutionalist and modernist Marxian critique with an analysis that owes much to the work of Baudrillard. Among other things, Baudrillard criticizes Marx for removing "use-value from history, making use-value a symbol of transformation beyond capitalism" (50). As McIntyre states, Baudrillard claims that "use-value . . . is just as fetishized as is exchange-value and cannot serve as an objective ground for exchange-value in some ideal world" (53). Thus, just as the apparent abstract equivalence of commodities is socially constituted, so too is the utility of the object (53). It follows, therefore, that this social constitution takes place under conditions of both markets and planning and that neither situation can be said to correspond to a state of "true" social needs.

or singular place where needs are created and of which they are an expression.[40] Certainly, markets and particular market agents participate in creating needs, but so does the activity of planning—for example, when the planners decide that some goods will be available in larger or smaller quantities, thereby creating the distinction between goods that are for "basic" consumption and other goods that represent forms of "luxury" consumption.

In this sense, the determination of use-value cannot be considered independent of either exchange-value or what might be called plan-value. At the same time, the needs that are "satisfied" (or not) by either markets or planning are only partly determined by those activities; they are also constituted by the diversity of identities and subjectivities—racial, gender, ethnic, class, and so on—that are produced in the two (capitalist and socialist) societies. Thus, a postmodern Marxism would refuse the distinction between markets and planning in terms of one (planning) being able to satisfy social needs that the other (markets) cannot and, instead, focus on the different ways in which each—together with many other social activities—participates in both determining and satisfying needs and desires in particular economic and social settings.

None of this is to deny what Marxists have long pointed out: that markets can be and often are disorderly, that such disorders can have negative consequences (since the lives of individuals, not to mention firms, sectors, regions, or entire nations, are often forcibly disrupted), and that the needs of many individuals and groups are often not met in particular market circumstances (hunger and starvation are not only possible but recurrent for significant sections of the population in many market economies, including the most developed). However, there is nothing either in the actual history or in the concept of socialist planning that avoids these "criticisms." There may, of course, be many situations where some form of planning is preferred to markets; what postmodern Marxian economists object to is the idea that planning is in general any more orderly than markets, that order is always preferable to disorder, and that either activity is capable (or not) of satisfying and of participating (or not) in the determination of social needs. What is open to question, therefore, is the terms in which modernist Marxists have distinguished between markets and planning and, on the basis of such distinctions, expressed a preference for socialism over capitalism.

[40] From a postmodern Marxian perspective, the body does not serve as the ground or origin of human "needs"—as, for example, when the "value of labor power" is interpreted as a kind of biological minimum. Building on Marx's view that the determination of the means of subsistence of the laborers includes a "historical and moral element" (Marx 1977, 1:275), the body can be seen as a site where needs, wants, and desires are constituted by a wide variety of social processes and activities, including those of markets and planning.

Capitalisms and Socialisms

Our view is that the postmodern moments of Marxian theory—those elements of the Marxian tradition that emphasize disorder (together with decentering, uncertainty, and much else that is downplayed or shunned by modernist Marxism)—are beginning to constitute key aspects of a new Marxian economic discourse. The distinctiveness of this discourse can be viewed by rethinking such oppositions as that between capitalism and socialism with this emphasis in mind. For example, Marx's analysis of a capitalist economy can be read more in terms of the idea of historical conjuncture and contingency than "laws of motion" and necessity. It is just this reading that Louis Althusser and his school have contributed to the Marxian tradition with the concept of overdetermination. In the work of Resnick and Wolff (1987), Gibson-Graham (1996), Callari (1986), Cullenberg (1994, 1996, 1998), Roberts (1987, 1988), Norton (1986, 1988, 1992), John Roche (1988), and Carole Biewener (1998), the creation and realization of economic value depend on forces—economic as well as noneconomic—that combine to produce a unique effect: the money-form of value, capital, surplus value, and so forth. For postmodern Marxism, there are no laws of motion of capitalism, no essences to be discovered in economic processes, no essential determinants of any economic effects, and no inexorable or preordained trajectory for the capitalist economy (and therefore, no necessary sequence of stages or phases of capitalism). For postmodern Marxism, likewise, there is no subject of history, no teleological historical process, and therefore no necessary end to any process of change or transition. If taken seriously, the notions of overdetermination and process without a subject—two of Althusser's main contributions—imply a radical contingency and uncertainty about social and economic processes.[41] In this sense, postmodern Marxism gives priority to disorder insofar as it becomes impossible to discern in advance, or even *ex post*, the necessary pattern of determinants or effects for any event and/or for historical change.

One implication for the contrast between capitalism and socialism is that postmodern Marxism sees all outcomes in either social formation as always contingent. Thus, it cannot be taken for granted nor understood as the necessary effects of the concept that, for example, socialist planning will mean more or less order, more or less certainty in comparison to capitalist markets. Likewise, capitalist markets imply nothing in particular about the necessity for economic crises, the meeting of individual

---

[41] Callari and Ruccio (1996), building on Althusser's insistence—especially in his later work—on the notion of the "aleatory," elaborate an approach to Marxian theory that they refer to as "postmodern materialism."

needs, and so forth. The effects of markets and planning depend crucially on the concrete conditions of existence of each and are not given in advance in the form of their respective concepts. In this sense, postmodernism unmoors Marxism from the modernist tendency to find abstract order in concrete disorderly events by emphasizing that the conjunctural analysis of overdetermined social sites is the Marxist method pure and simple. While many Marxists and other modernists find, of course, this "everythingism" to be nihilistic, postmodern Marxists reject this interpretation insofar as, far from denying or preventing theoretical or scientific analysis, their approach indicates its ever-present significance and possibility.[42] Indeed, postmodern Marxists borrow from Marx the insight, which he and Engels and certainly others limited to a description of life under capitalism, that overdetermination implies "ever-lasting uncertainty" (Marx and Engels 1978, 476) inasmuch as it implies that "effects" are never strictly deducible from their "causes" (or vice versa). Marxian views of capitalism and socialism, market and plan, and so forth could clearly benefit, in any event, from the deconstruction of all "inevitabilities," "necessary tendencies," and "laws of motion." Whatever light they may have shone on their objects, these concepts have fed into political views and social actions that have been at the heart of some of the failings of modernist Marxism.[43]

On the question of the disorderliness (or decentering) of the subject, a different—and postmodern—reading of commodity fetishism is possible. Amariglio and Callari (1993), for example, have argued that, far from setting up a dichotomy between false and true consciousness, Marx's discussion of commodity fetishism produces a new concept of the subject and his or her consciousness. This subject is socially constituted both prior to and in the act of exchange, and the consciousness that this subject possesses and enacts serves as a condition for the existence of (as well as a condition for the supersession of) commodity exchange. The socially constituted subject of commodity exchange therefore "sees" exchange in a certain way as a function of its overdetermination. But this sight has no privilege as being closer to or further from the "real" conditions that prevail. The ideological and discursive constitution of the subject as an exchanging subject, for example, is only one of many subjectivities enacted by subjects in a capitalist social formation, none of them more "correct" than any of the others in capturing the (partial or otherwise) "truth" of that perceived reality. The form of subjectivity described by

---

[42] For the charge of "everythingism" in the work of Resnick and Wolff and their spirited but careful response, see Carling 1990 and Resnick and Wolff 1992.

[43] See Gibson-Graham 1993; Callari and Ruccio 1996; Cullenberg 1992; Diskin 1996; and Gibson-Graham, Resnick, and Wolff 2001a for discussions of some of the theoretical and political failings of modernist Marxist conceptualizations and treatments of capitalism and socialism.

Marx in his discussion of commodity fetishism becomes, in this postmodern view, an "open" subject—a subject that is constantly being constructed anew (and in multiple and contradictory ways) and for which there is no "center" to the resulting construction. Thus, the form of subjectivity that serves to overdetermine the realm of commodity exchange is never finally "sutured," nor is it significantly different—at least in its moment of openness—from the forms of subjectivity that would prevail in noncommodity relations.

It is Althusser's essay on ideology and ideological state apparatuses (1971) that makes clear the impossibility for there to be an end to ideology. According to Althusser, the process of interpellation that constitutes subjects qua subjects exists in all social formations and is certainly not eliminated under socialism or communism, despite the possibility of halting general commodity relations. That is, Althusser's analysis of the process of subjectification implies as well the never-ending recomposition of the individual subject and, therefore, the impossibility of revealing the essence or center of the subject with the supposed end of commodity fetishism.[44] While Althusser's dismissal of any notion of commodity fetishism remains perhaps too closely tied to a "last instance" determination by the economy (Althusser and Balibar 1970), his strong criticism of the true/false consciousness distinction is built on the notion of a decentered subject. This decentered subject may exhibit many different subjectivities simultaneously (they are interpellated in different ways at different sites), none of which is given privilege as representing the subject's real essence, whether natural or historical. Althusser, too, employs a notion of the "open subject" insofar as he sees the processes of interpellation as incessant and without a goal or end to which they are moving. Indeed, there may never by a point of coalescence or unification of the different forms of subjectivity as a result of their overdetermination; this may explain why some Althusserians and post-Althusserians embrace the postmodern idea of the fragmented subject.

In any event, the difference between capitalism and socialism that modernist Marxists tend to draw—between the "really" fractured and alienated subject of capitalism and the potentially holistic and unalienated subject of socialism, "socialist man"—can be challenged by drawing out the postmodern moments in Marx's theories of commodity fetishism and ideology.[45] For postmodern Marxism, the difference between the subjects in

---

[44] See Lock 1996 and Montag 1996 for incisive commentaries on Althusser's notion of ideology.

[45] Or perhaps we should refer instead to the contributions toward such a theory that Marx developed in his discussions of commodity fetishism and of the ideology of "vulgar economics" in *Capital*—elements on which Althusser and others have been able to build.

the two social formations is a matter of the different elements of their overdetermination (for example, by capitalist class processes in the one, and by communal class processes in the other) and not of the absence or presence of subjective unity and true consciousness in either formation.

Finally, as Althusser, Hindess and Hirst (Hindess and Hirst 1975; Hindess 1977), Resnick and Wolff (1987), and others have argued, there is a distinct Marxian notion of knowledge that eschews the premises and logical consequences of classical—empiricist and rationalist—epistemology. We consider this notion of knowledge to be postmodern because it tends to demote the idea of certainty and replaces it with forms of cognition that tend toward uncertainty (at least in the sense of indeterminism). On this point, then, the distinction between capitalism and socialism as pertaining to the differential possibilities for knowledge (or lack thereof) is modernist in its basic premises. For modernist Marxism, the relativism that marks capitalism is attributed to the fact that it tends to fracture and segregate individuals and groups on the basis of the division of labor and membership in different classes. That is, capitalism produces "one-sided" individuals who lack the ability to perceive the whole and therefore to possess true knowledge. The possibility for seeing the totality, of course, rests historically with the class-conscious proletariat, and Marxism's conceit in this matter is that it claims to provide the working class with the "science" to turn its spontaneous perception of the many-sided (and therefore concrete) totality into a consistent theory of that totality and to eventually transform it. In modernist Marxism, then, socialism marks the moment of the historical transcendence of one-sidedness (abstractness) and allows potentially all of its members to see the whole. Thus, for example, planning can succeed where markets could not in discerning all of the needs underlying the plan and in calculating all of the effects of instituting it. The relativism (one-sidedness), uncertainty, and disorder of capitalism are overcome by rational planning whose objective basis—the victory of the proletariat, with its full appreciation of the totality—guarantees in advance the superiority of its knowledge and practice.

Postmodern Marxist economists could not but regard this view as unhelpful and ultimately damaging in distinguishing between capitalism and socialism. For it is clear, to postmodern Marxists at least, that socialism has been and will be beset with the multiplicity of knowledges and the radical uncertainty that goes along with the contingency of events and the persistence of ideology. Debilitating effects that have been visited both on peoples living under socialist regimes and on the very concept of socialism can be tied directly to the claim by the party or state to have privileged (and not partisan) objective knowledge. Socialist planning, in our view, will always be marked by the mediation of different knowledges and subjectivities, and the resulting plan, a contingent act if there ever was one, may need to declare itself as partisan, provisional, and uncertain of its effects if it is to avoid the disasters that have befallen planning mechanisms that have been infused with modernist explanations and ideals, utopian though they may have been.

In this sense, the totalizing promise of rational centralized planning is a modernist one. The declared partiality, relativism, and disorder of planning are, in contrast, postmodern.

7

Academic and Everyday Economic Knowledges

A SQUARE DEAL FOR ALL.

Phil Porter, "A Square Deal for All" (1909).
(Photo: Preston Thomas for Visual Ear.)

IN THE PRECEDING FIVE CHAPTERS, we focused on the postmodern moments that can be found within some of the diverse schools of thought that comprise the discipline of economics. But despite the appearances created by most historians of economic thought and economic methodologists, academic economists do not hold a monopoly on the production and dissemination of economic knowledges. Economic issues and themes are thought about and discussed by many people other than academic economists, within the academy and throughout society.

The current debate about globalization is a good example. Professors of economics, using both mainstream and heterodox approaches, have theorized and empirically investigated the new international economic relations that are often said to characterize the world today. Clearly, however, the analysis of the conditions and consequences of globalization is not confined to the world of academic economists. The individuals, groups, and organizations that have participated in the demonstrations in Seattle, Genoa, and elsewhere have conducted their own studies of globalization and have expressed views that often run counter to those held by academic economists. The same is true in think tanks, books by independent writers, human rights organizations, and elsewhere where the roles of foreign trade, international finance, and transnational corporations are being hotly debated. And even in colleges and universities, scholars from disciplines other than economics—including anthropology, sociology, and political science, not to mention art, theology, and literary criticism—have enjoined and become high-profile participants in the ongoing debate concerning the implications of contemporary globalization.

Such is the situation with respect to a wide variety of economic topics—from the effects of living wage propositions and the importance of federal budget deficits to the role of foreign sweatshops and the impact of international free trade agreements. In each case, quite specific economic ideas are held and produced not only by academic economists but also by activists, scholars, and others who operate outside the official discipline of economics. Notwithstanding this widespread interest in economic matters, economic educators largely ignore the opinions and views expressed by noneconomists, while academic economists frequently criticize them—often treating them with derision. And both groups routinely express their concern about the low level of "economic literacy" on the part of their students and the general public.

Is it really a problem of illiteracy, or is something else going on? Why is the reaction on the part of academic economists, when they pay attention to other economic ideas, ofttimes so strident and dismissive? What is it in the way that the discipline has been constituted by economic modernism that provokes such a reaction? Does postmodernism offer a different kind of engagement with the economic knowledges that are produced and disseminated outside the official discipline?

Our goal in this chapter is to answer these questions, first, by identifying the disciplinary protocols that govern academic economists' response to the economic knowledges that circulate beyond the sphere of the discipline and, then, by proposing an alternative way of proceeding, one that allows us to identify and analyze the artifacts of economic knowledges other than those of the discipline in terms of a different set of discursive structures. We begin our investigation with one academic economist's reaction to the "ersatz" economics of the "man in the street."

McCloskey, Economic Modernism, and "Ersatz" Economics

The rhetorician of economics Deirdre McCloskey has become best known for her insistent and persuasive attack on the "modernism" that has characterized economic discourse during much of this century, especially post–World War II neoclassical and Keynesian thought. In her call for economists to pay attention to the metaphors and narrative structures that comprise economic argument no less than they do the intellectual output of the humanities, McCloskey (19985a, 1990, and 1994) has clearly identified and criticized the tendency in modernist economics to fetishize so-called scientific ways of constructing discourse. Her criticism focuses primarily on the related points that scientific discourse, in any field, and without question in economics, relies on standard, recognizable literary and discursive forms of persuasion and that the preference for what passes for science should not be grounded in the presumption that economists do something called theory that somehow is not a function of the forms of rhetoric and literary construction.

McCloskey's appeal to economists to give up their modernist bias against exploring the implications of a rhetoric of economics leads her to the mostly pluralist view that, since the issue of distinguishing economics as a science from its nonscientific formulations cannot be a question of avoiding discursive forms or modes of persuasion, various economic schools of thought, perhaps especially those that constitute the mainstream, should give up the "sneering" that characterizes their attempts to lay claim to the necessary superiority of their efforts. In other words, McCloskey has established herself as perhaps one of the most eloquent— and, certainly within mainstream economics, one of the most important— defenders of those schools of economic thought (such as feminist economics and/or Austrian economics) whose ideas are often dismissed by those in the "core" of the profession as lacking scientific merit. It is not that McCloskey herself prefers such economic discourses. To the contrary, she remains a committed devotee of the Chicago School. It is instead that she regards the distinction between these other schools of thought and the mainstream to be more a matter of which forms of persuasion have had a better track record of working rather than one of category distinctions, in which the marginal economic discourses are said to be bad economics (or even not economics) in opposition to the mainstream, which claims for itself the title of true science.

Now, all of this might lead a reader to the conclusion that McCloskey would be willing to extend her pluralist antimodernism to include less formal economic discourses as well. After all, if there is a discernible rhetorical structure to most present forms of professional economic thought, then there is no reason a priori to suspect that such a rhetorical structure is not present in those forms of economic thinking (and writing and conversing) that are practiced outside the academic economics profession. Indeed, one would expect that a trained and astute rhetorician of economics like McCloskey would enjoy sinking her teeth into the project of bringing to light the metaphors and narrative structures that constitute the formulations of economic reasoning that can be found in the popular press, centers for policymaking, labor and business organizations, and in the last instance, in the expostulations of the "man in the street."

So, it is shocking, at least to us, to find that in the various versions of her textbook on price theory designed for use in the undergraduate economics curriculum (McCloskey 1985b), revised even after she established her reputation as the preeminent rhetorician of economics (1983a, 1983b, 1984, and 1985a), McCloskey would adamantly and aggressively identify something that she calls "ersatz" economics that, she claims, should both be distinguished from legitimate economic theorizing and be unmasked, thoroughly criticized for its mostly nonsensical, even irrational, formulations and effects. In McCloskey's view, ersatz economics, the economics of the "man in the street," has no redeeming features and must be avoided like the plague by fledgling undergraduate economists. In some startling turns of phrase, McCloskey likens ersatz economics to astrology and dismisses it as both wrongheaded and ultimately destructive in its effects on economic knowledge:

> The economist should persuade the open-minded noneconomist that these economic propositions are true by the same method that an astronomer would use to persuade them that astronomical propositions are true: refined common sense, consistent reasoning, and ascertainable fact.
>
> The economist faces the special obstacle that the people being persuaded are themselves economic bodies and have elaborate opinions of their own. The Earth's own opinion about the movement of the heavenly bodies would probably be that they all move around the Earth itself in circles. Untutored economic experience is a bad teacher of economics, just as the unaided eye is a bad teacher of astronomy.
>
> Practically everything that you thought you knew about economics before studying it is wrong . . .
>
> The vocabulary of such ersatz economics, the economics of the man in the street, contributes to the confusion . . .
>
> This book will attack ersatz economics again and again, with ever-increasing violence. (1985b, 3)

While McCloskey does not go so far as to claim that ersatz economics is inferior because it is vulgar, the discourse of the masses, there is no question that its informality and lack of rigor make it unsuitable for anyone serious enough about conducting economic analysis and making sound judgments about economic issues. Not only then is ersatz economics dismissed by McCloskey as not contributing to economic knowledge; it is also seen to be one of the prime causes of the gross misconceptions that noneconomists, untrained in the presumed rigors of mainstream theory, harbor in their approaches to everyday questions of economic activity and policy.

Nor is McCloskey alone in her contempt for what she terms ersatz economics. In fact, much of the jockeying for position of different economic schools in the history of economic thought has relied on various maneuvers to discredit other schools as lying closer to popular opinion, ideology, values, and the like than to rigorous science. As we argue below, many economists during the modernist age, and clearly into the present, have built cases against their professional opponents on the grounds that there is no substitute for formal methods of reasoning in constituting the scientific core of the economics discipline. But while it is true that the science/nonscience distinction has enabled those in the profession to subject one another (not to mention their colleagues in other disciplines) to scornful criticism or invective, often at will, it is also true that even harsher judgments than McCloskey's have been proffered to distance economic scientists from the popular charlatans who are often thought to occupy positions of power in policy institutions and the media in their effects on the public's understanding of economic theory and issues. That is, professional, academic economists often speak with utter disdain about "ersatz"—or "pop" or "airport"—economics, and spend not a little bit of time either in feigning disinterest or in viciously attacking the "mistakes" that policymakers and politicians, journalists, advocacy groups, lobbyists, and just plain folks are prone to make in their ignorance of proper economic method.

Paul Krugman, for example, wrote the original edition of *The Age of Diminished Expectations* (1990) in order to criticize what he calls airport economics (which he distinguishes both from the "Greek-letter" economics of academic economists and the "up-and-down" economics of business journalism). From the preface: "Along the way this book tries to convey a number of things that professional economists know but that the broader public generally does not" (1990, xii). Elsewhere, he baldly asserts, "economists are basically right and the general public basically wrong about international trade" (1993a, 362). On the same theme, he argues, "most of what a student is likely to read or hear about international economics is nonsense . . . the most important thing to teach our undergrads about trade is how to detect that nonsense. That is, our primary mission should be to *vaccinate* the minds of our undergraduates against the misconceptions that are so predominant in what passes for educated discussion about international trade," what he later refers to as "pop internationalism" (1990b, 23; emphasis added).

What we notice in these attacks—which can be seen in such events as the effete distaste with which so many notable economists in the United States originally greeted (and continue to treat) the diverse forces arrayed against the North American Free Trade Agreement (NAFTA), the World Trade Organization (WTO), and the contemporary contours of economic globalization in general to the disgust that academic economists express when mulling over popular opinion polls of their students and the general public concerning the usefulness of price and wage controls, the reasons for the decline in manufacturing jobs, and other economic questions—is that academic economists treat most expressions of ersatz economics to be unworthy of serious scientific study. In our view, these expressions of derision and dismissal are directly related to the effects of economic modernism: they represent and enact precisely the conception of disciplinarity with which many (if not most) academic economists conduct their research and teaching and engage divergent schools of economic thought, simply ignore or visit abuse on the work of academic colleagues in disciplines other than economics, and, especially it seems, denigrate the economic ideas that are produced and circulate outside the academy.

Perhaps the most striking among these effects is the tendency to portray ersatz economics as a nondiscourse, that is, as a mostly random set of irrational elocutions lacking both structure and consistency. Such a characterization is based on and enacts a particular treatment not only of ersatz economics but also of the discipline of economics itself. Ersatz economics, for example, is dismissed as nonknowledge precisely because—presumably—it does not follow the prescriptions for constituting scientific economic discourse. As an example of the mostly untrained mind, the statements that are said to characterize ersatz economics may sometimes mimic valid economic knowledge, but this is mostly accidental or clumsy parody. Ersatz economics' parodic nature is incomplete—or perhaps, instead, it is pastiche—insofar as it resembles the real thing only occasionally and, even then, without any regard to the consistent modalities of argument of the original. The dismissal of ersatz economics as a nondiscourse also presumes and performs a modernist narrative of the disciplinary self: the conclusions and policy proposals associated with academic economics are understood to be the products solely of formal, logical procedures, untainted by the mundane values and norms, subjective biases, political orientations, passions, or interests of its practitioners. It is therefore possible for academic economists to admit (as McCloskey and others have convincingly demonstrated) that the *modes of communication* within their discipline share the metaphors and strategies of persuasion present in the everyday world. However, whereas they consider ersatz economics to be thoroughly imbued with such tropes and linguistic devices, they still treat the methods and utterances of academic economic *science*—the procedures and positive statements associated with actually doing, instead of talking about or presenting the results of, academic economic research—as if they were immune from the contaminating effects of rhetoric.

One would think, then, that academic economists would prefer simply to ignore ersatz economics since, as is most often the case, it takes only one or two sentences spoken from the vantage point of scientific authority to demonstrate its fundamental absurdity and inconsistency. But, we note, the attacks on ersatz economics are quite vitriolic, leading us to suspect that something of consequence is at stake here in the academic economists' imagination, not to mention their (our) practices. There is something clearly transgressive about ersatz economics, enough to make someone as careful and respectful as McCloskey nearly foam at the mouth in expressing her reactions ("attack ersatz economics again and again, with ever-increasing violence"!). So, not only are the attacks on ersatz economics generally devoid of any serious attempt to make explicit the "rules of formation" of its discursivity (since it is denied, at one level, the status of discourse). They are also characterized by clear warnings against the dangers of even thinking in these ways since thoughts are sometimes put into practice, as academic economists' have contended in their onslaught against arguments even remotely critical of NAFTA, the WTO, and other recent international agreements to open world trade. Ersatz economics, then, is a transgression of the norms of the economics discipline (at least according to some of its practitioners) and, as such, must be defended against just as astronomy and the other natural sciences must be insulated and protected from the popularity of similar modes of expression such as astrology and magic.[1] The fact that ersatz economics may in fact hold pride of place in the minds of the public means that nothing short of a frontal attack—usually conducted with enormous pomp, if not ceremony—must be waged by academic economists to rid public discourse of the erratic shamanism implicit in ersatz economics. At least this is what appears to be the case if McCloskey's textbook (along with the pronouncements of Krugman and others) is viewed as our guide to the problem.[2]

---

[1] Mark Blaug also raises the specter of astrology's displacing "science" in his discussion of the methodology of economics: "Must we really conclude after centuries of systematic philosophizing about science that science equals myth and that anything goes in science as it does in dreams? If so, astrology is no worse or better than nuclear physics" (1980, 44).

[2] In a private communication (April 1995), McCloskey did admit that she might have gone "over the top" in her textbook. Later, in her response to the publication of an earlier version of this chapter, McCloskey reiterated that she was "too harsh on ersatz economics, and that economists of the mainstream are altogether too comfortable in their scorn for the life-world" (1999, 62). Our criticisms of her view, and our joining her together with other economists' dismissive conceptions of ersatz economics, are not intended as a personal attack (for, as we write above, such a stance seems to be inconsistent with other dimensions of her work, for which we have the greatest respect) but, rather, as a way of questioning and posing an alternative to the conception of ersatz economics that her "lapse" symbolizes. If there are differences between us that remain, they stem (at least partly) from the fact that, whereas McCloskey is inclined to borrow from the writings of such thinkers as Richard Rorty and Wayne Booth, our own work is more influenced by that of Michel Foucault and

In the remainder of this chapter, we discuss these two issues, that is, the discursive structure of ersatz economics and its transgressive—to the mainstream academicians—nature. Given the novelty of the change in perspective proposed here, we are interested primarily in exploring the problems that one might encounter in identifying the artifacts of ersatz economics and establishing the discursive regularity of ersatz economics as well as in distinguishing the forms and/or moments of transgression of economic discussion that take place outside the discipline. To state up front what we consider to be the implications of a discursive or postmodern perspective on these issues, the distinction between ersatz economics and its purported opposite (academic, scientific economic discourse) cannot be one of a mélange of unconnected and unfounded, biased, and value-laden opinions in contrast to the unified structure of a formal, rigorous, positive scientific discourse. Instead, the distinction must reside elsewhere, mostly in the *effects* of these two (or at least two) forms of economic argumentation, in that they lead to quite different and incommensurable (although not isolated or completely autonomous) processes and bodies of economic knowledge. Additionally, we suspect that much of the anger and fear that professional, academic economists have expressed toward ersatz economics has to do both with the latter's popularity and its occurrence in and among "the masses" as well as its sometimes antiauthoritarian, vaguely "left" or populist orientation (insofar as popular opinion on economic matters often calls attention to the permanence and growth of inequalities in income, status, and power).[3] That is, we think it is possible to find some of the transgressiveness of ersatz economics in the fact that it is not containable in either form or content within the bounds of mainstream economic discourse. And this overflowing or challenging of the boundaries is, indeed, threatening to many academic economists, as it puts into question both the disciplinary conceptions and the hegemonic positions—theoretical as well as occupational—that (we) academicians wish to hold in and out of the academy.

Louis Althusser. The result is that we probably hold divergent views concerning not only how discursive formations work (e.g., how statements are produced, which statements are included or excluded, etc.) but also how power is exercised in and through discourse.

[3] For example, according to the March 1985 *Gallup Report*, fully 70 percent of the respondents said that the percentage of Americans living below the poverty line was growing and 60 percent believed that the distribution of money and wealth in the United States "should be more fairly distributed among a larger percentage of the people." Of course, as the history of right-wing populism in the United States and elsewhere demonstrates, expressing concern about the existence of and increase over time in economic and social disparities does not necessarily lead to leftist politics. However, whether basically left-wing or right-wing (or, for that matter, a complex combination of the two), both tendencies often involve a critique of the status quo and the forms of authority—including academic economic discourse—with which it is associated.

"Ersatz" Economics and Economic Literacy

The ongoing, insistent, and even verbally violent efforts on the part of McCloskey and of other academic economists to eliminate what they consider to be ersatz economics and to replace it with economic science has not been matched by any comparable attempt either to theorize forms of economic knowledge other than their own or to investigate empirically the actual contents and procedures of the economic knowledges held by their students or by other noneconomists. How many economics instructors are even interested in asking their students what theories they invoke to understand or explain the economic dimensions of the society in which they live? And if they do pose such questions—"How would you define economics?" "What do you think is the appropriate policy to lower unemployment?"—isn't their (our) usual response to immediately challenge the students' "wrong" answers (sometimes accompanied by a look of bemusement, all too often with a chuckle or some other sign of ridicule or derision) and then to begin teaching them the "correct" answer and, perhaps even more important, mode of reasoning?

As the moniker suggests, *ersatz* economics—the economic knowledge that students enunciate in the classroom, that nonacademics bring to discussions of economic policy—does not need to be taken seriously, to be investigated for the knowledges that it may offer. Instead, it can be largely ignored, except as it serves as an obstacle to the reception of the proper "economic method." It is not surprising, therefore, that our survey of the last ten years of the *Journal of Economic Education* turned up not a single article that took as its object the discursive structure of ersatz economics, no article in which the author sought to investigate how high school or college students (let alone nonstudents) actually think about economics apart from academic economics. Of course, we did find a large number of studies in which the authors presented the results of "testing" the economic knowledge of students, many comparisons of the scores from "pretesting" and "posttesting" what students learn in high school and college economics courses. But the nature of the testing is always the same: students are asked a series of multiple-choice questions (e.g., from the TUCE, the *Test of Understanding in College Economics*, or the TEU, the *Test of Economic Understanding*, and the TEL, the *Test of Economic Literacy*, often given to secondary school students) before and after taking an economics course in order to determine how much they have "learned."

The issue that is never addressed is whether or not a process of "unlearning" is also taking place in the classroom, a process whereby prior knowledges are being set aside, deconstructed, and/or destroyed as a new knowledge is being put forward to take their place. Instead, economics education is portrayed, implicitly or explicitly, as a way of replacing nonknowledges—beliefs, opinions, half-baked ideas, myths, and so on—with knowledge—a combination of economic reasoning and positive conceptions of economic relationships and institutions. Thus, the idea of ersatz economics appears to eliminate any need for academic economists to examine the kinds of economic knowledges that their students, not to mention colleagues in other disciplines and people outside the academy, use to make sense of the economic dimensions of their lives and of the wider society.[4]

There is, however, ample evidence that students and others do have at least some form of knowledge of economic issues that does not derive from a formal course in economics. Not surprisingly, this evidence does not come from the kinds of tests economic educators are fond of—in which those who are tested are found to have more or less of a particular kind of knowledge, that which is set forth by "blue ribbon" panels of economists and enshrined in economics textbooks—but, rather, from opinion polls and surveys.[5] The *Gallup Report*, for example, regularly publishes the results of polls it conducts with representative samples of the U.S. population on a wide variety of economic questions: whether poverty is increasing or decreasing and where the blame for poverty should be placed (March 1985), if U.S. workers have received their fair share of the economic improvements in the U.S. economy (August 1997), should the U.S. government break up Microsoft into several companies (April 1999), the degree of confidence in U.S. economic institutions such as banks, big business, and labor (July 1985 and annually in different months), how NAFTA will affect jobs and wages (August 1993), whether or not minimum wages should be increased (May 1987 and February

---

[4] While recent studies of "genre" knowledges have focused attention on the rhetoric of disciplinary communication (see, e.g., Berkentotter and Huckin 1995), the tendency is still to emphasize the ways in which such genre conventions are learned and practiced—and not to consider the possibility that other forms of communication are perhaps disabled and displaced by socialization into disciplinary communities.

[5] Another source is child psychology. Berti and Bombi (1988), for example, have studied children's conceptions of such issues as work, buying and selling, wages and profits, and other aspects of economic life. As an illustration, Fabrizio (age ten) says that "things which people work on more cost more and things cost less which people get less tired making" (112). However, the fascinating research conducted by these child psychologists is ultimately compromised, we think, by a developmentalist approach that focuses on the "transition from a primitive to a more sophisticated and correct understanding" (x), which, in their view, is the set of ideas held by adults. Berti and Bombi set a standard for children's understandings of economics not unlike the neoclassical standard that is established for economic literacy campaigns. Other contributions to the burgeoning literature on the economic ideas and behaviors of children include Abramovitch, Freedman, and Pliner 1991; Ajello et al. 1987; Fox 1978; Furnham 1987; and Lunt and Furnham 1996.

1995), do labor unions help or hurt the economy (August 1997), and whether foreign trade between the United States and China will increase or decrease the number of jobs for U.S. workers (November 1999). In each case, the vast majority of those polled are able to answer the question (based on the polls we've examined, from 1985 onward, those with "no opinion" generally run between 2 and 12 percent), thus indicating a general awareness of and knowledge about economics.[6]

We recognize, however, that, from the perspective of ersatz economics put forward by McCloskey and others, the results of such polls can be interpreted in exactly the same terms that they apply to the ideas of their students: "prescientific" opinions and beliefs but not "real" economic knowledge. In fact, that is precisely the attitude adopted in the most comprehensive survey we have been able to find, the National Survey on the American Economic System conducted for the Advertising Council in 1974–75. Throughout the report, the authors lament the "fragmentary economic understanding" of the majority of respondents. And what is the criterion for such an overall assessment? In each case where those surveyed respond using terms that are not in the lexicon of academic economics, or arrive at judgments that appear to run counter to those of the majority of academic economists, the observation is that those surveyed have deficient economic knowledge.

As is often the case with surveys, the National Survey on the American Economic System may say as much about the attitudes of those who conducted the survey as it does about the ideas of those who were being surveyed.[7] Certainly in this case, the authors' own perception of their results seems to coincide with McCloskey's conception of ersatz economics, Krugman's scornful appraisal of "airport economics" and "pop internationalism," and with the authors of the pretesting/posttesting approaches published in the *Journal of Economic Education* whose overall orientation is that the majority of U.S. citizens have little knowledge of economics and what they know is generally misguided or just plain wrong. This is also the view of Lee Hansen, who, in reference to the "public's understanding of economics," can baldly state, "everyone judges it to be low" (1986, 152).

---

[6] A notable exception is the General Agreement on Tariffs and Trade (GATT). According to the Gallup Poll, 63 percent of respondents indicated that they did not "know enough" to favor or oppose the GATT treaty (December 1994). In the same month, however, only 4 percent held no opinion on whether or not foreign trade represented an opportunity or a threat to U.S. economic growth.

[7] A similar point is made by Edward Said (1978) concerning the conception of Orientalism produced within and by the West and about anthropology in considering ethnographies of the "other" (see, e.g., Clifford 1988).

Robert Blendon and his coauthors (1997) arrived at a similar judgment in their study of the gap that exists between the public's and economists' conceptions of the economy. Utilizing two surveys conducted in 1996, they convincingly demonstrate that, on most issues (from assessments of past economic performance to expectations about the intermediate and long-term economic future), the general public and economists hold "fundamentally different views" (112).[8] While acknowledging that at least six different factors may explain the divergent conceptions of the economy, and that "substantially more research needs to be done to understand the basis of the gap between public and expert views of the economy," the authors of the study conclude that their results "make it clear that economists need to do a better job educating the public about economic matters and spend more time communicating the implications of their research to the public" (117).

What is needed, in the crusade to stamp out and replace knowledges other than the "expert" ones, is more economic education—not only at the college level but also in high schools and even in elementary schools. Thus, beginning some ten years before the Advertising Council survey was conducted, a Development Economic Education Program for teachers and students was launched by the Joint Council on Economic Education in 3 school districts. By 1989 there were 1,836 districts enrolled in the program, covering 39 percent of the precollege student population. In 1999, the National Council on Economic Education launched its five-year Campaign for Economic Literacy for students, parents, and teachers. A major effort is thus under way whose goal is to disseminate "official" academic economics and to eliminate and replace what is considered to be ersatz economics.[9]

The campaign is justified by what the National Council on Economic Education considers to be the lack of a "basic understanding" of key economic concepts on the part of students and adults alike. According to the Standards in Economics Survey, conducted for the council by Louis Harris and Associates and funded by Merrill Lynch in 1999, only 16 percent of the adults and 10 percent of the high-school students who participated in the survey received a grade of A or B. Half of the adults and two-

---

[8] One of the few areas of agreement between the two groups was the perception, by large majorities, that the income gap between the rich and the poor had grown over the past twenty years (Blendon et al. 1997, 110).

[9] The theoretical underpinnings and the actual methods of this effort are discussed in Peterson (1982), Walstad and Soper (1991), and Walstad (1992). Julie Nelson and Steven M. Sheffrin (1991) have criticized the "ideological biases" in current versions of the TEL. Claire Sproul (1999), who teaches high-school economics and expresses her "strong support for economic literacy among pre-college students" (216), questions the exclusive focus on neoclassical economics in the Advanced Placement curriculum and examination.

thirds of the students received a failing grade. The average grade for adults was 57 percent, while for students the average grade dropped to 48 percent.[10] Thus, according to the authors, "there is long way to go to achieving a desirable level of economic literacy in America."

This concern provides an additional reason, alongside the elements of economic modernism concerning the protocols of disciplinarity that we saw above, for building and expanding a nationwide effort to displace or eradicate ersatz economics and replace it with correct economic knowledge. Economic educators are guided by a metanarrative concerning the benefits of economic literacy. According to the council, there is a "national imperative":

> The price of economic illiteracy is more than this country can afford: Young people unfamiliar with the basics of saving, investing, the uses of money and credit. Adults more likely to have money problems, career problems and credit problems, and less likely to make informed decisions as citizens and voters. (National Council on Economic Education 2001)

Economic educators thus supply themselves with ample warrant, concerning the quality of the private lives and public participation of young people and adults, to avoid the problems occasioned by economic illiteracy and to eliminate what they consider to be inadequate or ersatz economic thinking.

A major part of the council's work, besides training teachers and providing teaching materials, is the establishing of nationwide standards for economic literacy. The Economics America campaign involves twenty such standards, along with grade-level benchmarks.[11] A single example suffices to illustrate the approach that they have adopted. Standard 1 is described in the following fashion: "Productive resources are limited. Therefore, people can not have all the goods and services they want; as a result, they must choose some things and give up others."[12] The "keywords" related to this standard resemble those of any mainstream economics academic textbook and include the following: scarcity, choice, wants, opportunity cost, productive resources, natural resources, human resources, capital resources, human capital, and entrepreneurs.

---

[10] The questions and results of the survey are available on the council's web site: http://www.ncee.net/poll/ (accessed 30 July 2001). Readers themselves can take the test, which is immediately graded, at http://www.ncee.net/poll/econsurvey.html (accessed 30 July 2001).

[11] The standards are available from the National Council's web site, on a separate link: http://www.economicsamerica.org/standards/contents.html (accessed 30 July 2001).

[12] The question from the survey that tests this standard is as follows: "The resources used in the production of goods and services are limited, so society must: make choices about how to use resources; try to obtain additional resources; reduce their use of resources; don't know." (The first choice is the "correct" answer.)

The benchmarks for students in fourth grade include the following: "People make choices because they can't have everything they want" and "Entrepreneurs are people who organize other productive resources to make goods and services." By the end of eighth grade, students will also have learned that "Scarcity is the condition of not being able to have all of the goods and services that one wants. It exists because human wants for goods and services exceed the quantity of goods and services that can be produced using all available resources." And, finally, at the completion of grade twelve, students will also know that "Choices made by individuals, firms, or government officials often have long run unintended consequences that can partially or entirely offset the initial effects of the decision." A similar approach, establishing grade-level benchmarks that include "correct" and "incorrect" views (such as "Some students believe that they can have all the goods and services they want from their family or from the government because goods provided by family or by governments are free. But this view is mistaken") exists for all twenty standards.

The various facets of the project of creating economic literacy are largely defined in terms of replacing what academic economists and economic educators consider to be inadequate, ersatz economic knowledge with a "correct" set of economic knowledges, as elaborated by the mainstream schools of thought within academic economics. In our view, economic modernism serves to undergird this project in at least three ways: *(a)* a set of disciplinary protocols that creates a hierarchical structure of distinctions between science and nonscience; *(b)* a metanarrative of the salutary effects of adopting and following the methods and statements of academic economics; and *(c)* a conception of academic economics itself as consisting of a single set of correct methods and statements. The overall effect is to relegate ersatz economics to a subordinate position with respect to academic economics.

The Discursive Structure of Everyday Economics

But perhaps there is a different (and, in our view, more postmodern) approach, a way of understanding that "other" economics that does not relegate it to the status of ersatz knowledge. A first step in this direction is provided by Arjo Klamer and Thomas Leonard (1992), who discuss what they call "everyday economics" as a particular form of conversation and storytelling, one that is different from—indeed, incommensurate with—that of academic economics. Whereas in their view academic economists tell stories that are mechanical and highly stylized, everyday economics is replete with accounts that are historical and anthropomorphic, moral tales that have heroes and villains. Thus, both academic and every-day economics are taken to be forms of conversation and storytelling; where they differ is on the specific metaphors that are used to produce their respective knowledges.[13]

Klamer and Jennifer Meehan (1999), for their part, define "everyday economists" as "all those coping with economic issues on a daily basis" (69), among which they include consumers deciding whether to buy a commodity now or in the future, companies in the process of planning new investments, and politicians weighing the pros and cons of bills, treaties, and agreements concerning domestic and international economic matters. In their view, circles of both academic and everyday economists generate processes of knowledge, each of which has its own rhetorical devices, such as metaphors, narratives, and the selection of au-thority. What distinguishes the knowledges of the former from the "neatly systematized knowledges and empirical evidence" of academic econo-mists is that

> Everyday economists are most likely to personalize the economy; they think in terms of people doing things, of right and wrong, of victories and defeats, of special interests, and of identities. . . . These people, and we are all among them, think in dramatic terms, of winners, losers, and of power. (69)

In the case of the debate surrounding NAFTA, Klamer and Meehan argue that victory was achieved by the forces in favor of the treaty not because of the effectiveness of academic economic arguments in favor of free trade (they were "crowded out" of the debate). Rather, the battle was fought within the terms of the rhetoric of everyday economics, in which the "nar-rative of general interest and character" successfully challenged the "claims of special interest" (82).[14]

The consequence of adopting the "rhetorical" approach put forward by Klamer, Leonard, and Meehan is to call into question the hierarchical

---

[13] While we agree with Klamer and Leonard in terms of their overall approach, they probably overstate their case when they refer only to the formal, mechanistic side of aca-demic economics. Such an approach may be the *aspiration* of academic economists but, in our view, there is an abundance of heroes and villains, moral tales and historical epics to be found in existing statements concerning profit-maximizing firms, rent-seeking agents, wel-fare theorems, the role of Robinson Crusoe, and so on. For example, Susan Feiner has shown that, beneath the veneer of mathematical formalism, the neoclassical conception of the market actually "mirrors the fantasy mother of the unconscious" (1995, 156).

[14] The gist of Klamer and Meehan's is that academic economic thinking is relatively inef-fective in the public arena. Michael Bernstein (1999) offers a quite different view, however, arguing that the U.S. economics profession had a decisive impact during and after World War II, "not simply within the scholarly domain . . . but also in terms of the political and professional authority at home and imperial authority abroad that expertise both animates and cultivates" (104).

arrangement in which the "science" of academic economics is privileged (at least by academic economists and by politicians and policymakers who attempt to play the trump card of academic economics in policy discussions) over the "nonscience" of everyday economics. Suzanne Bergeron and Bruce Pietrykowski (1999) arrive at a similar conclusion in their comparison of academic economic discourse and the economic knowledges produced in *Mating*, Norman Rush's 1991 novel that discusses a range of economic issues, including distinctions between markets and planning and the role of gender in development. Their view is that "examination of alternative genres" of economic knowledge, including novels, "decenters the dominant discourses of economics" and "exposes all economic discourse as a particular type (or set of types) of language games" (149).[15]

The resulting horizontal arrangement between academic and everyday economics is also shared by Stephen Gudeman (1986), whose work on alternative "models of livelihood" challenges the privileged status of the models used by anthropologists to analyze the economies of their subjects. In Gudeman's view, modes of livelihood are "local" cultural constructions, and anthropologists would do well to interpret the models that social agents have already built rather than impose their own "universal" models of economic behavior and institutions, models that are often borrowed from the world of academic (especially mainstream neoclassical and Keynesian) economics. Building on this, Gudeman (in conversation with Alberto Rivera [1990]), challenges the argument of economic modernism—"which seeks to separate the 'amateur' from the 'professional' and the 'crackpot' from the 'scientist' " (190)—in order to "expand the community of conversationalists by drawing upon the work of both the marginalized modelers and the inscribers" (190).[16]

What both the rhetorical and local anthropological approaches point to is that what McCloskey and others consider to be ersatz economics has its own discursive structures; it is not merely a less-organized, incho-

---

[15] Like Klamer and Leonard, Bergeron and Pietrykowski insist on distinguishing the dramatic structure of novels and other forms of everyday economics from the more mechanical metaphors of academic economics. Thus, in their view, academic "economists can speak of unemployment and investment but not easily, not persuasively, of self-esteem, psychological power, guilt, or shame" (1999, 149). Our own perspective, drawn from many years of teaching the concepts and principles of mainstream economics, is that many—but, admittedly, not all—students *are* persuaded by the discursive production of self-esteem, psychological power, and other such "novelistic" themes that are dramatized in academic economic models of utility maximization, general equilibrium, and much else.

[16] Gudeman and Rivera (1990, 191) explain that "much of modern economics . . . starts from a Cartesian ego or from a reified model of the individual from which behavior in any aggregate is deduced; much has been lost by effacing the vocal presence of the other."

ate version of the knowledge produced by academic economists.[17] As we see it, one of the distinguishing characteristics of everyday economics is that it is often more *declarative* than the economics that is practiced in the academy: whereas academic economists tend to privilege the form of reasoning associated with economic science—the "economic way of thinking" they seek to impart to their students and lend to colleagues in other disciplines—and the formal methods that serve to guarantee scientific rigor, the practitioners of everyday economics tend to take firm positions on specific economic issues and problems. In this sense, McCloskey's "man in the street" emphasizes conclusions—specific observations about economic life, concrete explanations of economic events, advocacy of specific economic policies—instead of a general, scientific way of carrying out economic analysis.

The focus on conclusions involves a particular way of producing and narrating economic stories: concrete actors and agents are seen to make the decisions that lead to specific economic events. Academic economists tend to refer to the interaction of elements in an abstract system to explain economic events, such as the interplay of supply and demand that results in a market-clearing price. Everyday economists, on the contrary, look for and focus on the decisions and actions of "real" people and institutions: car manufacturers raise prices, the Fed lowers interest rates, IBM decides to lay off workers, Japan protects its markets, the U.S. Postal Service is inefficient, and so on. The emphasis is less on the elegance or parsimony of the form of argument than on the ways in which winners and losers can be identified and the responsibility for particular economic outcomes can be attributed to the activities of an actual agent (or set of agents) in the economy.

Another characteristic of everyday economics concerns the *interests* that are associated with, and perhaps even served by, economic knowledge. Academic economists tend to link economic analysis and policy prescriptions either with no interests or with a presumed general interest; that is, economic science is in some sense "above" what are considered to be any particularistic—for example, national, sectional, or class—interests.[18] It seems that the only time academic economics invoke interests is when they wish to denigrate ersatz economics (or, for that matter another

---

[17] The rhetorical and anthropological approaches discussed here have affinities with the *Alltagsgeschichte* (or "history of everyday life") movement within German historiography. See the essays collected in Lüdtke 1995 for a general explanation and specific examples.

[18] Leonard Silk invokes a similar argument as one of the possible explanations for why academic economists have had little success in educating the public on economic issues: "Economists are as politically biased as most other people, but they hide their biases behind a scientific curtain. This is not necessarily done from a deliberate and conscious desire to deceive. . . . But the public does recognize the biases of different economists and discounts their 'scientific' or 'positive' analyses for bias" (1986, 142).

school of economic thought) as the product of a fundamentally "limited" view, one that is confined to and biased by an idiosyncratic, "personal" standpoint. In everyday economics, however, interests are paramount. The presumption of economics produced outside the academy is that all economic knowledge—its own as well as that of the academics "who teach because they do not know how to do"—is, in a fundamental sense, interested. Even more, for nonacademics economic knowledge only has validity, that is, it only makes sense and is worth listening to or reading, if it announces (or at least can be linked to) a specific set of interests rather than hiding behind by a presumed disinterestedness (or general, universal interest—which, in the end, can be identified as someone's interest) on the part of the speaker or writer.[19]

A good example of the role of conclusions and interests in everyday economics is Molly Ivins's column titled "Workers Are Fed Up with Always Being Mr. Nice Guy" (2001; see the full text in appendix A). Ivins, a syndicated writer based in Austin, Texas, focuses her attention both on "some hideous things being done to human beings" in the U.S. economy and on the media's coverage of working conditions versus other topics. On the first point, using illustrations from the meatpacking industry and the trend in manufacturing toward operating plants twenty-four hours a day, she concludes, among other things, that the "stress on workers is grueling," profits seem to have a higher priority than people in U.S. society, and U.S. citizens are being "fleeced" by "banks and pharmaceutical companies and utilities and energy companies and our HMOs and big, international companies in general." Her second conclusion is that the media's discussion of the "stuff that actually makes a difference in people's lives," including labor issues, falls far short of their coverage of "fluff" stories, such as the plight of "the-whale-with-rope-around-its-jaw." Throughout her column, Ivins also makes explicit reference to the interests at stake— from her tongue-in-cheek characterization of the *Wall Street Journal* as "that reliable friend of the working man" to her facetious conclusion, "Hey, manufacturing has to compete in a world market these days."[20]

The idea that everyday economics, like Ivins's column, can be distinguished by its focus on conclusions and interests begins to overcome what is perhaps the major obstacle in attempting to make sense of forms of economic knowledge other than academic economics: that of recognition. It is possible, we think, to recognize the utterances that comprise

[19] This echoes Mikhail Bakhtin's approach to the language of everyday speech in which such factors as "*who* precisely is speaking, and under *what* concrete circumstances" (1981, 340) are of decisive significance.

[20] Along the way, Ivins also criticizes the "conventional wisdom" that the everyday economics of the so-called antiglobalization protestors in Genoa and elsewhere is deficient because it "has too many messages in it."

everyday economics as the products of specific economic discourses, produced according to their own rules of discursivity, displaying forms of discursive regularity that are no less (or, for that matter, more) coherent than those of academic economics. It is precisely these everyday economic discourses that give content and meaning to the way people think and talk about the economic decisions that they make (from financing a college education to purchasing a car) and the economic relationships and institutions with which their lives are intertwined (including the causes of a Teamsters strike, the effects of NAFTA, and the strategies to lower federal budget deficits).

Once this recognition is granted, it then becomes possible to look for and examine the *artifacts* of everyday economics, the texts and speech acts in which the discursive structures of economic meaning are embodied. These include the books and magazine articles written by nonacademic economists, editorial columns and newspaper accounts of economic events, discussions on talk shows, the lyrics of popular music, literary texts and visual arts (including poetry, novels, movies, and videos), and conversations and discussions in a wide variety of social settings, from the dinner table to the shop floor. In this sense, there is not a univocal everyday economics but an entire panoply of nonacademic discourses concerning economic issues.[21]

Table 7.1 includes specific examples from sixteen different genres in which everyday economic knowledges are regularly produced and disseminated.[22] Our purpose in this chapter is not to conduct a detailed analysis of each of the genres or specific artifacts that we collected and that are represented in the table. Rather, we want merely to suggest to readers the wide variety of discursive forms in which nonacademic or everyday economic ideas appear, today as in the past. They run the gamut from so-called high art (Shakespeare's *Merchant of Venice*) to cartoon series ("Dilbert"), self-styled political contestation (Haacke's "Global Marketing") to financial journalism *(Lou Dobbs Moneyline)*, print media *(Business Week)* to web sites (the Oneworld Guide to Transnational Corporations, *http://www.oneworld.org/guides/TNCs/index.html*) and computer games *(Railroad Tycoon 2: The Second Century)*, adult novels (Howard

[21] Similarly, academic economics is not limited to a single theory or method but, instead, includes a wide range of different—we would argue, incommensurable—discourses. See, e.g., the discussion by Amariglio, Resnick, and Wolff (1990).

[22] We consider these to be "artifacts of everyday economics" in the relatively straightforward sense that their content includes concepts, issues, events, and themes that many (if not most) people would take as pertaining to the "world" of economics. We leave for another project an analysis of the economic meanings associated with the "intratextual, intertextual, and extratextual dynamics" of the sort that has been pioneered by practitioners of the "new economic criticism" (Osteen and Woodmansee 1999).

TABLE 7.1
Artifacts of Everyday Economics

FAIRYTALES
Hans Christian Andersen,
    "The Money-Box"
Jakob and Wilhelm Grimm,
    "Rumpelstiltskin"
Johnny Bruce Grinols, "The Cold
    and the Gold"

STORIES
Joseph Conrad, "An Outpost of
    Progress"
F. Scott Fitzgerald, "The Diamond as
    Big as the Ritz"
Mark Twain, "The £1,000,000 Pound
    Bank-Note"

POETRY
Michael O'Connor, "Reaganomics
    Comes to Pittsburgh"
Brad Evans, "Out in the Cold"
Carl Sandburg, "Mill-Doors"

CARTOONS
Scott Adams, "Dilbert"
Rick Flores, "Ricardo's View"
Phil Porter, "A Square Deal for All"

ART
Will Barnett, "Factory District"
Peter Bruegel the Elder, "Elck"
    (Everyman)
Hans Haacke, "Global Marketing"

MOVIES
Modern Times
Roger & Me
The Full Monty

NOVELS
Daniel Defoe, *The Life and Adventures
    of Robinson Crusoe*
Howard Fast, *The Immigrants*
John Steinbeck, *The Grapes of Wrath*

WEB SITES
http://www.oneworld.org/guides/TNCs/
    index.html (Oneworld Guide to
    Transnational Corporations)
http://www.corpwatch.org/
    (CorpWatch)
http://www.eskimo.com/~rarnold/
    (Center for the Defense of Free
    Enterprise)

TELEVISION
"Lou Dobbs Moneyline"
"The Next Wave"
"Working"

Fast's *Immigrants*) and short stories (by such diverse authors as Joseph Conrad, F. Scott Fitzgerald, and Mark Twain) to children's books *(Casual Friday Paper Doll Book)* and fairy tales (Hans Christian Andersen's "The Money-Box"), and commercial movies (Charlie Chaplin's *Modern Times*) to documentaries (*The Money Story,* by the Federal Reserve Bank of St. Louis).[23]

[23] There are scant references to these artifacts, let alone scholarly analyses of them, in the work of economists. One exception is Moss 1979, on films. Sharma and Woodward (2001) discuss the "academic quality" of political economy web sites. A comprehensive guide to films about labor, compiled by a noneconomist, is Zaniello's *Working Stiffs, Union Maids, Reds, and Riffraff* (1996).

TABLE 7.1
Artifacts of Everyday Economics (*cont'd*)

DOCUMENTARIES	COMPUTER GAMES
Harlan County	*Railroad Tycoon 2: The Second Century*
The Money Lender$: Update 2000	*Theme Park*
The Money Story	*Age of Empires*
FABLES	PHOTOGRAPHY
Aesop, "The Ants and the Grasshopper"	Susan Neville, *Twilight in Arcadia*
Ambrose Bierce, "How Leisure Came"	Sebastiâo Salgado, *Workers*
Jean de La Fontaine, "The Miser Who Lost His Treasure"	Ben Shahn, "The Bowery, New York City, ca. 1933"
CHILDREN'S BOOKS	RADIO
Margaret Hall, *Credit Cards and Checks*	"Labor Express"
Kerry Milliron and Richard Waldrep, *Casual Friday Paper Doll Book*	"MarketWatch"
David M. Schwartz and Steven Kellogg, *If You Made a Million*	"Sound Money"
THEATER	PRINT
Moliere (Jean-Baptiste Poquelin), "The Miser"	*Business Week*
William Shakespeare, "The Merchant of Venice"	*Dollars and Sense*
Sophie Treadwell, "Machinal"	*Wall Street Journal*
NONFICTION	
Hernando de Soto, *The Mystery of Capital: Why Capitalism Triumphs in the West and Fails Everywhere Else*	
Doug Henwood, *Wall Street: How It Works and for Whom*	
Robert Linhart, *The Assembly Line*	

Sources: see appendix B.

A similar diversity of modes of expression characterizes one particular genre of everyday economic knowledge: music. Table 7.2 illustrates a wide range of lyrical forms (along with specific titles and artists in each category) in which we found concrete and, in many cases, quite elaborate statements about and analyses of economic themes and issues. Again, our goal here is not to carry out an in-depth investigation of the particular utterances contained in these songs but, instead, to document the existence of the variety of economic knowledges that are produced and circulate (much more widely than refereed articles and monographs) outside the purview of official academic economic protocols and institutions. What we can affirm is that the lyrics of the songs included in our table do demonstrate a "basic understanding" of such diverse phenomena as money, inflation,

TABLE 7.2
The Music of Everyday Economics

SOUL/MOTOWN
Ray Charles, "Busted"
Marvin Gaye, "Inner City Blues
    (Make Me Wanna Holler)"
Smoky Robinson and the Miracles,
    "Money (That's What I Want)"

MUSICALS
Richard Aldler and Jerry Ross,
    "Seven-and-a-Half Cents"
Bertolt Brecht and Han Eisler, "The
    Love Market"
Fred Ebb and John Kander, "Money"

FOLKY ROCK
Billy Bragg, "Northern Industrial Town"
Ani Difranco, "The Million You
    Never Made"
Wallflowers, "Somebody Else's Money"

LATIN
Ricardo Arjona, "Millonario de Luz"
Juan Luis Guerra y 4.40, "El Costo
    de la Vida"
Vico C, "La Recta Final"

INDIE ROCK
Quasi, "The Happy Prole"
Radiohead, "Dollars and Cents"
Sonic Youth, "The Sprawl"

HIP-HOP
Eminem, "If I Had"
Juvenile, "Rich Niggaz"
Notorious B.I.G., "Mo Money,
    Mo Problems"

COUNTRY–WESTERN
Alabama, "One More Time Around"
Garth Brooks, "Alabama Clay"
Aaron Tippin, "Working Man's Ph.D."

RAP
The Coup, "The Repo Man Sings
    for You"
Ice Cube, "A Bird in the Hand"
EPMD, "Bu$ine$$ Is Bu$ine$$"

BLUES
John Lee Hooker, "I Need Some Money"
B. B. King, "Recession Blues"
Bessie Smith, "Poor Man's Blues"

PUNK
Bad Brains, "Pay to Cum"
The Clash, "Lost in the Supermarket"
Dead Kennedys, "Kepone Factory"

POP
Billy Joel, "Easy Money"
Madonna, "Material Girl"
Sting, "We Work the Black Seam"

FOLK
Bruce Cockburn, "Mighty Trucks
    of Midnight"
Joe Glazer, "Automation"
Richard Thompson and Danny
    Thompson, "Last Shift"

ROCK
Dire Straits, "Money for Nothing"
Kinks, "Working at the Factory"
Bruce Springsteen, "My Hometown"

MISCELLANEOUS
Bang on a Can, *Industry*
Nations on Fire et al., *Land
    of Greed . . . World of Need*
OJays et al., *Wall Street's Greatest Hits*

Sources: see Appendix C

income distribution, trade, and so on—even when, from the perspective of many academic economists and economic educators, that understanding does not conform to official disciplinary protocols and does not contain many of the "keywords" that represent economic literacy.

From movies to music, the range of everyday economic discourses that can be evidenced in the modern-day equivalent of Bakhtin's "carnival" is not limited to the discursive formations of academe—indeed, it often includes quite stylized parodies of, and even concerted attacks on, the official academic language. Instead, it covers the most diverse genres, speaking positions, and social identities. While often chided and dismissed by academic economists, these heterogeneous economic knowledges serve to create a lively and contentious debate about economic issues in the wider society.

We should not have been surprised, therefore, to find a meaningful (and often fractious) discussion about matters pertaining to the economy in a visit by one of us to a local high school classroom. There we encountered students with opinions and ideas about a wide variety of economic topics, many of which did not coincide with the views expressed by academic economists. For example, one student saw markets as mostly chaotic and disorderly, because every time she went to buy something the price had changed—as compared to the fundamentally orderly, tendency-to-equilibrium conception of markets proffered by many schools of academic economic thought. Another student saw "individual greed" as the main cause of all the major economic problems in the United States—to which still another student responded that "self-interest" was a good thing, something that he had in fact "learned" in the first nine weeks of the course in economics in which our discussion with the students took place. (Perhaps we should have asked the teacher to leave the classroom during the course of the discussion?)

The Advertising Council survey to which we referred earlier turns out to be an excellent source for understanding the discursive structure of everyday economics. The main reason is that, in contrast to the usual "tests" of economic knowledge that we found in the *Journal of Economic Education* or that are used by the National Council on Economic Education, the survey was based on a series of open-ended questions in which respondents could choose their own terms. Thus, for example, the first question in the survey asked respondents to give a word or phrase to describe the U.S. economic system. While 41 percent used terms that were considered by the authors of the report to be "descriptive of a system" (free enterprise, capitalism, etc.), and thus indicative of more or less correct economic understanding, another 48 percent used phrases that the authors considered to be "personal," to reflect an "attitude" (in-

TABLE 7.3
Examples of Economic Language

	Academic Economics	*Everyday Economics*
System	Free enterprise Capitalism	Inflation Can't afford necessities Bad, not working, unstable
Good about System	Free enterprise Capitalism	Economic mobility Personal freedom
Role of Advertising	Informs consumers	Creates false wants Causes high prices
How profits are used	Reinvested For research	To buy goods/services To buy luxuries To live on
Definition of "private enterprise"	Private/not public ownership	Don't know

Source: Compton Advertising 1975.

flation, depression, bad, not working, etc.), and thus to represent an absence of economic literacy.[24] A wide variety of responses was also offered to all other questions in the survey—from the definition of profits to the merits of other economic systems compared to that of the United States—many of which the authors of the report correctly understood to fall outside the "language of economics" (see table 7.3). From our perspective, it is precisely the fact that the respondents often used terms and phrases that are not those of academic economists (and, in the case of private enterprise, a term from academic economics, the fact that almost one-quarter of respondents could not define what it was) which gives evidence that a different set of discursive structures, those of everyday economics, serves to construct the economic knowledge of people outside the academy.[25]

This examination of the content and nature of everyday economic discourses challenges not only McCloskey's and others' views of those dis-

---

[24] The other 11 percent used "mixed" phrases, referring both to a system and to an attitude.

[25] A similar issue arises in the case of literary and cultural studies where economic concepts and theories are often invoked and deployed—ranging, for example, from "symbolic economies" and "economies of desire" to the economics of "postindustrial society"—but not in a language that is recognized, much less understood or used, by most academic economists. See Amariglio and Ruccio 1999 for a discussion of the existence and effects of these different economic languages.

courses—by opening up the possibility that what is considered to be ersatz economics is constituted by quite different rules of formation—but also their conception of the economics discipline itself. If everyday economic knowledges are elaborated with an explicit view toward announcing and engaging the social context and identities of the speaking parties—thereby unmasking all pretenses to a purely objective, universal viewpoint on economic issues—this also serves to question the idea that the formation of academic economics is a purely logical, scientific procedure. Choices are made at every turn in the argument: choices to exclude (or not) issues of power, decisions to downplay (or highlight) instances where equilibrium cannot be reached, the presumption of certain knowledge (rather than uncertainty or simply no knowledge whatsoever), and so on. In each such case, a theoretical move is made that represents and enacts a particular set of interests and subject positions, concerned with matters of individual prestige, social influence, and political orientation no less than the rules of mathematics and adherence to conceptual rigor—in short, the disciplinary identity of academic economists. It is from this position that academic economists zealously guard their domain and rule everyday economics to be simply a form of nonknowledge.

Rethinking the Divide

However, the question still remains: why is everyday economics considered to be so dangerous, so transgressive, that it provokes such ire on the part of McCloskey and other academic economists?

Part of the answer may lie, as we have suggested earlier, in the differences in content between academic and everyday economics. For example, whereas academic economists tend to emphasize the gains from free trade for bilateral trading partners (and, as President Clinton correctly understood during his first term, six Nobel economics laureates were quite willing to support him by testifying to the merits of NAFTA), the majority of Americans were consistently opposed to the passage of the agreement with Mexico (see table 7.4).[26]

Another example concerns minimum wages. Students are often taught, especially by neoclassical economists, that minimum wages are an important cause of unemployment. However, in April 1987 a majority of Americans, 77 to 20 percent (the remaining 3 percent had no opinion),

[26] As the data in table 7.4 indicate, the full-scale campaign on behalf of NAFTA (perhaps together with Ross Perot's declining support in the presidential campaign) affected public opinion, especially in the final months before passage, leading to a decrease in the percentage of those opposed and an increase in the percentage of those either in favor or with no opinion.

TABLE 7.4
Free Trade with Mexico

	Favor	Oppose	No Opinion
November 1993	38%	46%	16%
September 1993	35	41	24
August 1993	26	64	10
July 1993	28	65	7
March 1993	31	63	6
September 1992	33	57	10

Source: *Gallup Poll Monthly* (November 1993).

favored increasing the minimum wage. Roughly a decade later, in three separate polls with different wordings, the percentages were virtually the same: 77 percent in favor, 21 percent opposed, 2 percent with no opinion (February 1995); 83 percent in favor, 15 percent opposed, and 2 percent with no opinion (April 1996); and 82 percent in favor, 16 percent opposed, and 2 percent with no opinion (October 2000). Indeed, "In every Gallup poll after the first minimum wage was passed, solid majorities expressed support for increases in the minimum wage that then prevailed" (*Gallup Poll Monthly*, February 1995, 14). So much for what is often alleged to be the fickleness of public opinion!

A third example comes from the survey conducted by Blendon and his coauthors (1997, 116). They note that the "public's lack of belief in market forces" runs counter to the lessons taught and the beliefs held by many academic economists. Thus, 69 percent of those surveyed expressed the belief that inflation is caused by companies trying to manipulate prices to increase profits, while only 20 percent thought price increases can be explained by supply and demand. Even more, nearly three-fourths of the public, held the view that the rise in gasoline prices was due not to the forces of supply and demand but to oil companies' attempt to raise profits—in contrast to 85 percent of the economists in the survey, who stated that the combination of supply and demand was the main cause behind the gasoline price increase.

There are many other examples we could cite in which everyday economics arrives at conclusions that are different from, and in many cases diametrically opposed to, the ideas put forward by the majority of academic economists. The fact is, however, there are also many instances in which the two discourses tend to coincide—a lesson which many liberal and left (e.g., Keynesian, feminist, radical, Marxist and other heterodox) economists have learned the hard way in the classroom and in attempting to get their views aired and favorably discussed in the media. The issue of decreasing the U.S. federal budget deficit (both the need for it and the particular means of achieving it) represents one example: according to the February 1994 *Gallup Poll Monthly*, 74 percent of Americans—despite repeated remonstrations from the White House, and not a few academic (especially Keynesian) economists—supported a constitutional amendment to require a balanced federal budget. Other examples of overlap between everyday economics and the views of perhaps the majority of academic economists include the role of accurate economic forecasting as an appropriate test of economic theory, the nature and role of welfare reform, the preferable amount of government regulation of the economy, the effects of equal pay/equal worth provisions, and the informational role of advertising. In these cases, popular opinion often appears to be closer to that of mainstream economists than to their academic colleagues on the left. In this sense, neither wing of the profession (nor even those of the ever-shifting middle) can sit comfortably in the presumption that their ideas are "naturally" in tune with or the correct palliative for the concerns expressed by the "man in the street." There would appear to be no simple, one-to-one mapping of ideas between academic economics and everyday economics.

What this hybridity suggests is that there must be another source of transgression, an additional cause of the degree to which mainstream academic economists feel the need to stamp out what they consider to be ersatz economics and to reeducate their students and the general public. The difference in language between everyday and academic economics suggests not only that nonacademic economists sometimes reach conclusions different from their academic counterparts but that, even when they reach similar conclusions, the knowledges of everyday economics represent a potential challenge to academic economics. Everyday economics, precisely because it is produced in and through a different set of discourses, always threatens to escape from the confines, to overflow the boundaries, of academic economics—and to turn against it. Since the knowledges of everyday economics are produced outside the academy, according to different concepts and procedures, they are not subject to the same mechanisms of control that academic economists impose on their own activity (and appear to want to extend elsewhere).

The case of NAFTA is once again instructive. According to the limits imposed by their own conception of appropriate scientific procedures (not to mention the views shared by the "community" of academic economists and the organizers of the conferences to which they were invited to present their work), academic economists tended to use the latest modeling technique of computable general equilibrium models to demonstrate the potential gains for both countries from a free trade agreement between the United States and Mexico.[27] The general population arrived at a quite different conception of the effects of NAFTA: 49 percent thought that U.S. wages would decline (another 28 said that there would be no effect on U.S. wages) while 68 percent believed that there would be fewer jobs in the United States as a result of the agreement. And this was on an issue in which there was a considerable campaign orchestrated from the White House (under two presidents, representing different political parties), not to mention economics classrooms across the nation, to convince the public of the merits of a free trade agreement!

But returning one final time to the Advertising Council survey, there is an additional element that we think might be fruitfully explored in attempting to explain the danger that academic economists perceive in everyday economics: the fear of the masses. Throughout the report, the authors emphasize the fact that, in comparison to their definition of economic knowledge, "most of the population discuss economic concepts in general, even vague, terms." Moreover, the authors go out of their way to note that specific demographic groups—"low income earners, those in lower level occupations, the old and retired, homemakers, those with low educational attainment, blacks, and those who are inactive in community affairs"—tend to use terms outside the "language of economics," to exhibit what they consider to be a "fragmentary and incomplete" knowledge, more than do other parts of the population—"those who have already attained some measure of success in American society" such as college-educated, upper-income people in high-level occupations. A good example is the definition of private enterprise: the first set of groups exhibited a much higher tendency not to be able to define that term—between 26 and 51 percent—than did the second—8 to 23 percent (see table 7.5).

What this seems to suggest is that the discursive divide between academic and everyday economics not only limits the extent to which academic economists can influence and shape the knowledge of others but also that the other, everyday economics to which it stands opposed represents more than just another knowledge or discourse: it is directly associated with people—a "general population" and, especially, parts of that population—who, since the beginning of the modern age, from the moment when academic economics first emerged, have been constituted as the rebellious masses, the "masterless men" (Bauman 1987). It is these people who, from their positions outside the academy, with their "ersatz" economics, represent a challenge not only to the modes of analysis and

---

[27] See Cypher 1993 and Klamer and Meehan 1999 for discussions of the role of academic economists in the "selling of NAFTA."

TABLE 7.5
Definition of "Private Enterprise"
by Selected Demographic Groups

	Private/Not Public Ownership	Don't Know
Total	50	24
Black	45	32
Skilled, operatives	48	26
Income under $7,000	41	36
8th grade education or less	30	51
Full-time homemaker	47	32
White	51	23
Professional, managerial	57	13
Income over $20,000	55	17
Completed college	61	8
Work	54	19

Source: Compton Advertising, 1975.

policies favored by academic economists but also to the very positions from which academic economists speak.

To be clear, the point of a discursive or postmodern approach to economic knowledges is not simply to celebrate or extol the enunciations of and positions taken in the name of everyday economics. We find ourselves disagreeing with the content of everyday economic knowledges probably just as often as McCloskey and other—both mainstream and heterodox—academic economists. Nor do we want to argue that the narrative elements of everyday economic discourses are more "persuasive" or "engaging" than the models and statistics of academic economics, or that academic economists will be more "successful" in the academic or public arenas if they listen more intently to everyday economists. Rather, from our viewpoint, one of the important effects of postmodernism is to challenge the terms in and through which academic economists have sought to subvert the discursive standing of everyday economics, to expose what such virulent and often violent responses disclose about the disciplinary identity of academic economics, and to open up a space in which the utterances of everyday economics can be differently read and heard—and thus engaged and elaborated in new ways—by both academic and everyday economists.[28]

From a postmodern perspective, the presence of economic "clowns," "charlatans," and "street performers" who deign to speak in languages other than the officially designated one—and, in this way, to mock and challenge the authority that academic economists attempt to bestow upon themselves—serves to remind us that economic discourses (no less than other discourses of the social and natural world) are inextricably bound up with the construction and contestation of social identities. The disciplinary identity that has been laboriously produced by college and university professors on the basis of economic modernism, no less than economic educators' metanarrative concerning the benefits of economic literacy, represents an attempt to centralize the language of economic discourse and, thereby, to place themselves in the privileged position of speaking for, to, and about what they consider to be the ill-informed, ignorant masses. Those who operate outside the academy appear to have failed, however, to exhibit the appropriate esteem and have dared to oppose the self-proclaimed authenticity and incontestability of academic economics.[29] They listen and appropriate the official teachings—and then proceed to make innumerable and far-reaching transformations to adapt them to their own interests and according to their own rules (de Certeau 1984).

In our view, thinking about the discursive structures and social identities of everyday economics in the postmodern terms we have explored in this chapter complicates the line that has been traditionally drawn between academic and everyday economic knowledges. It also leads to a different way of practicing and teaching economics, not only outside but also (and perhaps especially) inside the academy. An example of the kind of changes we see emerging is provided by Richard McIntyre (1999), who has outlined a way of delivering talks on economic issues to trade union

---

[28] Robert Garnett (1999b) usefully outlines some of the new questions and sensibilities opened up by the attempt (in which our own work in this chapter participates) to move beyond the old economics of knowledge, "with its view of the knowledge economy as a closed conversation among professionally licensed knowers" (4). He focuses on three sets of issues: *(a)* an attempt to "understand the boundary-work through which our profession continually reasserts the scientific quality and superiority of its knowledges vis-à-vis other, 'unscientific' genres of economic discourse"; *(b)* a posing of the question, "for whom are academic knowledges produced?" and *(c)* "a renewed appreciation of the two-way connections between knowledge and society" (4–5).

[29] Thus, in attempting to explain why, in his view, "many—(most?)—economists feel insecure in asserting their status as scientists" (they do?), Thomas Mayer (2001) suggests that "one reason is that much of the public refuses to accord them that status, or indeed to privilege professional economists' analysis of economic issues over its own cocktail-party chatter or over the thunderous profundities of editorial writers" (79).

audiences that begins with the premise that "what non-economists think about the economy is important" (237). At the same time, he is forced to negotiate the tensions concerning the expert status of academic economic science, which tends to silence the audience and yet provides his credentials as an authoritative speaker. Neither McIntyre nor we can pretend to offer a general solution to this problem. But we are convinced that the status and meanings of both academic and everyday economic knowledges will continue to change as the hold of economic modernism on the discipline of economics is disrupted.

Appendix A

Workers Are Fed Up with Always Being Mr. Nice Guy

MOLLY IVINS
August 2, 2001

AUSTIN, TEXAS—OK, it's a great country, but you've got to admit, it is a little strange. One of its strangest aspects is the relative attention paid to fluff compared to the stuff that actually makes a difference in people's lives. Take the-whale-with-rope-around-its-jaw.

I realize this is a trite, old argument—and I yield to no one in my fondness for dogs, cats, birds, fish, hamsters, etc.—but stay with me for a minute, because there is something truly weird going on. God bless all the humane societies, and the vegans who refuse to wear real leather, and the savers of uncuddly beasties, and everyone who puts time, care and thought into helping other creatures. PBS just ran a wonderfully dotty documentary on "The Natural History of the Chicken."

But an unscientific survey of the Internet since June 10 shows 239 articles about the-whale-with-rope-around-its-jaw, which also has been a popular feature on the nightly network news. The whale's plight, the efforts to rescue the whale and the attendant who-ha are a big-time media attraction, and in my opinion, more interesting than Rep. Gary Condit's love life.

During that time, I have seen exactly two articles about some hideous things being done to human beings in this country. One was the July/August cover of Mother Jones magazine titled "The most dangerous job in America," about conditions in the meatpacking industry that make Upton Sinclair's 1906 novel, "The Jungle," look tame. The slogan in meatpacking, where workers' body parts keep getting severed with depressing regularity, is, "The line must keep moving." Well, it's not just meatpacking.

The *Wall Street Journal*, that reliable friend of the working man, ran a front-page article by Timothy Aeppel last week on the trend in manufacturing toward plants that run 24 hours a day, seven days a week. Aeppel writes of "the unspoken reality of manufacturing: Increasingly, it is structured around the machines rather than the people who run them. The reason is economics. Every hour a costly plant sits idle is a drain on the company's bottom line, something no one can afford in the face of today's sharply slowing economy."

The most common pattern is 12-hour shifts, with a three-day weekend every other week. The stress on workers is grueling. Have you ever worked an eight-hour shift in a factory? Any idea what that feels like when you're getting on toward 65?

Aeppel reports: "Running factories non-stop can take a heavy toll on workers, disrupting homes and relationships. Single parents, Little League coaches, students as well as preachers must contort their lives to meet their schedules, or give up the things they love to do. The pressures affect not only the workers' quality of life, but also their health and safety."

Plastics, tires, toothpaste—one expert says it's a "massive conversion" to 24/7. What the corporations do is close down about 40 percent of their production facilities and consolidate the work in the remainder. Says Aeppel: "As plants become more automated, they are often designed to run non-stop." The *Journal* article then goes on to discuss whether alternating day/night 12-hour shifts causes fatigue, stress, depression, accidents and ill-health, as though there might be some doubt about it. Some unions have acceded to the 24/7 demands, while others fight it. Samuel Gompers must be rolling.

Sooner or later, we are going to have to rethink exactly what the point of this society is. If profits are above people, let's just put it out there. We already know illegal workers are cheaper than legal workers. Slave labor would be even cheaper. Hey, manufacturing has to compete in a world market these days.

When anti-globalization protesters first showed up, the media were like Freud on the subject of women: "What *do* these people want?" Since the G-8 summit in Genoa, Italy, they have settled on the conventional wisdom that the protesters may have some points, but their message is too confusing—has too many messages in it. Grave disapproval from the professional harrumphers. You can't have more than one point.

Unless, of course, what's happening permeates your whole life, causing everything from strokes to not being able to coach Little League. (More than one point there, sorry.) Can't anyone in the media think outside the damn box? Does anybody remember when labor was a beat, right along with business?

Why is "The Fleecing of America" always about some screw-up by government? Doesn't anyone notice that we're getting fleeced by banks and pharmaceutical companies and utilities and energy companies and our HMOs and big, international companies in general? Why is this a nonstory?

I know the whale has a rope around its jaw. That's sad. But there's an awful lot of people out here with the equivalent of ropes around their jaws, too.

Appendix B

References to Artifacts of Everyday Economics

Aesop. 1961. "The Ants and the Grasshopper." In *Aesop's Fables*, trans. J. Warrington, illus. J. Kiddell-Monroe, 10. New York: E. P. Dutton.

Andersen, H. C. 1892. "The Money-Box." In *Hans Andersen's Fairy Tales*. Trans. H. B. Paull, 45–47. London: Frederick Warne.

Barnet, W. 1977. *Factory District*. In *Graphic Works of the American Thirties: A Book of 100 Prints*, plate 18. New York: Da Capo Press.

Bierce, A. 2000. "How Leisure Came." In *The Collected Fables of Ambrose Bierce*, ed. S. T. Joshi, 71. Columbus: Ohio State University Press.

Bruegel the Elder. 1971. *Elck*. In M. Seidel and R. H. Marijnissen, *Bruegel*, plate 60. New York: G. P. Putnam and Sons.

Bullfrog. 1994. *Theme Park*. Electronic Arts.

CBS Radio. 2001. *Market Watch*.

Cable News Network. 2001. *Lou Dobbs Moneyline*. Hosted by Lou Dobbs.

Cattaneo, P. 1997. *The Full Monty*. Fox Searchlight.

Chaplin, C. 1936. *Modern Times*. United Artists.

Conrad, J. 1991. "An Outpost of Progress." In *The Collected Stories of Joseph Conrad*, ed. S. Hynes, 38–61. Hopewell: Ecco Press.

Defoe, D. 1965. *The Life and Adventures of Robinson Crusoe*. New York: Penguin.

de Soto, H. 2000. *The Mystery of Capital: Why Capitalism Triumphs in the West and Fails Everywhere Else*. New York: Basic Books.

Ensemble Studios. 1997. *Age of Empires*. Microsoft.

Evans, B. 2001. "Out in the Cold." http://www.comrade.org.uk/june2001/poetry/BradEvans.htm.

Fast, H. 1977. *The Immigrants*. New York: Dell.

Federal Reserve Bank of St. Louis. 1995. *The Money Story*. Federal Reserve Bank of St. Louis.

Fitzgerald, F. S. 2000. "The Diamond as Big as the Ritz." In *Novels and Stories, 1920–1922*, 913–53. New York: Library of America.

Flores, R. "Ricardo's View." Marion, Ind.: Workers Communications Press.

PopTop Software. 1999. *Railroad Tycoon 2: The Second Century*. Gathering of Developers.

Grimm, J., and W. Grimm. 1968. "Rumpelstiltskin." In *Grimm's Household Tales*, ed. and trans. M. Hunt, 221–24. Detroit: Singing Tree Press.

Grinols, J. B. 2000. "The Cold and the Gold." http://www.childrensfairytales.com/fairytales/fytl2.html

Haacke, H. 1989. *Artfairismes*. Paris: Editions du Centre Pompidou.

Hall, M. 2001. *Credit Cards and Checking (Earning, Saving, Spending)*. Chicago: Heinemann Library.

Henwood, D. 1997. *Wall Street: How It Works and for Whom*. New York: Verso.

Kopple, B. 1976. *Harlan County, USA*. First Run/Icarus Films.

Labor Beat. 2001. "Labor Express." Chicago: Labor Beat.

de La Fontaine, J. 1988. "The Miser Who Lost His Treasure." In *The Complete Fables of Jean de La Fontaine*, ed. and trans. N. B. Spector, 188–91. Evanston, Ill.: Northwestern University Press.

Linhart, R. 1981. *The Assembly Line*. Amherst: University of Massachusetts Press.

Milleron, K. and R. Waldrep. 2001. *Casual Friday Paper Doll Book (Punch and Play Book)*. New York: Random House.

Minnesota Public Radio. 2001. *Sound Money*. Cohosted by Debra Baer and Chris Farrell.

Moore, M. 1989. *Roger & Me*. New York: Warner Bros.

NBC. 1997. "Working."

Neville, S., and T. Miller. 2000. *Twilight in Arcadia: The Tobacco Industry in Indiana*. Bloomington: Indiana University Press.

Next Wave TV. 2001. *The Next Wave*. Hosted by Leonard Nimoy. Airs on CNBC.

O'Connor, M. 1990. "Reaganomics Comes to Pittsburgh." In *Working Classics: Poems on Industrial Life*, ed. P. Oresick and N. Coles, 172–73. Urbana: University of Illinois Press.

Porter, P. 1909. "A Square Deal for All." *American Monthly Review of Reviews* 40 (November): 547.

Richter, R. 2000. *The Money Lender$: Update 2000*. New York: Richter Productions.

Salgado, S. 1993. *Workers: An Archaeology of the Industrial Age*. New York: Aperture.

Sandburg, Carl. 1996. "Mill Doors." In *Selected Poems*, ed. G. and W. Hendrick, 6. New York: Harcourt Brace and Co.

Schwartz, D. M., and S. Kellogg. 1994. *If You Made a Million*. New York: Mulberry Books.

Shahn, B. 1975. *The Bowery, New York City, ca. 1933*. In *The Photographic Eye of Ben Shahn*, ed. D. Pratt, 23. Cambridge: Harvard University Press.

Shakespeare, W. 1951. *The Merchant of Venice*. In *The Complete Works of Shakespeare*, ed. H. Craig, 506–30. Chicago: Scott Foresman.

Steinbeck, J. 1976. *The Grapes of Wrath*. New York: Penguin.

Treadwell, S. 1993. *Machinal*. London: Nick Hern Books and Royal National Theatre.

Twain, Mark. 1996. "The £1,000,000 Bank-Note." In *The £1,000,000 Bank-Note and Other New Stories*, ed. S. F. Fishkin. Oxford: Oxford University Press.

References to the Music of Everyday Economics

Adler, R. and J. Ross. 2000. "Seven and a Half Cents." On *Pajama Game*. Sony.

Arjona, R. 1998. "Millonario de Luz." On *Sin Daños a Terceros*. Sony International.

Alabama. 1997. "One More Time Around." On *Dancin' on the Boulevard*. RCA.

Bad Brains. 1982. "Pay to Cum." On *Bad Brains*. ROIR.

Bang on a Can. 1995. *Industry*. Sony.

Bragg, B. 1996. "Northern Industrial Town." On *William Bloke*. Elektra.

Brecht, B., and H. Eisler. n.d. "The Love Market." On Frankie Armstrong and Dave von Ronk, *Let No One Deceive You: Songs of Bertolt Brecht*. Flying Fish.

Brooks, G. 1989. "Alabama Clay." On *Garth Brooks*. Liberty.

Charles, R. 1998. "Busted." On *In Concert*. Rhino.

The Clash. 1979. "Lost in the Supermarket." On *London Calling*. Epic.

Cockburn, B. 1991. "Mighty Trucks of Midnight." On *Nothing but a Burning Light*. Sony.

The Coup. 1998. "The Repo Man Sings for You." On *Steal This Album*. Dogday.

Dead Kennedys. 1981. "Kepone Factory." On *In God We Trust, Inc.* Alternative Tentacles.

Difranco, A. 1995. "The Million You Never Made." On *Not a Pretty Girl*. Righteous Babe.

Dire Straits. 1985. "Money for Nothing." On *Brothers in Arms*. Written by Mark Knopfler. Phonograph.

Ebb, F., and J. Kander. 1993. "Money." On *Cabaret*. First Night.

Eminem. 2001. "If I Had." On *Marshall Mathers LP*. Universal.

Gaye, M. 1972. "Inner City Blues (Make Me Wanna Holler)." On *Hits of Marvin Gaye*. Motown.

Glazer, J. 1983. "Automation." In *Songs for Labor*, comp. AFL-CIO Department of Education, 10. Washington, D.C.: AFL-CIO Pamphlet Division.

Hooker, J. L. 1995. "I Need Some Money." On *The Very Best of John Lee Hooker*. Rhino.

Ice Cube. 1991. "A Bird in the Hand." On *Death Certificate*. Priority.

J. L. Guerra y 4.40. 1992. "El Costo de la Vida." On *Areito*. RCA

Joel, B. 1983. "Easy Money." On *An Innocent Man*. Columbia.

Juvenile. 1998. "Rich Niggaz." On *400 Degreez*. Uptown/Univers.

King, B. B. 1992. "Recession Blues." On *King of the Blues*. MCA.

Kinks. 1986. "Working at the Factory." On *Think Visual*. MCA.

Madonna. 1984. "Material Girl." On *Like a Virgin*. Sire.

Nations on Fire et al. 1987. *Land of Greed . . . World of Need*. Dischord.

Notorious B.I.G. 1997. "Mo Money, Mo Problems." On *Mo Money, Mo Problems*. Bad Boy.

OJays et al. 1994. *Wall Street's Greatest Hits.* Sony.

PMD. 1996. "Bu$ine$$ Is Bu$ine$$." On *Business Is Business.* Relativity.

Quasi. 1998. "The Happy Prole." On *Featuring "Birds."* Up Records and Domino Records.

Radiohead. 2001. "Dollars and Cents." On *Amnesiac.* Capitol.

Smith, B. 1931. "Poor Man's Blues." On *Complete Recordings*, vol. 4. Columbia.

Smokey Robinson and the Miracles. 1961. "Money (That's What I Want)." On *Hi, We're the Miracles.* Motown.

Sonic Youth. 1988. "The Sprawl." On *Daydream Nation.* DGC.

Springsteen, B. 1984. "My Hometown." On *Born in the U.S.A.* Columbia.

Sting. 1985. "We Work the Black Seam." On *The Dream of the Blue Turtles.* A&M.

Thompson, R., and D. Thompson. 1997. "Last Shift" On *Industry.* Hannibal.

Tippin, A. 1993. "Working Man's Ph.D." On *Call of the Wild.* RCA.

Vico, C. 1994. "La Recta Final." On *Greatest Hits.* RCA International.

Wallflowers. 1992. "Somebody Else's Money." On *Wallflowers.* Virgin.

8

Economic Fragments

It is one thing to say, "Let's try this; it might help,"
and a much more dubious thing to say, "This is
what the age demands."
 —Richard Rorty, "Response to Daniel Conway"

But, after all, this fable asks not that it be believed,
only that we reflect on it.
 —Jean-François Lyotard, "A Postmodern Fable"

WE HOPE THAT, over the course of the preceding chapters, we have disinterred enough bodies and excavated a sufficient number of graves so that the mourners and other funereal spectators who have accompanied us thus far will be persuaded that the landscape of the economic graveyard has significantly changed. Changed but not necessarily improved. As we explained in the first chapter, postmodernism sounds the death knell for the idea of the progress of economics. We can't stake our discussion of the postmodern moments in modern economics on the argument that economics—whether in theory or in practice—will be improved as a result. Nor do we want to.

One reason for disavowing the promise (indeed, even the premise) of progress is that economics as such does not exist. From a postmodern perspective, the discipline of economics is an agonistic field of incommensurable discourses rather than a singular method or approach. Thus, throughout this book we refer to neoclassical, Keynesian, Austrian, feminist, Marxian, and institutionalist economics as distinct schools of thought that (together with many other theories, from rational expectations and new institutionalist to Sraffian and radical economics) make up what we consider to be the discipline of economics.[1] It is for this reason that we do not, in our writing (or, for that matter, in our speaking or teaching), use such phrases as "Economists think . . ." or "Economics

---

[1] We recognize, at the same time, that there has been considerable debate about the defining elements of each of these schools of thought. Both David Colander (2000) and John Davis (2001) argue that the term *neoclassical economics* should be declared dead since contemporary mainstream economics cannot be characterized by the key elements that historically have defined neoclassical theory.

can be defined as . . ." or other such unifying formulas.[2] And, while we are quite convinced that the field of different, contending discourses that comprises the discipline has changed over time (as some theories have faded into obscurity or disappeared altogether, others have been produced, and the remaining ones have changed in both character and relative prominence), we do not see (or, for that matter, promote or look forward to) a convergence of approaches, at the level of theory or methodology. If anything, our sense is that, today, there is a proliferation of economic theories and approaches that is unparalleled in the past century. The modern discipline of economics has thus become increasingly fractured and fragmented.[3]

The absence of a single, overarching criterion of what economics is or what economists do means that there is no element to which one can attribute the appellation of progress (or, by the same token, for those who bemoan the shape of contemporary economics, of regress). Nor do we take this as a sign of weakness or failure. Postmodernism suggests that economics has changed—it has become "other," different from itself—at least in part as a result of grappling with the aporias and undecidables that have erupted during the "normal" course of economists' work on such varied topics as certain knowledge, representations of the human body, appropriate conceptions of knowing and acting subjects, the role of values in economic inquiry, drawing distinctions between capitalism and socialism, the relationship between academic and everyday knowledges, and so on. Pursuing these postmodern moments—recognizing them and allowing them to flourish and develop, moving beyond the limits associated with economic modernism—will, in our view, lead to further changes within the discipline of economics.

But it is only from the perspective of a postmodern sensibility (however unintended or self-conscious) that such changes would be seen as improvements, as a form of progress. As we have seen at numerous points throughout this book, the moments that we have defined as postmodern have been criticized or simply ignored by economists who remain wedded to the protocols and procedures—the epistemological and methodological strictures—of modernism. From their perspective, postmodern approaches to economic concepts and ways of theorizing imply (correctly,

---

[2] We are much more inclined to refer to specific schools of thought—"Marxists think . . ." or "Neoclassical economics can be defined as . . ."—and, even then, we are quick to point out the diversity of perspectives and approaches that exists within each school of thought.

[3] While we hold to this view—based on our reading of the literature, participation in conferences, and conversations with colleagues inside and outside the academy—we are not aware of any study that quantifies the number of schools of thought either now or at any point in the past.

in our view) nihilism, an undermining of the very possibility of carrying out economic analysis. Yet one of the things we have endeavored to show over the course of the preceding chapters is that, while postmodernism as critique does call into question and close off some paths (especially those based on or associated with the modernist "isms" of essentialism, scientism, determinism, humanism, and so on), it also uncovers and opens up other avenues of analysis, thereby creating a new and distinct set of theoretical possibilities.

So it is a particular standpoint or sensibility that is responsible for allowing or encouraging one to consider postmodernism to be a congenial development of or, conversely, an unwelcome incursion into economic analysis. But as we see it, such a standpoint is neither given nor absolute. It is not given in the sense it is both a condition and a consequence not only of modern and postmodern sensibilities in the wider culture but of changes, including the existence of both modern and postmodern moments, within economic discourse itself. Thus, the modalities of economic inquiry can be seen as, at least partly, the consequence of larger cultural currents—the forms of art and architecture that economists view, the literature they read, the philosophical currents from which they borrow, and much more. Just as economics has been affected by the modern "experience of space and time, of the self and others, of life's possibilities and perils" depicted (in different ways) by Stephen Kern (1983), Marshall Berman (1988), and Stephen Toulmin (1990), so it is also the product of the various elements of the postmodern condition or logic analyzed (again, in diverse ways) by Jean-François Lyotard (1984), David Harvey (1989), and Fredric Jameson (1991). On this score, economists' engagements with the cultural matrices and artifacts of the societies in which they live and work create distinct (complex and changing) reactions to the modern and postmodern methods and procedures whereby economic analysis can be and is carried out.

Which is not to deny a certain "relative autonomy" of economic discourse. As we have seen in previous chapters, the actual practice of economics—solving conceptual problems, responding to criticisms from other schools of thought, developing "better" tools of empirical investigation or theoretical analysis, analyzing new situations or institutions—has, over the course of its history, brought forth both modern and postmodern concepts and strategies. These, in turn, shape economists' responses to the possibility of following, at each juncture, modern or postmodern paths of analysis.

Instead of taking economists' standpoints with respect to modernism and postmodernism as given, we prefer to see them as endogenous elements of developments and changes within economics and of the larger culture within which economics is practiced. Similarly, we don't want to treat any of these standpoints or sensibilities as universal or absolute. A relative openness to postmodernism in one dimension may be and often is created through and/or accompanied by the strictest modernism in other dimensions (and vice versa). A good example is the neoclassical approach to the body that we analyzed in chapter 3. Inspired by modernist standards and protocols of neoclassical economic science (from a commitment to the foundations of knowledge to the essentialism underlying general equilibrium), Arrow and Debreu ended up fragmenting and dispersing the orders and capabilities of the human body. That is, starting from some of the key elements of economic modernism, they produced what we consider to be a distinctly postmodern conception of the body. At the same time, Arrow, Debreu, and other neoclassical economists held (and, in most quarters, continue to hold) securely to a modernist conception of rationality on the part of economic agents. A similar nonabsoluteness—"unevenness" or "relativity"—with respect to modernism and postmodernism applies to all of the cases we discussed in preceding chapters: Keynes (where we find a postmodern notion of uncertainty and a modernist treatment of the body), feminists (who engage in a postmodern decentering of knowing and acting subjects but, in many cases, continue to rely a modernist view of the central role of individual agency), institutionalists (for whom a postmodern understanding of the cultural relativity of values exists alongside a modernist invoking of values as the origin of economic inquiry), Marxists (who carry out a postmodern analysis of the social construction of "bourgeois" and other forms of economic subjectivity and yet express a modernist preference for order over disorder in treating the distinctions between capitalism and socialism), and rhetoric (in which encouraging a postmodern pluralism among academic economists is accompanied by a modernist attack on "ersatz" economic knowledges).

Our point is not to deplore a lack of consistency or rigor occasioned by the coexistence of modern and postmodern moments within each of these schools of thought. We hold to no such singular standard. But we do think this "pastiche" of elements indicates that the emergence of what we consider to be postmodern concepts or ideas is not necessarily self-conscious or intentional (we would not claim that Arrow and Debreu—or, for that matter, any of the other economists whose work we have discussed—set out, purposefully or by design, to upend the protocols of modernism or to move in a postmodern direction). Economists of various schools of thought have produced and pursued postmodern lines of analysis as a result of both their economic practice and their engagement with the larger culture. Perhaps even more important, the combination of elements of modernism and postmodernism in contemporary economics shows that there is plenty of room, within and across the various schools of thought, to recognize and extend the postmodern moments that have existed historically and that continue to emerge in contemporary discussions.

Yet, to repeat our earlier warning, we do not want to suggest that following these postmodern leads will improve either the way economists think about or conduct economic analysis. Although we certainly believe that both economic methodology and practice have changed—and will to continue to change—as the effects of new configurations of modern and postmodern moments are felt across the discipline. We should also be as clear as possible about other, related arguments we are *not* making on behalf of postmodernism. Our interest in exploring the postmodern moments in economics does *not*, for example, emerge from a sense that postmodern thought more or less adequately captures new forms of economy that exist "out there." First, we are wary of many of the analyses that, in the name of postmodernism, seek to demonstrate that one or another element of the contemporary economic landscape—the globalization of product or financial markets, the commodification of culture, the proliferation of post-Fordist manufacturing facilities and networks, or the rise of the Internet—represents a fundamental break from the previous forms of economic organization. While we do not want to deny that economic life within and between countries has changed and continues to change in all sorts of important ways (markets, prices, enterprises, subjectivities, information, and so on are not, for us, universals, economic phenomena that transcend time and space), we observe too many parallels with and continuities from previous periods to accept the verdict that a new, postmodern economy has simply replaced the old.[4] Second, and perhaps more important, once we relinquish the "mirror of nature" view of knowledge, then we are lead in the direction of emphasizing the constitutive, as against the representational, view of economic thinking. Thus, to return to a prior theme concerning the agonistic field of economics, each of the theories that exists within and comprises the discipline of economics can be said to produce a specific and different discourse of the economy. Where, for example, feminist economists construct an economy in which agents engage in both self-interested and altruistic behavior (in both markets and households), neoclassicals focus on rational decision-making and equilibrium outcomes, and Marxists see commodity fetishism and class appropriations and distributions of surplus labor. In other words, different groups of economists create, within discourse, different economies—with differ-

---

[4] We do not have the space, nor is it appropriate given our aims in this book, to elaborate this argument concerning the emergence or not of a new—postmodern, postindustrial, or information—economy. One of us has analyzed one dimension, the issue of the novelty of contemporary globalization, in a separate paper (Ruccio 2003).

Figure 8.1. Modernism and Postmodernism in Economics.

ent problems, different solutions, and so on. A postmodern approach to
economics no more mirrors the "real economy," whether new or old, than
any of the existing theories within contemporary economics.

At the same time, we don't want to maintain that postmodernism is
independent of economists' attempts to conceptualize and analyze what
they take to be the economy "out there." First, the postmodern moments
that we have analyzed during the course of this book have arisen within
economic practice, as economists have grappled with their existing representations of the economy and, in turn, have refined them and constructed
new ones. Thus, economists of different theoretical orientations have produced postmodern notions of uncertainty, the body, the role and nature of
knowing and acting subjects, values, order and disorder, and the distinctions between academic and everyday economic knowledges during the
course of creating and developing their respective objects of analysis (and,
we should add, challenging those of other schools of thought). Second,
these postmodern moments have served to modify—in less or more fundamental ways—the manner in which economic actors, institutions, practices, and policies are theorized and empirically investigated within the
diverse schools of thought that make up the discipline of economics. Finally, the postmodern discursive representations that have emerged within
economic theory affect—through the theories that are disseminated, the
problems that are recognized, the policies that are advocated, and so on—
the course of economic (and, more broadly, social) development.

However consequential this "postmodern turn" is, for how economics
is thought about and practiced, it does not, in our view, do away with the
existing distinctions and divisions among economic theories. Rather (as
we illustrate in figure 8.1), we see both modernism and postmodernism as
being intertwined with, layered upon and cutting across, the various theories that together make up contemporary economics. What this means is
that economists of different schools of thought—Keynesian, neoclassical,
feminist, institutionalist, Marxist, Austrian, and still others that lie beyond
the purview of this book—will continue to debate and disagree about the
methods and procedures of economic analysis and of the problems and
prospects of "real" economic institutions and practices; at the same time,
each theory has been (and, for the foreseeable future, will continue to be)

subject to and recast in terms of more or less modern and postmodern versions or interpretations. Thus, while we don't envision (or, for that matter, seek to promote) a separate postmodern economic theory, we do think that the differences between modern and postmodern approaches within each school of thought have been and will continue to be significant.

The implication is that economists associated with each theory may and often will agree with one another on some issues and disagree on many others. For example, as we have seen, Marxist economists can be expected to share a condemnation of the presence and effects of capitalist exploitation (and a critique of other economists who, from a Marxist perspective, ignore or seek to deny the existence of such exploitation) but to differ with respect to the degree of order and disorder in capitalist markets and socialist planning or of the status of economic "laws" or the use of "modern" mathematical methods. What this does is create a new pattern of dispersions—points of disjuncture and encounter—across the disciplinary landscape. Just as Marxist economists and literary critics may have more in common, at least in some areas (such as the role of history, a concern with "modes of production," and so on), than Marxist economists have with their Austrian counterparts, so postmodern Marxists and Austrians will find new points of convergence with one another and grounds for disagreement with their modernist colleagues.

If we have tended to stress the incommensurability among—the gulf that separates the discursive constructions offered by—different economic theories, postmodernism serves as both a reminder of the porosity of such theories and a vehicle in and through which new points of contact can and do take place across (but, of course, never eliminating) theoretical divisions. What we have in mind, on the first score, is that individual economic theories never achieve the completeness or autonomy that, on modernist grounds, is part of their self-definition. Instead, each economic theory is, at least in part, defined in terms of the traces and differences with respect to other economic theories. It is as if written into the margins of each discourse concerning the economy are all the discourses that it is not (and cannot be). More concretely, the entry points, concepts, and logics of individual economic theories acquire meaning not only in relation to the other terms that make up those theories but also through the effects of other theories. Thus, each theory is constituted by the self-conscious borrowings and unintended migrations from, the discussions and debates between, the tensions and conflicts over theory, method, and policy that take place with the practitioners of adjacent and rival schools of thought.[5]

Another way of stating this is that each economic theory tends to create a remainder, an array of silences and indeterminacies, that necessarily

[5] And, we would add, the effects of other theories of the social, cultural, and natural world.

refers to and can only be supplemented by other theories. This becomes a different way of understanding the proliferation of discourses within and beyond the discipline of economics. Whereas modernism attributes theoretical differences and disagreements largely if not entirely to normative issues, a postmodern perspective suggests that any economic theory is parasitic on and calls forth its "other."[6] Thus, over the course of the history of economic thought, new theories have emerged from the aporias and unstable meanings that have arisen during the course of change (call it progress or not) within existing theories. It is not surprising, therefore, that today, when neoclassical economics has become by many accounts the predominant theory in the United States and around the world, a wide variety of nonneoclassical theories and methods (from Austrian to Marxist and game theory to experimental economics) are growing and receiving attention within the discipline. In a similar manner, we can see that the statements that are not (and cannot be) made within academic economics have led to a burgeoning of "economic talk" among other academics (in sociology, geography, anthropology, literature, cultural studies, and related disciplines), economic activists (on issues ranging from "fair" international trade and antisweatshop campaigns to alternative currencies and living wages), and the many other "everyday economists" whose work we discussed in chapter 7.

Postmodernism thus represents a way of rethinking the boundaries that exist between and among economic theories, inside and outside the academy. It also creates new points of theoretical encounter. Of course, economic modernism itself has served as a bridge between otherwise different, and often opposed, theoretical orientations. As we have seen, modernist preferences for order, centering, certainty, and much else were—and continue to be—shared by economists in a wide variety of discourses. The emergence of postmodern moments has both undermined that supposed consensus (demonstrating that is was never as solid or uniform as many had believed) and created the grounds for new forms of communication among schools of thought. In recent years especially, economists working in diverse theoretical traditions have discovered shared suspicions toward and begun to explore alternatives to the modernist protocols that have been a hallmark of (or, at least, the set of official "rules" that were said to govern) much work in their respective approaches.[7]

----

[6] Normative issues are singularly important for explaining theoretical disagreements since, in terms of positive analysis, the modernist standards of science promise (or, at least, create the possibility for) the elimination of error, the progress of science, and the convergence among approaches,

[7] In this, postmodernism shares much with feminism in serving as a contemporary vehicle for discussions across theoretical paradigms that seek to devise alternatives to some of the key concepts and methods prevalent within the discipline.

Some recent conversations illustrate this emergent tendency. One is the dialogue between institutionalist and Marxist economists. As George De-Martino (1999) explains in his introduction to a symposium published in the *Journal of Economic Issues*, the intellectual exchange between these two theoretical traditions has a long (if contentious) history. What is new are the postmodern terms of the contemporary discussion. All three participants in that symposium —Robert Garnett (1999a), Stephen Cullenberg (1999), and William Waller (1999)—argue that the critique of the "essentialist tendencies" in their respective paradigms is a common theme that has far-reaching consequences for a wide variety of issues, from notions of causality and totality to theories of economic value. In addition, as Garnett explains, it has become possible "to cultivate a decentered, postmodern vision of the dialogue itself—as a plural, heterodox space in which theorists of both traditions can work in loose yet productive collaboration" (818–19).

A good example of this new type of collaboration (as well of the use of postmodern-inspired concepts to rethink the role and nature of economic agencies and institutions) is the work of Fikret Adaman and Yahya Madra (2002), who focus on spheres of economic activity that are not covered either by a price mechanism of markets or by governmental transactions, what they call the "third sphere."[8] Inspired by elements of both the institutionalist and Marxian traditions, Adaman and Madra's analysis is based on the general idea that economic models are, at one and the same time, representative and constitutive: they are models of the economy *and* models for shaping the economy. They then argue that, while the existing literature concerning third sector activities has attempted to reduce such activities to one or another behavioral essence (whether self-interest, altruism, or tit-for-tat reciprocity), the very proliferation of such essences has led to "the disintegration of the methodological consistency of individualism" (1070). [9] But, according to Adaman and Madra, it is precisely the investigation of the heterogeneity of activities and behaviors encompassed by the third sector—making the various institutional contexts and

---

[8] These include, according to the authors, "voluntary contributions to charities, services donated to self-help organizations, gifts and counter-gifts, inheritance, domestic work, childcare, and intra-community support networks" (Adaman and Madra 2002, 1045).

[9] Their conclusion is similar to that of Davis (2001), who argues both that mainstream economics no longer has a theory of the individual and that the solution is to build on the heterodox tradition of "thinking about individuals as socially embedded." Davis's critique clearly echoes and builds on the postmodern moments concerning subjectivity that we have discussed at various points in preceding chapters. However, in calling for a "viable, post-Lockean defense of the individual" (an argument he develops at length in *The Theory of the Individual in Economics* [2003]), he fails to explore another postmodern possibility, of moving beyond the individual subject and rethinking the economy as a "process without a subject."

subjectivities of that sector "visible"—that will create the possibility for exploring and creating "associative, egalitarian, and solidaristic alternatives to market- and state-based economies" (1071).

Two other examples are conversations in which we have been involved. Both started out as conferences—one involving economists and literary critics, the other mostly economists—the results of which were later published in edited volumes. The inspiration behind *The New Economic Criticism* (Woodmansee and Osteen 1999b) was that modes of literary analysis were increasingly being deployed to make sense of texts within economics and, simultaneously, the use of economic concepts and themes in literary analysis was expanding. As we explained in our contribution to that volume (Ruccio and Amariglio 1999), the interdisciplinary discussion and exchange of ideas in the new economic criticism conference was not always effortless or smooth. Nor do we want to argue that postmodernism was the only factor in the intellectual climate that made such a gathering possible (shared interests in both Marxism and feminism on the part of at least some participants created the grounds for various aspects of the cross-disciplinary borrowing and dialogue). But, in our view, the existence of postmodern moments in economics is closely associated both with the attempt to unearth and investigate the discursive protocols and rhetorical strategies of economic texts and with the recognition that the development and use of economic concepts and themes exceed the discipline of economics, particularly as it has been defined by modernism. The result is a new interdisciplinary dialogue that may not involve anything like a "unified theory or set of theories," a single "major statement" (Woodmansee and Osteen 1999a, 28) but, instead, an unsettling of totalizing strategies with respect to the analysis of economic concepts and themes—from value and exchange to the activities of giving and consuming—on both sides of the disciplinary divide.

The third example of the theoretical engagements and interactions that are made possible by postmodernism was a conference that we ourselves (along with our colleague and friend at the University of California–Riverside, Stephen Cullenberg) organized on the topic of postmodernism, economics, and knowledge (Cullenberg, Amariglio, and Ruccio 2001). Once again, the conversation ranged widely, not only over issues (from diverse attempts to define modernism and postmodernism to reconceptualizations of gender, rationality, the gift, and international trade) but, especially, over theoretical perspectives and methodologies (from "old Chicago," institutionalist, and post-Keynesian to postcolonial, Marxist, and feminist approaches to economics)—exactly the kind of "loose but productive collaboration" that Garnett described above. The important point, for the purposes of this discussion, is that such a collaboration is possible even when, as with that gathering of participants and collection of authors, there is no shared foundation underpinning their work. Perhaps there are readers who, in perusing the chapters of that edited volume, will be able to weave a cloth of overlapping themes or concerns. Our own view, however, is different: we find no common perspective among the authors—no mutual conception of the problems with economic modernism, no similar view of the prospects for postmodernism, not even a shared commitment to talk with one another under the same rules or guidelines—and yet the conversation did (and, at least among most of us, continues to) take place.

Indeed, the presumption or search for a firm footing or underlying agreement (whether explicit or implicit) may itself betray a modernist conceit. This conception of the possibility of intellectual exchange unhinged from a common framework is akin to other postmodern themes that we have uncovered during the course of this book. We have shown, for example, that agents' actions or behaviors can be investigated and explained even though they may not be preceded by (or, by the same token, need to be explained in terms of) rational thought; that the various functions and capacities of the human body are enhanced in and for economic discourse precisely when no natural configuration of the body is asserted; that the regendering of knowing and acting agents becomes possible precisely when the subject itself is displaced from the center of economic analysis; that a relativist, nonoriginary conception of value may itself serve to reenliven the discussion of the role of values in economic discourse; that it is possible to choose (and to persuade others of the advantages of) socialism over capitalism by dispensing with the contrasts between order and disorder; and, finally, that academic and everyday economic knowledges can be distinguished and compared without presuming that they are characterized by the same discursive structure. These are all cases when not only does the absence of foundation or agreement not stop the conversation within and across economic discourses; it may even be productive of new and more expansive conversations.

Conversations and encounters, rather than a new home. That's what we have in mind. Postmodernism does not represent a Cockaigne or domicile, a respite from or solution to the ravages of existing approaches, a simple answer to the tumult and turmoil occasioned by the current state of the discipline. Economic modernism may lie in tatters, challenged from various quarters, but we are hesitant to argue that postmodernism shows the way forward. What we can say is that the conversations and encounters occasioned by postmodernism chart a path through the economic landscape that we have found particularly fecund and engaging. For us, postmodern styles and forms of criticism have stimulated not only new conversations with colleagues inside and outside the discipline of economics but also new encounters with the objects of economic discourse. They have served to open up our interest in and investigations of a wide variety of issues and themes, from the role of uncertainty to the utterances of everyday economists.

To return one last time to our opening metaphor: the postmodern moments of modern economics may represent nothing more than a row of freshly dug graves. But, resting on our shovels, we can survey the landscape, imagining that the buried corpses offer new ways of both thinking about and doing economics.

References

Abolafia, M. Y. 1989. "Markets as Cultures: An Ethnographic Approach." In *The Laws of the Markets*, ed. M. Callon, 69–85. Oxford: Blackwell.

Abramovitch, R., J. L. Freedman, and P. Pliner. 1991. "Children and Money: Getting an Allowance, Credit versus Cash, and Knowledge of Pricing." *Journal of Economic Psychology* 12:27–45.

Adaman, F., and Y. M. Madra. 2002. "Theorizing the 'Third Sphere': A Critique of the Persistence of the 'Economistic Fallacy.' " *Journal of Economic Issues* 36:1045–78.

Aerni, A. L., R. L. Bartlett, M. Lewis, K. McGoldrick, and J. Shackelford. 1999. "Toward a Feminist Pedagogy in Economics." *Feminist Economics* 5, no. 1: 29–44.

Agarwal, B. 1997. " 'Bargaining' and Gender Relations: Within and Beyond the Household." *Feminist Economics* 3, no. 1: 1–51.

Aglietta, M. 1979. *A Theory of Capitalist Regulation*. Trans. D. Fernbach. London: New Left Books.

Ajello, A. M., A. S. Bombi, C. Ponecorvo, and C. Zucchermaglio. 1987. "Teaching Economics in Primary School: The Concepts of Work and Profit." *International Journal of Behavioural Development* 10, no. 1: 51–69.

Albelda, R. 1997. *Economics and Feminism: Disturbances in the Field*. New York: Twayne.

Albritton, R. 1999. *Dialectics and Deconstruction in Political Economy*. New York: St. Martin's.

Alston, R. M., J. R. Kearl, and M. B. Vaughan. 1992. "Is There a Consensus among Economists in the 1990's?" *American Economic Review* 82, no. 2: 203–9.

Althusser, L. 1970. *For Marx*. Trans. Ben Brewster. New York: Vintage.

———. 1971. *Lenin and Philosophy and Other Essays*. New York: Monthly Review Press.

Althusser, L., and E. Balibar. 1970. *Reading Capital*. Trans. Ben Brewster. London: New Left Books.

Amariglio, J. 1988. "The Body, Economic Discourse, and Power: An Economist's Introduction to Foucault." *History of Political Economy* 20, no. 4: 583–613.

———. 1990. "Economics as a Postmodern Discourse." In *Economics as Discourse: An Analysis of the Language of Economists*, ed. Warren J. Samuels, 15–46. Boston: Kluwer.

———. 1998. "Poststructuralism." In *The Handbook of Economic Methodology*, ed. J. B. Davis, D. W. Hands, and U. Mäki, 382–88. Cheltenham, U.K.: Edward Elgar.

———. 2001. "Writing in Thirds." In *Postmodernism, Economics, and Knowledge*, ed. S. Cullenberg, J. Amariglio, and D. F. Ruccio, 129–40. London: Routledge.

Amariglio, J., and A. Callari. 1993. "Marxian Value Theory and the Problem of the Subject: The Role of Commodity Fetishism." In *Fetishism as Cultural Discourse*, ed. E. Apter and W. Pietz, 186–216. Ithaca, N.Y.: Cornell University Press.

Amariglio, J., A. Callari, and S. Cullenberg. 1989. "Analytical Marxism: A Critical Overview." *Review of Social Economy* 47, no. 4: 415–32.

Amariglio, J., S. A. Resnick, and R. D. Wolff. 1990. "Division and Difference in the 'Discipline' of Economics." *Critical Inquiry* 17 (autumn): 108–37.

Amin, A., ed. 1994. *Post-Fordism: A Reader*. Cambridge, Mass.: Blackwell.

Andrew, E. G. 1995. *The Genealogy of Values: The Aesthetic Economy of Nietzsche and Proust*. Lanham, Md.: Rowman and Littlefield.

Appadurai, A. 1986a. "Introduction: Commodities and the Politics of Value." In *The Social Life of Things: Commodities in Cultural Perspective*, ed. A. Appadurai, 3–63. Cambridge: Cambridge University Press.

———, ed. 1986b. *The Social Life of Things: Commodities in Cultural Perspective*. Cambridge: Cambridge University Press.

Appiah, K. A. 1992. *In My Father's House: Africa in the Philosophy of Culture*. Oxford: Oxford University Press.

Arrow, K. 1971. *Essays in the Theory of Risk-Bearing*. Chicago: Markham.

———. 1990. "Economic Theory and the Hypothesis of Rationality." In *The New Palgrave: Utility and Probability*, ed. J. Eatwell, M. Milgate, and P. Newman, 25–37. New York: W. W. Norton.

Arrow, K., and F. Hahn. 1971. *General Competitive Analysis*. San Francisco: Holden Day.

Arthur, C. J., and G. Reuten, eds. 1998. *The Circulation of Capital: Essays on Volume Two of Marx's "Capital."* New York: St. Martin's.

Backhouse, R. 1992. "The Constructivist Critique of Economic Methodology." *Methodus* 4, no. 1: 65–82.

———. 1995. "Should Economists Embrace Postmodernism?" In *Keynes, Knowledge, and Uncertainty*, ed. S. Dow and J. Hillard, 357–66. Cheltenham, U.K.: Edward Elgar.

Badgett, M. V. L. 1995a. "Gender, Sexuality, and Sexual Orientation: All in the Feminist Family?" *Feminist Economics* 1, no. 1: 121–39.

———. 1995b. "The Last of the Modernists?" *Feminist Economics* 1, no. 2: 63–65.

———. 1998. "Towards Lesbian, Gay, and Bisexual Perspectives in Economics: Why and How They May Make a Difference." *Feminist Economics* 4, no. 2: 49–54.

Bakhtin, M. M. 1981. *The Dialogic Imagination: Four Essays*. Ed. M. Holquist. Trans. M. Holquist and C. Emerson. Austin: University of Texas Press.

Baran. P. A., and P. M. Sweezy. 1968. *Monopoly Capital*. New York: Monthly Review Press.

Bardhan, P. K., and J. E. Roemer, eds. 1993. *Market Socialism: The Current Debate*. Oxford: Oxford University Press.

Barnes, B. 1985. *About Science*. Oxford: Blackwell.

Bataille, G. 1986. *Erotism, Death and Sensuality*. Trans. M. Dalwood. San Francisco: City Lights Books.

————. 1991. *The Accursed Share: An Essay on General Economy.* Vol. 1. Trans. R. Hurley. New York: Zone Books.

Baudrillard, J. 1975. *The Mirror of Production.* Trans. M. Poster. St. Louis: Telos Press.

————. 1981. *For a Critique of the Political Economy of the Sign.* Trans. C. Levin. St. Louis: Telos Press.

Bauman, Z. 1987. *Legislators and Interpreters: On Modernity, Post-modernity, and Intellectuals.* Ithaca, N.Y.: Cornell University Press.

Bausor, R. . 1985. "The Limits of Rationality." *Social Concept* 2 (March): 66–83.

————. 1986. "Time and Equilibrium." In *The Reconstruction of Economic Theory,* ed. P. Mirowski, 93–136. Boston: Kluwer-Nijhoff.

Becker, G. 1991. *A Treatise on the Family.* Enlarged ed. Cambridge: Harvard University Press.

Beed, C., et al. 1991. "Symposium: Postmodernism, Economics, and Canon Creation." *Journal of Post Keynesian Economics* 13, no. 4: 459–94.

Benería, L. 1995. "Towards a Greater Integration of Gender in Economics." *World Development* 23 (November): 1839–50.

Benhabib, S., J. Butler, N. Fraser, and D. Cornell. 1995. *Feminist Contentions: A Philosophical Encounter.* London: Routledge.

Beniger, J. R. 1986. *The Control Revolution: Technological and Economic Origins of the Information Society.* Cambridge: Harvard University Press.

Bergeron, S. 2001. "Political Economy Discourses of Globalization and Feminist Politics." *Signs* 26, no. 4: 983–1006.

————. 2002. "Challenging the World Bank's Narrative of Inclusion." In *World (Bank) Literatures,* ed. A. Kumar. Minneapolis: University of Minnesota Press.

Bergeron, S., and B. Pietrykowski. 1999. "Can There Be Genre Difference in Economic Literature?" In *What Do Economists Know? New Economics of Knowledge,* ed. R. F. Garnett Jr., 139–52. London: Routledge.

Bergstrom, T. C. 1996. "Economics in a Family Way." *Journal of Economic Literature* 34:1903–34.

Berkentotter, C., and T. N. Huckin, eds. 1995. *Genre Knowledge in Disciplinary Communication: Cognition/Culture/Power.* Hillsdale, N.J.: Lawrence Erlbaum Associates.

Berman, M. 1982. *All That Is Solid Melts into Air: The Experience of Modernity.* New York: Simon and Schuster.

Bernstein, M. 1999. Economic Knowledge, Professional Authority, and the State: The Case of American Economics during and after World War II." In *What Do Economists Know? New Economics of Knowledge,* ed. R. F. Garnett Jr., 103–23. London: Routledge.

Berti, A. E., and A. S. Bombi. 1988. *The Child's Construction of Economics.* Trans. G. Duveen. Cambridge: Cambridge University Press.

Bertens, H. 1995. *The Idea of the Postmodern: A History.* London: Routledge.

Best, S., and D. Kellner. 1991. *Postmodern Theory: Critical Interrogations.* New York: Guilford Press.

Biewener, C. 1998. "Socially Contingent Value." In *Marxian Economics: A Reappraisal,* vol. 2, *Price, Profits, and Dynamics,* ed. R. Bellofiore, 57–69. New York: St. Martin's.

Biewener, C. 1999. "A Postmodern Encounter: Poststructuralist Feminism and the Decentering of Marxism." *Socialist Review* 27, nos. 1–2: 71–97.

Birke, L. 2000. *Feminism and the Biological Body*. New Brunswick, N.J.: Rutgers University Press.

Blank, R. M. 1993. "What Should Mainstream Economists Learn from Feminist Theory?" In *Beyond Economic Man*, ed. M. A. Ferber and J. A. Nelson, 133–43. Chicago: University of Chicago Press.

Blaug, M. 1980. *The Methodology of Economics, or How Economists Explain*. Cambridge: Cambridge University Press.

———. 1998. "Disturbing Currents in Modern Economics." *Challenge* 41 (May–June): 11–34.

Blendon, R. J., J. M. Benson, M. Bridie, R. Morin, D. E. Altman, D. Gitterman, M. Brossard, and M. James. 1997. "Bridging the Gap between the Public's and Economists' Views of the Economy." *Journal of Economic Perspectives* 11, no. 3: 105–18.

Boettke, P. J. 1996. "What Is Wrong with Neoclassical Economics (and What Is Still Wrong with Austrian Economics)?" In *Beyond Neoclassical Economics: Heterodox Approaches to Economic Theory*, ed. F. E. Foldvary, 22–40. Cheltenham, U.K.: Edward Elgar.

Booth, W. J. 1993. *Households: On the Moral Architecture of the Economy*. Ithaca, N.Y.: Cornell University Press.

Bordo, S. R. 1987. *The Flight to Objectivity: Essays on Cartesianism and Culture*. Albany: State University of New York Press.

Bourdieu, P. 1984. *Distinction: A Social Critique of the Judgement of Taste*. Cambridge: Harvard University Press.

Brooks, P. 1993. *Body Works: Objects of Desire in Modern Narrative*. Cambridge: Harvard University Press.

Brown, S. 1995. *Postmodern Marketing*. London: Routledge.

Brown, V. 1994a. *Adam Smith's Discourse: Canonicity, Commerce and Conscience*. London: Routledge.

———. 1994b. "The Economy as Text." In *New Directions in Economic Methodology*, ed. R. E. Backhouse, 368–82. London: Routledge.

Buchanan, A. 1982. *Marx and Justice*. Totowa, N.J.: Rowman and Allenheld.

Buchanan, J. M. 2001. "Game Theory, Mathematics, and Economics." *Journal of Economic Methodology* 8, no. 10: 27–32.

Burczak, T. 1994. "The Postmodern Moments of F. A. Hayek's Economics." *Economics and Philosophy* 10, no. 1: 31–58.

———. 2001a. "Profit Expectations and Confidence: Some Unresolved Issues in the Austrian/Post-Keynesian Debate." *Review of Political Economy* 13, no. 1: 59–80.

———. 2001b. "Response to Butos and Koppl: Expectations, Exogeneity, and Evolution." *Review of Political Economy* 13, no. 1: 87–90.

Bush, P. 1993. "The Methodology of Institutional Economics: A Pragmatic Instrumentalist Perspective." In *Institutional Economics: Theory, Method, Policy*, ed. M. Tool, 59–107. Boston: Kluwer.

Butler, J. 1990. *Gender Trouble: Feminism and the Subversion of Identity*. London: Routledge.

———. 1993. *Bodies That Matter: On the Discursive Limits of Sex*. London: Routledge.

Caldwell, B. 1982. *Beyond Positivism: Economic Methodology in the Twentieth Century*. London: George Allen and Unwin.

Callari, A. 1986. "History, Epistemology, and Marx's Theory of Value." In *Research in Political Economy*, vol. 9, ed. P. Zarembka. Greenwich, Conn.: JAI Press.

———. Forthcoming. "The Ghost of the Gift: The Unlikelihood of Economics." In *The Question of the Gift*, ed. M. Osteen. London: Routledge.

Callari, A., and D. F. Ruccio. 1996. "Introduction: Postmodern Materialism and the Future of Marxist Theory." In *Postmodern Materialism and the Future of Marxist Theory: Essays in the Althusserian Tradition*, ed. A. Callari and D. F. Ruccio, 1–48. Hanover, N.H.: Wesleyan University Press.

Caputo, J. D., ed. 1997. *Deconstruction in a Nutshell: A Conversation with Jacques Derrida*. New York: Fordham University Press.

Carabelli, A. 1988. *On Keynes's Method*. London: Macmillan.

———. 1995. "Uncertainty and Measurement in Keynes: Probability and Organicness." In *Keynes, Knowledge, and Uncertainty*, ed. S. Dow and J. Hillard, 137–60.

Caravale, G. A. 1991. *Marx and Modern Economic Analysis*. 2 vols. Cheltenham, U.K.: Edward Elgar.

Carling, Alan. 1990. "In Defence of Rational Choice: A Reply to Ellen Meiksins Wood." *New Left Review*, no. 184 (November–December): 97–109.

Carnap, R. 1950. *Logical Foundations of Probability*. Chicago: University of Chicago Press.

———. 1966. *An Introduction to the Philosophy of Science*, ed. M. Gardner. New York: Basic Books.

Carrier, J. G., ed. 1997. *Meanings of the Market: The Free Market in Western Culture*. New York: Berg.

Castells, M. 1996–98. *The Information Age: Economy, Society, and Culture*. 3 vols. Oxford: Blackwell.

Charusheela, S. 2001. "Women's Choices and the Ethnocentrism/Relativism Dilemma." In *Postmodernism, Economics, and Knowledge*, ed. S. Cullenberg, J. Amariglio, and D. F. Ruccio, 197–220. London: Routledge.

Cilliers, P. 1998. *Complexity and Postmodernism: Understanding Complex Systems*. London: Routledge.

Cixous, H. 1997. "Sorties: Out and Out: Attacks/Ways Out/Forays." In *The Logic of the Gift: Toward an Ethic of Generosity*, ed. A. D. Schrift, 148–73. London: Routledge.

Clarke, S. 1994. *Marx's Theory of Crisis*. New York: St. Martin's.

Cleland, T. M. 1930. Appendix. *Fortune*, February, 180–81.

Clifford, J. 1988. *The Predicament of Culture: Twentieth-Century Ethnography, Literature, and Art*. Cambridge: Harvard University Press.

Clower, R. W. 1994. "Economics as an Inductive Science." *Southern Economic Journal* 60 (April): 805–14.

Coddington, A. 1975. "Creaking Semaphore and Beyond: A Consideration of Shackle's 'Epistemics and Economics.' " *British Journal of Philosophy of Science* 26 (June): 151–63.

———. 1976. "Keynesian Economics: The Search for First Principles." *Journal of Economic Literature* 14:1258–73.

———. 1982. "Deficient Foresight: A Troublesome Theme in Keynesian Economics." *American Economic Review* 72, no. 3: 480–87.

Cohen-Rosenfield, L. 1968. *From Beast-Machine to Man-Machine: Animal Soul in French Letters from Descartes to La Mettrie.* New York: Octagon Books.

Colander, D. 2000. "The Death of Neoclassical Economics. *Journal of the History of Economic Thought* 22, no. 2: 127–43.

Compton Advertising, Inc. 1975. *National Survey on the American Economic System: A Study of Understanding and Attitudes of the American People.* New York: Advertising Council.

Connor, S. 1989. *Postmodernist Culture: An Introduction to Theories of the Contemporary.* Oxford: Blackwell.

———. 1993. "The Necessity of Value." In *Principled Positions: Postmodernism and the Rediscovery of Value*, ed. J. Squires, 31–49. London: Lawrence and Wishart.

Cooper, B. P., and M. S. Murphy. 1999. " 'Libidinal Economics': Lyotard and Accounting for the Unaccountable." In *The New Economic Criticism: Studies at the Intersection of Literature and Economics*, ed. M. Woodmansee and M. Osteen, 229–241. London: Routledge.

Cooper, R., and G. Burrell. 1988. "Modernism, Postmodernism, and Organizational Analysis: An Introduction." *Organization Studies* 9, no. 1: 91–112.

Cooper, R. W., D. V. DeJong, R. Forsythe, and T. W. Ross. 1990. "Selection Criteria in Coordination Games: Some Experimental Results." *American Economic Review* 80, no. 1: 218–33.

Corlett, W. 2000. *Class Action: Reading Labor, Theory, and Value.* Ithaca, N.Y.: Cornell University Press.

Cornwall, R. 1997. "Deconstructing Silence: The Queer Political Economy of the Social Articulation of Desire." *Review of Radical Political Economics* 29, no. 1: 1–30.

———. 1998. "A Primer on Queer Theory for Economists Interested in Social Identities." *Feminist Economics* 4, no. 2: 73–82.

Crotty, J. 1993. "Are Keynesian Uncertainty and Macrotheory Compatible? Conventional Decision Making, Institutional Structures, and Conditional Stability in Keynesian Macromodels." In *Macroeconomics on the Minsky Frontier*, ed. R. Pollin and G. Dymski. Ann Arbor: University of Michigan Press.

———. 1994. "Are Keynesian Uncertainty and Macrotheory Compatible?" In *New Perspectives in Monetary Economics: Explorations in the Tradition of Hyman P. Minsky*, ed. R. Pollin and G. Dymski, 105–39. Ann Arbor: University of Michigan Press.

Cullenberg, S. 1992. "Socialism's Burden: Toward a 'Thin' Definition of Socialism." *Rethinking Marxism* 5, no. 2: 64–83.

————. 1994. *The Falling Rate of Profit: Recasting the Marxian Debate*. London: Pluto Press.

————. 1996. "Althusser and the Decentering of the Marxist Totality." In *Postmodern Materialism and the Future of Marxist Theory: Essays in the Althusserian Tradition*, ed. A. Callari and D. F. Ruccio, 120–49. Hanover, N.H.: Wesleyan University Press.

————. 1998. "Decentering the Marxian Debate over the Falling Rate of Profit: A New Approach." In *Marxian Economics: A Reappraisal. Essays on Volume II of Capital*, vol. 2, *Price, Profits, and Dynamics*, ed. R. Bellofiore, 163–76. New York: St. Martin's.

————. 1999. "Overdetermination, Totality, and Institutions: A Genealogy of a Marxist Institutionalist Economics." *Journal of Economic Issues* 33:801–15.

Cullenberg, S., J. Amariglio, and D. F. Ruccio, eds. 2001. *Postmodernism, Economics, and Knowledge*. London: Routledge.

Cullenberg, S., and I. Dasgupta. 2001. "From Myth to Metaphor: A Semiological Analysis of the Cambridge Capital Controversy." In *Postmodernism, Economics, and Knowledge*, ed. S. Cullenberg, J. Amariglio, and D. F. Ruccio, 337–53. London: Routledge.

Culler, J. 1983. *On Deconstruction: Theory and Criticism after Structuralism*. Ithaca, N.Y.: Cornell University Press.

Cypher, J. M. 1993. "The Ideology of Economic Science in the Selling of NAFTA: The Political Economy of Elite Decision-Making." *Review of Radical Political Economics* 25, no. 4: 146–64.

Daston, L. 1987. "The Domestication of Risk: Mathematical Probability and Insurance 1650–1830." In *The Probabilistic Revolution*, vol. 1, *Ideas in History*, ed. L. Kruger et al., 237–60. Cambridge: MIT Press.

Davidson, P. 1978. *Money and the Real World*. 2d ed. London: Macmillan.

————. 1981. "Keynesian Economics." In *The Crisis in Economic Theory*, ed. D. Bell and I. Kristol, 151–73. New York: Basic Books.

————. 1991. "Is Probability Theory Relevant for Uncertainty? A Post Keynesian Perspective." *Journal of Economic Perspectives* 5, no. 1: 129–43.

Davis, J. B. 1994. *Keynes's Philosophical Development*. Cambridge: Cambridge University Press.

————. 2001. "The Emperor's Clothes." Presidential address to the History of Economics Society, 1 July, Wake Forest University. Photocopy.

————. 2003. *The Theory of the Individual in Economics*. London: Routledge.

de Certeau, M. 1984. *The Practice of Everyday Life*. Trans. S. Rendall. Berkeley and Los Angeles: University of California Press.

de Finetti, B. 1964. "Foresight: Its Logical Laws, Its Subjective Sources. In *Studies in Subjective Probability*, ed. H. E. Kyburg, Jr., and H. E. Smokler, 93–158. New York: John Wiley and Sons.

Debreu, G. 1959. *Theory of Value: An Axiomatic Analysis of Economic Equilibrium*. New Haven: Yale University Press.

Defoe, D. 1965. *The Life and Adventures of Robinson Crusoe*. New York: Penguin.

Deleuze, G. 1983. *Nietzsche and Philosophy*. Trans. H. Tomlinson. New York: Columbia University Press.

Deleuze, G. 1988. *Spinoza: Practical Philosophy*. Trans. R. Hurley. San Francisco: City Lights Books.

Deleuze, G., and F. Guattari, 1983. *Anti-Oedipus: Capitalism and Schizophrenia*. Trans. R. Hurley, M. Seem, and H. R. Lane. Minneapolis: University of Minnesota Press.

DeMartino, G. 1993. "Beneath 'First Principles': Controversies within the New Macroeconomics." *Journal of Economic Issues* 27:1127–53.

———. 1999. "Anti-essentialist Marxism and Radical Institutionalism: Introduction to the Symposium." *Journal of Economic Issues* 33:797–800.

———. 2000. *Global Economy, Global Justice: Theoretical Objections and Policy Alternatives to Neoliberalism*. London: Routledge.

Derrida, J. 1976. *Of Grammatology*. Trans. G. C. Spivak. Baltimore: Johns Hopkins University Press.

———. 1978. *Writing and Difference*. Trans. A. Bass. Chicago: University of Chicago Press.

———. 1992. *Given Time: The Time of the King*. Vol. 1, *Counterfeit Money*. Trans. Peggy Kamuf. Chicago: University of Chicago Press.

Desai, M. 1991. "Human Development: Concepts and Measurement." *European Economic Review* 35, nos. 2–3: 350–57.

Descombes, V. 1980. *Modern French Philosophy*. Cambridge: Cambridge University Press.

Dewey, J. 1938. *Logic: The Theory of Inquiry*. New York: Henry Holt.

———. 1939. *Theory of Valuation*. Chicago: University of Chicago Press.

———. 1944. "Some Questions about Value." *Journal of Philosophy* 41:449–55.

———. 1949. "The Field of 'Value.' " In *Value: A Cooperative Inquiry*, ed. R. Lepley, 64–77. New York: Columbia University Press.

Dilley, R., ed. 1992. *Contesting Markets: Analyses of Ideology, Discourse, and Practice*. Edinburgh: Edinburgh University Press.

Dimand, M. A., R. W. Dimand, and E. L. Forget, eds. 1995. *Women of Value: Feminist Essays on the History of Women in Economics*. Cheltenham, U.K.: Edward Elgar.

Dirlik, A. 2000. "Globalization as the End and the Beginning of History: The Contradictory Implications of a New Paradigm." *Rethinking Marxism* 12, no. 4: 4–22.

Diskin, J. 1996. "Rethinking Socialism: What's in a Name?" In *Postmodern Materialism and the Future of Marxist Theory: Essays in the Althusserian Tradition*, ed. A. Callari and D. F. Ruccio, 278–99. Hanover, N.H.: Wesleyan University Press.

Dobb, M. 1973. *Theories of Value and Distribution since Adam Smith*. Cambridge: Cambridge University Press.

Docherty, T., ed. 1993. *Postmodernism: A Reader*. New York: Columbia University Press.

Douglas, M., and B. Isherwood. 1979. *The World of Goods: Towards an Anthropology of Consumption*. London: Allen Lane.

Dow, S. C. 1991. "Are There Any Signs of Postmodernism within Economics?" *Methodus* 3, no. 1: 81–85.

———. 2001. "Modernism and Postmodernism: A Dialectical Analysis." In *Postmodernism, Economics, and Knowledge*, ed. S. Cullenberg, J. Amariglio, and D. F. Ruccio, 71–76. London: Routledge.

Dow, S. C., and A. Dow. 1985. "Animal Spirits and Rationality." In *Keynes's Economics: Methodological Issues*, ed. T. Lawson and H. Pesaran, 46–65. London: Croom Helm.

Dow, S. C., and J. Hillard, eds. 1995. *Keynes, Knowledge, and Uncertainty*. Cheltenham, U.K.: Edward Elgar.

Dreyfus, H., and P. Rabinow. 1983. *Michel Foucault: Beyond Structuralism and Hermeneutics*. Chicago: University of Chicago Press.

Dugger, W. M. 1979. "Methodological Differences between Institutional and Neoclassical Economics." *Journal of Economic Issues* 13:899–909.

———, ed. 1989. *Radical Institutionalism: Contemporary Voices*. New York: Greenwood Press.

Dupré, J. 1993. *The Disorder of Things: Metaphysical Foundations of the Disunity of Science*. Cambridge: Harvard University Press.

Eagleton, T. 1996. *The Illusions of Postmodernism*. Oxford: Blackwell.

Easterlin, R. A. 1997. "The Story of a Reluctant Economist." *American Economist* 41 (fall): 11–21.

Eatwell, J., and M. Milgate. 1983. "Unemployment and the Market Equilibrium." In *Keynes's Economics and the Theory of Value and Distribution*, ed. J. Eatwell and M. Milgate, 260–80. Oxford: Oxford University Press.

Eichner, A. 1983. *Why Economics Is Not Yet a Science*. Armonk, N.Y.: M. E. Sharpe.

Elkins, J. 1999. *Pictures of the Body: Pain and Metamorphosis*. Stanford: Stanford University Press.

Elliott, J. 1986. "On the Possibility of Marx's Moral Critique of Capitalism." *Review of Social Economy* 44, no. 2: 130–45.

Elson, D., ed. 1995. *Male Bias in the Development Process*. 2d ed. New York: Manchester University Press.

Elster, J. 1985. *Making Sense of Marx*. Cambridge: Cambridge University Press.

———, ed. 1986. *The Multiple Self*. Cambridge: Cambridge University Press.

England, P. 1993. "The Separative Self: Androcentric Bias in Neoclassical Assumptions." In *Beyond Economic Man: Feminist Theory and Economics*, ed. M. A. Ferber and J. A. Nelson, 37–53. Chicago: University of Chicago Press.

Esteva, G., and M. S. Prakash. 1998. *Grassroots Post-Modernism: Remaking the Soil of Cultures*. London: Zed Books.

Faigley, L. 1992. *Fragments of Rationality: Postmodernity and the Subject of Composition*. Pittsburgh: University of Pittsburgh Press.

Farjoun, E., and M. Machover. 1983. *Laws of Chaos: A Probabilistic Approach to Political Economy*. London: Verso.

Feher, M., with R. Naddaff and N. Tazi, eds. 1989. *Fragments for a History of the Body*. 3 vols. New York: Zone Books.

Feiner, S. F. 1994. "Reading Neoclassical Economics: Toward an Erotic Economy of Sharing." *Studies in Psychoanalytic Theory* 3 (fall): 50–67.

———. 1995. "Reading Neoclassical Economics: Toward an Erotic Economy of Sharing." In *Out of the Margin: Feminist Perspectives on Economics*, ed.

E. Kuiper and J. Sap, with S. Feiner, N. Ott, and Z. Tzannatos, 151–66. London: Routledge.

———. 1999. "A Portrait of Homo Economicus as a Young Man." In *The New Economic Criticism: Studies at the Intersection of Literature and Economics*, ed. M. Woodmansee and M. Osteen, 193–209. London: Routledge.

Feiner, S. F., and B. B. Roberts. 1990. "Hidden by the Invisible Hand: Neoclassical Economic Theory and the Textbook Treatment of Race and Gender." *Gender and Society* 4, no. 2: 159–81.

Ferguson, H. 1990. *The Science of Pleasure: Cosmos and Psyche in the Bourgeois World View*. London: Routledge.

Feyerabend, P. 1978. *Against Method*. London: Verso.

———. 1999. *Conquest of Abundance: A Tale of Abstraction versus the Richness of Being*. Chicago: University of Chicago Press.

Fitzgibbons, A. 1988. *Keynes's Vision: A New Political Economy*. Oxford: Clarendon Press.

Flax, J. 1987. "Postmodernism and Gender Relations in Feminist Theory." *Signs* 12, no. 4: 621–43.

———. 1990. *Thinking Fragments: Psychoanalysis, Feminism, and Postmodernism in the Contemporary West*. Berkeley and Los Angeles: University of California Press.

———. 1993. *Disputed Subjects: Essays on Psychoanalysis, Politics, and Philosophy*. London: Routledge.

Fleetwood, S., ed. 1999. *Critical Realism in Economics: Development and Debate*. London: Routledge.

Folbre, N. 1988. "The Black Four of Hearts: Toward a New Paradigm of Household Economics." In *A Home Divided: Women and Income in the Third World*, ed. D. Dwyer and J. Bruce, 248–62. Stanford: Stanford University Press.

———. 1993. "Socialism, Feminist and Scientific." In *Beyond Economic Man: Feminist Theory and Economics*, ed. M. A. Ferber and J. A. Nelson, 94–110. Chicago: University of Chicago Press.

———. 1994. *Who Pays for the Kids? Gender and the Structures of Constraint*. London: Routledge.

———. 1997. "Gender Coalitions: Extrafamily Influences on Intrafamily Inequality." In *Intrahousehold Resource Allocation in Developing Countries: Methods, Models, and Policy*, ed. L. Haddad et al. Baltimore: Johns Hopkins University Press.

Folbre, N., and H. Hartmann. 1988. "The Rhetoric of Self-Interest: Ideology and Gender in Economic Theory." In *The Consequences of Economic Rhetoric*, ed. A. Klamer, D. N. McCloskey, and R. M. Solow, 184–203. Cambridge: Cambridge University Press.

Foley, D. K. 1986. *Understanding Capital: Marx's Economic Theory*. Cambridge: Harvard University Press.

Foucault, M. 1972. *The Archaeology of Knowledge and The Discourse on Language*. Trans. A. M. S. Smith. New York: Harper and Row.

———. 1973. *The Order of Things: An Archaeology of the Human Sciences*. Trans. A. Sheridan. New York: Vintage.

————. 1979. *Discipline and Punish: The Birth of the Prison*. Trans. A. Sheridan. New York: Vintage.

————. 1980. *Power/Knowledge: Selected Interviews and Other Writings, 1972–1977*. Trans. C. Gordon, L. Marshall, J. Mepham, and K. Soper. New York: Pantheon.

————. 1988. *The History of Sexuality*, vol. 3, *The Care of the Self*. Trans. R. Hurley. New York: Vintage.

Fox, K. F. A. 1978. "What Children Bring to School: The Beginnings of Economic Education." *Social Education* 42:478–81.

Fraad, H., S. A. Resnick, and R. D. Wolff. 1994. *Bringing It All Back Home: Class, Gender, and Power in the Modern Household*. Boulder, Colo.: Pluto Press.

Frank, A. 1990. "Bringing Bodies Back In: A Decade Review." *Theory, Culture, and Society* 7:131–62.

Frank, R. H., T. Gilovich, and D. T. Regan. 1993. "Does Studying Economics Inhibit Cooperation?" *Journal of Economic Perspectives* 7, no. 2: 159–71.

————. 1996. "Do Economists Make Bad Citizens?" *Journal of Economic Perspectives* 10, no. 1: 187–92.

Frey, B. 2001. "Why Economists Disregard Economic Methodology." *Journal of Economic Methodology* 8, no. 1: 41–47.

Friedman, M. 1953. "The Methodology of Positive Economics." In *Essays in Positive Economics*, 3–43. Chicago: University of Chicago Press.

Fuchs, V. R., A. B. Krueger, and J. M. Poterba. 1998. "Economists' Views about Parameters, Values, and Policies: Survey Results in Labor and Public Economics." *Journal of Economic Literature* 36:1387–1425.

Furnham, A. 1987. "School Children's Perception of Economic Justice: A Cross-Cultural Comparison." *Journal of Economic Psychology* 8:457–67.

Gablik, S. 1984. *Has Modernism Failed?* New York: Thames and Hudson.

Gagnier, R., and J. Dupré. 2001. "Chacun Son Goux? or, Some Skeptical Reflections on Flat Bodies and Heavy Metal." In *Postmodernism, Knowledge, and Economics*, ed. S. Cullenberg, J. Amariglio, and D. F. Ruccio, 182–93. London: Routledge.

Gallagher, C. 1987. "The Body versus the Social Body in the Works of Thomas Malthus." In *The Making of the Modern Body: Sexuality and Society in the Nineteenth Century*, ed. C. Gallagher and T. Laqueur, 83–106. Berkeley and Los Angeles: University of California Press.

Gallup Poll. Various years. *Gallup Poll Monthly*. Princeton, N.J.: Gallup Poll.

Gärdenfors, P., and N.-E. Sahlin. 1988. "Unreliable Probabilities, Risk Taking, and Decision Making." In *Decision, Probability, and Utility: Selected Readings*, ed. P. Gärdenfors and N.-E. Sahlin, 313–34. Cambridge: Cambridge University Press.

Garnett, R. F., Jr. 1999a. "Postmodernism and Theories of Value: New Grounds for Institutionalist/Marxist Dialogue?" *Journal of Economic Issues* 33:817–34.

————, ed. 1999b. *What Do Economists Know? New Economics of Knowledge*. London: Routledge.

Gasché, R. 1986. *The Tain of the Mirror: Derrida and the Philosophy of Reflection*. Cambridge: Harvard University Press.

Geiger, G. R. 1949. "Values and Inquiry." In *Value: A Cooperative Inquiry*, ed. R. Lepley, 93–111. New York: Columbia University Press.

Geras, N. 1985. "The Controversy about Marx and Justice." *New Left Review*, no. 150 (March–April): 47–85.

Gergen, K. J. 1991. *The Saturated Self: Dilemmas of Identity in Contemporary Life*. Basic Books.

Gerrard, B. 1992. "From *A Treatise on Probability* to the *General Theory*: Continuity or Change in Keynes's Thought." In *The Philosophy and Economics of J. M. Keynes*, ed. B. Gerrard and J. Hillard, 80–95. Cheltenham, U.K.: Edward Elgar.

———, ed. 1993. *The Economics of Rationality*. London: Routledge.

Ghiselin, M. T. 1978. "The Economy of the Body." *American Economic Review* 68, no. 2: 233–37.

Gibson-Graham, J. K. 1993. "Waiting for the Revolution; or, How to Smash Capitalism While Working at Home in Your Spare Time." *Rethinking Marxism* 6, no. 2: 10–24.

———. 1996. *The End of Capitalism (as We Knew It): A Feminist Critique of Political Economy*. Oxford: Blackwell.

Gibson-Graham, J.-K., and P. O'Neill. 2001. "Exploring a New Class Politics of the Enterprise." In *Re/presenting Class: Essays in Postmodern Marxism*, ed. J. K. Gibson-Graham, S. A. Resnick, and R. D. Wolff, 56–80. Durham, N.C.: Duke University Press.

———, eds. 2000. *Class and Its Others*. Minneapolis: University of Minnesota Press.

Gibson-Graham, J.-K., S. A. Resnick, and R. D. Wolff. 2001a. "Toward a Poststructuralist Political Economy." In *Re/presenting Class: Essays in Postmodern Marxism*, ed. J. K. Gibson-Graham, S. A. Resnick, and R. D. Wolff, 1–22. Durham, N.C.: Duke University Press.

———, eds. 2001b. *Re/presenting Class: Essays in Postmodern Marxism*. Durham, N.C.: Duke University Press.

Giddens, A. 1990. *The Consequences of Modernity*. Stanford: Stanford University Press.

Gintis, H. 1992. "The Analytical Foundations of Contemporary Political Economy: A Comment on Hunt." In *Radical Economics*, ed. B. Roberts and S. Feiner, 108–16. Boston: Kluwer.

Godelier, M. 1999. *The Enigma of the Gift*. Trans. N. Scott. Chicago: University of Chicago Press.

Gordon. W. 1984. "The Role of Institutional Economics." *Journal of Economic Issues* 18:369–81.

———. 1990. "The Role of Tool's Social Value Principle." *Journal of Economic Issues* 24:879–86.

Grapard, U. 1995. "Robinson Crusoe: The Quintessential Economic Man?" *Feminist Economics* 1, no. 1: 32–53.

———. 2001. "The Trouble with Women and Economics: A Postmodern Perspective on Charlotte Perkins Gilman." In *Postmodernism, Economics, and Knowledge*, ed. S. Cullenberg, J. Amariglio, and D. F. Ruccio, 261–85. London: Routledge.

Griswold, C. L., Jr. 1999. *Adam Smith and the Virtues of Enlightenment*. Cambridge: Cambridge University Press.

Grosz, E. 1994. *Volatile Bodies: Toward a Corporeal Feminism*. Bloomington: University of Indiana Press.

Gruchy, A. G. 1987. *The Reconstruction of Economics: An Analysis of the Fundamentals of Institutional Economics*. New York: Greenwood Press.

Gudeman, S. 1986. *Economics as Culture: Models and Metaphors of Livelihood*. Boston: Routledge and Kegan Paul.

———. 2001. "Postmodern Gifts." In *Postmodernism, Economics, and Knowledge*, ed. S. Cullenberg, J. Amariglio, and D. F. Ruccio, 459–74. London: Routledge.

Gudeman, S., and A. Rivera. 1990. *Conversations in Colombia: The Domestic Economy in Life and Text*. Cambridge: Cambridge University Press.

Guillory, J. 1993. *Cultural Capital: The Problem of Literary Canon Formation*. Chicago: University of Chicago Press.

Hacking, I. 1990a. "Probability." In *The New Palgrave: Utility and Probability*, ed. J. Eatwell, M. Milgate, and P. Newman, 163–77. New York: W. W. Norton.

———. 1990b. *The Taming of Chance*. Cambridge: Cambridge University Press.

Hahn, F. 1981. "General Equilibrium Theory." In *The Crisis in Economic Theory*, ed. D. Bell and I. Kristol, 123–38. New York: Basic Books.

Hammond, P. J. 1990. "Uncertainty." In *The New Palgrave: Utility and Probability*, ed. J. Eatwell, M. Milgate, and P. Newman, 280–94. New York: W. W. Norton.

Hands, D. W. 1997. "Frank Knight's Pluralism." In *Pluralism and Economics: New Perspectives in History and Methodology*, ed. A. Salanti and E. Screpanti, 194–206. Cheltenham, U.K.: Edward Elgar.

Hansen, W. L. 1986. "What Knowledge Is Most Worth Knowing—for Economics Majors?" *American Economic Review* 76, no. 2: 149–52.

Haraway, D. J. 1991. *Simians, Cyborgs, and Women: The Reinvention of Nature*. London: Routledge.

Harding, S. 1986. *The Science Question in Feminism*. Ithaca, N.Y.: Cornell University Press.

———. 1991. *Whose Science? Whose Knowledge? Thinking from Women's Lives*. Ithaca, N.Y.: Cornell University Press.

———. 1995. "Can Feminist Thought Make Economics More Objective?" *Feminist Economics* 1, no. 1: 7–32.

———. 1998. *Is Science Multicultural? Postcolonialisms, Feminisms, and Epistemologies*. Bloomington: Indiana University Press.

Hargreaves Heap, S. P. 1993. "Post-modernity and New Conceptions of Rationality in Economics." In *The Economics of Rationality*, ed. Bill Gerrard, 68–90. London: Routledge.

———. 2001. "Postmodernity, Rationality, and Justice." In *Postmodernism, Economics, and Knowledge*, ed. S. Cullenberg, J. Amariglio, and D. F. Ruccio, 354–73. London: Routledge.

Hargreaves Heap, S. P., and Y. Varoufakis. 1995. *Game Theory: A Critical Introduction*. London: Routledge.

Harsanyi, J. C. 1995. "Games with Incomplete Information." *American Economic Review* 85, no. 3: 291–303.

Harvey, D. 1984. *The Limits to Capital*. Oxford: Blackwell.

———. 1989. *The Condition of Postmodernity*. Oxford: Blackwell.

Hayden, F. G. 1989. "Institutionalism for What: To Understand Inevitable Progress or for Policy Relevance?" *Journal of Economic Issues* 23:633–45.

Hayles, N. K., ed. 1991. *Chaos and Order: Complex Dynamics in Literature and Science*. Chicago: University of Chicago Press.

Heidegger, M. 1991. *Nietzsche*. Trans. D. F. Krell. 2 vols. San Francisco: Harper Collins.

Henderson, W. 1995. *Economics as Literature*. London: Routledge.

Henderson, W., T. Dudley-Evans, and R. Backhouse, eds. 1993. *Economics and Language*. London: Routledge.

Hewitson, G. 1994. "Deconstructing Robinson Crusoe: A Feminist Interrogation of 'Rational Economic Man.' " *Australian Feminist Studies* 20 (summer): 131–49.

———. 1999. *Feminist Economics: Interrogating the Masculinity of Rational Economic Man*. Cheltenham, U.K.: Edward Elgar.

———. 2001. "The Disavowal of the Sexed Body in Neoclassical Economics." In *Postmodernism, Knowledge, and Economics*, ed. S. Cullenberg, D. F. Ruccio, and J. Amariglio, 221–45. London: Routledge.

Hicks, J. R. 1939. *Value and Capital*. Oxford: Oxford University Press.

Hicks, J. R., and R. G. D. Allen. 1934. "A Reconsideration of the Theory of Value." *Economica* 1:52–76, 196–219.

Hillard, J. 1992. "Keynes, Orthodoxy, and Uncertainty." In *The Philosophy and Economics of J. M. Keynes*, ed. B. Gerrard and J. Hillard, 59–79. Cheltenham, U.K.: Edward Elgar.

Hillman, D., and C. Mazzio, eds. 1997. *The Body in Parts: Fantasies of Corporeality in Early Modern Europe*. London: Routledge.

Hindess, B. 1977. *Philosophy and Methodology in the Social Sciences*. Hassocks, Sussex: Harvester Press.

———. 1987. *Freedom, Equality, and the Market*. London: Tavistock.

Hindess, B., and P. Q. Hirst. 1975. *Pre-capitalist Modes of Production*. London: Routledge and Kegan Paul.

Hirshleifer, J. 1985. "The Expanding Domain of Economics." *American Economic Review* 75, no. 6: 53–68.

Hodgson, G. 1993. "Commentary." In *Institutional Economics: Theory, Method, Policy*, ed. M. Tool, 108–18. Boston: Kluwer.

Hollinger, D. A. 1994. "The Knower and the Artificer, with Postscript 1993." In *Modernist Impulses in the Human Sciences, 1870–1930*, ed. D. Ross, 26–53. Baltimore: Johns Hopkins University Press.

Hollis, M., and E. Nell. 1975. *Rational Economic Man: A Philosophical Critique of Neo-classical Economics*. Cambridge: Cambridge University Press.

Hopwood, A. G., and P. Miller, eds. 1994. *Accounting as Social and Institutional Practice*. Cambridge: Cambridge University Press.

Horwitz, S. 1995. "Feminist Economics: An Austrian Perspective." *Journal of Economic Methodology* 2, no. 2: 259–79.

Howard, M. C., and J. E. King. 1975. *The Political Economy of Marx*. Harlow, Essex: Longman Group.

Howes, D., ed. 1996. *Cross-Cultural Consumption: Global Markets, Local Realities*. London: Routledge.

Hudson, L. 1972. *The Cult of the Fact: A Psychologist's Autobiographical Critique of His Discipline*. New York: Harper and Row.

Hume, D. 1970. *Writings on Economics*. Ed. E. Rotwein. Madison: University of Wisconsin Press.

Hunt, E. K. 1979. "Marx as a Social Economist: The Labor Theory of Value." *Review of Social Economy* 37, no. 3: 275–94.

———. 1982. "Marx's Concept of Human Nature and the Labor Theory of Value." *Review of Radical Political Economy* 14, no. 2: 7–25.

———. 1992. "Analytical Marxism." In *Radical Economics*, ed. B. Roberts and S. Feiner, 91–107. Boston: Kluwer.

Hutchison, T. W. 1979. *Knowledge and Ignorance in Economics*. Chicago: University of Chicago Press.

Hyman, P. 1994. "Feminist Critiques of Orthodox Economics: A Survey." *New Zealand Economic Papers* 28, no. 1: 53–80.

Ingrao, B. 1997. "Comment." In *Pluralism and Economics: New Perspectives in History and Methodology*, ed. A. Salanti and E. Screpanti, 227–31. Cheltenham, U.K.: Edward Elgar.

Ingrao, B., and G. Israel. 1990. *The Invisible Hand*. Trans. I. McGilvray. Cambridge: MIT Press.

Irigaray, L. 1985. *This Sex Which Is Not One*. Trans. C. Porter and C. Burke. Ithaca, N.Y.: Cornell University Press.

Ivins, M. 2001. "Workers Are Fed Up with Always Being Mr. Nice Guy." *Chicago Tribune*, 2 August, sec. 1, 23.

Jackson, S. 1997. "Stitch Bitch: The Patchwork Girl." http://web.mit.edu/m-i-t/articles/jackson.html (accessed 17 February 2003).

Jaggar, A. M. 1997. "Love and Knowledge: Emotion in Feminist Epistemology." In *Feminist Social Thought: A Reader*, ed. D. T. Meyers, 385–405. London: Routledge.

Jameson, F. 1991. *Postmodernism; or, The Cultural Logic of Late Capitalism*. Durham, N.C.: Duke University Press.

Jeffrey, R. C. 1988. "Probable Knowledge." In *Decision, Probability, and Utility: Selected Readings*, ed. P. Gärdenfors and N.-E. Sahlin, 86–96. Cambridge: Cambridge University Press.

Jencks, C. 1987. *The Language of Post-modern Architecture*. 5th ed. New York: Rizzoli.

Jevons, W. S. 1971. *The Theory of Political Economy*. Harmondsworth, Middlesex: Penguin.

Justman, S. 1993. *The Autonomous Male of Adam Smith*. Norman: University of Oklahoma Press.

Kantor, B. 1979. "Rational Expectations and Economic Thought." *Journal of Economic Literature* 17:1422–41.

Katzner, D. W. 1991a. "In Defense of Formalization in Economics." *Methodus* 3, no. 1: 17–24.

Katzner, D. W. 1991b. "Our Mad Rush to Measure: How Did we Get into This Mess?" *Methodus* 3, no. 2: 18–26.

Kayatekin, S., and D. F. Ruccio. 1998. "Global Fragments: Subjectivity and Class Politics in Discourses of Globalization." *Economy and Society* 27 (February): 74–96.

Keller, E. F. 1985. *Reflections on Gender and Science.* New Haven: Yale University Press.

Kern, S. 1983. *The Culture of Time and Space, 1880–1918.* Cambridge: Harvard University Press.

Keynes, J. M. 1921. *A Treatise on Probability.* London: Macmillan.

———. 1937. "The General Theory of Employment." *Quarterly Journal of Economics* 51, no. 2: 209–23.

———. 1964. *The General Theory of Employment, Interest, and Money.* New York: Harcourt, Brace and World.

———. 1973–79. *The Collected Writings of John Maynard Keynes.* Ed. D. E. Moggridge. 29 vols. London: Macmillan.

Kirzner, I. M. 1994. "On *The Economics of Time and Ignorance.*" In *The Market Process: Essays in Contemporary Austrian Economics,* ed. P. J. Boettke and D. L. Prychitko, 38–51. Cheltenham, U.K.: Edward Elgar.

———. 1998. "The Driving Force of the Market: The Idea of 'Competition' in Contemporary Economic Theory and in the Austrian Theory of the Market Process." In *Why Economists Disagree: An Introduction to Alternative Schools of Thought,* ed. D. L. Prychitko, 37–52. Albany: State University of New York Press.

Klamer, A. 1983. *Conversations with Economists: New Classical Economists and Their Opponents Speak Out on the Current Controversy in Macroeconomics.* Totowa, N.J.: Rowman and Allanheld.

———. 1995. "Feminist Interpretative Economics." In *Out of the Margin: Feminist Perspectives in Economics,* ed. E. Kuiper and J. Sap, with S. Feiner, N. Ott, and Z. Tzannatos, 167–71. London: Routledge.

———. 2001. "Late Modernism and the Loss of Character in Economics." In *Postmodernism, Economics, and Knowledge,* ed. S. Cullenberg, J. Amariglio, and D. F. Ruccio, 77–101. London: Routledge.

———, ed. 1996. *The Value of Culture: On the Relationship between Economics and the Arts.* Amsterdam. Amsterdam University Press.

Klamer, A., and T. C. Leonard. 1992. "Everyday versus Academic Rhetoric in Economics." George Washington University, November. Photocopy.

Klamer, A, D. N. McCloskey, and R. M. Solow, eds. 1988. *The Consequences of Economic Rhetoric.* Cambridge: Cambridge University Press.

Klamer, A., and J. Meehan. 1999. "The Crowding Out of Academic Economics: The Case of NAFTA." In *What Do Economists Know? New Economics of Knowledge,* ed. R. F. Garnett Jr., 65–85. London: Routledge.

Klein, B., R. Crawford, and A. Alchian. 1986. "Vertical Integration, Appropriable Rents, and the Competitive Contracting Process." In *The Economic Nature of the Firm,* ed. L. Putterman, 230–49. Cambridge: Cambridge University Press.

Klein, D. B., ed. 1999. "Introduction: What Do Economists Contribute?" In *What Do Economists Contribute?* 1–26. New York: New York University Press.

Klotz, H. 1988. *The History of Postmodern Architecture*. Trans. R. Donnell. Cambridge: MIT Press.

Knight, F. 1921. *Risk, Uncertainty, and Profit*. Boston: Houghton Mifflin.

Komter, A. E. 1996a. "Women, Gifts, and Power." In *The Gift: An Interdisciplinary Perspective*, ed. A. E. Komter, 119–31. Amsterdam: Amsterdam University Press.

———. 1996b. Introduction to *The Gift: An Interdisciplinary Perspective*, ed. A. E. Komter, 1–12. Amsterdam: Amsterdam University Press.

———, ed. 1996c. *The Gift: An Interdisciplinary Perspective*. Amsterdam: Amsterdam University Press.

Koopmans, T. C. 1957. *Three Essays on the State of Economic Science*. New York: McGraw Hill.

Koppl, R. 1991. "Retrospectives: Animal Spirits." *Journal of Economic Perspectives* 5, no. 3: 203–10.

Koppl, R., and W. Butos. 2001. "Confidence in Keynes and Hayek: Reply to Burczak." *Review of Political Economy* 13, no. 1: 81–86.

Kopytoff, I. 1986. "The Cultural Biography of Things: Commoditization as a Process." In *The Social Life of Things: Commodities in Cultural Perspective*, ed. A. Appadurai, 64–91. Cambridge: Cambridge University Press.

Koritz, A., and D. Koritz. 1999. "Symbolic Economics: Adventures in the Metaphorical Marketplace." In *The New Economic Criticism: Studies at the Intersection of Literature and Economics*, ed. M. Woodmansee and M. Osteen. London: Routledge.

Kreps, D. M. 1990. *Game Theory and Economic Modelling*. Oxford: Clarendon Press.

———. 1997. "Economics—the Current Position." *Daedalus* 126, no. 1: 59–85.

Krips, H. 1987. *The Metaphysics of Quantum Theory*. Oxford: Oxford University Press.

Krüger, L., L. J. Daston, and M. Heidelberger, eds. 1987. *The Probabilistic Revolution*, vol. 1, *Ideas in History*. Cambridge: MIT Press.

Krüger, L., G. Gigerenzer, and M. S. Morgan, eds. 1987. *The Probabilistic Revolution*, vol. 2, *Ideas in the Sciences*. Cambridge: MIT Press.

Krugman, P. 1990. *The Age of Diminished Expectations: U.S. Economic Policy in the 1990s*. Cambridge: MIT Press.

———. 1993a. "The Narrow and Broad Arguments for Free Trade." *American Economic Review* 83, no. 2: 362–66.

———. 1993b. "What Do Undergrads Need to Know about Trade?" *American Economic Review* 83, no. 2: 23–26.

Kuhn, T. S. 1970. *The Structure of Scientific Revolutions*. 2d ed. Chicago: University of Chicago Press.

La Mettrie, J. O. de. 1912. *Man a Machine*. Trans. M. W. Calkins. Chicago: Open Court.

Lachmann, L. M. 1998. "From Mises to Shackle: An Essay on Austrian Economics and the Kaleidic Society." In *Why Economists Disagree: An Introduction to Alternative Schools of Thought*, ed. D. L. Prychitko, 53–64. Albany: State University of New York Press.

Latour, B. 1993. *We Have Never Been Modern*. Trans. C. Porter. Cambridge: Harvard University Press.

Latour, B., and S. Woolgar. 1986. *Laboratory Life: The Social Construction of Facts*. Princeton: Princeton University Press.

Lavoie, D., ed. 1991. *Economics and Hermeneutics*. London: Routledge.

Lawson, T. 1985. "Uncertainty and Economic Analysis." *Economic Journal* 95 (December): 909–27.

———. 1988. "Probability and Uncertainty in Economic Analysis." *Journal of Post Keynesian Economics* 11, no. 1: 38–65.

———. 1997. *Economics and Reality*. London: Routledge.

Lecourt, D. 1975. *Marxism and Epistemology*. London: New Left Books.

Leder, D. 1990. *The Absent Body*. Chicago: University of Chicago Press.

Leijonhufvud, A. 1968. *On Keynesian Economics and the Economics of Keynes: A Study in Monetary Theory*. Oxford: Oxford University Press.

Lepley, R., ed. 1949. *Value: A Cooperative Inquiry*. New York: Columbia University Press.

———, ed. 1957. *The Language of Value*. New York: Columbia University Press.

Levin, L. B. 1995. "Toward a Feminist, Post-Keynesian Theory of Investment." In *Out of the Margin: Feminist Perspectives on Economics*, ed. E. Kuiper and J. Sap, with S. Feiner, N. Ott, and Z. Tzannatos, 100–119. London: Routledge.

Levine, D. 1992. "Radical Theories of Accumulation and Crisis: A Comment on Norton." In *Radical Economics*, ed. B. Roberts and S. Feiner, 194–98. Boston: Kluwer.

Lock, G. 1996. "Subject, Interpellation, and Ideology." In *Postmodern Materialism and the Future of Marxist Theory: Essays in the Althusserian Tradition*, ed. A. Callari and D. F. Ruccio, 69–90. Hanover, N.H.: Wesleyan University Press.

Longino, H. 1990. *Science as Social Knowledge: Values and Objectivity in Scientific Inquiry*. Princeton: Princeton University Press.

Lüdtke, W., ed. 1995. *The History of Everyday Life: Reconstructing Historical Experiences and Ways of Life*. Trans. W. Templer. Princeton: Princeton University Press.

Lunt, P., and A. Furnham. 1996. *The Economic Beliefs and Behaviours of Young People*. Cheltenham, U.K.: Edward Elgar.

Lynch, M., and S. Woolgar, eds. 1990. *Representation in Scientific Practice*. Cambridge: MIT Press.

Lyotard, J.-F. 1984. *The Postmodern Condition: A Report on Knowledge*. Trans. G. Bennington and B. Massumi. Foreword by F. Jameson. Minneapolis: University of Minnesota Press.

——— 1993. *Libidinal Economy*. Trans. I. H Grant. Bloomington: University of Indiana Press.

———. 1997. "A Postmodern Fable." In *Postmodern Fables*, trans. G. Van Den Abbeele, 83–101. Minneapolis: University of Minnesota Press.

MacCannell, J. F., and L. Zakarin, eds. 1994. *Thinking Bodies*. Stanford: Stanford University Press.

MacIntyre, A. 1984. *After Virtue*. Notre Dame: University of Notre Dame Press.

Maddock, R., and M. Carter. 1982. "A Child's Guide to Rational Expectations." *Journal of Economic Literature* 20:39–51.

Magnani, M. 1983. " 'Keynesian Fundamentalism': A Critique." In *Keynes's Economics and the Theory of Value and Distribution*, ed. J. Eatwell and M. Milgate, 247–59. Oxford: Oxford University Press.

Mäki, U. 1998. "Instrumentalism." In *The Handbook of Economic Methodology*, ed. J. B. Davis, D. W. Hands, and U. Mäki, 253–56. Cheltenham, U.K.: Edward Elgar.

———. N.d. "Economics Imperialism: Concept and Constraints." Photocopy.

Mandel, E. 1970. *Marxist Economic Theory*, 2 vols. Trans. B. Pearce. New York: Monthly Review Press.

———. 1975. *Late Capitalism*. London: Verso.

Manuel, F. E., and F. P. Manuel. 1979. *Utopian Thought in the Western World*. Cambridge: Harvard University Press.

Marris, P. 1996. *The Politics of Uncertainty: Attachment in Private and Public Life*. London: Routledge.

Marshall, A. 1961. *Principles of Economics*. 8th ed. London: Macmillan.

Martin, E. 1992. *The Woman in the Body*. Boston: Beacon Press.

Marx, K. 1968. *Theories of Surplus-Value*. Vol. 4 of *Capital*. Part 2. Moscow: Progress Publishers.

———. 1977. *Capital*. 3 vols. Trans. B. Fowkes. New York: Vintage.

Marx, K., and F. Engels. 1978. "Manifesto of the Communist Party." In *The Marx-Engels Reader*, ed. R. Tucker. 2d ed. New York: W. W. Norton.

Marzola, A., and F. Silva, eds. 1994. *John Maynard Keynes: Language and Method*. Cheltenham, U.K.: Edward Elgar.

Matthaei, J. 1992. "Marxist-Feminist Contributions to Radical Economics." In *Radical Economics*, ed. B. Roberts and S. Feiner, 117–44. Boston: Kluwer.

———. 1995. "The Sexual Division of Labor, Sexuality, and Lesbian/Gay Liberation: Toward a Marxist-Feminist Analysis of Sexuality in U. S. Capitalism." *Review of Radical Political Economics* 27, no. 2: 1–37.

———. 1998. "Some Comments on the Role of Lesbianism in Feminist Economic Transformation." *Feminist Economics* 4, no. 2: 83–88.

Mauss, M. 1950. *The Gift: Forms and Functions of Exchange in Ancient Societies*. Trans. I. Cunnison. London: Routledge and Kegan Paul.

Mayer, T. 2001. "Improving Communication in Economics: A Task for Methodologists." *Journal of Economic Methodology* 8, no. 10: 77–84.

Mayhew, A. 1987. "Culture: Core Concept under Attack." *Journal of Economic Issues* 24:587–603.

———. 1998. "Veblen and the Anthropological Perspective." In *The Founding of Institutional Economics: The Leisure Class and Sovereignty*, ed. W. Samuels, 234–49. London: Routledge.

McClintock, A., A. Mufti, and E. Shohat, eds. 1997. *Dangerous Liaisons: Gender, Nation, and Postcolonial Perspectives*. Minneapolis: University of Minnesota Press.

McCloskey, D. N. 1983a. "The Rhetoric of Economics." *Journal of Economic Literature* 21:481–517.

———. 1983b. "The Character of Argument in Modern Economics: How Muth Persuades." In *Argument in Transition: Proceedings of the Third Sum-*

mer Conference on Argumentation. Annandale, Va.: Speech Communications Association.

———. 1984. "The Literary Character of Economics." *Daedalus* 113, no. 3: 97–119.

———. 1985a. *The Rhetoric of Economics.* Madison: University of Wisconsin Press.

———. 1985b. *The Applied Theory of Price.* 2d ed. New York: Macmillan.

———. 1990. *If You're So Smart: The Narrative of Economic Expertise.* Chicago: University of Chicago Press.

———. 1993. "Some Consequences of a Conjective Economics." In *Beyond Economic Man: Feminist Theory and Economics,* ed. M. A. Ferber and J. A. Nelson, 69–93. Chicago: University of Chicago Press.

———. 1994. *Knowledge and Persuasion in Economics.* Cambridge: Cambridge University Press.

———. 1996. *The Vices of Economists, The Virtues of the Bourgeoisie.* Amsterdam: Amsterdam University Press.

———. 1999. "Jack, David, and Judith Looking at Me Looking at Them." In *What Do Economists Know? New Economics of Knowledge,* ed. R. F. Garnett Jr., 60–64. London: Routledge.

———. 2001. "The Genealogy of Postmodernism: An Economist's Guide." In *Postmodernism, Economics, and Knowledge,* ed. S. Cullenberg, J. Amariglio, and D. F. Ruccio, 102–28. London: Routledge.

McIntyre, R. 1992. "Consumption in Contemporary Capitalism: Beyond Marx and Veblen." *Review of Social Economy* 50, no. 1: 40–60.

———. 1999. "A Working Knowledge of Economics?" In *What Do Economists Know? New Economics of Knowledge,* ed. R. F. Garnett Jr., 236–50. London: Routledge.

McNally, D. 1993. *Against the Market: Political Economy, Market Socialism, and the Marxist Critique.* New York: Verso.

Mehta, J. 1993. "Meaning in the Context of Bargaining Games—Narratives in Opposition." In *Economics and Language,* ed. W. Henderson, T. Dudley-Evans, and R. Backhouse, 85–99. London: Routledge.

———. 1999. "Look at Me Look at You." In *What Do Economists Know? New Economics of Knowledge,* ed. R. F. Garnett Jr. 37–59. London: Routledge.

———. 2001. "A Disorderly Household—Voicing the Noise." In *Postmodernism, Economics, and Knowledge,* ed. S. Cullenberg, J. Amariglio, and D. F. Ruccio, 374–98. London: Routledge.

Ménard, C. 1980. "Three Forms of Resistance to Statistics: Say, Cournot, Walras." *History of Political Economy* 12, no. 4: 524–41.

Milberg, W. 1988. "The Language of Economics: Deconstructing the Neoclassical Text." *Social Concept* 4 (June): 33–57.

———. 2001. "Decentering the Market Metaphor in International Economics." In *Postmodernism, Economics. and Knowledge,* ed. S. Cullenberg, J. Amariglio, and D. F. Ruccio, 407–30. London: Routledge.

Miller, D. 1992. *Material Culture and Mass Consumption.* Oxford: Blackwell.

Miller, G. J. 1997. "The Impact of Economics on Contemporary Political Science." *Journal of Economic Literature* 35:1173–204.

Miller, R. 1984. *Analyzing Marx*. Princeton: Princeton University Press.

Milward, B. 2000. *Marxian Political Economy: Theory, History, and Contemporary Relevance*. New York: St. Martin's.

Mini, P. 1991. *Keynes, Bloomsbury, and "The General Theory."* New York: St. Martin's.

Mirowski, P. 1987. "The Philosophical Bases of Institutional Economics." *Journal of Economic Issues* 21:1001–38.

———. 1989. *More Heat Than Light: Economics as Social Physics, Physics as Nature's Economics*. Cambridge: Cambridge University Press.

———. 1990. "Learning the Meaning of a Dollar: Conservation Principles and the Social Theory of Value in Economic Theory." *Social Research* 57, no. 3: 689–717.

———. 1997. "A History of Classical and Frequentist Approaches to Probability in Economics." In *The State of the History of Economics*, ed. J. Henderson, 19–38. London: Routledge.

———. 2001. "Refusing the Gift." In *Postmodernism, Economics, and Knowledge*, ed. S. Cullenberg, J. Amariglio, and D. F. Ruccio, 431–58. London: Routledge.

Mitchell, E. T. 1949. "Criticisms by Mitchell." In *Value: A Cooperative Inquiry*, ed. R. Lepley, 400–14. New York: Columbia University Press.

Moggridge, D. E. 1992. "Correspondence." *Journal of Economic Perspectives* 6, no. 3: 207–8.

Montag, W. 1996. "Beyond Force and Consent: Althusser, Spinoza, Hobbes." In *Postmodern Materialism and the Future of Marxist Theory: Essays in the Althusserian Tradition*, ed. A. Callari and D. F. Ruccio, 91–106. Hanover, N.H.: Wesleyan University Press.

Moore, G. E. 1903. *Principia Ethica*. Cambridge: Cambridge University Press.

Morgan, M. S. 1987. "The Probabilistic Revolution in Economics—An Overview." In *The Probabilistic Revolution*, vol. 2, *Ideas in the Sciences*, ed. L. Kruger, G. Gigerenzer, and M. S. Morgan, 135–37. Cambridge: MIT Press.

———. 1990. *The History of Econometric Ideas*. Cambridge: Cambridge University Press.

Morris, D. 1993. *The Culture of Pain*. Berkeley and Los Angeles: University of California Press.

Moseley, F. 1991. *The Falling Rate of Profit in the Postwar United States Economy*. New York: St. Martin's.

Moseley, N. 1990. *Hopeful Monsters*. London: Martin Secker and Warburg.

Moss, L. S. 1979. "Film and the Transmission of Economic Knowledge: A Report." *Journal of Economic Perspectives* 17, no. 3: 1005–19.

Muth, J. 1961. "Rational Expectations and the Theory of Price Movements." *Econometrica* 29 (July): 315–35.

Nancy, J.-L. 1994. "Corpus." In *Thinking Bodies*, ed. J. K. MacCanell and L. Zakarin, 17–31. Stanford: Stanford University Press.

National Council on Economic Education. 2001. http://www.ncee.net.

Neale, W. 1990. "Absolute Cultural Relativism: Firm Foundation for Valuing and Policy." *Journal of Economic Issues* 24:333–44.

Nelson, J. 1993. "The Study of Choice or the Study of Provisioning? Gender and the Definition of Economics." In *Beyond Economic Man*, ed. M. Ferber and J. Nelson, 23–36. Chicago: University of Chicago Press.

———. 1994. "I, Thou, and Them: Capabilities, Altruism, and Norms in the Economics of Marriage." *American Economic Review* 84, no. 2: 126–31.

———. 1996. *Feminism, Objectivity, and Economics*. London: Routledge.

Nelson, J. A., and S. M. Sheffrin. 1991. "Economic Literacy or Economic Ideology?" *Journal of Economic Perspectives* 5, no. 3: 157–65.

Nicholson, L., ed. 1990. *Feminism/Postmodernism*. London: Routledge.

Nietzsche, F. 1956. *The Birth of Tragedy and the Genealogy of Morals*. Trans. F. Golffing. Garden City, N.Y.: Doubleday.

———. 1966. *Beyond Good and Evil*. Trans. W. Kaufman. New York: Vintage.

———. 1967. *The Will to Power*. New York: Random House.

Norris, C. 1988. *Derrida*. Cambridge: Harvard University Press.

———. 1990. *What's Wrong with Postmodernism: Critical Theory and the Ends of Philosophy*. Baltimore: Johns Hopkins University Press.

———. 1991. *Deconstruction: Theory and Practice*. London: Routledge.

Norris, C., and A. Benjamin. 1989. *What Is Deconstruction?* New York: John Wiley and Son.

North, D. C. 1990. *Institutions, Institutional Change, and Economic Performance*. Cambridge: Cambridge University Press.

Norton, B. 1986. "Steindl, Levine, and the Inner Logic of Accumulation: A Marxian Critique." *Social Concept* 3 (December): 43–66.

———. 1988. "Epochs and Essences: A Review of Marxist Long-Wave and Stagnation Theories." *Cambridge Journal of Economics* 12:203–44.

———. 1992. "Radical Theories of Accumulation and Crisis: Developments and Directions." In *Radical Economics*, ed. B. Roberts and S. Feiner, 155–198. Boston: Kluwer.

———. 1995. "Late Capitalism and Postmodernism: Jameson/Mandel." In *Marxism in the Postmodern Age: Confronting the New World Order*, ed. A. Callari, S. Cullenberg, and C. Biewener, 59–70. New York: Guilford Press.

———. 2001. "Reading Marx for Class." In *Re/presenting Class: Essays in Postmodern Marxism*, ed. J. K. Gibson-Graham, S. A. Resnick, and R. D. Wolff, 23–55. Durham, N.C.: Duke University Press.

O'Donnell, R. M. 1991. "Keynes on Probability, Expectations, and Uncertainty." In *Keynes as Philosopher-Economist*, ed. R. M. O'Donnell, 3–60. New York: St. Martin's.

Ortner, S. B. 1972. "Is Female to Male as Nature Is to Culture?" *Feminist Studies* 1, no. 2: 5–31.

———. 1995. "So, *Is* Female to Male as Nature Is to Culture?" Paper presented at the American Anthropological Association Meetings, Washington, D.C.

———. 1996. *Making Gender: The Politics and Erotics of Culture*. Boston: Beacon Press.

Osteen, M., and M. Woodmansee. 1999. "Taking Account of the New Economic Criticism: An Historical Introduction." In *The New Economic Criticism: Studies at the Intersection of Literature and Economics*, ed. M. Woodmansee and M. Osteen, 3–50. London: Routledge.

Ozawa, T. 1992. "Correspondence." *Journal of Economic Perspectives* 6, no. 3: 210–11.

Park, M.-S., and S. Kayatekin. 2002. "Organicism, Uncertainty, and 'Societal Interactionism': A Derridean Perspective." In *Beyond Keynes*, vol. 2, *Keynes, Uncertainty, and the Global Economy*, ed. S. Dow and J. Hillard. Cheltenham, U.K.: Edward Elgar.

Peffer, R. G. 1990. *Marxism, Morality, and Social Justice*. Princeton: Princeton University Press.

Peterson, J., and D. Brown, eds. 1994. *The Economic Status of Women under Capitalism: Institutional Economics and Feminist Theory*. Cheltenham, U.K.: Edward Elgar.

Peterson, W. H., ed. 1982. *Economic Education: Investing in the Future*. Knoxville: University of Tennessee Press.

Pickering, A. 1997. "Concepts and the Mangle of Practice: Constructing Quaternions." In *Mathematics, Science, and Postclassical Theory*, ed. B. H. Smith and A. Plotnitsky. Durham, N.C.: Duke University Press.

Pietrykowski, B. 1994. "Consuming Culture: Postmodernism, Post-Fordism, and Economics." *Rethinking Marxism* 7, no. 1: 62–80.

Plotnitsky, A. 1994. *Complementarity: Anti-epistemology after Bohr and Derrida*. Durham, N.C.: Duke University Press.

Polanyi, K. 1957. *The Great Transformation*. Boston: Beacon Press.

Poovey, M. 1998. *A History of the Modern Fact: Problems of Knowledge in the Sciences of Wealth and Society*. Chicago: University of Chicago Press.

Porter, T. A. 1990. "The Quantification of Uncertainty after 1700: Statistics Socially Constructed?" In *Acting under Uncertainty: Multidisciplinary Conceptions*, ed. G. M. von Furstenberg, 45–75. Boston: Kluwer.

Porter, T. M. 1995. *Trust in Numbers: The Pursuit of Objectivity in Science and Public Life*. Princeton: Princeton University Press.

Portoghesi, P. 1983. *Postmodern: The Architecture of the Postindustrial Society*. New York: Rizzoli.

Posner, R. A. 1992. *Sex and Reason*. Cambridge: Harvard University Press.

Power, M., ed. 1994. *Accounting and Science: Natural Inquiry and Commercial Reason*. Cambridge: Cambridge University Press.

Pujol, M. 1992. *Feminism and Anti-feminism in Early Economic Thought*. Cheltenham, U.K.: Edward Elgar.

———. 1995. "Into the Margin!" In *Out of the Margin: Feminist Perspectives in Economics*, ed. E. Kuiper and J. Sap, with S. Feiner, N. Ott, and Z. Tzannatos, 17–34. London: Routledge.

Rabinbach, A. 1990. *The Human Motor, Energy, Fatigue, and the Origins of Modernity*. New York: Basic Books.

Rabinow, P., ed. 1984. *The Foucault Reader*. New York: Random House.

Ramsey, F. 1978. "Truth and Probability." In *Philosophical Papers: F. P. Ramsey*, ed. D. H. Mellor, 52–94. London: Routledge and Kegan Paul.

Ramstad, Y. 1989. " 'Reasonable Value' versus 'Instrumental Value': Competing Paradigms in Institutional Economics." *Journal of Economic Issues* 23:761–77.

Ramstad, Y. 1995. "John R. Commons's Puzzling Inconsequentiality as an Economic Theorist." *Journal of Economic Issues* 29:991–1012.

Rayner, S. 1990. "Risk in Cultural Perspective." In *Acting under Uncertainty: Multidisciplinary Conceptions*, ed. G. M. von Furstenberg, 161–79. Boston: Kluwer.

Resnick, S. A., and R. D. Wolff. 1987. *Knowledge and Class: A Marxian Critique of Political Economy*. Chicago: University of Chicago Press.

———. 1988. "Communism: Between Class and Classless." *Rethinking Marxism* 1, no. 1: 14–42.

———. 1992. "Everythingism, or Better Still, Overdetermination." *New Left Review*, no. 195 (September–October): 124–26.

———. 1993. "State Capitalism in the USSR? A High-Stakes Debate." *Rethinking Marxism* 6, no. 2: 46–68.

———. 2001. "Struggles in the USSR: Communisms Attempted and Undone." In *Re/presenting Class: Essays in Postmodern Marxism*, ed. J. K. Gibson-Graham, S. A. Resnick, and R. D. Wolff, 264–90. Durham, N.C.: Duke University Press.

Riesman, D. 1960. *Thorstein Veblen: A Critical Interpretation*. New York: Seabury Press.

Riley, D. 1988. *Am I That Name? Feminism and the Category of "Women" in History*. Minneapolis: University of Minnesota Press.

Roberts, B. 1987. "Marx after Steedman: Separating Marxism from 'Surplus Theory.'" *Capital and Class* 32:84–103.

———. 1988. "What Is Profit?" *Rethinking Marxism* 1, no. 1: 136–51.

Roche, J. 1988. "Value, Money, and Credit in the First Part of *Capital*." *Rethinking Marxism* 1, no. 4: 126–43.

Roemer, J. E. 1988. *Free to Lose: An Introduction to Marxist Economic Philosophy*. Cambridge: Harvard University Press.

———, ed. 1996. *Equal Shares: Making Market Socialism Work*. New York: Verso.

Rorty, R. 1979. *Philosophy and the Mirror of Nature*. Princeton: Princeton University Press.

———1982. "Pragmatism, Relativism, and Irrationalism." In *Consequences of Pragmatism*. Minneapolis: University of Minnesota Press.

———. 1991. *Objectivity, Relativism, and Truth: Philosophical Papers*. Vol. 1. Cambridge: Cambridge University Press.

———. 2001. "Response to Daniel Conway." In *Richard Rorty: Critical Dialogues*, ed. M. Festenstein and S. Thompson, 89–92. Cambridge, Mass.: Polity Press.

Rose, M. A. 1991. *The Post-Modern and the Post-Industrial: A Critical Analysis*. Cambridge: Cambridge University Press.

Rosenau, P. M. 1992. *Post-modernism and the Social Sciences: Insights, Inroads, and Intrusions*. Princeton: Princeton University Press.

Ross, D., ed. 1994. *Modernist Impulses in the Human Sciences, 1870–1930*. Baltimore: Johns Hopkins University Press.

Rossetti, J. 1990. "Deconstructing Robert Lucas." In *Economics as Discourse: An Analysis of the Language of Economists*, ed. W. Samuels, 225–43. Boston: Kluwer.

————. 1992. "Deconstruction, Rhetoric, and Economics." In *Post-Popperian Methodology of Economics: Recovering Practice*, ed. N. de Marchi, 211–34. Boston: Kluwer.

————. 2001. "Postmodernism and Feminist Economics." In *Postmodernism, Economics, and Knowledge*, ed. S. Cullenberg, J. Amariglio, and D. F. Ruccio, 305–26. London: Routledge.

Rotman, B. 1993. *Ad Infinitum, The Ghost in Turing's Machine*. Stanford: Stanford University Press.

Ruccio, D. F. 1986a. "Planning and Class in Transitional Societies." *Research in Political Economy*, vol. 9, 235–52. Greenwich: JAI Press.

————. 1986b. "Essentialism and Socialist Economic Planning: A Methodological Critique of Optimal Planning Theory." *Research in the History of Economic Thought and Methodology*, vol. 4, 85–108. Greenwich: JAI Press.

————. 1988. "The Merchant of Venice, or Marxism in the Mathematical Mode." *Rethinking Marxism* 1, no. 4: 37–68.

————. 1991. "Postmodernism and Economics." *Journal of Post Keynesian Economics* 13, no. 4: 495–510.

————. 1992. "Failure of Socialism, Future of Socialists?" *Rethinking Marxism* 5, no. 2: 7–22.

————. 1995. "Marx's Critical/Dialectical Procedure: A Review Essay." *Research in the History of Economic Thought and Methodology*, vol. 13, 311–17. Greenwich: JAI Press.

————. 1998. "Deconstruction." In *The Handbook of Economic Methodology*, ed. J. B. Davis, D. W. Hands, and U. Mäki, 89–92. Cheltenham, U.K.: Edward Elgar.

————. 2003. "Globalization and Imperialism." *Rethinking Marxism* 15, no. 1, forthcoming.

Ruccio, D. F., and J. Amariglio. 1999. "Literary/Cultural 'Economies,' Economic Discourse, and the Question of Marxism." In *The New Economic Criticism: Studies at the Intersection of Literature and Economics*, ed. M. Woodmansee and M. Osteen, 381–400. London: Routledge.

Ruccio, D. F., and A. Callari, eds. 1996. *Postmodern Materialism and the Future of Marxist Theory: Essays in the Althusserian Tradition*. Middletown, Conn.: Wesleyan University Press.

Ruccio, D. F., J. Graham, and J. Amariglio. 1996. " 'The Good, the Bad, and the Different': Reflections on Economic and Aesthetic Value." In *The Value of Culture: On the Relationship between Economics and Arts*, ed. A. Klamer, 56–73. Amsterdam: Amsterdam University Press.

Russell, B., and A. N. Whitehead. 1910–13. *Principia Mathematica*. 3 vols. Cambridge: Cambridge University Press.

Rutherford, M. 1998. "Institutionalism." In *The Handbook of Economic Methodology*, ed. J. B. Davis, D. W. Hands, and U. Mäki, 249–52. Cheltenham, U.K.: Edward Elgar.

Sahlins, M. 1976. *Culture and Practical Reason*. Chicago: University of Chicago Press.

Said, E. 1978. *Orientalism*. New York: Vintage.

Salanti, A., and E. Screpanti, eds. 1997. *Pluralism and Economics: New Perspectives in History and Methodology*. Cheltenham, U.K.: Edward Elgar.

Samson, M. 1995. "Towards a 'Friday' Model of International Trade: A Feminist Deconstruction of Race and Gender Bias in the Robinson Crusoe Trade Allegory." *Canadian Journal of Economics* 28, no. 1: 143–58.

Samuels, W. 1988. "An Essay on the Nature and Significance of the Normative Nature of Economics." *Journal of Post Keynesian Economics* 10, no. 3: 347–54.

———. 1990. "The Self-Referentiability of Thorstein Veblen's Theory of the Preconceptions of Economic Science." *Journal of Economic Issues* 24:695–718.

———. 1996. "Postmodernism and Economics: A Middlebrow View." *Journal of Economic Methodology* 3, no. 1: 113–20.

———, ed. 1990. *Economics as Discourse: An Analysis of the Language of Economists*. Boston: Kluwer.

———, ed. 1998. *The Founding of Institutional Economics: The Leisure Class and Sovereignty*. London: Routledge.

Samuelson, P. A. 1983. *Foundations of Economic Analysis*. Cambridge: Harvard University Press.

———. 1997. "Credo of a Lucky Textbook Author." *Journal of Economic Perspectives* 11, no. 2: 153–60.

———. 1998. "How *Foundations* Came to Be." *Journal of Economic Literature* 36:1375–86.

Sandler, I. 1996. *Art of the Postmodern Era: From the Late 1960s to the Early 1990s*. New York: Harper and Row.

Sargent, T. J. 1993. *Bounded Rationality in Macroeconomics*. Oxford: Clarendon Press.

Sass, L. A. 1992. *Madness and Modernism: Insanity in the Light of Modern Art, Literature, and Thought*. Cambridge: Harvard University Press.

Savage, L. J. 1954. *The Foundations of Statistics*. New York: Wiley.

Scarry, E. 1985. *The Body in Pain: The Making and Unmaking of the World*. Oxford: Oxford University Press.

Schick, F. 1988. "Self-Knowledge, Uncertainty, and Choice." In *Decision, Probability, and Utility: Selected Readings*, ed. P. Gärdenfors and N.-E. Sahlin, 270–86. Cambridge: Cambridge University Press.

Schlicht, E. 1998. *On Custom in the Economy*. Oxford: Oxford University Press.

Schrift, A. D. 1997a. "Introduction: Why Gift?" In *The Logic of the Gift*, ed. A. D. Schrift, 1–22. London: Routledge.

———, ed. 1997b. *The Logic of the Gift*. London: Routledge.

Sen, A. 1977. "Rational Fools: A Critique of the Behavioural Foundations of Economic Theory." *Philosophy and Public Affairs* 6, no. 4: 317–44.

———. 1985. *Commodities and Capabilities*. New York: North-Holland.

———. 1987. *On Ethics and Economics*. Oxford: Blackwell.

———. 1990. "Rational Behavior." In *The New Palgrave: Utility and Probability*, ed. J. Eatwell, M. Milgate, and P. Newman, 198–216. New York: W. W. Norton.

———. 1991. "Economic Methodology: Heterogeneity and Relevance." *Methodus* 3, no. 1: 67–80.

———. 1992. *Inequality Reexamined*. Cambridge: Harvard University Press.

Sent, E.-M. 1997. "Sargent versus Simon: Bounded Rationality Unbound." *Cambridge Journal of Economics* 21, no. 3: 323–38.

———. 1998. "Sargent and the Unbearable Lightness of Symmetry." *Journal of Economic Methodology* 5, no. 1: 93–114.

Shackle, G. L. S. 1961. *Decision, Order, and Time in Human Affairs*. Cambridge: Cambridge University Press.

———. 1966. *The Nature of Economic Thought: Selected Papers, 1955–64*. Cambridge: Cambridge University Press.

———. 1972. *Epistemics and Economics*. Cambridge: Cambridge University Press.

———. 1990. *Time, Expectations, and Uncertainty in Economics: Selected Essays*. Ed. J. L. Ford. Cheltenham, U.K.: Edward Elgar.

Shaikh, A. M., and E. A. Tonak. 1994. *Measuring the Wealth of Nations: The Political Economy of National Accounts*. Cambridge: Cambridge University Press.

Shapiro, M. J. 1993. *Reading "Adam Smith": Desire, History, and Value*. Modernity and Political Thought, vol. 4. Newbury Park, Calif.: Sage Publications.

Shapiro, N. 1978. "Keynes and Equilibrium Economics." *Australian Economic Papers* 17 (December): 207–23.

Sharma, A., and R. Woodward. 2001. *New Political Economy* 6, no. 1: 119–30.

Shildrick, M., and J. Price, eds. 1998. *Vital Signs: Feminist Reconfigurations of the Bio/logical Body*. Edinburgh: Edinburgh University Press.

Shiller, R. J. 1981. "Do Stock Prices Move Too Much to Be Justified by Subsequent Changes in Dividends?" *American Economic Review* 71, no. 3: 421–36.

———. 1990. "Market Volatility and Investor Behavior." *American Economic Review* 80, no. 2: 58–62.

Shuklian, S. 1995. "Marx, Dewey, and the Instrumentalist Approach to Political Economy." *Journal of Economic Issues* 29:781–806.

Shumway, D. 1993. *Michel Foucault*. Charlottesville: University Press of Virginia.

Silk, L. 1986. "Communicating Economic Ideas and Controversies." *American Economic Review* 76, no. 2: 141–44.

Sim, S., ed. 1999. *The Routledge Dictionary of Postmodern Thought*. London: Routledge.

Simon, H. A. 1976. "From Substantive to Procedural Rationality." In *Method and Appraisal in Economics*, ed. S. Latsis, 129–48. Cambridge: Cambridge University Press.

———. 1978. "Rationality as Process and Product of Thought." *American Economic Review* 68, no. 2: 1–16.

———. 1991. *Models of My Life*. New York: Basic Books.

Skidelsky, R. 1983. *John Maynard Keynes*, vol. 1, *Hopes Betrayed, 1883–1920*. London: Macmillan.

Smart, B. 1993. *Michel Foucault*. London: Routledge.

Smith, A. 1965 (1776). *The Wealth of Nations*. New York: Random House.

———. 1976. *The Theory of Moral Sentiments*. Indianapolis: Liberty Classics.

Smith, B. H. 1988. *Contingencies of Value*. Cambridge: Harvard University Press.

Smith, D. 1990. *The Conceptual Practices of Power: A Feminist Sociology of Knowledge*. Boston: Northeastern University Press.

Sofianou, E. 1995. "Postmodernism and the Notion of Rationality in Economics." *Cambridge Journal of Economics* 19, no. 3: 373–89.

Solo, R. A. 1991. *The Philosophy of Science and Economics*. Armonk, N.Y.: M. E. Sharpe.

Solow, R. M. 1991. "Discussion Notes on 'Formalization.' " *Methodus* 3, no. 1: 30–1.

Spary, E. 1996. "Political, Natural, and Bodily Economies." In *Cultures of Natural History*, ed. N. Jardine, J. A. Secord, and E. C. Spary, 178–96. Cambridge: Cambridge University Press.

Spivak, G. C. 1999. *A Critique of Postcolonial Reason: A Critique of the Vanishing Present*. Cambridge: Harvard University Press.

Sproul, C. 1999. "Mandating Knowledge: The Role of the Advanced Placement Exam in Secondary Economics Education." In *What Do Economists Know? New Economics of Knowledge*, ed. R. F. Garnett Jr., 215–22. London: Routledge.

Squires, J., ed. 1993. *Principled Positions: Postmodernism and the Rediscovery of Value*. London: Lawrence and Wishart.

Stafford, B. M. 1991. *Body Criticism: Imaging the Unseen in Enlightenment Art and Medicine*. Cambridge: MIT Press.

Stanfield, J. R. 1986. *The Economic Thought of Karl Polanyi: Lives and Livelihoods*. New York: St. Martin's.

———. 1989. "Recent U.S. Marxist Economics in Veblenian Perspective." In *Radical Institutionalism: Contemporary Voices*, ed. W. M. Dugger, 83–104. New York: Greenwood Press.

Stigler, S. M. 1986. *The History of Statistics: The Measurement of Uncertainty before 1900*. Cambridge: Harvard University Press.

Strassman, D. 1993. "Not a Free Market: The Rhetoric of Disciplinary Authority in Economics." In *Beyond Economic Man: Feminist Theory and Economics*, ed. M. A. Ferber and J. A. Nelson, 54–68. Chicago: University of Chicago Press.

Strassman, D., and L. Polanyi. 1995. "The Economist as Storyteller: What the Texts Reveal." In *Out of the Margin: Feminist Perspectives in Economics*, ed. E. Kuiper and J. Sap, with S. Feiner, N. Ott, and Z. Tzannatos, 129–50. London: Routledge.

Strathern, M. 1990. *The Gender of the Gift*. Berkeley and Los Angeles: University of California Press.

Sugden, R. 1991. "Rational Choice: A Survey." *Economic Journal* 101 (July): 751–85.

Sweezy, P. M. 1970. *The Theory of Capitalist Development*. New York: Monthly Review Press.

Thaler, R. H. 1994. *Quasi Rational Economics*. New York: Russell Sage Foundation.

Thompson, G. 1982. "The Firm as a 'Dispersed' Social Agency." *Economy and Society* 11 (August): 233–50.

Tilman, R. 1974. "Value Theory, Planning, and Reform: Ayres as Incrementalist and Utopian." In *Journal of Economic Issues* 8:689–706.

Todd, J. 1986. *Sensibility: An Introduction*. London: Methuen.

Tool, M. R. 1986. *Essays in Social Value Theory: A Neoinstitutionalist Contribution*. Armonk, N.Y.: M. E. Sharpe.

———. 1993a. "The Theory of Instrumental Value: Extensions, Clarifications." In *Institutional Economics: Theory, Method, Policy*, ed. M. Tool, 199–59. Boston: Kluwer.

———. 2000. *Value and Economic Progress: The Institutional Economics of J. Fagg Foster*. Boston: Kluwer.

———, ed. 1993b. *Institutional Economics: Theory, Method, Policy*. Boston: Kluwer.

Toulmin, S. 1990. *Cosmopolis: The Hidden Agenda of Modernity*. Chicago: University of Chicago Press.

Tribe, K. 1978. *Land, Labour, and Economic Discourse*. London: Routledge and Kegan Paul.

van Staveren, Irene. 1999. *Caring for Economics: An Aristotelian Perspective*. Delft, The Netherlands: Uitgeverij Eburon.

Vandevelde, A., ed. 2000. *Gifts and Interests*. Leuven: Peeters.

Varoufakis, Y. 1993. "Modern and Postmodern Challenges to Game Theory." *Erkenntnis* 38, no. 3: 371–404.

———. 2002. "Why Critics of Economics Can Ill-Afford the 'Postmodern Turn.' " *Post-autistic Economics Review*, no. 13, article 1. http://www.btinternet.com/pae_news/review/issue13.htm (accessed 11 June 2002).

Vaughn, K. I. 1987. "Invisible Hand." In *The New Palgrave: The Invisible Hand*, ed. J. Eatwell, M. Milgate, and P. Newman, 168–172. New York: W. W. Norton.

Waller, W. T., Jr. 1982. "The Evolution of the Veblenian Dichotomy." *Journal of Economic Issues* 16:757–71.

———. 1989. "Methodological Aspects of Radical Institutionalism." In *Radical Institutionalism: Contemporary Voices*, ed. W. M. Dugger, 39–49. New York: Greenwood Press.

———. 1999. "Institutional Economics, Feminism, and Overdetermination." *Journal of Economic Issues* 33:835–44.

Waller, W., and A. Jennings. 1990. "On the Possibility of a Feminist Economics: The Convergence of Institutional and Feminist Methodology." *Journal of Economic Issues* 24:613–22.

Walstad, W. B. 1992. "Economics Instruction in High Schools." *Journal of Economic Literature* 30:2019–51.

Walstad, W. B., and J. C. Soper, eds. 1991. *Effective Economic Education in the Schools*. Washington, D.C.: Joint Council on Economic Education and National Education Association.

Watkins, E. 1998. *Everyday Exchanges: Marketwork and Capitalist Common Sense*. Stanford: Stanford University Press.

Weatherford, R. 1982. *Philosophical Foundations of Probability Theory*. London: Routledge and Kegan Paul.

Weedon, C. 1997. *Feminist Practice and Poststructuralist Theory*. 2d ed. Oxford: Blackwell.

Weeks, J. 1981. *Capital and Exploitation*. London: Edward Arnold.

Weiner, A. B. 1976. *Women of Value, Men of Renown: New Perspectives in Tro-briand Exchange*. Austin: University of Texas Press.

———. 1988. *The Trobrianders of Papua New Guinea*. Chicago: Holt, Rinehart and Winston.

———. 1992. *Inalienable Possessions: The Paradox of Keeping While Giving*. Berkeley and Los Angeles: University of California Press.

Weintraub, E. R. 1979. *Microfoundations*. Cambridge: Cambridge University Press.

———. 1985. *General Equilibrium Analysis*. Cambridge: Cambridge University Press.

———. 1991. *Stabilizing Dynamics*. Cambridge: Cambridge University Press.

———. 1992. "Roger Backhouse's Straw Herring." *Methodus* 4, no. 2: 53–57.

———. 1997. "Is 'Is a Precursor of' a Transitive Relation?" In *Mathematics, Science, and Postclassical Theory*, ed. B. H. Smith and A. Plotnitsky, 173–88. Durham, N.C.: Duke University Press.

West, C. 1989. *The American Evasion of Philosophy: A Genealogy of Pragmatism*. Madison: University of Wisconsin Press.

Wheale, N., ed. 1995. *The Postmodern Arts: An Introductory Reader*. London: Routledge.

White, H. 1975. *Metahistory: The Historical Imagination in Nineteenth-Century Europe*. Baltimore: Johns Hopkins University Press.

White, M. V. 1994. "The Moment of Richard Jennings: The Production of Jevons's Marginalist Economic Agent." In *Natural Images in Economic Thought: "Markets Read in Tooth and Claw,"* ed. P. Mirowski, 197–230. Cambridge: Cambridge University Press.

Wilber, C. K., and R. S. Harrison. 1978. "The Methodological Basis of Institutional Economics: Pattern Model, Storytelling, and Holism." *Journal of Economic Issues* 12:61–89.

Wilde, L. 1998. *Ethical Marxism and Its Radical Critics*. New York: St. Martin's.

Wiles, M. 1981. " 'Rational Expectations' as a Counterrevolution." In *The Crisis in Economic Theory*, ed. D. Bell and I. Kristol, 81–96. New York: Basic Books.

Williams, R. M. 1993. "Race, Deconstruction, and the Emergent Agenda of Feminist Economics." In *Beyond Economic Man*, ed. M. A. Ferber and J. A. Nelson, ed. 144–53. Chicago: University of Chicago Press.

Williamson, O. E. 1985. *The Economic Institutions of Capitalism: Firms, Markets, Relational Contracting*. New York: Free Press.

Wilson, H. T. 1991. *Marx's Critical/Dialectical Procedure*. London: Routledge.

Wilson, L. 1996. "John Dewey's Pragmatism and Economic Method: Modernism and Postmodernism in Economics." Ph.D. diss., University of Massachusetts, Amherst.

Winslow, E. G. 1986. "Keynes and Freud: Psychoanalysis and Keynes's Account of the 'Animal Spirits' of Capitalism." *Social Research* 53, no. 4: 549–78.

Winterson, J. 1997. *Gut Symmetries: A Novel*. New York: Alfred A. Knopf.

Wise, M. N. 1995. *The Values of Precision*. Princeton: Princeton University Press.

Wittgenstein, L. 1922. *Tractatus Logico-Philosophicus*. London: Routledge and Kegan Paul.

Wittig, M. 1992. *The Straight Mind and Other Essays*. London: Harvester Wheatsheaf.

Wolff, R. D., and S. A. Resnick. 1987. *Economics: Marxian versus Neoclassical*. Baltimore: Johns Hopkins University Press.

Wolff, R. D., B. Roberts, and A. Callari. 1982. "Marx's (not Ricardo's) Transformation Problem: A Radical Reconceptualization." *History of Political Economy* 14, no. 4: 564–82.

———. 1998. "The Transformation Trinity: Value, Value Form, and Price." In *Marxian Economics: A Reappraisal. Essays on Volume II of Capital*, vol. 2, *Price, Profits, and Dynamics*, ed. R. Bellofiore, 43–56. New York: St. Martin's.

Wong, S. 1978. *The Foundations of Paul Samuelson's Revealed Preference Theory*. Boston: Routledge and Kegan Paul.

Wood, A. 1972. "The Marxian Critique of Justice." *Philosophy and Public Affairs* 1, no. 3: 244–82.

———. 1984. "Marx and Morality." In *Darwin, Marx, and Freud*, ed. A. Caplan and B. Jennings, 131–44. New York: Plenum Press.

Woodmansee, M., and M. Osteen. 1999a. "Taking Account of the New Economic Criticism: An Historical Introduction." In *The New Economic Criticism: Studies at the Intersection of Literature and Economics*, 3–50. London: Routledge.

———, eds. 1999b. *The New Economic Criticism: Studies at the Intersection of Literature and Economics*. London: Routledge.

Woolf, V. 1924. *Mr. Bennett and Mrs. Brown*. London: Hogarth Press.

Xenos, N. 1989. *Scarcity and Modernity*. London: Routledge.

Yonay, Y. P. 1998. *The Struggle over the Soul of Economics: Institutionalist and Neoclassical Economists in America between the Wars*. Princeton: Princeton University Press.

Zaniello, T. 1996. *Working Stiffs, Union Maids, Reds, and Riffraff: An Organized Guide to Films about Labor*. Ithaca, N.Y.: Cornell University Press.

Zelizer, V. A. 1994. *The Social Meaning of Money*. New York: Basic Books.

Index

academic economics, 53, 252–88, 290, 296; and attack on "ersatz" economics, 255–60, 281; as disinterested, 257, 268; and everyday economics, 259, 275–79, 281 299; and fear of the masses, 279; and globalization debate, 252–53; postmodern notion of, 294; privileging of, 267, 281; public dissemination of, 263–65; and testing of economic knowledge, 260–62

Adaman, Fikret, 297

Adorno, Theodor, 6

Advertising Council, 262–63, 274, 279

Aiken, Henry David, 171

alienation: in capitalism, 216; and commodity fetishism, 232; Marx on, 231

Allen, R.G.D., 103

Althusser, Louis, 108; and critique of theoretical humanism, 47–48, 109; and decentered subject, 49, 249; and Marxian epistemology, 250; and overdetermination, 46, 247; "process without a subject" in, 247; *Reading Capital*, 40n.58

altruism, 8; in neoclassical theory of the household, 147; and self-interest, 148

Amariglio, Jack, 10n, 48n.73, 50, 174n.5, 248, 298

Andrew, Edward, 171n.2, 205n.35

"animal spirits": and Freudian psychoanalysis, 73n.13; in Keynes, 63, 72n.11, 72n.12, 104; in Marx, 72n.11

anthropology: and institutionalist economics, 185n; of markets, 236–37

aporias: deconstruction of, 18; in economics, 2, 3, 54, 290, 296

Aristotle, 117n, 172, 209n

Arrow, Kenneth, 33n, 52; criticism of Knight, 61, 63; the fragmented body in, 110, 113–19, 292; *General Competitive Equilibrium* (with Hahn), 110, 117–18

Arrow-Debreu model, 111; postmodern conception of body in, 113–19, 134

artifacts of everyday economics, examples of, 259, 269, 270, 271, 272–73, 285–88

ascetic ideal: in Nietzsche's genealogy of morals, 204–06, 210; science as part of, 212

Austrian economics, 43n.67, 76, 219–21, 254, 289, 294, 296; the body in, 93, 110; and critique of neoclassical economics, 219–21; disorder and order in, 219, 221; and feminist economics, 139n; and Keynes, 77n.22; modernism of, 89; postmodern moments of, 220; subjectivism of, 93, 221

Ayres, C. E., 171, 175, 183, 198

Bachelard, Gaston, 39

Backhouse, Roger: *Economics and Language*, 26; on power in economics, 41n.62

Bacon, Francis, *Three Figures and a Portrait*, 120

Badgett, M.V.L., 130

Bakhtin, Mikhail, 269n.19, 274

Balibar, Etienne, 109, 249

Barnes, Barry, 43

Bataille, Georges, 125, 156n; *Erotism*, 128; on labor and libidinality, 127–28

Baudrillard, Jean, 237n.27, 245n.39; and productionism of Marxism, 125

Becker, Gary, 46; as "postmodern economist," 7

Benería, Lourdes, 153n

Benhabib, Seyla, 141

Beniger, James, 12n24

Bentham, Jeremy, 104

Bergeron, Suzanne, 16n, 153n, 164; 267

Berman, Marshall, 291

Bernstein, Michael, 266n.14

Berti, A. E., 261n.5

Biewener, Carole, 48n.74, 247

Blank, Rebecca, 165n

Blaug, Mark, 33n.52, 98n, 99n, 258n.1; on postmodernism, 54

Blendon, Robert, 263, 277

body: in Arrow and Debreu, 110–19, 292; in classical economics, 93–94, 120–24; and denial of the feminine, 142, 161;

body (cont'd)
desiring, 96–100, 102, 109, 110, 140–
41; disappearance in modern economics
of, 92–109; discursivity of, 100, 108; in
economics, 102, 145–46, 290, 299; in
feminist economics, 100, 129–33; feminists on, 49, 162; Foucault on, 48, 203n;
as fragmented and decentered in economics, 13n, 23, 92–134; "full," 101, 123,
136; gendering of, 129–33; 162–63; as
inside-out, 112, 119; in Keynes, 72, 292;
laboring, 96, 109, 124–29; machinic conception of, 116–17; in Marx, 128–29;
mind and, 140–46; in neoclassical economics, 53, 92–136, 143–44, 162; nor-
mativity of European, male, 100; as organic unity, 123; postmodern conception
of, 92–136, 292, 294; and power, 143–
44; producing, 110–17; in Smith, 92; social, 121, 146; story of "fall from grace"
in economics of, 102–9; unfixity of, 108,
128n. See also subject
Boettke, Peter: 221n.8
Bombi, A. S., 261n.5
Booth, William James, 143n
Bordo, Susan, 72
bounded rationality, 1, 91n
bounded uncertainty, in Shackle,
66–67
Bourdieu, Pierre, 245
Brooks, Peter: Body Works, 98; on story of
"fall" of body in modernity, 101–2
Brown, Stephen, 4n
Brown, Vivienne, 75n.18; Adam Smith's
Discourse, 25
Buchanan, James, 32n.49
Burczak, Theodore, 52n.80, 77n.22
Bush, Paul, and institutionalist conception
of science, 197–98
Butler, Judith, 48–49, 168; on bodies and
discourse, 100; and decentered subject,
49, 167

Caldwell, Bruce, 99
Callari, Antonio, 159, 176n, 226n.16, 247;
on Althusser's "postmodern materialism," 247n; on commodity fetishism,
248; on the impossibility of the gift, 155,
158
Canguilhem, Georges, 39
capitalism, 4, 5, 216–51; and accumulation
of capital, 216, 228–29, 241; alienation

in, 216–17, 223; anarchy of production
in, 216–17, 223, 225, 230; circulation
and production in, 222–25, 230; class
processes of, 250; and commodity fetishism, 216, 232–33; competition in, 225–
30, 239–44; creation of "false" needs in,
216; crises in, 216, 224–27, 230; decentered subject in, 232; disorderliness of,
88, 223, 225–27, 250; and distinction
from socialism, 216–17, 230, 250, 290;
distribution in, 230; enterprises in, 224–
29, 239–44; exploitation in, 217, 228,
229–30; fragmentation in, 216–17, 223,
225; and globalization, 6, 9, 228; instability of, 216, 226–27, 229; irrationality
of, 226–27, 229; "late," 5, 10; markets
in, 216, 225, 230; in Marxian economics, 216–51; 292; order in, 111, 223,
226–27, 229, 236; and self-expansion of
value, 228; as self-reproducing economy,
163–64; surplus-value in, 223–24, 226,
228–29; uncertainty in, 223; value in,
224, 226
Carabelli, Anna, 78, 80, 85n.30
caring: economic value of, 156; in feminized subjectivity, 148; and gift economy, 155
Carnap, Rudolf, 35–38; "as if" hypotheses
in, 34–35; An Introduction to the Philosophy of Science, 35; reductionism in, 36;
theory of probability of, 81
Carson, David, The End of Print, 20–21
Carter, Michael, 90
Cartesian ego/subject: and Marxian economics, 231; in modern economics, 167,
267n.16
Castells, Manuel, 6n.10
cause(s): in Carnap, 35, 38, 38n; and determinism, 45; language of, 34; as not deducible from effects, 248; and overdetermination, 73
centering: in Marxian economics, 222; of
subject, 67, 231–33
certainty: as discursive construction, 80; in
Keynesian economics, 55; and Marxist
epistemology, 250; in neoclassical economics, 55; and probability, 57; and
rational decision-making, 88; and
uncertainty, 58
Charusheela, S., 42n.64
Chicago School, 188, 191, 254,
298

Cilliers, Paul, 11n.23
civil society, 144; feminizing of, 142; and "invisible hand," 218
Cixous, Hélène, 138; on the gift and the masculinism of "return," 156
class(es), 6n.12; in capitalism, 217n.1; and economic determinism, 47; as entry point, 46; fundamental and subsumed, 240; and morality, 180; in socialism, 217n.1, 234
classical political economy: the body in, 93–94, 102, 109–10, 112, 121–24; desire and labor in, 102, 124; passions, interests, and sentiments in, 102–3, 121, 123; and Robinson Crusoe, 140; and value theory, 124, 174; the "whole human" in, 102
Cleland, T. M., 18–19
Clower, Robert, 2n.5
Coddington, Alan, 65, 69–70, 74, 86
Colander, David, 289n
commodification: and alienation, 232; as cause of decentered subject, 14; of culture, 293; as key feature of postmodernism, 5–8. See also markets
commodity fetishism, 232–33; in capitalism, 216; and "false consciousness," 232; postmodern reading of, 248–49
Commons, John R., 175, 186n, 198n.32, 214; concept of "reasonable value" in, 183
competition: Austrian view of, 221; disorderly, 239–44; between enterprises, 228, 239–41; in Marxian economics, 226–29, 234–44; neoclassical view of, 221; as normative ideal, 179; orderly process of, 242; within enterprises, 241
Cooper, Brian, 12n.25
Corlett, William, 231n.19
Cornwall, Richard, on queer political economy, 130n
Cournot, Augustin, 60
Crotty, James, 58n.7
Cullenberg, Stephen, 11n20, 26n.43, 50, 52n.80, 225n, 240, 247; 297–98
culture, 6n.12; and capitalism, 9; and commodification, 7; spread of global capitalist, 18

Dasgupta, Indraneel, 11n.20
Daston, Lorraine, 60n.8
Davidson, Paul, 58n.7, 66, 71

Davis, John, 85n.30, 289n, 297n.9; Theory of the Individual in Economics, 297n.9
Debreu, Gerard: fragmented body in, 110, 113, 116, 118, 119, 292; Theory of Value, 33n.52, 110, 115; uncertainty in, 57n.4
decentering: of body in Marx, 128–29; of body in neoclassical economics, 92–134; of capitalist enterprises, 243; of economic agents, 87–88; of economic totalities, 51, 164; in feminist economics, 138–39, 160, 292; and the gift, 139; as postmodern moment, 247; of self, 10, 12, 14–16; of social life, 12, 16, 49; of subject, 49, 53, 59, 164, 166–67, 232, 248; and uncertainty, 59, 87–88. See also fragmenting
de Certeau, Michel, 281
de Chirico, Giorgio, Hector and Andromache, 105
decision-making: by capitalist enterprises, 228; and certainty, 88; desires and emotions and, 141; in Shackle, 65, 67; and uncertainty, 87. See also rational choice
deconstruction: in the arts, 7n.15; of formal systems, 76; of human subject, 49; and indeterminacy, 22; as postmodern style, 17, 18, 20–22; of "totalization," 28
de Finetti, Bruno, 82
Defoe, Daniel, 140, 141
Deleuze, Gilles, 119n.16, 125, 211–12; on bodies and wills, 209n; on distinction between morals and ethics, 203n; on Nietzschean conception of knowledge, 207
DeMartino, George, 194, 220n.6, 297; on humanism and moral objectivism, 196
Derrida, Jacques, 47, 58; and deconstruction, 18, 20; on impossibility of the gift, 155; on textuality of the world, 76n.20
Descartes, Réne, 72n.11
Descombes, Vincent, Modern French Philosophy, 204
desire: channeled through mind, 142; domesticated (tamed) by reason, 140–41, 143; "economies of," 275n.25; and power, 143; as primary cause of value, 106
determinism, 30, 291; in Carnap, 35; as discursive construction, 80; economic, 45–47, 231; as form of essentialism, 45; in

determinism (*cont'd*)
  Marxian economics, 231; Nietzsche's rejection of, 208; postmodern critique of, 45–46
Dewey, John: as antiepistemologist, 190; difference of Nietzsche and, 202; and economic methodology, 173; on indistinction between value-judgments and scientific inquiry, 189; and institutionalist economics, 173, 181n.18; and instrumentalism, 189–90; modernist readings of, 188; postmodernism and/of, 172, 188, 202, 215; pragmatism of, 172–73, 178, 187–92, 198n.32; Rorty's reading of, 191–92; "Some Questions about Value," 171; and Veblen's institutionalism, 188
Dirlik, Arif, 16n
discourse(s): constitution of body by/through, 100; and impossibility of knowledge, 78; as "mirror of nature," 58; and notions of disorder and order, 89; probability as a construction of, 80–81, 83, 86; and subjectivity, 91, 170; uncertainty as a construction of, 74–78, 86–87; undecidability of, 76. *See also* knowledge(s)
discursive formation, 39, 259n.2; interpretation of, 81; rules of scientific, 43, 58
disequilibrium: irreducibility of, 53; Keynes on, 51n.76, 73; in mainstream economics, 219; permanent, 220; as postmodern moment, 219
disorder, 29; in Austrian economics, 219, 221; of competition, 239–44; discursivity of, 89; and "invisible hand," 218; in Keynes, 80; in markets, 225, 234–39, 246; in Marxist theories of capitalism and socialism, 53, 218, 222–225, 227, 233, 246, 299; in neoclassical economics, 227; and planning, 246; in post-Keynesian economics, 88, 219; postmodern notions of, 247, 294; and uncertainty, 88–89
Dobb, Maurice, 125
Douglas, Mary, 245
Dow, A., 71
Dow, Sheila, 10n, 50, 71
Dudley-Evans, Tony, *Economics and Language*, 26
Dugger, William, 175
Dupré, John, 134n.25

Eagleton, Terry, 217n.2, 232n.22
Easterlin, Richard, 33n.53, 51n.78
Eatwell, John, 70
econometrics, 44, 56n; Keynes's reservations about, 73; and probability, 60n.9
economic agent(s): as altruistic, 147–48; cultural embeddedness of, 175; feminized notions of, 150; fundamental uncertainty of, 59; masculinity of, 161; in neoclassical economics, 50, 226; and rational expectations, 90–91; and self-interest, 90, 147–48, 226; as "separative self," 147; and uncertainty, 62, 87–88
economic discourse(s), 2, 3, 205, 291, 296; and "ersatz" economics, 258; heterogeneity of, 3; masculinism of value in, 156; production of subjectivity in, 161; and social identities, 281; and uncertainty, 70. *See also* economics
economic knowledge(s), 1, 2, 261n.5, 293; "genres" of, 267; multiplicity of, 59; postmodernism of, 280; regendering of, 137–39; testing of students', 260–62
economic literacy, 253, 260–65, 275, 281; and Campaign for Economic Literacy, 263; and Development Economic Education Program, 263; and Economics America campaign, 264–65; and Joint Council on Economic Education, 263; and *Journal of Economic Education*, 260, 262, 274; and National Council on Economic Education, 263–64, 274; and National Survey on the American Economic System, 262; and *Test of Economic Literacy* (TEL), 260; and *Test of Economic Understanding* (TEU), 260; and *Test of Understanding in College Economics* (TUCE), 260
economic methodology: and Dewey's pragmatism, 173, 187; of institutionalist economics, 197
economic modernism. *See* modernist economics
economics: as a discipline, 289–90, 293, 296; as free marketplace of ideas, 138, 146; imperialism of, 51; modernism of, 53; as a science, 2, 51, 70, 200, 256–57; as value-laden (normative), 176, 200. *See also* economic discourse(s)
economic scientist(s): body of, 146; detachment of, 151; expert knowledge of, 71; gendered choices of, 170; Knight on, 62;

as phallocentric, 162; and rational expectations, 90–91; and uncertainty, 88
economics education: and "ersatz" economics, 261; and metanarrative of economic literacy, 264; and "unlearning," 260
economy: control of body by, 146; decentering of, 164; as machine, 145, as master of man, 163; nonmarket forms of, 185; as organism, 145; as process without a subject, 139, 170, 297n.9; as self-reproducing, 158–59; as totality, 163–64
Eichner, Albert, 91
Elliott, John, 175, 180
Elson, Diane, 153n
Elster, Jon, on the "multiple self," 119
empiricism, 40; in feminist economics, 139, 153, 166–67
Engels, Friedrich, 127n, 180, 248
England, Paula, 155, 169; criticism of "separative self" in neoclassical economics by, 147; on gender bias of rationality, 149
Enlightenment, 2, 10, 16, 26, 47, 48, 108, 199–200, 202, 207
enterprises: in capitalism, 224–29; competition between and within, 228–29, 239–41; decentered, 243; and distributions of surplus-value, 240–41; inside and outside of, 241–42; order within, 236, 242
entry point, 46, 49, 64
epistemology, 26; Cartesian, 72; classical, 26, 250; empiricist, 40, 58, 87; Marxist, 39n, 250; modernist, 40, 58, 67, 172; Nietzsche on, 207; norms of, 39, 43, 87; pluralism of, 190, 213; positivist, 40, 58, 87; privilege of, 44; rationalist, 34, 40, 58, 87; realist, 87; and subjectivism, 67; and uncertainty, 87; and values, 190
ersatz economics, 43, 252–88; distinction from academic economics of, 259, 267; efforts to eliminate, 263–65; as irrational, 257; lack of rigor of, 255, 257; Mc-Closkey's attack on, 255–56; as obstacle to "economic method," 260; and opinion polls, 262; popularity of, 259; postmodern approach to, 265; as structured discourse, 258–59, 267, 276; of students, 260. See also everyday economics
essence(s): contrasted with appearance(s), 28, 31, 32, 43; scientific observations as, 34

essentialism, 30–31, 54, 291; in Carnap, 34–39; determinism as form of, 45; of facts, 36; in institutionalism, 188; of labor in Marxism, 125, 129; and limits of knowledge, 39; of nature, 37; in philosophy of science, 34–35; postmodern critique of, 33–34, 40, 43, 297; of rational thought, 88; of will in Nietzsche, 208
Esteva, Gustavo, 9n
ethics: as context-specific, 12; objectivist approach to, 194; and postmodernism, 18
everyday economics, 43, 53, 252–88; 290, 296, 300; as a Bakhtinian "carnival," 274; and coincidence with academic economics, 277–78; declarativeness of, 268; as different from academic economics, 265–66, 275–79, 299; discursive coherence of, 270, 274; focus on conclusions in, 268–69; genres of, 270; and globalization debate, 252–53; interests in, 268–69, 276; personal nature of, 274–76; postmodernism of, 280, 294; as storytelling, 265; transgressiveness of, 258–59, 276, 278. See also ersatz economics
exchange: the gift and equivalent, 154, 155; identities and subjectivities constituted by, 159; impossibility of, 158, 160; uncertainty of, 159–60

fact(s): in Carnap, 35; cult of the, 36n; as interpretations, 209; Nietzsche on values and, 209–10; privileging of, 36; radical separation of values and, 199; social construction of, 27n.42; as theory-laden, 198; and values in Dewey, 189
Faigley, Lester, 15n.29
Farjoun, Emmanuel, 223n.13, 239n
Feiner, Susan, 102n, 156, 266n.13; on homo economicus as gendered, 149
feminism: and bodies, 100; on decentered subjects, 167; on the "maleness" of abstract subject, 141, 168; on masculinization of thought, 145; postmodern, 139, 166; poststructuralist, 48–49
feminist economics, 7, 30, 41, 42n.64, 47n.71, 50, 137–170, 254, 277, 289, 293, 294, 298; altruism in, 293; and critique of masculinism in economics, 138, 147, 153, 169; and decentered subject, 165–66, 292; empiricism in, 139, 153,

feminist economics (*cont'd*)
161; and fragmented subjects, 53,
147, 150, 153, 165–66, 169; gendered
subjectivity and body in, 129–33; 137,
147–50, 152, 169; the gift in, 138–39,
155, 158; humanism in, 153, 161;
mainstream dismissal of, 254; modernism of, 166, 292; and neoclassical economics, 139, 147–50, 160, 169; and
objectivity, 151–52, 169; postmodern
moments of, 138–39, 150, 152; 296n.7;
(re)gendering of economic knowledge
in, 137, 150, 153; and "separative
self," 147
Ferguson, Harvie, 122n, 123
Feuerbach, Ludwig, 231
Feyerabend, Paul, 2n.4, 39, 43
Feynman, Richard, 2n.5
Fitzgerald, F. Scott, 271
Fitzgibbons, Athol, 79
Flax, Jane, 48, 167–68
Folbre, Nancy, 148–50, 155
formalism, 4, 30, 33–34; in the arts and
philosophy, 81; associated with rigor,
33n.52; and displacement of the body,
103; in economics, 52, 54; Keynes' reservations about, 73; Knight's neglect of,
63; mathematical, 30n.45; in neoclassical economics, 139; probability and, 81;
Shackle's critique of, 64–65
formal modeling, 7–8, 33; and knowledge
production, 34; in neoclassical economics, 139
Foster, J. Fagg, 183
Foucault, Michel, 87, 122n; on the body,
97–98, 108; and "the care of the self,"
203n; and critique of theoretical humanism, 47–48, 109–10, 214–15; and decentered subject, 49; and epistemes, 47; on
power/knowledge, 16, 41, 48, 110
foundationalism, 30; critique of, 40, 43; in
feminist economics, 165; in neoclassical
economics, 165, 292
fragmenting, 216; of body in neoclassical
economics, 92–136; of economics, 290;
in feminist economics, 138; of knowledge, 221; of subjectivity, 167
Frank, Robert, 100
Frankfurt School, 6, 231
Freud, Sigmund: and construction of ego,
208; on overdetermination, 73
Frey, Bruno, 25n

Friedman, Milton, 34; instrumentalism of,
187; modernist reading of Deweyan pragmatism by, 187–88, 191; and realism of
assumptions, 179n.13
Frye, Thomas, *Henry Crispe of the Custom
House*, 123
Fuchs, V. R., 3n.8

Gagnier, Regenia, 134n.27
Galen, 72n.11
Gallagher, Catherine, on Smith, Malthus,
and the "social body," 121n
Gallup Poll Monthly, 278; Gallup Poll in,
262n.6, 277
Gallup Report, 259n.3, 261
game(s), 11, 16, 20, 82, 169, 267, 296;
and probabilities, 82; and rationality assumptions, 53; theory of, 21, 32n.49,
46n.69; 59, 219n; and uncertainty, 59
Gärdenfors, Peter, 78
Garnett, Robert, 52n.80, 175n.8, 281n.28,
297–98; on modernist and postmodernist notions of value, 184–85
Geiger, George R., 184n.23
Gellert, Hugo, "Primary Accumulation," 126
gender, 48; and essentialism, 49; in feminist economics, 137–70; and regendering
of mainstream economics, 138. *See also*
sex(uality)
General Agreement on Tariffs and Trade
(GATT), 262n.6
general equilibrium, 119, 227; and coordination of the body, 111, 113–19; essentialism of, 292; Shackle's criticism of,
65; uncertainty and, 57n.4, 89
Georgescu-Roegen, Nicholas, 151
Gergen, Kenneth, 13
Gerrard, Bill, 69
Ghiselin, Michael, 95n
Gibson-Graham, J. K., 16n, 47n.70, 161,
170, 231n.19, 244n.38, 247; and feminist rethinking of Marxian political economy, 162–64; and forms of capitalist
competition, 240; on metaphors of
"body economic," 145n.12
Giddens, Anthony, 28n
gift, 9; alternative to exchange of, 138–39;
and decentering of modern economics,
139; as "feminine economy," 138, 156;
and feminist economics, 154–55, 157;
gendering of, 157; impossibility of, 139,
155, 158; indeterminacy of, 158, 160;

markets and, 138–39, 154; masculinism of, 156–58; postmodern implications of, 139; reciprocity and, 154–55; social embeddedness of, 139, 153; theories of, 156

gift giving: and "exchange of women," 157; potlatch and aggressiveness of, 156

Gilovich, T., 100

globalization, 5, 6, 16, 293; in academic and everyday economics, 252–53; masculinist discourses of, 164; and postmodern condition, 15; struggle against, 257

Godelier, Maurice, 156n

Gordon, Wendell, 194, 195, 213; and critique of Tool's absolutist social value theory, 177, 183–84, 187, 192

Graham, Julie, 174n.5

Grapard, Ulla, 52n.79

Griswold, Charles, 172n

Grosz, Elizabeth, 48, 100, 119n.16, 131n.23

growth of knowledge, 3, 42; cause of social progress, 11; and history of economic thought, 52; and theoretical humanism, 48

Gruchy, Allan, 178

Guattari, Felix, 119n.16, 125

Gudeman, Stephen: on community in economics, 155; on "models of livelihood," 267

Guillory, John, 174n.7

Hacking, Ian, 60n.9, 74n.16, 80

Hahn, Frank, *General Competitive Equilibrium* (with Arrow), 110, 117–18

Hamilton, Rowan, 32n.51

Hammond, Peter, 57n.4

Hands, D. Wade, 52n.80

Hansen, Lee, 262

Haraway, Donna, 151, 168

Harding, Sandra, 43, 144n, 151, 168; on feminist notions of objectivity, 152

Hargreaves Heap, Shaun, 53, 219n

Harrison, Robert, 197

Harsanyi, John, 46n.69

Hartmann, Heidi, 148, 155

Harvey, David, 291; *The Condition of Postmodernity*, 6n.13

Hayden, F. Gregory, 186

Hayek, Friedrich von, 52n.80, 76, 77n.22, 235

Heidegger, Martin, 209n; on "will to power" in Nietzsche, 206n

Heisenberg's uncertainty principle, 27

Henderson, Willie: *Economics and Language*, 26; *Economics as Literature*, 25

heterodox economics, 5, 30, 41, 50, 53, 236, 277; gender biases in, 139n

Hewitson, Gillian, 47n.71, 137n.2, 140n, 161, 163–64, 170; and neoclassical construction of gendered subjectivity, 131–32, 162; on poststructuralist feminism, 49 130–31

Hicks, John R., 90; and purge of hedonistic utility from economics, 98–99, 103

"high modernism," 5, 11n.20, 22, 29; in Becker's economics, 7

Hindess, Barry, 250

Hirshliefer, Jack, 51n.77

Hirst, Paul, 250

history: dialectic of, 208; as process without a subject, 48; randomness of, 66

history of economic thought, 44–45; marginalized bodies in, 100; passions and reason in, 140; story of disappearance of body in, 92–109; teleology of, 107

Hodgson, Geoffrey, 198n.31

Hollinger, David, 42n.65

homo economicus: centrality of, 51, 135; feminist criticisms of, 47n.71, 102n, 137, 149, 169; and humanism, 50; postmodern critique of, 47; regendering of, 137

Horkheimer, Max, 6

household(s): altruism in, 147; mainstream economics' neglect of the, 138; in neoclassical economics, 147, 152; as private sphere, 143; selfishness within, 148

Hudson, Liam, 35n

humanism, 30, 50, 291; of Austrian economics, 221; and criticism of positivism, 199, 215; of critics of neoclassical economics, 109; critique of theoretical, 47–50, 174; in feminist economics, 130, 153; of institutionalist "holism," 201; in Marxism, 129; of neoclassical economics, 142, 221; Nietzsche's rejection of, 201, 203, 207–8, 211, 215; nonabsolutist institutionalist assault on, 214–15; and values, 195

Hume, David: the body and moral refinement in, 121–22; on the desire for labor, 124n.19

Hutchison, T. W., 2, 3

identity: constituted by exchange and gift
giving, 159; feminist rethinking of, 48,
150; queer, 150; social, 6n.12; as unstable, 49. *See also* subject
incommensurability, 84, 86; of academic
and "ersatz" economics, 259, 265; of discourses, 40, 59 86, 295; of epistemologies, 213; of probabilities, 83; of subjectivity, 165; and uncertainty, 59, 67
indeterminacy, 29; of exchange, 160; of the
gift, 158, 160; Keynes on, 51n.76; in
mainstream economics, 219; and postmodern condition, 16; as postmodern
moment, 56, 219; in probability theory,
82; in science, 11
individual, 47; bourgeois, 231; in neoclassical economics, 140; "one-sidedness" of,
250; as origin of knowledge, 151; as origin of uncertainty, 77. *See also* subject
Ingrao, Bruna, 40n.60
institutionalist economics, 30, 50, 171–
215, 289, 294, 298; as absolutist, 172,
189; on conventions in markets, 237;
Deweyan pragmatism in, 172, 181n.18,
188–89; holism of, 197, 201–02, 208;
and instrumentalism, 178–79, 182; and
Marxian economics, 176n, 180, 297;
modernism of, 188; Nietzsche and, 172,
202, 213–15; nonabsolutist strands of,
185, 213–14; postmodern moments of,
172, 184–86, 215; pragmatism in, 176,
188; privileging of values over facts in,
176, 215; and science, 189, 196–99; on
social provisioning, 175–76, 185; social
value theory in, 177–82, 193, 199–200;
and value/values, 53, 171–215, 292
"invisible hand": and general equilibrium,
227; Marxian critique of, 223; in neoclassical economics, 111, 218; order and
disorder of, 218; story of, 225. *See also*
markets
Irigaray, Luce, 138; on masculinism of universal concepts, 168, 170
irony: as master trope of modernism, 218;
and story of the "invisible hand," 225
Isherwood, Baron, 245
Ivins, Molly, "Workers Are Fed Up with Always Being Mr. Nice Guy," 269, 283–84

Jackson, Shelley: *The Patchwork Girl*, 134;
and postmodern notion of the body,
133–34

Jaggar, Alison, 152n
James, William, 188
Jameson, Fredric, 5–6, 6n.10, 7–8, 14, 16,
217n.2, 291; on Becker as "postmodern-
ist," 7; on postmodernism as cultural
form of capitalism, 5
Jeffrey, Richard, 77n.21
Jevons, William Stanley, 106, 116; *Theory
of Political Economy*, 104
Journal of Economic Issues, 297
Journal of Philosophy, 171
Journal of Post Keynesian Economics,
51n.76
Justman, Stewart, 142n.8

Kantor, Brian, 65
Katzner, Donald, on mathematical formalism in economics, 25n, 30n, 33n.52
Kayatekin, Serap, 6n.12, 76n.20
Keller, Evelyn Fox, 151
Kern, Stephen, 291
Keynes, John Maynard, 51n.76, 55–58,
67–74, 135n.29; "animal spirits" in, 63,
68, 72, 84, 104; on conventions, 69, 84;
discursive notion of probability in, 81,
84; disequilibrium in, 73; on evidence,
81–82; fundamentalist reading of, 69–
70; *General Theory*, 57, 68–69, 78–79,
83–84, 85n.29, 86; on limits to knowledge, 71–72, 84; on long-term expectations, 67–68; modernism of, 73, 86;
"My Early Beliefs," 84; nihilism of, 67,
69–71, 74, 84–85, 89, 91; postmodern
moments of, 69, 71, 74, 79–80, 83, 85,
292; on probability, 78–85; *Quarterly
Journal of Economics* article, 68–69,
83–84, 86; separation of knowledge and
action in, 72–73; *Treatise on Probability*,
78–79, 83–84, 85n.29, 86; "true uncertainty" in, 56–57, 74; on uncertainty,
53, 55–58, 60, 62, 67–74, 76n.20, 78–
79, 83–86, 292
Keynesian economics, 277, 289, 294;
knowledge in, 55–91; and Marxian economics, 218; modernism of, 89, 218,
253; postmodern moments of, 53; uncertainty in, 55–91
Kirzner, Israel, 221n.9
Klamer, Arjo, 10n, 27, 58, 90, 172; *The
Consequences of Economic Rhetoric*,
26; *Conversations with Economists*, 26;
on disappearance of subjects from "late

modernist" economics, 96–97; on everyday economics, 265–66, 267n.15

Klein, Daniel, 43n.67

Knight, Frank, 52n.80; antimodernism of, 67; on expectations, 62; and free choice, 63; modernism of, 61, 64, 67, 69, 86; and objectivity of uncertainty, 78; and postmodernism, 64; *Risk, Uncertainty, and Profit*, 61; on uncertainty, 61–64

knowledge(s), 2, 3, 33n.51, 170; in Austrian economics, 221; certainty of, 55, 290; and decentered subject, 15; discursivity of, 17, 77, 86, 91; disjoint from action, 72; in feminist economics, 138, 150–51; fragmentation of, 138, 150, 221; gendered, 137, 145; impossibility of, 78, 88, 221; as incomplete, 38–40; indeterminancy of, 16; instrumentalism and, 173n, 178–79; in Keynesian economics, 55–91; limits to, 38–39, 59, 63, 70–72; masculinist forms of, 138, 150–51; as "mirror of nature," 58, 144, 172, 293; multiplicity of, 16, 88; Nietzsche on, 207, 210, 213; objective, 138, 147, 200; and postmodernism, 10, 89, 250; power and persuasion in, 41–42; "problem of," 26, 207, 213; production of, 16, 21, 26, 30, 32, 34, 40–41, 58, 87; Shackle on, 64–66; "situated," 15, 23; in socialism, 250; and uncertainty, 55–91; and the unknown, 59, 62; values and, 201. *See also* discourse(s); science

Komter, Aafke, 157n.23

Koopmans, Tjalling, 2n.6, 17n.31

Koppl, Roger, 68n, 72n.11, 77n.22

Kreps, David, 41n.61

Krueger, A. B., 3n.8

Krugman, Paul, 256, 258, 262; *The Age of Diminished Expectations*, 256

Kuhn, Thomas, 39, 43

labor: disutility of, 93, 104, 123n; as fatiguing, 125–26; as liberating, 126; as source of economic value, 104, 106, 124–25; as subcategory of utility, 106

La Mettrie, Julien Offray de, *Man a Machine*, 117n

language: ambiguity of, 35; as a neutral medium, 31–32: as reflection of nature, 36

Latour, Bruno, 43

Lavoie, Don, *Economics and Hermeneutics*, 26

Lawson, Tony, 34n; on uncertainty in Keynes, 69–70, 74, 79, 86

Lecourt, Dominique, *Marxism and Epistemology*, 39n

Leonard, Thomas, 265–66, 267n.16

Lepley, Ray: *The Language of Value*, 171n.1; *Value: A Comparative Inquiry*, 171

Levin, Lee, 161, 162, 164, 170

Levine, David, 227n

Lévi-Strauss, Claude, 138

Longino, Helen, 151

Lotze, Rudolph Hermann, 171n.2

Lukács, Georg, 6, 231

Lucas, Robert, 20n.36, 90

Lyotard, Jean-François, 17, 47, 119n.16, 291; *Libidinal Economy*, 12n.25; *The Postmodern Condition*, 10–12

Machover, Moshe, 223n.13, 239n

MacIntyre, Alasdair, 180n.15, 202

Maddock, Rodney, 90

Madra, Yahya, 297

Magnani, Marco, 65

mainstream economics: modernism of, 50, 71, 86; order and disorder in, 219; and positive/normative distinction, 172, 179; postmodern moments of, 53

Mäki, Uskali, 51n.77, 187

Malinowski, Bronislaw, 157n.22

Malthus, Thomas Robert, 121n

Mandel, Ernest, on "late capitalism," 6

Manuel, Frank E., 31n.46

Manuel, Fritzie P., 31n.46

Marcuse, Herbert, 6

marginalist(s): conception of the desiring body for, 93, 104; nonutilitarianism of, 98; passions and reason for, 140; revolution, 3, 98. *See also* neoclassical economics

markets: altruism within, 148; in Austrian economics, 221–22, 235; in capitalism, 216; decentralized, 218–19; and disequilibrium, 219–20; disorder of, 217–19, 229–30, 234, 238, 246; distortion of needs by, 245–46; equilibrium in, 226–27; and gift, 138, 154; habit and ritual in, 236–38; in Marxian economics, 222, 234–39; in neoclassical economics, 218–22, 236; orderliness of, 218, 236–38; vs. planning, 229–30, 234–39; in post-Keynesian economics, 219–20, 222; as

markets (*cont'd*)
  self-regulating, 154; social embed
  dedness of, 238; uncertainty of, 230; as
  unplanned, 224;
Marris, Peter, 75n.17
Marshall, Alfred, *Principles of Economics*,
  100n
Martin, Emily, 133n.25
Marx, Karl: the body in, 109, 128–29,
  246n; *Capital*, vol. 1, 126, 226; *Capital*,
  vol. 2, 224; *Capital*, vol. 3, 226, 239–40,
  242; on commodity fetishism, 248–49;
  on competition, 226, 239, 241–42, 244;
  "early," 231, 245; *Economic and Philosophic Manuscripts*, 125–26; and ethics,
  180; on "ever-lasting uncertainty," 248;
  labor theory of value in, 124–25; on
  needs, 245; postmodern moments of,
  233–51
Marxian economics, 5, 30, 41, 46, 50,
  216–51, 277, 289, 294, 296, 298; on accumulation of capital, 225, 239; on anarchy of production, 225, 230; body (laboring) in, 124–29; capitalism vs.
  socialism in, 216–51, 292, 295; on capitalist enterprises, 224–27, 239–44; centered subject in, 232; circulation and production in, 222–25; class in, 225, 231;
  293; on competition, 226–30, 239–44;
  and crisis theory, 224–26; and critique of
  bourgeois individualism, 125, 231; and
  critique of "invisible hand," 223, 227;
  decentered subject in, 232; economic determinism in, 231; exploitation in, 230,
  295; habit and ritual in, 237–38; and institutionalist economics, 176n, 180, 297;
  labor theory of value in, 124–25; and literary theory, 217n.2, 295; and markets,
  225, 230, 234–39, 246; masculinism of,
  139n, 148; modernism of, 125, 218,
  222–23, 225, 227, 229–32, 238, 248,
  292; moral relativism of, 180–81; needs
  in, 244–46; order and disorder in, 218,
  222, 225–227, 229, 233, 248, 292, 295;
  and planning, 234–39, 246; postmodern
  moments of, 222, 233–51, 292; on rate
  of profit, 224–27, 229; stability over instability in, 218; and subjectivity, 230–
  33; surplus-value in, 224–27, 229; uncertainty in, 222, 224; utopian imaginary
  of, 233; value (economic) in, 124–29,

223, 226, 229–30; values (normative) in,
  180, 195
Marzola, A., *John Maynard Keynes:
  Language and Method*, 26
masculinism, 49, 50; in economic knowledge, 138; in economic subjectivity, 138;
  of economies based on "return," 156; of
  gift theory, 156; and ideal of detachment, 151; in neoclassical economics,
  130, 150, 156, 165; of self-reproducing
  economy, 164; of structural adjustment
  programs, 153n; of universal concepts,
  168
mathematics: in economics, 4, 33, 41n.61;
  elevated over "feminine" ways of
  knowing in economics, 151; and nine
  -teenth-century neoclassical economics,
  106
Matthaei, Julie, 130; on economic construction of gay/straight sexualities, 129
Mauss, Marcel, 138, 154, 156, 157n
Mayer, Thomas, 281n.29
Mayhew, Anne, 175, 196, 213; and critique of Tool's absolutist social value theory, 177, 183–84, 187, 192; cultural relativism of, 184, 215
McCloskey, Deirdre, 10n, 11n.20, 32n.52,
  52, 58, 146n.14; and "conjective" knowledge, 151; *The Consequences of Economic Rhetoric*, 26; and critique of "ersatz" economics, 255, 257–58, 260,
  262, 267–68, 275–76, 280; *Knowledge
  and Persuasion in Economics*, 26; on
  market's support of "feminine virtues,"
  142n.8; on modernism in economics, 50,
  253–54; and persuasion in economics,
  254, 257; *The Rhetoric of Economics*,
  26; self-criticism of, 258n.
McIntyre, Richard, 244n.39; 281–82
meaning(s): contingency of, 32, 81; instability of, 296; and Nietzschean perspectivism, 210, 213; and postmodern style, 18;
  undecidability of, 17
Meehan, Jennifer, 266, 279n
Mehta, Judith, 20–21, 22n.37, 53, 82n,
  114n
Ménard, Claude, 60–61
Menger, Carl, 93, 104
metanarratives: humanism and, 14;
  Lyotard on "grand,"10, 12; of social
  justice, 174

methodological individualism, 175, 179, 225n

Mies van der Rohe, Ludwig, 22–23

Milgate, Murray, 70

Mill, John Stuart, 102, 104

Millberg, William, 26n.40, 236n

Miller, Gary, 46n.68

mind: and "animal spirits," 72; body's control over, 142; control of the body by, 63, 140–44; multiplicity of, 59; uncertainty and, 59, 63; unity of, 59

Mirowski, Philip, 82, 106, 176n, 183n.21, 213; on dissolution of gift into exchange, 155; on scientism of institutionalist economics, 198–99; social value theory of, 156

Mitchell, Edward Thomas, 171

Mitchell, Wesley Clair, 188–89, 198n.32

models (economic), 44; as constitutive of knowledge, 297; gendered nature of mathematical, 138

modernism(s), 4, 5, 12, 18, 29; culture of, 2; in economics, 51–53, 290; in institutionalism 188; and limits to knowledge, 38; and metaphor of the machine, 65; Nietzsche's criticism of, 203; postmodern critique of, 27–29; and primacy of reason, 64; and representation of truth, 31; time and space in, 64, 291

modernist economics, 1, 2, 3, 53–54, 253, 282, 299; centering, certainty, and order in, 296; centrality of body to, 94; and fear of nihilism, 56; and feminist economics, 139, 152, 165; homo economicus and homo scientis in, 137; humanism of, 221; Keynesianism and 70, 73, 74, 218; Marxian economics as, 218, 229–30, 232; and neoclassical economics as, 218; optimism of, 218–19; order and disorder in, 226; and rational choice, 219; and separation of morality and science, 199; and subjectivity, 230; three phases of, 107; and uncertainty, 56, 59, 64, 71, 86, 89, 91

Moore, Charles, *Piazza d'Italia*, 22, 24

Moore, G. E., *Principia Ethica*, 81

moral theory: modernist, 172; of Nietzsche, 201–15; Platonic, 172n, and rule of Reason, 199–201. *See also* ethics; values

Morgan, Mary, 56n, 60n.9, 91

Morris, David, 104

Murphy, Margueritte, 12n.25

Muth, John, 89

National Bureau of Economic Research, 51n.78

nature: laws of, 37; neoclassical economics as close to, 143; women as, 142

Neale, Walter, 184n.23

needs: in Marxian economics, 181, 216, 244–46; postmodern view of, 245–46

Nelson, Julie, 130, 149, 155; and gender-value compass, 148–49; on masculinist ideal of detachment, 151

neoclassical economics, 4, 5, 52, 64, 144, 289; and Austrian economics, 219–21; and Benthamite utilitarianism, 104; body in, 13n.26, 53, 92–136, 292; competition in, 221; disappearance of the body in, 95, 102–9; dominance of, 51, 296; equilibrium in, 175, 293; ethical relativism of, 179–80; and feminist economics, 137, 139; homo economicus, in 50, 135, 137, 149; humanism of, 142–43; markets in, 218–222, 236–37; and Marxian economics, 218, 227; masculinism of, 148–50, 154, 161, 165; methodological individualism of, 175, 179; modernism of, 52, 218, 253; naturalism of, 142–43; order and disorder in, 218, 226–27; postmodern moments of, 53; and problem of fragmented subjectivity, 167; rational decision-making in, 237, 293; and reduction of value to price, 174; and Robinson Crusoe, 140, 162; self-interest in, 226, and "separative self," 147; story of desire and reason in, 139–47; subjective value theory of, 106; subjectivity constructed within, 161–62; and uncertainty, 57–58, 86–87; value principle of, 179–80, 195. *See also* mainstream economics; marginalist(s); modernist economics

neotraditionalists, 27

new classical (macro)economics, 96; uncertainty in, 58–59, 71, 87, 89–91

new institutionalist economics, 237n.28, 289

Newman, Barnet, *Vir Heroicus Sublimus*, 97

Nietzsche, Friedrich, 49, 191; on the ascetic ideal, 204–6; *Beyond Good and Evil*, 202; chance and necessity in, 74n.16; as critic of science; 203, 211–12; economics of, 205n.35; and institutionalist economics, 213–15; and moral relativism, 211; on morals and Reason, 201–215; and "noble" moralities, 206, 211; *On the Genealogy of Morals*, 202, 205n.35; perspectivism of, 172, 210–13; rejection of humanism by, 201, 203, 207–8, 211, 215; and rejection of "teleologies and determinisms," 208; on "slave moralities," 205, 207, 211; on stupidity of modernism, 203; on values, 171–72, 176, 195–96, 207; will to nothingness in, 206, 209, 212; *The Will to Power*, 207; will to power in, 206–8, 232n.22; will to truth in, 204–5, 207

nihilism: of Austrian economics, 221; of deconstruction, 22; in Keynes, 69; moral, 181; of post-Keynesian economics, 219; of postmodern economics, 291; of postmodern Marxism, 248; of uncertainty, 56, 59, 62, 69–70, 86, 88–89

noncapitalism, 9, 217

Norris, Christopher, 232n.23

North American Free Trade Agreement (NAFTA), 256–57, 266; and everyday economics, 266, 276, 278–79

Norton, Bruce, 6n.10, 227n, 241, 247; on forms of capitalist competition, 240

objectivity: in feminist standpoint theory, 152; gendered conception of, 144–45

O'Donnell, Rod, 78–79

O'Neill, Phillip, 240, 244n.38

order: discursive constitution of, 89; and "invisible hand," 218; in Keynes, 80; in markets, 218, 234–39, 246; in Marxist theories of capitalism and socialism, 53, 218, 222–23, 227, 229, 233, 246, 299; in neoclassical economics, 227; and planning, 229; in post-Keynesian economics, 220; postmodern notions of, 294; privileged over disorder, 29, 88, 218, 246; and uncertainty, 88–89

Ortner, Sherry, 142n.7

Osteen, Mark, *The New Economic Criticism*, 26, 298

overdetermination, 58, 164; of the body in Marx, 128; and critique of determinism,

46; and "ever-lasting uncertainty," 248; Freud's notion of, 73; of habit and ritual, 238; of knowledges, 88; and radical contingency of economic processes, 247

Ozawa, Terutomo, 72n.11

Pareto, Vilfredo, 98

Pareto efficiency, 227

Park, Man-Seop, 76n.20

Peirce, Charles S., 183n.21, 188, 198, 199n.32; chance and necessity in, 75n.16

Pepper, Stephen, 171

perspectivism: in Carnap, 35; in Nietzsche, 172, 210–12

philosophy of science, 31, 34, 39; and critique of scientism, 43

Pickering, Andrew, 32n.51

Pietrykowski, Bruce, 6n.14, 267

Planck, Max, 1n.1

planning: in capitalism, 229–30; and class conflict, 234; contingency of, 250; disorder of, 234–35, 244; vs. markets, 229–30, 234–39; and needs, 244–46; postmodern Marxist notion of, 250–51; in socialism, 216, 223, 229–30, 234–39, 244, 250–51

Plato, 163

Polanyi, Karl, 9n, 172, 175, 185

Polanyi, Livia, 152

Pop art, 7

Popper, Karl, 199

Porter, Theodore, 77n.23

positive/normative distinction, 172, 176; challenged by institutionalists, 179, 213; and ethical relativism, 186; Marxist rejection of, 180; and positivism, 199

positivism, 34, 40; and Deweyan pragmatism, 187; humanist criticisms of, 199, 215; and institutionalism, 198–99; and story of separation of reason from values, 177, 199–202, 212; and value-free science, 176

Posner, Richard, 46

postcolonial, 5; economics, 41, 298; subjects, 6n12, 9n; theory, 41n.64

post-Enlightenment thought, 48, 140; and feminizing of civil society, 142

post-Fordism, 5, 6n.10, 8, 293; Fordism and, 6n.14

postindustrialization, 6, 12n.24, 275n.25; 293n

Post-Keynesian economics, 51n.76, 85, 298; on conventions in markets, 237; disequilibrium in, 219–20; empiricism of, 91; and expectations, 88, 91; humanism of, 91; institutions in, 220; modernism of, 91; nihilism of, 219; and objectivity of uncertainty, 78; order and disorder in, 91, 219–20; and uncertainty, 53, 86, 88

postmodernism, 3–7, 299; as antimodernism, 27–8, 30, 52; in arts and architecture, 4, 7, 22; as "condition," 4, 10–16, 18; as critique of determinism, 45–47; as critique of essentialism, 32–33, 40, 43; as critique of foundationalism, 40; as critique of modernism, 4, 27–30, 291; and critique of scientism, 42–44; as critique of theoretical humanism, 47–50; and decentered subjects, 167; of Deweyan pragmatism, 187–88; and discursivity of subjectivity, 91; in economics, 50–51, 54; and epistemology, 58; 91, 280; as historical phase, 3–5, 10; "key features of," 4; and knowledges, 91; as latest stage of modernism, 29; multiplicity of, 29–30; as nonmodernism, 28, 30, 52; as refusal of representation, 32–33; as style, 4, 17–25; and uncertainty, 55, 74, 85, 91; and "values vacuum," 174

postmodern moment(s), 3, 29, 219; of Austrian economics, 221; in/of economics, 5, 29, 30, 52–54, 252, 289–91, 293–94, 296, 298, 300; of feminist economics, 138; of institutionalist economics, 172; of Keynes(ian) economics, 53, 55, 74, 80, 83, 85; of Marxian economics, 222, 233–51; in modernism, 28–29; of neoclassical economics, 53; in Shackle, 64; of uncertainty, 55–56, 58, 74, 80, 85

poststructuralism: and critiques of humanism, 52; and postmodernism, 18; Rorty's use of, 191; and textuality of the world, 44; and theories of the gift, 156

Poterba, J. M., 3n.8

power, 48: in discourse, 259n.2; and reason, 144; as result of will, 144

pragmatism: antiessentialism of, 191; Deweyan, 172–73, 180, 187–92, 197–98, 213–14; and institutionalist economics, 171, 176, 188; modernist readings of, 188; and Nietzsche, 214; of Peirce, 75n.16; Veblen's notion of, 180. See also Dewey, John

Prakash, Madhu Suri, 9n

prediction, 4, 34, 38n; and disconfirmation, 35; and uncertainty, 91

preferences: of economic scientists, 25; endogenous determination of, 169–70; exogeneity of, 245; as neoclassical entry point, 64; as unruly, 143

probability, 45, 56; and Bayesianism, 78; and certainty, 57; discursive notion of, 79, 80, 83; and games of chance, 82; incommensurability of, 83; Keynes on, 56, 78–83; Knight on, 61; limits to, 62; as logical arguments, 79; objectivist notions of, 79–80; and rational choice, 60 "rationalist" notions of, 80; Shackle on, 66; subjectivist notions of, 77–80, 82; and uncertainty, 58, 60, 62, 66; as undecidable, 81

profit: as composite notion, 242; ambiguity of, 243

progress, 10; in economics, 2, 4, 54, 289–90; and postmodernism, 289; subjective development and, 141; valuation as the source of, 196

Quarterly Journal of Economics, 68

Rabinbach, Anson, 117n, 125–26; The Human Motor, 127n

radical economics, 139n, 226, 277, 289

Ramsey, Frank, 77n.31, 82

Ramstad, Yngve, 175, 183, 186n, 192

rational choice, 219; and probability, 61; under uncertainty, 87; universality of, 90

rational expectations, and uncertainty, 59, 63, 87, 89–91

rationalism, 34, 40

rationality: in Arrow and Debreu, 292; distinction from irrationality of, 87; gender bias of, 138, 149–50, 165; habit and ritual of, 237; Knight on, 62; in modernist Marxism, 218; overdetermination of, 87; in socialism, 216–17, 223; subordinated to dictates of the body, 142; and uncertainty, 58–59, 87, 89–90

realism of assumptions, 34, 179n.13

Reason: and separation from values, 199–201; "will to nothingness" of, 204–6

reciprocity: as embedded in community, 155; and exchange, 155, 156; as part of feminized subjectivity, 148; regendering of, 158

Regan, D., 100

Reisman, David, 188

relativism, 16; of capitalism, 250; cultural, 184, 196; epistemological, 54, 190; in institutionalist economics, 186, 194–95, 214; and irreducibility of difference, 214; of Marxian economics, 180–81; moral (or ethical), 178, 186, 190, 194, 211; of neoclassical value principle, 179–80; and Nietzsche's perspectivism, 210–11, 213

representation: and essentialism, 30–33; Foucault on, 47; impossibility of, 18; language as, 31; postmodern critique of, 29, 33; and self-consciousness of science, 31

Resnick, Stephen, 39, 46, 47n.70, 52, 58, 231n.19, 247; on fundamental and subsumed class processes, 240n; and Marxist epistemology, 250

Ricardo, David, 104, 108, 226n.16

Riley, Denise, 167, 168

risk in economics, 56; Knight on, 61–62; and uncertainty, 57, 60, 62

Rivera, Alberto, 267

Robbins, Lionel, 61

Roberts, Bruce, 176n, 226n.16, 240, 247

Robinson Crusoe, in economics, 140, 141n, 161, 266n.13

Roche, John, 247

Roemer, John, 220n.7

Rorty, Richard: on absence of epistemological difference between facts and values, 191, 198; on foundationalism, 40n.59; and modernist epistemology, 58; notion of "mirror of nature" in, 178; and Nietzsche, 172, 191–92, 213; postmodern reading of Deweyan pragmatism by, 172, 188, 191–92, 197, 214

Rosenau, Pauline, 50n

Ross, Dorothy, 27n.43

Rossetti, Jane, 20n, 32n.50

Rotman, Brian, on embodiment in formal mathematics, 111

Rotwein, Eugene: on hedonism of preferences, 100; on Hume, 122

Ruccio, David F., 6n.12, 20n, 50, 174n.5, 247n, 293n, 298

Rush, Norman, *Mating*, 267

Russell, Bertrand, *Principia Mathematica* (with Whitehead), 81

Rutherford, Malcolm, 173n, 198n.32

Sade, Marquis de, 104n

Sahlin, Nils-Eric, 78

Sahlins, Marshall, 237n.27

Salanti, Andrea, *Pluralism in Economics*, 26n.40

Samuels, Warren, 22, 178, 213–15; *Economics as Discourse*, 25

Samuelson, Paul, 1–4, 31n.47, 52, 90; and disappearance of body from economics, 96, 98–99, 103, 111–12, 119; *Economics*, 1n.1; *Foundations of Economic Analysis*, 1n.1, 98; revealed preference theory of, 98, 103, 112; on utility, 96, 112

Sargent, Thomas, 90, 91n

Sass, Louis, 14n.29

Savage, Leonard, 82

Say's Law, 67

Scarry, Elaine, 128n

Schick, Frederic, 66

Schrift, Alan, 155n

science: discursivity of, 12; epistemological privilege of, 43, 197; gendered conception of, 145; hermeneutic conception of, 198–99; institutionalist conception of, 196–99, 215; and moral discourse, 188, 200; Nietzsche's criticism of, 203, 211–12; positivist, 198, 215; and postmodernism, 10; self-interest in, 146

scientific knowledge: as accumulation of laws, 38; and objectivity, 59; power and persuasion in, 40–42; and uncertainty, 59. *See also* knowledge(s)

scientific laws: contingency of, 39; distinction between facts and, 35; of nature, 37

scientism, 4, 30, 291; in economics, 54; of institutionalist economics, 198–99; postmodern critique of, 42–43; and scientific practice, 42

Screpanti, Ernesto, *Pluralism in Economics*, 26n.40

self-interest: feminist economists' criticism of, 138; generosity and caring not reducible to, 155; as key feature of neoclassical economics, 147; masculinism of, 148, 150; teaching economic students about, 100. *See also* economic agents; individual

self-reflexivity, 17, 22–24, 27; in economics, 26; and knowledge production, 26

Sen, Amartya, 7n.16, 33n.52, 112, 179; on capabilities of bodies, 94; 33n.52; on "imperialism" of economics, 7n.16; on uncertainty in economics, 17n.31

sex(uality), 48; and bodies in neoclassical economics, 162; and distinction from gender in feminism, 131; economics and gay/straight, 129. *See also* gender

Shackle, G.L.S., 221; attack on formalism by, 64–65; criticism of determinism by, 65–66; on freedom of (uncertain) agents, 57, 63–65, 67, 88; humanism of, 77n.22; on knowledge, 66, 88; modernism of, 64–65, 69, 86; nihilism of, 89, 91; postmodernism in, 64, 67, 74, 77n.22; on "potential surprise," 66; probability in, 64; subjectivism of, 67; on uncertainty, 57, 62–67; 78, 88, 221

Shapiro, Michael, 93n

Shuklian, Steve, 180

Silk, Leonard, 268n.18

Silva, F., *John Maynard Keynes: Language and Method*, 26

Simon, Herbert, 14n.27, 63, 89; and bounded rationality, 1n.1

Smith, Adam, 51, 108, 111, 141, 142n.7, 172, 218, 231; on beneficence and drudgery of labor, 126–27; the body in, 92, 93n, 102, 120–21, 124; labor theory of value of, 92, 104; passions and reason in, 140; sympathy in, 121; *Theory of Moral Sentiments*, 85n.29, 102, 109, 121–22; *The Wealth of Nations*, 85n.29, 126–27

Smith, Barbara Herrnstein, 174n.7

Smith, Dorothy, 168

Smith, Kiki, *Las Animas*, 132

socialism, 216–51; absence of commodity fetishism in, 233; absence of crises in, 230; centered subject in, 232–33; communal appropriation of surplus in, 217; disorder and order in, 223; distinction from capitalism of, 216–17, 250, 290; and markets, 216, 230; in Marxian economics, 216–51; 292; needs in, 245; planning in, 216–17, 223, 234–35, 250; production for use in, 233, 245; rationality of, 216–17, 230; self-realization in, 217, 223; and "socialist man," 249; stability of, 216–17; subject in, 249–50; true knowledge in, 223; and uncertainty in, 230, 250

Socrates, 202, 206; and dualism of faith and knowledge, 204–05

Solo, Robert, 32n48

Solow, Robert, 33n.52; *The Consequences of Economic Rhetoric*, 26

space: feminist knowledges of, 163; postmodern compression of, 13

Spary, Emma, 145n.12

Spinoza, B., 203n, 209n

Spivak, Gayatri Chakravorty, 42n.64

Squires, J., 173

Sraffian economics, 116, 289

Standards in Economics Survey, 263

standpoint theory, in feminism, 15–16, 152

Stanfield, J. Ron, 172, 180

Strassmann, Diana, on gendered storytelling in neoclassical economics, 152

Strathern, Marilyn, on gendering of gift exchange, 157–58

structuralism, 49

subject: abstract universal, 138, 141; and alienation, 231–32; in capitalism, 230, 232, 249; centered, 67, 109, 231–33; and commodity fetishism, 232–33, 248–49; contingency of, 231; decentered, 13n, 14–16, 29, 49, 53, 59, 166–67, 232, 248; desiring, 110, 140; discursive construction of, 91, 164, 167, 170; (dis)-embodiment of, 150–52; essentialism of human, 49; 231; in exchange and gift giving, 159; in feminist economics, 53, 137–70; fragmented, 13, 15, 49, 53, 138, 165, 167, 169, 249; gendering of, 137, 142, 145, 165, 169; in Marxian economics, 230–33; masculinist forms of, 138, 148–49, 152, 169; multiplicity of, 166–67; in neoclassical economics, 47, 64, 110, 140, 166; "open," 166–68, 249; postmodern, 13, 59, 166–70, 294; rational, 110, 140; regendered, 138, 169, 299; saturated, 13, 16; in socialism, 230, 232–33, 249; as starting point for economic theory, 154, 161, 165; and theoretical humanism, 47–48; and uncertainty, 58–59, 63, 66–67, 89–90; unity of, 14, 29, 59, 89; as unstable, 49, 53. *See also* economic agents; individual

subject/object distinction, 28, 67

surplus labor: appropriation and distribution of, 293; communal appropriation of, 217

surplus-value, 223; and commodity fetishism, 233; and competition within and between capitalist enterprises, 240–41;

surplus-value (*cont'd*)
  distributions of, 240–41, 244. *See also*
  profit

teleology: in Marxism, 231; of narrative of
  body's disappearance in economics,
  107–9; Nietzsche's rejection of, 208
time: as discursive construct, 78; and the
  gift, 160; postmodern compression of,
  13
Todd, Janet: *Sensibility*, 120–21; on sensibility of female bodies, 122n
Tool, Marc, 175, 186; absolutism of, 177,
  188–89, 192, 213; critique of Marxism
  by, 180–81; *Essays in Social Value Theory*, 179n.14; instrumental value principle of, 177–78, 182, 187–89, 194–95;
  modernism of, 178; on neoclassical
  value principle, 179; social value theory
  of, 177–82, 193, 213
Toulmin, Stephen, 291
Townsend, Hugh, 80
Tribe, Keith, 51–52
Turgot, A.R.J., 31n.46

uncertainty, 17, 54, 55–91, 300; in Austrian economics, 89, 221; and challenge
  to rationality, 58–59; and decentered subject, 59, 87–88; discursivity of, 74, 76,
  78, 80, 87; and disorder, 88–89; and exchange, 159–60; and expectations, 17,
  62, 71, 89–91; as fact of nature, 40, 63,
  86; and freedom, 63, 66; "fundamental"
  or "true," 46, 53, 56–58, 62, 66, 74,
  221; as ignorance, 71, 83; Keynes on,
  51n.76, 56–57, 67–74, 79, 83; Knight
  on, 61–63; lack of universality of, 75;
  and limits to knowledge, 63, 66, 71, 86;
  in Marxian economics, 222, 224, 247; in
  mercantilist thought, 60; nihilism of, 56,
  59, 62, 69–71, 86–89; objectivism of,
  76–78, 219; as postmodern moment in
  economics, 53, 56, 79, 85, 89, 91, 247;
  294; and predictions, 91; and probability, 58, 62, 66, 79; Shackle on, 64–67,
  88; subjectivism of, 76–77, 219; and subjectivity, 15, 49, 58–59, 63–64, 66, 76;
  as threat to economic theory, 86, 89; undecidability of, 74, 76
undecidability: and deconstruction, 18; of
  discourse, 76; in economics, 2, 3, 54, 56,

290; and the gift, 155; in Keynes, 84;
  and probability, 81
utilitarianism, 141; of Bentham, 104; and
  question of passions vs. reason, 140
utility, 106; disappearance of, 98; and disutility of labor, 93, 104; hedonism of,
  98–99, 103; as initiating cause, 104; and
  reordering of body of classical economics, 93; and uncertainty, 59; as value referent of neoclassical economics, 179

value (economic): body in debates over, 94,
  111–12; in classical economics, 93–94;
  difference from and connection to "values"; 174n; in institutionalist economics,
  175, 184–86; labor theory of, 92, 124;
  in Marxian economics, 124–29; 175,
  223, 229, 242; in neoclassical economics, 93–94, 111, 112, 174; objective and
  subjective theories of, 94, 104, 106, 109;
  postmodern notion of, 174n.5, 184;
values, 51, 200, 290; contingency of, 32;
  and Deweyan pragmatism, 172–3, 187–
  92; discursivity and extradiscursivity of,
  193–95; and facts, 189, 198–99, 209;
  and humanism, 195–96, 199; in institutionalist economics, 53, 171–215; instrumentalism and, 177, 183–84, 187–92,
  198; in Marxism, 180, 195; in neoclassical economics, 195; in Nietzsche, 171–
  73, 195–96, 206–15; objectivity of, 192–
  95, 199; as origin of inquiry, 201, 292;
  postmodernism and, 184, 191, 294; relativism and, 182–86, 193, 299; universal,
  182–86; and wills, 206–10
Van Gogh, Vincent, *Still Life with Apples,
  Meat, and Bread Roll*, 7, 8
van Staveren, Irene, 156
Varoufakis, Yanis, 53, 219n
Veblen, Thorstein, 109, 175, 182n, 183, 185n,
  188, 191, 198n.32, 202, 213–14, 244n.39;
  on conspicuous consumption, 245; and Darwinian notions of evolution, 188

Waller, William, 178, 182n.20, 213, 297
Walras, Léon, 60–61, 104, 106, 111
Ward, Benjamin, 197
Warhol, Andy, *Campbell Soup*, 1, 7, 9
Weedon, Chris, 41n.63
Weiner, Annette, 157n.22
Weintraub, E. Roy, 2n.3, 24, 40n.60;
  41n.62

West, Cornel, postmodern reading of Deweyan pragmatism by, 188–89, 214

Wheale, Nigel, 17n.32

White, Hayden, 218n.3

Whitehead, Alfred North, *Principia Mathematica* (with Russell), 81

Wilber, Charles, 197

Wildavsky, Adam, 44n.67

Wiles, Mark, 90

will(s): as active forces, 209; to knowledge, 41, 147; to nothingness, 206, 209, 211; to power, 206–8, 232n.22; to truth, 204–5; and values, 208–15

Williams, Rhonda, critique of Nelson's humanism by, 130

Wilson, Lucas, 214; on Deweyan pragmatisms in economics, 173, 187–92

Winslow, E. G., 71, 72n.12

Wise, M. Norton, 11n.22

Wittgenstein, Ludwig, 191; *Tractatus Logico-Philosophicus*, 81

Wittig, Monique, on masculinism of universal concepts, 168, 170

Wolff, Richard, 39, 46, 47n.70, 52, 58, 176n, 226n.16, 231n.19, 247; on fundamental and subsumed class processes, 240n; and Marxist epistemology, 250

Wong, Stanley, 99, 112n

Woodmansee, Martha, *The New Economic Criticism*, 26, 298

Woolf, Virginia, 57

World Trade Organization (WTO), 256–57

Yonay, Yuval, 181n.18, 198n.32